Unintended Lessons of Revolution

UNINTENDED

Student Teachers and Political Radicalism in

LESSONS OF

Twentieth-Century Mexico **TANALÍS PADILLA**

REVOLUTION

Duke University Press   Durham and London   2021

Printed in the United States of America on acid-free paper ∞
Designed by Aimee C. Harrison
Typeset in Garamond Premier Pro and Helvetica Neue by Westchester Publishing Services

Library of Congress Cataloging-in-Publication Data
Names: Padilla, Tanalís, [date] author.
Title: Unintended lessons of revolution: student teachers and political radicalism in twentieth-century Mexico / Tanalís Padilla.
Description: Durham: Duke University Press, 2021. | Includes bibliographical references and index.
Identifiers: LCCN 2021011881 (print)
LCCN 2021011882 (ebook)
ISBN 9781478013860 (hardcover)
ISBN 9781478014799 (paperback)
ISBN 9781478022084 (ebook)
ISBN 9781478091684 (ebook other)
Subjects: LCSH: Education, Rural—Social aspects—Mexico—History—20th century. | Teachers colleges—Mexico—History—20th century. | Boarding schools—Mexico—History—20th century. | Peasants—Education—Social aspects—Mexico—History—20th century. | Teachers—Political activity—Mexico—History—20th century. | BISAC: HISTORY / Latin America / Mexico
Classification: LCC LC5148. M45 P236 2021 (print) | LCC LC5148. M45 (ebook) | DDC 370.9173/4—dc23
LC record available at https://lccn.loc.gov/2021011881
LC ebook record available at https://lccn.loc.gov/2021011882

This title is freely available in an open access edition made possible by a generous contribution from the Massachusetts Institute of Technology Libraries.

Cover art: (*Foreground*) Mural at the rural normal of Ayotzinapa, Guerrero. Photograph by the author. (*Background*) Rural normal of Galeana, Nuevo León, 1934. Archivo General de la Nación, Photographic Archive, Normales Rurales, c2, Sobre 9.

In memory of my mother, Eva, herself a radical teacher

To Ayotzinapa's Missing 43: May your families one day find justice

Contents

Acknowledgments

Intellectually, politically, and personally, the topic of this book picked me as much as I picked it. The question of rural teachers first began to tug at me in the early 2000s when I was working on my first book about a postrevolutionary agrarian movement. The more I delved into Mexico's twentieth-century history of campesino resistance, the more I encountered the countryside's teachers, as organic intellectuals, as advisers, and as leaders. My search for answers about their persistent presence led me to the rural normales, utterly unique institutions whose politicized student body often made headlines for mounting roadblocks, staging demonstrations, or otherwise disrupting business as usual. From predominantly poor backgrounds, the youths who attended these boarding schools couched their demand for an education in the language of socialism, an ethos that, I came to learn, was a constituting element of their school culture. The fact that their student association defined itself as Marxist-Leninist was fascinating to me, having grown up in a Marxist household but coming of age after the fall of the Berlin Wall when, even among the leftist groups with which I participated, many insisted on a new analytic paradigm. And then there was my own childhood in rural Mexico, where I attended my town's public elementary school, precisely the type where rural *normalistas* would have been sent to teach. Precarious in so many ways, it was better off than most rural schoolhouses because it went up to sixth grade. Still, its predominantly campesino and indigenous student body was unstable. Youngsters were pulled out during harvest season to help their families, and many had to join the labor market before reaching sixth grade. I remember clearly my sixth-grade cohort being half the size of the first-grade class.

In various ways these dynamics shaped my connection to the world of rural *normalismo*, and I am ever indebted to those who assisted me in reconstructing it. In Mexico, numerous *compañeros* and *compañeras*, colleagues and friends, helped me navigate the vast network of schools, teachers, students, and archives necessary to write this book. Luis Hernández Navarro was an ever generous source of contacts, stimulating discussion, and a treasure trove of knowledge about Mexico's education policy—past and present. His own work with, and participation in, the democratic teachers' movement, is a powerful example of the best tradition of the committed intellectual. I feel fortunate to call him a friend. My research in various parts of Mexico would not have been possible without the kindness of people like Alma Gómez Caballero, who opened her home to me and introduced me to other normalistas who, like herself, participated in local and national struggles. In Oaxaca, Rogelio Vargas Garfias led me through the rich and multifaceted world of the state's militant teachers. His warmth and tireless struggle are inspiring amid the seemingly insurmountable odds faced by teachers and students in Mexico's poorest regions. I will likewise always be grateful to those dissident teachers who accompanied me through hard-to-reach parts of the countryside. Those journeys, those conversations, and the people I met will long remain with me. In Zacatecas, I am grateful to Martín Escobedo for his help accessing the local archives of San Marcos. Marcelo Hernández Santos, Sergio Ortíz Briano, and Hallier Arnulfo Morales Dueñas have also been enormously supportive. Always eager to help clarify some of normalismo's intricacies, they have been valuable colleagues in the process of writing this book. I am likewise grateful to Siddharta Camargo, who generously provided fruitful contacts for key parts of this research. In Morelos, Guillermo Franco Solís helped guide me through the fascinating world of Amilcingo's rural *normal*. During my visits to various rural normales current students gave me tours of their campuses and shared their experiences of study and struggle. I am grateful that they allowed me in, even during delicate moments such as when they had shuttered a campus as protest. In the wake of different acts of state repression, student leaders spoke to me with pride and determination, even as their precautionary measures and a tendency to look over their shoulder revealed the extent to which violence was a part of their condition. Those interactions gave me a complex sense of their schools' present and sharpened the lens with which to see their past. Throughout the research and writing process, I have benefited enormously from conversations with Hugo Aboites, Ariadna Acevedo Rodrigo, Jorge Cázares, Alicia Civera, Francisco López Bárcenas, César Navarro, Jesús Vargas, and Lev Velázquez. I am grateful for their time and intellectual generosity. I thank Tracy Goode and Irving Reynoso for their research support as well as the numerous archivists and librarians who went out of their way make my searches fruitful. Friends like Enrique Dávalos, Guillermo Peimbert, Víctor Hugo Sánchez Reséndiz, and Javier Villanueva have brought me support, fun, and hours of stimulating conversation. My travels to Mexico have long been enriched by their presence. My aunt and uncle, Hilda Moreno and Arturo Padilla, remain generous with their home and ever present with logistical support. Their welcoming arms have been a great source of comfort.

Through the many years working on this project, I have received support from several institutions. The Woodrow Wilson Career Enhancement Fellowship Program helped fund my initial research in Mexico, the Institute for Historical Studies at the University of Texas at Austin provided the time and space to begin the writing process, and a fellowship at Wellesley's Newhouse Center for the Humanities supported my writing as I finished the first draft of this manuscript. Dartmouth College, where I was a faculty member until 2015, provided financial support for several research trips, and the Massachusetts Institute of Technology (MIT), my new institutional home, has been generous in its funding and leave time, both crucial to finishing this book.

The thinking, drafting, writing, and rewriting process for this book took place in conversation with many colleagues and friends. Claudia Rueda has been an ever-present sounding board for ideas, a generous draft reader, and an incisive source of feedback, often helping me out of the corners I wrote myself into. Our in-person and long-distance writing sessions helped fend off some of the loneliness inherent in the writing process. Over many years now, Louise Walker has been an incredibly generous draft reader. Her keen eye, a ruthlessly helpful commentary, and an acute sense of the larger picture have been crucial to honing my ideas. With immense care, Cindy Forster read almost the entire draft of this manuscript. She is deeply attuned to the voices from below and the logic to which they point, and her feedback and her own work as a historian have influenced my thinking in fundamental ways. Christina Jiménez also read most of this manuscript. Her comments, encouragement, and ever-positive outlook were an important part of the process. Alex Aviña has time and again engaged thoughtfully and constructively with so many of my questions—big and small. His solidarity and *compañerismo* have meant a lot to me. At a crucial moment in the life of this book, Kirsten Weld provided invaluable observations that sharpened its focus. It has been a privilege to count on her feedback and be part of the Latin Americanist community of historians she has helped create through the writing workshops at Harvard. I have also benefited enormously from the wider community of Mexicanist historians and am especially grateful to Ray Craib, Shane Dillingham, Gil Joseph, Steve Lewis, Ken Maffitt, Jocelyn Olcott, Wil Pansters, Pablo Piccato, Thom Rath, Ben Smith, and Mary Kay Vaughan. With kindness and wisdom, Gisela Fosado, Duke's editorial director, has guided this project through publication. I am immensely grateful to her, Ale Mejía, Ellen Goldlust, and Duke University Press's wonderful editorial production team. To Brooke Larson (who subsequently revealed herself) and Duke's other anonymous reviewer, thank you for engaging deeply with this manuscript, asking tough questions, and making invaluable suggestions.

My colleagues in the History Department at MIT have been nothing short of wonderful. Welcoming me with warmth and kindness, they have been crucially supportive and enthusiastic about my work. Craig Wilder, a longtime friend and colleague, continues to be a wise and generous mentor. He has been immensely helpful in thinking about parallels between the United States and Mexico on the dynamics of education as it relates to historically subjugated populations. Jeff Ravel's warmth, generous spirit, and enthusiastic engagement have greatly enriched my time at MIT. His own knowledge of Latin American history has made for some especially compelling discussions about my work and the dynamics of the region more generally. Deeply thoughtful and thoroughly kind in his feedback, Chris Capozzola has time and again provided invaluable commentary on this project. Emma Teng's continuous commitment to Latin American studies at MIT has been crucial to fortifying the institute's vibrant intellectual community and increasing the possibilities of connecting research, teaching, and community engagement. Directly and indirectly, this project has been supported by numerous staff members. I am especially grateful to Ece Turnator, MIT's humanities and digital scholarship librarian, for consistently going above and beyond the call of duty to help track down obscure works. At Dartmouth College, Jill Baron also proved amazing in her skill and dogged pursuit of sources. Karen Gardener, whom I had the privilege of working alongside during my tenure as director of graduate studies at MIT, was thorough, patient, and ever on top of tasks big and small. Her conscientious nature made it possible to strike a productive balance between research and administrative work.

My lasting friendship with numerous colleagues has been an immense source of strength, not to mention fun. I am especially grateful to Aimee Bahng, Laura Brown, Joe Cullon, Kendra Field, Jennifer Fluri, Reena Gold-three, Jean Kim, Annelise Orleck, Rashauna Johnson, Russell Rickford, Naaborko Sackeyfio-Lenoch, Justin Steil, and Franny Sullivan, who have been there in good times and bad, providing support and sharing in joy. Since we first met as we began teaching at Dartmouth, Celia Naylor has been a kindred spirit. Her camaraderie, generous spirit, humor, and audacity have accompanied me in countless ways. I look forward to many more years of work, visits, and travel, hopefully more of the latter two.

In the fullest dimension of the term, Bobby has been a true compañero. Not only has he read multiple drafts of this work, talked through my ideas in their rawest form, helped refine them to acquire coherence, and offered immensely constructive feedback, but he has consistently undertaken the lion's share of domestic and family duties. His unassuming, loving, and supportive acts made possible the focus this book so often required. Camilo, our son, who has lived with this work the entirety of his short life, handled the absences it brought with a patience otherwise uncharacteristic of his eager personality. To be sure, he found ways of joining the process, constantly matching my early waking hours by insisting he could sit quietly by my side and draw. I will always cherish these predawn work sessions even if they were never quite as quiet as he promised. *Hijo*, I'm finally done "making my book." I hope one day you will read it.

My mother, Eva, did not live to see this work's completion. But her spirit shaped it in many ways. Tireless in her devotion as a mother and committed in her work as a public schoolteacher, she was also daring and unabashed in her relationship to the world. Witnessing her tireless labor as a Los Angeles public schoolteacher, I learned early on how deficient education budgets rested on the backs of teachers, not to mention their students. She was not one to hold back on political explanations even when I was too young to understand them, and her accounts of how racism and capitalism shaped the world instilled in me an early indignity toward injustice. I consider it a great fortune to have been born to a resilient, radical schoolteacher like her.

Abbreviations

CNED	National Central of Democratic Students (Central Nacional de Estudiantes Demócraticos)
CREN	Regional Normal Teaching Center (Centro Regional de Enseñanza Normal)
FECSM	Mexican Federation of Socialist Campesino Students (Federación de Estudiantes Campesinos Socialistas de México)
GPG	Popular Guerrilla Group (Grupo Popular Guerrillero)
IPN	National Polytechnic Institute (Instituto Politécnico Nacional)
MAR	Revolutionary Action Movement (Movimiento de Acción Revolucionaria)
MRM	Revolutionary Teachers Movement (Movimiento Revolucionario del Magisterio)
PAN	National Action Party (Partido Acción Nacional)
PP	Popular Party (Partido Popular)
PPS	Popular Socialist Party (Partido Popular Socialista)
PST	Socialist Workers' Party (Partido Socialista de los Trabajadores)
PRI	Institutional Revolutionary Party (Partido Revolucionario Institucional)

SEP   Ministry of Public Education (Secretaría de Educación Pública)
SNTE   National Union of Education Workers (Sindicato Nacional de Trabajadores de la Educación)
UGOCM   General Union of Mexican Workers and Campesinos (Unión General de Obreros y Campesinos de México)

Ayotzinapa and the Legacy of Revolution

IN THE AFTERNOON OF September 26, 2014, dozens of students from the teacher-training college of Ayotzinapa in Mexico's coastal state of Guerrero set out to commandeer several buses to use as transportation to Mexico City. As they had in years past, they would attend the annual commemoration of the 1968 massacre in which the army killed hundreds of students demonstrating in Tlatelolco's plaza. Frowned on by the authorities and begrudgingly tolerated by bus companies as the cost of doing business, such bus takeovers by students of the country's seventeen rural normales were common practice. These boarding schools, created in the 1920s for the sons and daughters of campesinos, have long enjoyed a reputation for political militancy. This latest action appeared as another exploit in this tradition. However, later that night, as the Ayotzinapa students tried to depart the city of Iguala with the five buses they had garnered, they found themselves encircled by a massive armed operation. Local police blocked their exit while uniformed agents and plainclothes gunmen shot at them. The army dispatch at the nearby military base that had, in concert with federal and state police, been tracking the students since they left their school earlier that afternoon, did nothing. By morning, three Ayotzinapa students lay dead, one with his face torn off.

Forty-three other students had disappeared, last seen being dragged off in the presence of federal and state authorities.[1]

Gruesome as it was, this event was hardly remarkable in a country whose war on drugs—officially declared in 2006—had, by then, left over 100,000 people dead and 25,000 more disappeared.[2] Indeed, federal officials quickly dismissed the attack as a local cartel conflict: if students from Ayotzinapa had been victims, they must have had some connection to illicit activity. After all, the normalistas' penchant for disruption was widely known. Remarkably, however, this official narrative did not quell public ire, nor did the victims' families accept it. Over the following months, thousands took to the streets demanding justice and the return of the forty-three disappeared Ayotzinapa students. Why this event and not the thousands of other deaths and disappearances sparked the unprecedented protests has much to do with the identity of the forty-three disappeared, the immediate actions of their peers, and the history of the schools where they studied.[3]

Founded in 1926, the rural *normal* of Ayotzinapa was one of thirty-five teacher-training schools the Mexican government built in the two decades following the 1910–20 revolution. This civil war ended the thirty-five-year dictatorship of Porfirio Díaz (1876–1911) and brought to power a nationalist government whose ensuing project deployed teachers as agents of state consolidation. The institutions that would train these educators acquired many of their defining characteristics during the presidency of Lázaro Cárdenas (1934–40), whose numerous progressive reforms included socialist education. Although socialist education was short-lived as official policy and never clearly defined by its state architects, at rural normales its meaning was simple and enduring: justice. Education for the poor, a student voice in institutional practices, and class consciousness constituted defining elements of *normalista* culture, reproduced in subsequent decades thanks to student collective action.

These dynamics were at play that fateful September night. Commandeering buses from private companies was not just a means to acquire transportation but also a lesson in protest, one the student association passed on to each incoming class. The Tlatelolco commemoration that the Ayotzinapa students planned to attend, moreover, offered a history lesson, an important one for rural normalistas whose besieged schools had for decades produced numerous campesino and labor activists, some killed or jailed by the state (figure I.1). Tlatelolco's anniversary provided a venue to dramatize the myriad ways the government had betrayed the 1917 Constitution and the revolutionary principles on which the modern Mexican state was founded.

FIGURE I.1 Mural at the rural normal of Ayotzinapa, Guerrero, that depicts the 1970s guerrilla leader Lucio Cabañas and the images of the Missing 43. The legend reads, "We are an army of dreamers." Photograph by author.

The betrayal was decades in the making. President Enrique Peña Nieto (2012–18), whose administration marked the return of the Institutional Revolutionary Party (Partido Revolucionario Institucional, PRI), which had ruled the country from 1929 to 2000, epitomized many of its sins. It was corrupt, authoritarian, and technocratic, and its long relationship to drug trafficking had spun out of control, a dynamic reflected in the dizzying numbers of people killed and disappeared in the preceding decade.[4] In this context, the violence against Ayotzinapa's students was the proverbial straw that broke the camel's back. Their condition as students, the sheer scale of the attack against them, and the state's involvement in it elicited the specter of Tlatelolco, the site of a massacre that still haunts the PRI. Building on their long tradition of protest, rural normalistas mobilized immediately, sparking a level of outcry the state could not contain.

There are few weapons the poor can wield against the powerful, but in those the rural normalistas are well versed. In addition to compelling bus drivers to take them to demonstrations, they have frequently blocked roads, taken over tollbooths to let drivers pass for free, commandeered and distributed merchandise from cargo trucks, and sequestered transport vehicles in their schoolyards. And they have long organized school strikes and walkouts. Students undertook most of these actions merely to force the authorities to allocate the necessary budgets for the schools' subsistence—funds they are entitled to but often receive only after a fight. While normalista persistence and loud protest have ensured their schools' survival, they also produced a black legend. For decades, the government and the press have labeled these institutions centers of agitation and guerrilla seedbeds; the authorities have threatened to turn them into pig farms or schools for tourist technicians and have characterized those who study and teach there as agitators, subversives, and, more recently, pseudostudents or hooligans. Indeed, in the public debates that raged as the families of Ayotzinapa's Missing 43 searched for their sons, official narratives sought to blame the victims. What, other than trouble, could students expect with their disruptive behavior and blatant disregard for private property?

To the narrative that criminalized the victims, protesters counterposed the crimes of the state. "Fue el estado" ("It was the state") became the massive rallying cry. Here the Tlatelolco massacre, the anniversary of which the Ayotzinapa normalistas sought to honor, intensified the rage. Still an open wound, Tlatelolco resonated across social sectors, partly because its victims were students.[5] Just as significant was the rural normalistas' tradition of protest. Within moments of the September 26 attack, with a fellow classmate's blood-soaked body still on the ground, students called a press conference and safeguarded the crime scene. Before most could even describe the events as they transpired that night, normalistas had activated their school networks across the country, publicized this latest aggression against them, and reminded the nation of their schools' history. That history is the subject of this book.

A RADICAL TRADITION

Since their founding, rural normales have been hosts to national sagas. Emerging from the state's revolutionary project, they trained teachers who were intended to shape a modern patriotic citizenry by organizing civic festivals, promoting hygiene and health campaigns, and replacing superstition with science. But the popular longings driving the Mexican Revolution also permeated these institutions and by the 1930s became constituting elements of their institutional logic. Land reform, education for the poor, and community leadership stood as guiding principles of the teachers they trained. Over the coming decades, the tensions between state consolidation and revolutionary justice produced a telling contradiction. The very schools meant to shape a loyal citizenry became hotbeds of political radicalism, and their graduates appeared consistently linked to militant protests, including guerrilla struggles. How and why did the rural normales stray from the state's original design?

The answer lies in four interrelated processes. First, while rural normales were founded for the purposes of state consolidation, they were grounded in the notion of agrarian justice. Built on expropriated haciendas, these schools were enshrined with an air of poetic justice. In the palatial estates that previously exploited their parents, adolescents of campesino origin—one of the requirements to study at these institutions—would now gain an education.[6] State officials linked education to rural development, adopting pedagogical principles that connected the classroom to the community, cooperativism to individual discipline, and learning to laboring. These qualities, insisted Mexico's early twentieth-century educational architects, would reinforce a "rural spirit," one that harnessed campesinos' commitment to the land but directed it to modern, efficient ends.[7] This framework sparked a uniquely student-campesino consciousness that came to challenge a modern national project increasingly devoid of justice.

Second, the state's prescribed mission comingled with a transformation in students' own identity. At rural normales, the children of campesinos became professionals, male and female students shed gender norms and absorbed different ones, and ethnic identities expanded or narrowed as normalistas navigated the contradictions of *mestizaje*, the dominant ideology that Mexico constituted a harmonious mixture of Spanish and indigenous heritage. Field trips exposed students to different parts of the country, and dorm life alongside two hundred to five hundred other youth gave them a degree of autonomy they did not have at home. Such exposure and social fluidity denaturalized hierarchy and created both the possibility and expectation of change.

Third, rural normales hosted broad contradictions that made struggle a fact of daily life. The imposing architecture of the ex-haciendas that housed these schools contrasted with the spartan nature of daily life. Boarding-houses rarely had enough beds for all of the students; the newly arrived slept on cardboard. Food was meager, running water and electricity infrequent. To secure their basic needs, students continuously petitioned the government, leading them to mobilize for resources as much as they studied for classes. By underfunding and abandoning rural normales, the state assured that the individual upward mobility the schools promised could be secured only through collective struggle.

Finally, these contradictions extended beyond normalistas' time as students. Upon their graduation, the Ministry of Public Education (Secretaría de Educación Pública, SEP) dispatched the young teachers to communities whose children they would teach, whose living conditions they would improve, and whose inhabitants they would organize and uplift. It was a daunting task, one made virtually impossible after 1940 as the state took less interest in the countryside, except as it might serve the cities. In lieu of the funding, infrastructure, and resources—including a dignified teaching salary—that might buttress rural education, the SEP appealed to teachers' missionary duty. They were of campesino origin after all; sacrifice must not be foreign to them.

Rural teachers navigated this contradiction in myriad ways. As did the rest of the population, most migrated to urban centers, where they pursued professional advancement and could teach in more manageable conditions. Plenty became regional caciques (political bosses), *charros* (official unionists), or corrupt politicians.[8] Some pursued justice relentlessly, willing to lose life and limb in the process. In the minority, these militant teachers and students exerted an outsized role, and their legacy is most associated with the rural normales. This association is partly based on rural normalistas' constant protest to garner resources for their schools' survival. But it is also a measure of how these schools served as an uncomfortable reminder of the countryside's abandonment.

Unintended Lessons of Revolution details the culture of student militancy that was forged and reproduced in Mexico's rural normales. Rural normalistas occupied an intermediary position between city and countryside, and their lived experience, tactics of struggle, and notions of justice drew on the campesino, student, and labor worlds. The ideology they fashioned highlights key continuities between the old left (whose relationship to the Communist Party looked to the Soviet Union as a model, saw workers as the principal revolutionary protagonists, and privileged structure over agency) and the new left (which was more inspired by anti-imperialist struggles, especially Cuba; saw students and campesinos as essential agents of change; and believed the conditions for revolution should be made rather than awaited). At rural normales the relationship between the two became manifest not because of the content or style of classroom lessons—which were in many ways quite traditional—but because of the nature of students' collective living experience in institutions conceived of within the framework of revolutionary justice. As an ethos more than a pedagogy, Mexico's brief 1930s experiment with socialist education proved transcendent. So, too, the Mexican Federation of Socialist Campesino Students (Federación de Estudiantes Campesinos Socialistas de México, FECSM) formed in 1935 to advocate for the rights of students at rural normales. In the tradition of the old left, the federation was hierarchical, sought discipline from its members, imposed mandatory meetings and activities, and had a vanguardist strategy. Within rural normales it became a primary vehicle to challenge the state, transmit historical knowledge, and offer analytical tools that denaturalized poverty. It challenged the powerful to reckon with the vision of the oppressed.

That challenge propelled a radical political culture at rural normales, schools that, like other progressive institutions from Latin America's old left, became venues "where the abstractions of liberty and equality could be embodied as felt experiences, where individual rights and collective social justice would be viscerally understood and mutually dependent," what Greg Grandin characterized as insurgent politics.[9] That from the start rural normales were materially precarious, besieged by the right and dependent for their survival on students petitioning the state, punctured liberal individualist notions that education was an independent, self-sufficient endeavor. Insurgent politics also tied schooling to action, giving students a sense that conditions in the world could be changed. This process spurred political consciousness, not because students learned a critical pedagogy that they then applied as teachers,

but because they came to understand their very schools as historically constituted through social relationships of power.[10]

The question of consciousness, an awareness of one's material reality that
spurs action, is a central theme in this story. Scholars of labor, agrarian, student, and guerrilla movements have long noted the multifaceted, contingent,
and contradictory nature of critical consciousness and its manifestations.[11]
Consciousness is not, as E. P. Thompson famously put it, tied to the ups and
downs of an economic curve but is an accumulation of lived experiences.[12] It
is also not a static or binary characteristic that subjects either do or do not
possess. Consciousness is a process with multiple origins and expressions, always dependent on the particularities of time and place.[13] Finally, consciousness is a constantly evolving process, one honed or transformed in the act of
struggle, one that itself generates new possibilities.[14] This is why the tactics,
rhetoric, and demands of particular movements change over time and why
radical revolutionary language coexists with seemingly innocuous strategies
of "reaching the people."[15] In their rhetoric, historical actors often borrow
from the only available political discourse, even if it originates with elites.[16]
Other times the language of struggle comes from utopian ideals spurred by
insurrections of the dispossessed, whether failed or successful.[17] Whatever
its manifestations, context is key to understanding the puzzle of collective
action.[18]

For the indigenous and campesino students of this study, that context was
the network of rural normales, schools that came to harbor shared politicized
cultural norms. This institutional world determined much of their praxis, a
condition that goes a long way in explaining why, after graduation, individual teachers' paths diverged so widely and why, for many, upward mobility
came to supersede collective action. But even within the schools, the politicized environment did not mean all students were militant actors. Indeed,
as is historically the case, relentless activists are the minority and achieve
change only when their message resonates with a larger group and when
that larger group is willing to act. At rural normales the self-consciously political student leadership organized through the FECSM achieved collective
action not because it promised liberation but because it secured the basic
material needs for their institutions' survival and reproduction. To be sure,
the FECSM did articulate radical principles—in its calls for socialism, for
example—and organized militant actions such as land takeovers alongside
campesinos that posited a fundamental restructuring of society and cultivated alliances to achieve it. But for most normalistas those lessons served as a
framework to justify and secure their own rights: adequate living conditions

in their boarding schools, competent teachers and sufficient learning supplies, pedagogical and recreational infrastructure, and a dignified job upon graduation. To achieve this, the FECSM constantly called for strikes. Since its representative body drew from rural normales across the country, these strikes extended nationally and forced the upper echelons of the SEP to the negotiating table.

The politicized culture that became such an enduring feature of rural normales is a measure of how far the schools' constituting logic—which foregrounded the countryside—contrasted with the state's actions that privileged cities. Unable and unwilling to resolve this contradiction, the government propagated a narrative that stigmatized these schools and their students like no others, even as many rural normal graduates went on to serve as cogs in the ruling party's governing apparatus. In the 1940s the authorities revived reactionary 1930s tropes demonizing teachers' role as community leaders; the press added red-scare tales of Bolshevik takeovers in the 1950s and of Cuban subversion in the 1960s; and the SEP topped it off by insisting that unqualified teachers bore responsibility for the nation's educational shortcomings, especially the dismal situation in the countryside.

The logic established a clear continuity between the portrayal of ungrateful campesino youth who, at rural normales, continued to challenge the state rather than appreciate the opportunity and resources to study and teachers who would not succumb to SEP appeals for self-sacrifice and insisted on higher pay, better working conditions, and more benefits. Teachers' very struggle for union democracy, which, under the leadership and with the participation of rural normal graduates, saw especially strong episodes in the mid-1950s and again in the late 1970s, provided an additional layer with which to demonize them in the public eye.[19] On the one hand, the National Union of Education Workers (Sindicato Nacional de Trabajadores de la Educación, SNTE)—the powerful official teachers' union, whose historic allegiance to the state produced (often dubious) labor concessions meant to control its base and harness support for the PRI—offered proof of teachers' collective corruption. On the other, when teachers challenged SNTE cronyism by mounting struggles for independent unions, they were stigmatized for putting their labor interests above children's educational needs.

But stigmatizing rural normales and blaming teachers for Mexico's low education levels obscure the extent to which the school system itself reflected structural inequality, which after 1940 became increasingly acute and was driven by three policy strategies that marked most of the twentieth century. First, in contrast to President Cárdenas, who in the 1930s treated rural education as part and parcel of community development, which included land distribution, support for the *ejido* (communal landholdings), and the establishment of cooperatives, subsequent administrations addressed schooling in isolation. After 1940 the SEP continued to build schoolhouses throughout the country, often at an accelerated pace. The SEP also trained an increasing number of teachers to populate the new classrooms. But a village teacher could do little against the broader forces of hunger, lack of infrastructure, and families who could not send their children to school because their immediate economic survival depended on the entire household's labor. The staggeringly low rates of elementary school completion are a testament to these larger dynamics.[20] Teacher absenteeism was another. Sent to remote communities, educators found themselves in a situation that was tantamount to exile. Rural living conditions did not correspond to the upward mobility their education had promised. Their paychecks alone might take a year to arrive. Their salary level, moreover, was set on a lower scale than that of urban teachers. With this situation, SEP appeals to missionary duty and self-sacrifice rang hollow. Teachers consistently sought transfers to urban areas where they would have better pay and working conditions and could seek additional schooling to qualify for positions in secondary schools or as principals, SEP bureaucrats, or regional inspectors.

A second dynamic, the state's policy toward the countryside, aggravated this process since it stymied the efforts of those teachers willing to brave difficult conditions. Absent after 1940 was any type of deliberate or sustained strategy to develop social infrastructure in the countryside. Indeed, at every turn the state undermined campesinos' basic ability to subsist off the land. Not only did agrarian redistribution slow after Cárdenas, but presidents Manuel Ávila Camacho (1940–46) and Miguel Alemán (1946–52) eased laws designed to prevent land concentration by expanding expropriation limits for export-crop cultivation. Through subsidized inputs for production and infrastructure projects, the state helped agribusiness establish its dominance in the countryside, much of it geared to serve the US market.[21] The 1941 Rockefeller-sponsored Green Revolution also focused its aid efforts on large-scale farms. Campesinos could in no way compete with a mechanized industry whose high-yielding seeds depended on sustained irrigation and high levels of fertilizers and chemical pesticides, the costs of which both the public and private sector sponsored.[22] The 1942–64 US-Mexico Bracero Program, which sent hundreds of laborers north, and the 1965 Border Industrialization Program, which led to the proliferation of northern assembly plants, offered jobs to rural migrants that usually paid more than the income they might derive from their own land cultivation. But such opportunities did nothing for rural development's social infrastructure. On the contrary, to the extent that such opportunities helped laborers provide a better future for their children, that future lay with an education in the cities. By the 1960s Mexico went from being a predominantly rural to a predominantly urban nation, a trend that continued throughout the century. Material support for rural teachers and their schoolhouses as venues to promote community development had by then long been abandoned—but not the rhetoric. The SEP continued to invoke teachers' sense of missionary duty by which they were to endure rural poverty and isolation for the greater good of the nation. Such appeals may have had some resonance had they been part of a deliberate national effort in which shared sacrifice produced a more equitable collective well-being. But the state made these appeals at a time of unbridled prosperity, whose fruits accentuated inequality and were based on a transfer of wealth from the countryside to the city.[23]

Finally, Mexico's education spending itself operated under a palliative rather than transformative logic. The state expanded educational opportunities without implementing the structural reform consistently demanded by campesino, labor, student, and indigenous movements. Public education compensated for the lack of other benefits—health care, social security, adequate housing, stable employment, a living wage—ones the country's majorities would never enjoy.[24] Over the latter part of the twentieth century, education spending ebbed and flowed depending on the presidential administration, but even when it increased, that rise did not improve its quality nor offer more equitable access.[25] Nor did it always correspond to significant intergenerational social mobility.[26] Intertwined with this dynamic was the nature of the PRI, whose power and organizational logic came from a corporatist structure that relied on union networks affiliated to the state. The official teachers' union, the SNTE, constituted Mexico's (and Latin America's) largest union. Aside from teachers, it included schools' technical, manual, and clerical personnel; nonmanagement and some lower-level SEP administrative workers; and academic and nonacademic employees of institutes, research centers, and museums.[27] Its infamously corrupt leadership—whose general secretaries comfortably navigated the halls of power, often using the SNTE as a springboard into political office—supported the PRI in exchange for concessions to their membership.[28] Those concessions were again palliative, translating into increased opportunities for individual upward mobility rather than collective material improvements, much less union democracy. When adjusted for inflation, for example, teachers' pay did not achieve its

1921 levels until the early 1960s; during the crucial years of educational expansion, this allowed the state to hire three teachers for the price of one.[29] In lieu of raises and other benefits demanded by dissident teachers in the 1950s, the SEP offered opportunities for professional development that corresponded to individual merit-based pay. The SNTE's involvement in academic matters—so censured by technocrats as interfering with educational efficiency—acted in tandem with this dynamic. The SNTE assured, guided, and directed opportunities for upward mobility to control its base.[30] These opportunities, moreover, came in the cities, partly because that was where the accrediting institutions were located but, more important, because that was where the higher-paying jobs lay.[31]

It is within these three structural dynamics—school construction devoid of rural development, support for agribusiness at the cost of the campesino economy, and the corporatist logic of education spending—that we must understand rural normales and their consistently politicized student body. Mexico's urbanizing political economy marked rural normales as relics of a past project even as they provided crucial opportunities for students to navigate the contradictions of national development. For this opportunity students had to fight: they had to fight to secure material resources, to ensure rural normales remained schools for the poor, and to prevent the reduction of spots for incoming students. Far from static, their frameworks of struggle changed with each passing decade and acquired new dimensions, ones rooted in the Mexican Revolution and the structural changes carried out under Cárdenas, spurred by subsequent battles to preserve the popular elements of the 1917 Constitution, given new impetus by the anti-imperialist and socialist ideals of the 1960s, and engaged with the guerrilla struggles of the 1970s.

OLD DIVIDES, NEW QUESTIONS

Mexico's education system of the 1920s and 1930s enjoys a robust tradition of study.[32] For subsequent decades, however, historians have turned their attention to student protest rather than to educational policy or schools as institutions.[33] The relationship between the two remains largely unexamined, a lacuna this work seeks to fill. How rural normales become repositories of political militancy, how this ethos was reproduced, and how it survived amid sea-change transformations constitute this book's guiding questions. To answer them, I center the experience of the indigenous and campesino students who participated in school mobilizations, engaged in popular struggle, and perpetuated political traditions. Their experience, in turn, I contextualize within the broader forces that conditioned their vision and actions. My story begins with the revolutionary state consolidation in the 1920s–1930s, continues through the 1940–68 Mexican miracle, and takes us through the guerrilla groups of the 1970s—three periods historians tend to treat separately. Focusing on the countryside or Mexico City and alternatively treating campesinos, students, workers, or the middle class, recent histories have uncovered the multifaceted protest and state repression that accompanied the betrayal of the revolution's social reforms.[34] Seeking to expand these geographic, temporal, and social divides, I take a *longue durée* approach that is national in scope and that examines subjects whose changing identity—from campesino, to student, to teacher—defies neat categorizations. In this way, *Unintended Lessons of Revolution* addresses key questions raised, but still unanswered, by this recent literature.

First, while the recent scholarship on popular unrest has revealed the 1940–68 *pax priísta* (peace of the PRI) to be a myth, uncertain still are the effects of those struggles. Put another way, what is the relationship between the protest that we now know marked the Mexican miracle and the institutions meant to fulfill the revolution's social reforms?[35] To answer this question, this study considers Mexico's revolutionary twentieth century as a distinct historical period.[36] In a rather bold fashion, historians Greg Grandin and Gilbert Joseph have posited a long Cold War time frame that extends, in Joseph's words, "back to the Mexican Revolution, the twentieth-century's first great social revolution," and by some measures "has not yet ended."[37] This new Cold War historiography understands Latin American politicization not as resulting from US-Soviet rivalry but as emerging from local historical dynamics in conversation with global events. The 1910 revolution inaugurated Latin America's transition from nineteenth-century authoritarian liberalism to revolutionary nationalism as popular struggles throughout the region challenged landed oligarchs, their exclusionary institutions, and the racial hierarchies that structured social domination.[38] No institution better represents nationalism's inclusionary vision than Mexico's rural normales, the boarding schools that trained agents of state consolidation while bringing education to the children of the historically subjugated campesino and indigenous population. This ostensibly inclusionary vision housed serious contradictions, namely, the assimilationist framework of mestizaje on which it was based. How indigenous students navigated a system that demanded they shed their languages, traditions, and worldview and the alternative educational proposals that indigenous communities would themselves make by century's end reveals the dynamic nature of the educational process and the differing visions originating from above and from below.

Second, a history of rural normales provides a unique opportunity to hone in on the question of political consciousness and examine its expansive nature amid a group whose identity drew from the agrarian, student, and labor worlds. Utterly unique in their evolution, student practices, and institutional mores, rural normales display the fate of leftist foundational principles in a changing national landscape. First conceived as a means to produce campesino teachers and soon expanded within the logic of socialist education, rural normales endured reactionary backlash, survived despite state neglect, housed teachers and students-turned-guerrillas, and persisted in their Marxist-Leninist rhetoric even as many on the left abandoned such language in the 1990s. Their origins in a particularly radical period of revolutionary state consolidation, their almost mythical status in the official revolutionary narrative, and the role of the FECSM within and across these schools made social justice both an effective and a compelling framework by which to elicit the state's material support. Ideology and praxis, the collective and the individual, material interests and radical ideals constituted ever-evolving dialectics. While rural normales hosted an array of student types—from militant, to reformist, to indifferent, to conservative—all had to contend with a politicized institutional universe overseen and enforced by the student association. For those who chose activism, the road to politicization began with a rather modest venture: demands for better food, dormitories, and pedagogical resources. For many that is where it ended. But for many others the notion that campesinos were entitled to an education coalesced with longer memories of family exploitation, concurrent agrarian struggles, student mobilizations, teachers' movements, and anti-imperialist notions that produced a militant consciousness that the state battled to contain.

Finally, *Unintended Lessons of Revolution* broadens the framework of transnational comparisons for both radical actors and institutions within authoritarian systems. If previous notions of the pax priísta prompted views of Mexican exceptionalism, recent debates alternately characterize the seventy-one-year PRI rule as a *dictadura* (dictatorship) or a *dictablanda* (soft dictatorship). The former stresses the state's coercion, its physical and symbolic violence, and an evolving repressive apparatus.[39] The latter, in contrast, emphasizes a loose political control, a "cultivated but thin hegemony," and an uneven ability to co-opt and points to the PRI's irregular process of state domination, in which repression was limited, controlled, and hidden.[40] My own view is that this debate sets up a false dichotomy for a regime that was both staunchly repressive *and* remarkably flexible.[41] While rendering Mexico's authoritarianism soft risks minimizing state repression as proponents of the dictadura view maintain, overemphasizing its likeness to other Latin American dictatorships risks diminishing the fundamental significance of the 1910 revolution as a social upheaval. The extent to which the PRI was more restrained in its repression owes much to the popular revolution that earlier in the century broke the church-oligarchy-army triumvirate that in the southern cone structured state terror.[42] More useful for making transnational comparisons is understanding the Cold War as counterrevolution, a process that was hard and soft, in which anticommunism served both to attenuate old-left notions of democracy that linked political and economic rights and to marshal elite power with broader conservative traditions such as status anxiety, racism, and fear of loosening social mores.[43] In this context, rural normalistas harnessed the principles inherent in the twentieth century's first great social revolution to defend their schools, a process that led them to question capitalism's socioeconomic structures. The political consciousness they acquired in the course of their struggle became increasingly articulated through larger ideological and subjective frameworks tied to national and international battles in Latin America's century of revolution.

In this sense, contrary to interpretations of the PRI as a successful political center that oversaw a society largely devoid of Cold War politicization, *Unintended Lessons of Revolutions* shows how that political center was itself historically constituted through violence and co-optation.[44] Time and again, elites harnessed Cold War narratives about the containment of communists, foreign agitators, and those intent on tarnishing the nation's image to battle popular sectors fighting for their constitutional rights. It was a counterrevolutionary process that sought to break the link between political and economic rights propelled by the radical elements of Mexico's 1910 insurrection. While the PRI's tried-and-true strategy of co-optation was by definition a less violent method of suppressing dissent, its success depended on the ever-looming threat of violence—the violence of the stick or the violence of poverty.

In this context of resistance, repression, and co-optation, what does it mean, then, to tell the history of rural normales from the perspective of radical actors? Why not focus on their conservative, quiescent, officialist, or corrupt graduates, those who helped shape the dominant political and economic system rather than those who challenged it? Or, indeed, why not devote equal time to both? The latter position is attractive especially to those who conceive of historical writing as a quest to find balance between all perspectives, an endeavor in which the historian is a free agent "floating above, taking notes with equanimity."[45] This question of objectivity has itself been the subject of historical examination revealing the extent to which its proponents have been dominant groups at the center and its challengers those at the margins of the status quo.[46] Without subscribing to the trappings of historical relativism, it is imperative to interrogate the power of dominant narratives and the extent to which they act to silence the past, to use Michel-Rolph Trouillot's haunting analysis of power and the production of history.[47] One way of silencing the past is to erase the radical possibilities presented by the struggles of the dispossessed. Another is to attenuate those possibilities by placing them on equal footing with endeavors that aligned with the status quo. Finally, there is the temptation to evaluate radical actors by whether or not their movement succeeded, a measure that, as Robin Kelley puts it, would render virtually all of them failures "because the basic power relations they sought to change remain pretty much intact." Rather than regarding this as a fatalistic assessment, however, Kelley reminds us that precisely these alternative visions drive new generations of struggle.[48]

For these reasons, I have chosen to privilege normalista radical voices— the ways they contended with and created their institutional world; the debates, strategies, and contradictions they encountered; their interactions and confrontations with those who occupied the seats of power; and the inspiration they drew from local, national, and international struggles. Within the capitalist forces that structured the political economy of education, these dynamics shaped their history. The unrest of campesino students created an institutional culture that slowed down the erosion of revolutionary rights, awakened an expansive form of consciousness, and continues to reveal the counterrevolutionary process that resulted in neoliberalism's imposition. Their perspective, their struggle, brings into sharp relief the power relations that created the past and produced the present, puncturing the dominant narrative that sees teachers primarily as a reflection of an officialist leadership.

SOURCES AND STRUCTURE

The story that follows draws on seven different source bodies, including intelligence documents that were declassified in 2002.[49] Within this collection, reports on rural normales are extensive—in some instances produced daily—and focus primarily on student political activity. Their content provides essential chronology, numbers, and information on government views of and strategy toward these schools. My other source bodies include press reports, US State Department records, SEP documents, local school archives, published memoirs, and over fifty oral histories that I conducted. Documents from the SEP are extensive and provide additional material for context, policy, and state vision. While the SEP's National Archive (Archivo Histórico de la Secretaría de Educación Pública) collections are vast, few go beyond the early 1940s, especially for normales.[50] To fill this void, I traveled to rural normales throughout the country, working at the handful of schools that had available archives. Varying in quantity, organization, and accessibility, these collections housed an array of national directives, curricula, institutional correspondence, student files, meeting reports, and petitions that help fill the post-1940s void in the SEP's National Archive. Despite my time at individual schools and the fact that some rural normales—Salaices and Saucillo in the north, Ayotzinapa and Amilcingo in the coastal and central south, and Tamazulapan or Mactumactzá in the indigenous south—at times occupy prominent places in this account, the history told here is a national one that privileges the rural normal system, its student networks, and federal policy over microhistories of individual schools.[51]

These archival sources help contextualize and cross-reference the oral histories on which this book is also based, gathered beginning in 2006 and for over a decade thereafter from normalistas across the country; those interviewed for this work span from generations who studied in the 1930s to those graduating as recently as 2019. Working with oral histories requires, as Alessandro Portelli wrote, operating at different levels: reconstructing the past, analyzing how events are narrated, and "connecting what we know about the facts with what we know about the narratives."[52] While written documentation also necessitates context and attention to narrative structure, oral history has an added complexity since it is mediated by memory. "Less about *events* and more about their *meaning*," oral testimonies are thus intrinsically different from written documents and therefore specifically useful.[53] Recounted decades later, normalista accounts are often contradictory, partial, and usually romanticized. If turned into analytical categories, however, these apparent limitations can help decipher the meaning students attached to particular experiences. Concerned as this work is with political consciousness—itself expansive, contradictory, and contingent—student reflections provide an essential way to understand individuals' relationship to the student body, institutional norms, changing frameworks of social justice, and national education policy.

Political participation tends to play an outsized role in student accounts about life at the normales. This narrative quality reflects an objective reality:

the obligatory encounter with the FECSM, the socialist student organization whose hold on dorm life meant students confronted a politicized world from the moment they arrived at the normal. Coming at a turbulent moment in a youngster's life—living away from home for the first time, learning to live as part of a collective, and preparing to make the most of this opportunity to study—the experience was gripping for many. Others took it simply as another component of their education—the particular variant of dorm culture—and thus recount FECSM assemblies, school strikes, and student marches in the most matter-of-fact manner. For still others, such practices, ideological formation, and public speaking and organizing skills became a tool kit and source of knowledge deployed years later either in the classroom, in dissident political groups, or even in official government circles.[54]

A telling insight into the politicized world comes from a normalista opposed to it. A 1987 graduate of the rural normal of Panotla in Tlaxcala, and that school's director when I interviewed her in 2012, Victoria Ramírez recounted her own experience as a student:

> The most difficult part was not so much the separation from my family—which was hard. The most difficult thing was when I saw that there was a student committee and that there was going to be a strike, and we were going to commandeer buses, and the school director and teachers were worth peanuts. . . . I came from a strong, authoritarian home, in which the father and mother had to be obeyed, and from a [junior high] school where there were rules, where there was a principal and a teacher who you had to obey. Seeing what for me was total student impunity just didn't make sense.

Narrating these events twenty-five years later while she herself was barred from campus as students shuttered the school during a strike, Ramírez stated that then, as now, students had to participate in such mobilizations. The fierce debates about actions and strategies that others recall as part of the collective decision-making process are absent from her account. And yet when I asked what her parents thought of her participation, her narrative converged with those from across the political spectrum: "It was that sense of justice. Even when [my parents] told me I was in danger, and they warned the [student] committee that if anything happened to me they were the ones responsible, my parents never withdrew me. Well, there was one moment when my father said, 'Come home, leave.' But where to?! I had to stay. It was a challenge to myself. And it was also that sense of justice. In that, the normalistas are right."

Which is the same thing that parents say today, 'The government won't give [resources], it lets students starve.' . . . That was my parents." Half guarding her, half supporting normalista petitions, Ramírez's parents accompanied her on marches, at mobilizations in Mexico City, and at conventions at other normales.[55] While she was disdainful of collective action—students should come together according to individual preferences, Ramírez emphasized— her account underscores a key dynamic at the center of this study: how the precarity of rural normales as institutions, and the lack of other educational options in the countryside, made student mobilizations there a necessity.

The story that follows is largely chronological. Chapter 1 sets the stage by exploring Mexico's early twentieth-century educational architects, their new pedagogical approaches in the wake of the revolution, and their place in a wider transnational context of state formation. It likewise provides a panoramic picture of rural normales, their changing structure and unique place within Mexico's larger teacher-training system. Chapter 2 delves into the rural normales' early history in the 1920s and their consolidation under radical Cardenista principles in the 1930s. It shows how socialist education had a lasting effect on an institutional culture whose mores the FECSM preserved and reproduced, setting the stage for the schools' long-lasting politicized culture.

Chapter 3 begins in 1940 as post-Cardenista regimes steered state policy to the right. In this context, the number of rural normales was reduced by almost half, and new educational reforms ended socialist pedagogy and co-education, decreased the schools' autonomy, and replaced previous appeals to social justice with appeals to national unity. Significantly, the Cold War would give the right new tools with which to demonize activist teachers, a context that established rural normales as bulwarks of the revolution.

By the late 1950s, two decades of state neglect of campesinos had produced an increasingly urbanizing nation, concentrating teachers in the cities while the greatest need for them lay in the countryside. Chapter 4 telescopes outward and, through the lens of education, assesses the different sectors vying to define the course of the revolution. Loath to address educational needs through structural reform as rural normalistas demanded, the state doubled down on its appeal to teachers' missionary duty and self-sacrifice. Normalistas and teachers fought back, prompting the state to paint them as dangerous subversives. At the same time, the government's own effort to expand primary education emboldened old foes—namely, the Catholic Church and powerful business groups—which harnessed the panic over the 1959 Cuban Revolution in an effort to roll back previous limits on private and religious education.

During the 1960s new repertoires of struggle emerged in rural normales. This decade, which crystallized the association between these institutions and the radical protest of their students, is the focus of chapters 5 and 6. Key to this dynamic were the joint teacher-student-campesino land takeovers in northern Mexico, which soon gave way to a regional guerrilla group in the northern state of Chihuahua. Chapter 5 examines the nature of rural normalistas' participation in this state's agrarian struggle to highlight how student protest characterized Mexico's periphery before the widely recognized 1968 movement in the capital. It shows how the rural background of normalistas marked them in unique ways as they drew on two politically rich categories, that of the campesino with its deep roots in the Mexican Revolution and that of the student, which during the 1960s acquired such charged meaning. Chapter 6 follows this dynamic at the national level through the FECSM-led strikes. By analyzing the nature of normalista demands and the experience of those who participated in the struggle, I show how their unrest manifested elements of old- and new-left politics.

Chapter 7 explores the state's effort to contain rural normalista organizing with particular attention to the 1969 SEP reform that reduced the country's rural normales from twenty-nine to fifteen, disbanded the FECSM, and implemented unprecedented harsh disciplinary measures at the remaining schools. Given this severe blow to student power, chapter 8 traces normalista efforts to recover and reconstitute the FECSM. It shows how student organizing became more militant but also more fractured. President Luis Echeverría's (1970–76) democratic opening provided a space for normalistas to regroup. In this context, normalistas—together with campesino activists—achieved the creation of a new rural normal in the state of Morelos. But the 1970s also saw the proliferation of guerrilla groups, to whom the 1968 Tlatelolco massacre signaled the impossibility of working within the system. Many rural normalistas collaborated with or joined these armed movements, a dynamic that cemented their radical reputation. By the decade's end, state surveillance, infiltration, and demonization of rural normales marked the system.

The epilogue recounts the SEP's decentralization process, which, coupled with the economic crisis of the 1980s, paved the way for the increasing neoliberal restructuring of education. It addresses the latest changes to the rural normal system and other educational reforms of the subsequent three decades, closing with a discussion of some of the recent episodes of normalista protest and repression.

THREE YEARS BEFORE the Missing 43 became a worldwide symbol of Mexico's state and narco-violence, police killed two Ayotzinapa students who, along with their peers, had blocked the Mexico City–Acapulco highway in December 2011. The normalistas were protesting the Guerrero governor's stonewalling of their yearly negotiation over school resources. The killings shook but did not deter Ayotzinapa students, who closed their school in protest and organized subsequent mobilizations. Among the banners the normalistas prepared, one depicted their peers' deaths as part of a larger history of campesino massacres. The image they drew up included several blood-soaked corpses; in addition to the two normalistas, bodies represented the 1995 Aguas Blancas massacre, in which police killed seventeen campesinos en route to a demonstration, and the 1998 El Charco massacre, in which soldiers killed eleven indigenous Mixtecs participating in a community assembly. The banner shows yet another body outline, this one with a question mark, an open interrogation about the next instance of state terror.

Even as this sign illustrated how much Ayotzinapa students understood themselves as a persecuted group, they likely never imagined the nature and scale of the attack that came in Iguala on the night of September 26 and elicited such far-reaching national and international condemnation. Some of the survivors of both attacks stated that, had the police been prosecuted for the 2011 killings, the 2014 ones might not have happened, or at least not so brazenly. That assertion may be difficult to maintain, but, along with the student banner, it reflects normalistas' keen understanding of the long relationship among protest, state violence, and impunity. Ayotzinapa laid that dynamic bare for the world to see. The mobilizations it inspired, in turn, added another lesson in resistance to institutions that, for a century, have made justice for campesinos a constituting element of their existence.

1

Normales, Education, and National Projects

DIEGO RIVERA'S 1924 MURAL *La maestra rural* (The Rural Teacher), which adorns one of the first floor walls of Mexico's Ministry of Public Education (SEP), lays out what would become an iconic image of the rural schoolteacher: against a backdrop of campesinos tilling the land, sitting on the ground as part of a human circle, a teacher leads a makeshift classroom (figure 1.1). Her pupils, indigenous men and women, children, and elders, reveal the community dimension of rural education. Alongside this open-air classroom, a member of the rural defense league, mounted on a horse, rifle in hand, dutifully protects two of the poor's most prized revolutionary achievements: land and access to education.

Mexico's 1910 revolution was at heart an agrarian struggle. While the Constitutionalists—the northern-led bourgeois faction—triumphed over the popular forces led by Emiliano Zapata and Francisco Villa, the decade-long mass uprising made clear the need for broad social reforms. Thanks to the Zapatistas and Villistas, who fought not only to oust dictator Porfirio Díaz but to overturn the exploitative structures that undergirded his rule, progressive articles regarding labor, land, and subsoil protections permeated the 1917 Constitution, along with the right to free, secular elementary education. As the new government consolidated its rule during the 1920s, workers

FIGURE 1.1 Mural by Diego Rivera entitled *La maestra rural*, located on one of the first-floor patio walls of the SEP. Photograph by author.

and campesinos continued to press for reform; in many parts of the country, this coalesced into radical projects spearheaded by or in conjunction with local socialist organizations.[1]

In the 1920s the SEP's policies and programs identified the teacher with social reform, as the agent who would guide grassroots demands. In the coming years, the SEP came to house an array of progressive thinkers. Ranging from humanists, to Marxists, to idealists, these pedagogues—several of them former teachers—believed in the redemptive power of education. While many operated under a paternalist framework, they understood schools as part of a broader project of economic justice demanded by the poor. Primary schoolteachers had already played a part in both the resistance to the Díaz dictatorship and the revolutionary leadership. Otilio Montaño, the author of the Plan of Ayala, the political program of Zapata's campesino army, best exemplifies the dynamic by which teachers could become vocal advocates of the poor.[2] Perhaps more than any other social group, teachers pushed for and were receptive to principles of social justice. Belonging to the lower rungs of the professional class, they were poorly paid and little recognized. Unlike other intellectual groups, James Cockcroft points out, "teachers lack the 'social distance' that separates middle class professionals from workers [and can awaken] the respect and trust of their less lettered brethren."[3] When the SEP later made it a specific policy to recruit the sons and daughters of campesinos to become rural teachers, it established an institutional connection between the countryside's educators and the poor.

For much of the revolutionary intelligentsia, education functioned as part of a modernizing project to transform a mostly poor, apparently backward, and unsettlingly diverse population—85 percent of whom lived in the countryside—into modern citizens. The SEP would be a key institution in this monumental undertaking, and José Vasconcelos, its first minister (1921–24), conceived of education as a way to regenerate the nation's soul.[4] Teachers were central to this project, he believed, for only they possessed the spiritual authority and self-sacrifice necessary to wade through a social morass characterized, on the one hand, by the rich, the bearers of culture whose own privilege precluded a social conscience, and, on the other hand, by the poor, whose ignorance paralyzed them.[5] For Vasconcelos, devotion rather than academic preparation made a great educator, and he expressed a general disdain for intellectuals indifferent to social ills.[6] He envisioned teachers who simply "gathered the poor and without more incentive than a will to enlighten . . . instructed without reserve, no matter how limited their own knowledge."[7] These types of teachers indeed emerged, as often in fact as in fiction, but always in lore.

By articulating social justice as an organizing principle, the state provided the space for those motivated by ethics, idealism, and social responsibility to influence the nationalist project. This process was especially apparent among Mexico's muralists, whom the SEP commissioned to paint the walls of government buildings. There, artists like Diego Rivera, José Clemente Orozco, and David Alfaro Siqueiros depicted a conception of Mexican history and society and a vision of the future in which the masses were central protagonists. They exalted Mexico's pre-Columbian civilization and depicted a reality whose essence was indigenous and campesino. Rivera especially celebrated bucolic scenes, traditional work instruments, and local handicrafts or festivities, in images that became iconic symbols of Mexican culture. While the muralists promoted these signifiers of Mexico's past, they painted a modern socialist future in which workers secured their liberation from capitalist exploitation. In the Marxist vision held by many artists, science eliminated superstition and triumphed over the Catholic Church's religious hold. Principles of social justice, to be overseen by the very agencies whose walls these scenes adorned, constituted an important organizing motif that "mimicked and [was] mimicked by" emerging official versions of history.[8]

La maestra rural is one of the first paintings in Mexico's art history to depict women in a progressive light. Shown on the front line of the battle to create a new society, the model who posed for Rivera's mural was herself a young indigenous woman intent on joining the literacy brigades created in the wake of the revolution.[9] The centrality of the female teacher in this iconic image is more than a depiction of a job traditionally accessible to women. It is an example of revolutionary citizenship, the process by which historically marginalized groups insisted "on material revolutionary benefits, recognition as political, 'public' actors, and official appreciation of their centrality to the new regime's revolutionary project."[10] This process upended social hierarchies, for despite the revolutionary intelligentsia's attempts to demarcate the boundaries of a now more inclusive national project, popular sectors were anxious to see the ten-year revolutionary war bear fruit and pushed further to define the nature of such projects and the course they would take. In this context, rural teachers constituted the intermediary figures between state directives and popular longings. Their class background and state mandate made them receptive to community needs and contributed to their role as organic intellectuals who could provide the bureaucratic know-how and social leadership to make the revolution's reforms a reality. And while community leadership roles of the type teachers were supposed to inhabit were gendered male, early educational architects insisted that rural normales be coeducational, thus paving the way for women to also occupy such positions. As one graduate put it, "Rural normales broke many taboos. Before that, a woman's job was to get married and have kids. . . . Now you had young girls moving away from their families to attend school, working in the fields, doing carpentry and blacksmithing, then being sent to a community where the teacher was everything."[11]

The Mexican revolutionary school instilled long-term lessons in social and political participation, opening up previously unthinkable spaces for the poor that challenged ethnic and gender boundaries. This chapter begins by tracing the early pedagogical approaches that laid the foundation for Mexico's twentieth-century education project. For the first two decades after the revolution, that project focused on the countryside and was intimately tied to the process of state consolidation. Taking an agrarian approach that posited campesinos as the subjects of transformation, rural normales tended to subsume indigenous identity under the broader category of the rural poor. This chapter teases out those assumptions and shows the racialized nature of revolutionary nationalism in a transnational context. As the century wore on and the revolutionary regime changed course, rural normales lost their central role in the educational project but preserved a unique identity. To show their place in the contemporary teacher-training landscape, the chapter then turns to their evolving curriculum and oppositional character concluding with a brief account of their students as self-conscious participants in Mexico's national drama.

NEW PEDAGOGICAL APPROACHES

The Mexican Revolution spawned a dramatic effort to extend public education throughout the country. "We must follow the methods of the great venerable Spanish educators, like Las Casas, Vasco de Quiroga and Motolinía, who adapted the Indian to European civilization," declared Vasconcelos in 1922.[12] The metaphor was not coincidental (though somewhat ironic given the revolutionary government's anticlericalism) and illustrates the ambitious transformation SEP officials envisioned. The appropriation of a religious structure itself constituted a syncretic exercise to promote gradual change.[13] In the years to come, *El Maestro Rural*, the SEP's publication, disseminated a missionary identity among teachers to foster enthusiasm for life in poor rural communities. The magazine created an archetype both of the campesino, a peon in need of redemption, and of the teacher as the immanent savior. "Victims of their own rhetoric and of the state's strategic decision to utilize the symbolic and operational structure of Christianity," wrote Guillermo Palacios in his analysis of the publication, "rural teachers frequently conceived of themselves as heroic bearers of messages of salvation who undauntedly confronted the classic dangers of fantastical adventures."[14] On-the-ground realities in local communities may have tempered such fervor, but in their efforts to adapt, teachers both translated official dicta into practical action and served as barometers for the SEP to evaluate its own policy.[15]

The vast cultural and educational project of the 1920s stimulated discussion of new pedagogical theories. Especially prominent in the early part of the decade was action pedagogy, John Dewey's philosophy that students learn best by doing. Popularized and adapted to the Mexican context by Moisés Sáenz, undersecretary of education from 1924 to 1933 and a student of Dewey's at Columbia University, action pedagogy provided an important vehicle for other educational philosophies that crystallized in the 1930s and had lasting legacies thereafter. Adopted as official policy in 1923, action pedagogy seemed especially suited to the countryside, where the natural environment would be the canvas on which students could paint a new reality.[16] Emphasizing that instruction should not be overly academic, action pedagogy stood as an explicit critique of nineteenth-century education, with its vertical imposition of discipline and European aesthetic. Instead, new norms valued student freedom and interaction with the surrounding environment, which could offer practical knowledge and address the needs of the community. As figures like Sáenz linked education and rural development, action pedagogy connected the classroom to the community, collective interests to individual discipline, and learning to laboring. The goal, he stated, was to create a rural spirit, "to have children love the earth, to prefer the countryside to the city, to have them profit from the land so they will feel inextricably tied to it."[17] By infusing agricultural work with new value and attaching to it theoretical and practical significance, action pedagogy strengthened the idea of the teacher as a community leader. Earlier, Dewey himself had observed about Mexico, "there is no educational movement in the world which exhibits more of the spirit of intimate union of school activities with those of the community."[18]

Pedagogical approaches acquired a more materialist basis in the 1930s with figures like Rafael Ramírez, head of the mobile instructor training institutes known as cultural missions, from 1927 to 1935, and Narciso Bassols, minister of education from 1931 to 1934. Ramírez emphasized technical support that would improve campesino agricultural production, which, in turn, was to be organized through collectivist or cooperative principles. Rather than being spiritual guides, teachers were to have practical knowledge, be agitators, and mobilize communities to unleash their productive capacity. Rural education would in its essence be agricultural and pursue as its highest principles "a social regime in which there are neither poor nor rich, where all workers enjoy life's advantages."[19] Bassols, a committed Marxist, likewise emphasized wealth redistribution and departed sharply from Vasconcelos's cultural approach. The Spanish conquest, he maintained, had inaugurated an educational tradition based on exploitation, damaging the rich spiritual tradition of indigenous culture. After independence the political system's emphasis on the individual had further undermined the "customs, culture, and needs" of rural communities, laying the basis for the violent contrasts between cities and the countryside. "It is not possible to seriously resolve any of our nation's important questions without taking into consideration the economic and cultural state of our campesinos," declared Bassols. Indeed, through the revolution, he continued, "the countryside had imposed its educational longings."[20]

Both Ramírez and Bassols applied an assimilationist approach when it came to the indigenous population, with Ramírez emphasizing Spanish-language instruction and Bassols espousing classical principles of mestizaje by which education was to preserve the indigenous virtues and values while drawing on the technical resources of Western civilization. While the SEP's implementation of socialist education in 1934 accentuated some of these positivist notions, the progressive nature of President Lázaro Cárdenas's regime created a space for those who advocated indigenous and multilingual education. In the latter part of the decade, there were a series of regional congresses where self-identified indigenous community leaders addressed public forums.[21] Approaches based on cultural pluralism, whereby indigenous people taught or were taught in their own language and preserved political and social forms of organization, made some headway in the context of predominantly assimilationist practices.[22] Mexico displayed international leadership on this question when it hosted the First Indigenous Inter-American Congress in Pátzcuaro, Michoacán, in April 1940. There, 250 delegates from nineteen countries met to discuss joint approaches to improve the lives of indigenous people while maintaining cultural particularities. Sáenz, one of the conference's principal organizers, advocated for a policy based on social and political activism that pushed for full participation by indigenous people in national transformations.[23] The Mexican Communist Party, too, critiqued the policy of formal mestizaje, arguing for bilingual education and respect for indigenous social and cultural forms of organization. Turning the assimilationist logic on its head, one of the party's recommendations was to better educate mestizos so "they know the capabilities of indigenous people and understand the urgent need to establish close alliances with them in order to protect Mexico and its Revolution."[24] While this view was in the minority at the conference—and in Mexico was soon superseded by the apolitical and scientific approach advocated by anthropologists like Manuel Gamio—it provided a basis for progressive approaches that would take root in later decades.

NORMALES AND NATION BUILDING

In Mexico, as in other countries, education is intimately tied to the process of national formation. During the early nineteenth century, as most Latin American nations gained their independence, governing groups debated how to forge a sense of unity among the disparate peoples inhabiting the newly drawn national boundaries. Of European inspiration, the dominant liberal ideology cast the challenge as one in which modern, civilizing elites would bring order, progress, and modernity to the unruly, backward, and culturally inferior populations—be they indigenous, Afro-descendant, mixed-race, or rough-and-tumble frontier populations. Several national constitutions made primary education—seen as the tool to achieve this—obligatory, the responsibility of municipalities, to be financed through local taxes. However, the lack of resources and infrastructure, along with political instability, and the general poverty of the mass population meant that such legislation was rarely translated into practice. For most of the nineteenth century, education remained a decentralized patchwork of institutions in private or religious hands and was accessible mostly to urban elites. The impulse to centralize education gathered momentum in the latter part of the nineteenth century as governments strengthened civil over religious institutions and used tax revenues generated by export booms to finance schools. Positivist legacies and governments that were in the hands of white elites gave way to the twentieth-century *estado docente*, an educating state that had a remarkably similar structure throughout Latin America. Ministries of public instruction presided over a hierarchical system of primary education whose affiliated leadership was named directly by the executive. These bodies, in turn, ran public schools, created their curriculum and even set rules for private schools. The establishment of normal schools constituted a key part of this process as they provided state control over the selection and training of teachers. Vast centralized bureaucracies, teaching's status as a state profession, and the lack of local say over teachers have been long-standing legacies of this structure.[25]

Twentieth-century nation-building projects continued to be predicated on the ideal of a homogeneous population. Increasingly, however, this framework celebrated native cultures, racial mixture, and the unique essence of individual Latin American nations. As such, education policy was one of assimilation, projected onto rural areas as means of incorporating diverse populations into national development, teaching indigenous people the dominant language, and replacing long-standing traditions with modern ways. But the desired ethnic uniformity was never achieved. Not only was the state's reach uneven, but community resistance and cultural pride ensured the preservation of indigenous languages and traditions across generations. Not until the 1970s, as UNESCO (the United Nations Educational, Scientific, and Cultural Organization) critiqued national bureaucratic policies that stifled local initiatives along with the vocal push of indigenous people, did communities begin to have a voice in the education projects that affected them.[26]

Throughout the twentieth century, Mexico's rural normales operated under an assimilationist framework. They were for campesinos, who, it was assumed, were mestizo if they spoke Spanish.[27] While rural normales early on made efforts to recruit indigenous students, the schools' constituting logic continued to be tied to justice for the campesino class, a characteristic consolidated under President Cárdenas in the 1930s.[28] But even before Cárdenas's more radical policies, the popular vindications inherent in Mexico's 1910 revolution drove early educational architects to identify teachers with social justice. As agents of social and political literacy, their role could no longer be limited to the classroom. Aside from the focus on the countryside, a key innovation of the revolution's school—referred to as *la casa del pueblo* (the people's house)—was its attention to the entire community. Adult literacy, hygiene, land reform, and civic celebrations were as much the teacher's responsibility as instructing children in the basics of reading, writing, and arithmetic. Influenced by the architects of the Soviet Union's education reform, Vasconcelos adopted similar strategies of cultural dissemination in Mexico, which included sponsoring the publication of literature at low prices, creating libraries and systematizing literacy campaigns, and organizing popular festivals, puppetry, and open-air theater. While Vasconcelos, unlike his Soviet counterpart, Anatoly Lunacharsky, did not prioritize the politics of class struggle, many of those involved in the cultural missions—mobile instruction brigades composed of teachers, workshop instructors, agricultural experts, and song, theater, and art promoters—traveled to the Soviet Union and were inspired by the possibilities of socialism, a message theater troupes reproduced throughout the countryside. Radical pedagogy, didactic revolutionary plays, and instructions on how to organize community members to claim their land and labor rights also reached the countryside's teachers through the pages of the SEP's bimonthly publication *El Maestro Rural*, whose articles were often penned by teachers from normales.[29] At some rural normales, teachers developed reading materials whose content explained basic Marxist principles like surplus value, class struggle, and exploitation, even before the state's adoption of socialist education in 1934.[30]

The cultural missions and the rural normales constituted the backbone of the state's education project during the 1920s and 1930s. Marxist analysis and a socialist vision would acquire long-lasting legacies partly because they became intertwined with commonsense notions of justice promoted by revolutionary state discourse. Article 3 of the 1917 Constitution, for example, established the population's right to a free, secular primary education and decreed that the state was responsible for providing it. Radical elements coexisted alongside civic lessons aimed at replacing local allegiances with a national identity. The education process thus constituted an effort to expand and centralize state power while incorporating historically neglected populations, a strategy that did not always draw a clear distinction between indigenous and campesino populations. To the extent that it did, it was usually language that constituted the strongest marker of who the SEP considered indigenous.

Still, early approaches conceived of education in terms of cultural rather than racial hierarchies, which provided some overlap in how SEP officials approached indigenous and campesino education. Rejecting the social Darwinism of many of their Western counterparts, revolutionary educators attributed campesino and indigenous penury to oppression rather than racial inferiority.[31] As such, these populations could be redeemed through incorporation, a process that, unlike in the United States and Canada, was meant to cultivate rather than sever ethnic affiliations and targeted entire communities instead of focusing on individuals.[32] A critic of segregated education as practiced in the United States, Vasconcelos declared that in Mexico the indigenous population would not be pushed aside into reservations but had to be incorporated into the national project.[33] Rural normal graduates would be the agents of this incorporation, and their importance is reflected in the growth of these institutions, which from the early 1920s to 1940 developed from makeshift, ambulatory missions into formal, coeducational boarding schools, often housed in expropriated haciendas. At their height in 1936, rural normales, then known as regional campesino schools, numbered thirty-five.[34]

Mexico's educational undertaking did not go unnoticed. In the United States, social reformers, including those who would contribute foundational theories to the civil rights movement, drew inspiration from Mexico's integrationist approach. Many lauded the central government's strong interventionist impulse in light of the United States' failures to use federal institutions to dismantle southern segregation.[35] In Latin America, countries with high proportions of indigenous peoples were especially interested in Mexico's rural normales. In the early 1940s, as Peru prepared to establish its own teacher-training centers, it sent representatives to Mexico, "a country with unmistakable similarities to Peru and where rural normales have been functioning for more than twenty years."[36] Likewise, in the 1930s, as Bolivia transitioned from a liberal to a military-socialist government seeking to expand school coverage to indigenous communities, it, too, sent representatives to Mexico. Prominent Mexican pedagogues like Sáenz themselves visited Bolivia, showing special interest in Warisata, the *ayllu* (kin- and territorial-based community) school founded in 1931 with an Aymara communalist curriculum taught by indigenous teachers.[37] Other international connections dated a decade earlier. For example, Minister Vasconcelos invited the Chilean poet—later Nobel laureate—Gabriela Mistral to participate in the cultural missions. Mistral lauded Mexico's focus on indigenous education and hailed pedagogical practices that included farming, workshops, and small industry, an approach, she observed, that imbued youth at normales with the ability to bridge intellectual and artisan knowledge, which was, for her, "the most far-reaching human quality."[38]

Work still needs to be done on the transnational networks of these different educational projects.[39] But independent of specific connections, across Latin America, not to mention regions with dramatically different histories, such as the US South or China, there are discernible parallels in peripheral-area normal schools designed under the logic of national consolidation.[40] The students in Chile's rural normales also hailed from lower socioeconomic groups for whom a university education was inaccessible both for financial reasons and because of the years of prerequisite schooling.[41] Where these institutions drew from historically subjugated populations, as did African

American normal schools during Reconstruction, they not only provided a means of social mobility but created a cadre of educator-activists who would go on to become community leaders and challenge racist educational norms.[42] Moreover, boarding-school life and pedagogical training that combined academics, agriculture, and small industry, along with the modernizing or redemptive task assigned to graduates, often imbued teachers with a particular esprit de corps and a sense of collective mission. In some cases, this quality translated to political radicalism after graduation; in Chile the country's seventeen rural normales were known for their politicized student body and were promptly closed by Augusto Pinochet after his 1973 military coup.[43]

This context renders the story of Mexico's rural normales both unique and broadly representative of larger social processes. Their main particularity lies in how rural normales articulated the principles of the Mexican Revolution—evident in the primacy of the campesino identity to which rural normalistas laid claim, the enduring discourse of teachers as agents of community change, and the socialist signifiers preserved from the radical 1930s. In more generalizable terms, rural normales showcase the relationship between education and political consciousness, the varying mechanisms through which marginalized populations lay claim to their rights, and the way legacies of struggle grow roots and endure over time.

THE EVOLVING TEACHER-TRAINING SYSTEM

The significance of Mexico's rural normales lay not only in the revolutionary ideals they housed but also in their design as institutions by which the federal government extended its charge over education. During much of the nineteenth century, the Lancaster Society had run teacher-training institutes in Mexico, and it was not until 1887 that the country saw its first federally controlled normal, the Teachers' Normal School.[44] In 1907, on the eve of the revolution, Mexico had twenty-six normales, most controlled by the states rather than the federal government; both their locations and their graduates were concentrated in the state capitals and Mexico City.[45] As the federal government built schoolhouses throughout the countryside during the 1920s and 1930s, it began recruiting and forming a teaching body with different characteristics from the Porfirian-era normal graduates. The new teachers had little formal education, and their authority came more from their ability to provide community leadership and act as links to federal land, union, or credit agencies. Rural normales themselves began as makeshift institutions whose study plans in the 1920s consisted of two years of coursework focusing on three broad areas: core academic subjects such as language, math, social studies, and art; basic pedagogical techniques; and farming, workshops, and small industries, with home economics classes for women. During the 1930s the study plan was expanded to allow for a greater diversity of subjects and categories, while the new socialist curriculum added courses like Economy and History of the Working Class, Socialist Orientation and Worker and Campesino Legislation, Institutions and Social Problems, and Technical Investigation for Communal Improvement.[46] Aside from formalizing teacher training, rural normales were to integrate adjacent communities into their programmatic activities and conduct social, geographic, and economic studies of the regions where they were established. Their name change to regional campesino schools during this period partly reflects that goal. Their personnel, along with that of the cultural missions, had a central role in coordinating education policy across the country, while socialist education was itself a decisive centralizing impulse since it articulated a unified ideological message with a pedagogy of social and economic transformation.[47] The more radical educational principles went hand in hand with Cárdenas's progressive social legislation, itself structured under a strong executive and state party.

The central role of rural normales underwent a major shift during the 1940s as radical Cardenista policies waned, the centrality of agricultural training diminished, and socialist education and coeducation were overturned. The guiding philosophy became national unity, a framework meant to downplay class struggle and teachers' leadership roles and to establish academics rather than community development as the principal focus. Urban normales, presumably of better academic quality, became the model around which to promote curricular uniformity. The years of normal study were expanded to six, with the first three equivalent to *secundaria* (junior high school) and the latter three providing professional teacher training. Since most elementary schools in the countryside did not go up to sixth grade, two complementary years were added to rural normales, where students could complete fifth and sixth grade. Socialist subjects pertaining to political economy, working-class history, and agrarian legislation were eliminated and replaced by subjects such as pedology, psychology of learning, instruction techniques, psychometrics of pedagogy, and science and sociology of education.[48] The uniformity of the urban and rural curriculum did not mean agricultural training at rural normales was eliminated; instead, it was given a status equivalent to workshops at urban normales. Although this change was initially celebrated by students and teachers at rural normales because it elevated the institutions' academic status, a persistent lack of funding would perpetually associate rural normales with an inferior academic reputation.

The SEP's efforts to centralize education continued through the 1940s as the state expanded its construction of other normales and pushed for the consolidation of a national teachers' union. Urban rather than rural normales now became the flagship institutions. The National Teachers School, established in 1925, was expanded and in 1945 housed in a grand new building. The SEP also founded the Higher Normal School of Mexico in 1942 to train teachers for normales or postelementary education and, in 1947, the National Preschool Teachers School.[49] Additionally, in 1944 the SEP created the Federal Institute for Teacher Training, meant to formalize the education of the staggeringly high numbers of teachers who taught without a formal degree (the majority in the countryside).[50] In a related process, 1943 saw the foundation of the National Union of Education Workers (SNTE), whose vast structure absorbed previous regional, administrative, and professional education unions that had been ideologically diverse. The SNTE's growth went hand in hand with the expansion of the central government's control over education since not only did the new schools it built and the new teachers it hired add to the SNTE's membership, but the union increasingly fought for the incorporation of municipal and state teachers into the federal ranks. This process entailed standardizing teacher-training programs, rank and promotion requirements, and the elementary school curriculum itself. The political implications would be enormous, for, like other unions under the umbrella of the Institutional Revolutionary Party (PRI), the SNTE's leadership acted more in accordance with party leadership than with the interests of its rank and file. At the same time, as the union grew to be the country's largest, it developed enormous power, which it wielded through a say in curricular, professional, and teaching-degree requirements. In the curricular changes discussed in the following, the SNTE always had a seat at the table.

By 1954, when the SEP held a national conference to assess the country's normal education, officials spoke of a system in chaos. There were seven different types of normales (for preschool, elementary, secondary, specialized, and physical education, as well as music, in addition to the accrediting Federal Institute of Teacher Training), and the SEP had not managed to implement a coordinating logic among them; the relationship among federal, state, and private control over teacher-training institutions was unclear; course plans were unwieldy, and teaching methods ineffective; and the number of normalistas who did not complete the degree was staggeringly high—about 70 percent at most normales—an indication that students used these institutions not to become teachers but to have some sort of schooling, especially in the countryside, where junior high schools were sparse. Officials acknowledged the mistake of having unified the urban and rural normal curriculum since the measure facilitated transfers to the National Teachers School in Mexico City, whose attrition rate was only 30 percent. A commission charged with revamping the curriculum recommended that the junior high school years be separated from the normal training and that the latter's curriculum be reduced and simplified, with the first year devoted to general education requirements and the latter two years emphasizing pedagogical techniques and hands-on teacher training. Electives would be reduced and designed for the needs of the region in which the schools were located; instruction was to be less rote and instead based on research and discussion.[51]

Over the following decades, Mexico's teacher-training system grew increasingly complex as additional types of normales were created, entrance and schooling requirements changed, years of study expanded, and the character of the teaching degree transformed. In 1964 there were 166 normales that trained elementary schoolteachers, of which 38 were federal (including the 29 rural normales), 41 state-run, and 87 private.[52] In 1969 the SEP implemented some of the changes proposed at its 1954 normal education congress. For example, the secundaria and normal tracks were separated, and an additional year was added to the professional training. A new type of teacher-training institution, known as the *regional normal*, was created for the urban periphery. Specifically designed without the boarding-school structure, these normales were to replace the rural ones, whose numbers were reduced from twenty-nine to fifteen in 1969. Curricular changes were once again implemented in the early 1970s. The new course load sought to both improve core knowledge in the areas of math, science, social studies, art, and literature and link that knowledge base to instructional techniques in each subject. With this change, courses in general education subjects such as math, science, philosophy, and history were increased, and pedagogy courses decreased. In 1973 a teacher-training degree was given the rank of *bachillerato* (roughly equivalent to a high school) diploma, making teachers eligible to apply to universities, a change meant to expand the intellectual and professional possibilities of those who had gone to a normal out of economic necessity rather than a desire to teach.[53]

Today, a degree from a normal school has the status of *licenciatura*, roughly equivalent to a college degree. This reform came in 1984 when new entrance requirements made a high school education mandatory, a change that was at once meant to increase normalistas' core knowledge base, allow

students to better develop their research and teaching skill, and elevate normales to the realm of higher education. It also had the effect of reducing the
number of teachers since the few years needed to obtain a degree had been
a key appeal of the teaching profession. Just as significant was the 1980s economic crisis, which seriously depressed teachers' salaries.[54] Conflicts that had
been brewing since the late 1970s came to a head by the end of the 1980s and
included disputes between government officials and the SNTE's leadership,
as well as between the union leadership and its base. Citing the unwieldy
nature of the SEP as a state bureaucracy and the need to reform an ossified
educational structure and imbue it with a truly federalist structure in which
local governments had a say, then president Carlos Salinas de Gortari (1988–
94) implemented the 1992 National Agreement to Modernize Elementary
and Normal Education, with which it handed to state governments some
functions and responsibilities previously in the hands of the SEP.[55] The federal government would still determine the curriculum, but the states would
now administer budgets, oversee schools, and be in charge of personnel. The
centralizing impulse that began in the 1920s, it seemed, had come full circle.

"AS LONG AS THERE IS POVERTY . . ."

Rural normales are among the few institutions of higher education that continue to operate under a boarding-school structure, a characteristic that, in
recent decades, makes them especially distinctive. Those admitted are entitled to free room and board, a modest stipend, and some basic supplies such
as shoes and uniforms. While a handful of rural normales are now coeducational, most are still divided by gender. The school grounds include teacher
housing, agricultural lands, and farm animals that students attend with varying
degrees of curricular formality. Most rural normales are located outside major
urban areas, although given the swelling nature of cities and the expanding
road infrastructure during the past few decades, the schools are accessible
through public transportation. Upon graduation, the young teachers are expected to work in the countryside or in marginal communities, where, until
President Enrique Peña Nieto's 2013 education reform, the SEP guaranteed
them a job.

As institutions, rural normales hold a special place in the national narrative. A whole mystique surrounds their early graduates, often referred to
as "education missionaries" or "apostles of agrarian revolution."[56] While not
all of the countryside's educators were trained at rural normales, the selfless
teacher who braved difficult, often dangerous conditions in remote territories

to bring educational enlightenment became the archetype of the rural normal graduate. The central role President Cárdenas gave rural teachers in his 1930s progressive agenda cemented their association with social justice. In addition, during Cárdenas's presidency the rural normales were designated explicitly for the sons and daughters of campesinos, the poor who had historically been denied an education. Over subsequent decades the category of campesino grew more expansive, and the changing demographics marked by the increasing urbanization made the urban poor eligible to study there.[57] Whereas for most of the twentieth century a campesino identity was the most prominent signifier of rural normalistas, students from rural normales in the southern parts of Mexico also increasingly identify as indigenous. Moreover, since 2000 the SEP has granted formal recognition to three indigenous normales in Chiapas, Oaxaca, and Michoacán.[58] The latter's student association joined the Mexican Federation of Socialist Campesino Students (FECSM) and thus participates in nationwide rural normalista mobilizations.[59]

Significantly, rural normales' lore of political militancy persists and today is most dramatically evident in the numerous murals that adorn their school walls. Large images of Karl Marx, Friedrich Engels, Vladimir Lenin, and Che Guevara—sometimes located prominently in amphitheaters or cafeterias—are common (figure 1.2), as is the hammer and sickle, the communist symbol representing proletarian and peasant unity. Some schools also celebrate rural teachers-turned-guerrillas as well as the indigenous Zapatista insurgents from the southern state of Chiapas. A power fist with the FECSM acronym is ubiquitous, and murals depicting the ravages of capitalism or celebrating popular struggles mark the exterior of classroom walls, dorms, and fences. Such radical themes have a didactic quality and hearken back to the artistic production of the 1920s and 1930s that condemned capitalist exploitation, celebrated popular struggle, and presented education as a means of breaking the system's oppressive shackles.[60] In this way, the murals at rural normales stand as part of a larger tradition of Mexican public art that figures prominently on government buildings and flagship educational institutions such as the National Autonomous University of Mexico, the National Polytechnic Institute, the National Preparatory School, and the National Teachers School. Unlike the murals at these institutions—commissioned by the state and undertaken by famous artists—those at rural normales are crafted by grassroots collectives in conjunction with normalistas. They are rustic and ever changing and pointedly condemn the current power structure (figure 1.3). As in other contested territories (such as the autonomous Zapatista

FIGURE 1.2 Mural at the rural normal of Ayotzinapa, Guerrero, depicting Vladimir Lenin, Friedrich Engels, and Karl Marx on the left and Ernesto "Che" Guevara, Lucio Cabañas, and Genaro Vázquez on the right. Photograph by author.

communities in Chiapas), there is a self-conscious declaration of a distinct identity, an imagined community of sorts in which past and present collide.[61] Today the schools have murals demanding justice for Ayotzinapa's Missing 43 and consistently showcase the names and seals of the seventeen remaining rural normales.

If today's murals tell a political story, normalistas' published memoirs give a sense of their graduates' esprit de corps, celebrate rural normales as institutions of singular importance, and, through an air of youthful nostalgia, reflect on the grand and the mundane. Self-published, limited in circulation, and compiled by and about male normalistas, these works are at once an exercise in reminiscing and an intervention in the historical record of a project they consider in peril.[62] Such works tend to highlight rural normalistas' commitment to teach in remote communities, celebrate the democratic quality of the schools as evidenced by student participation in institutional life, detail early interaction with surrounding communities, discuss the FECSM as a

FIGURE 1.3 Mural at the rural normal of Amilcingo, Morelos. The caption reads "We all have blood, the poor in our veins and the rich on their hands." Photograph by author.

fixture of institutional life, and condemn the 1969 closure of half of their schools, with many remarking that it was the state's retaliation for the 1968 student movement. As with oral histories, certain memory frames mediate their accounts, and personal redemptive narratives are interwoven with official historical tropes. The notably gendered production of these publications, for example, is consistent with the extent to which the rural teacher, as a community leader, was conceived as male even while the teaching profession had historically been largely female.[63] The very act of compiling and publishing such works reflects a deliberate effort to account for one's role in a transcendent national undertaking, a quality less evident in women teachers, whose leadership has been either historically sidelined or conceived of as complementary, or whose labor is considered an extension of their caregiving roles. There is likewise a generational divide in normalistas' narratives. While older graduates celebrate their own actions and deeds as students, they do not always approve of current normalistas' mobilizations. Instead, many present the view that past generations were both more committed to the countryside and less reckless in their political acts. The former characterization speaks to an internalization of the missionary narrative, contradicted by the fact that while their teaching careers began in the countryside, most migrated to the cities. The latter assertion provides a glimpse into how, for so many, the activism they participated in as students did not continue after graduation.

Still, the overwhelming consensus for normalistas across generations and the political spectrum is the invaluable nature of rural normales as life-changing institutions for the poor, a quality expressed more in material than in professional terms. The painstaking detail with which older generations remember the type of food they consumed, the mattress—or cardboard—on which they slept, or the uniform and shoes they were given contrasts with the vagueness of their accounts about the classes they took, the pedagogical materials they worked with, or the types of teachers they had. Spartan in every way, these conditions nonetheless contrasted with the crushing poverty of the campesino life from which they came. At least in the boarding schools, most relate, they had scheduled meals, a bed to themselves, and a change of clothes. Younger generations—those who have studied since the 1970s—tend to speak less about such immediate material needs and more in terms of their general lack of life options. "If it wasn't for the normal, I would have had to migrate to the United States," state many.[64] Current students put it more ominously: "It was the normal or working for a drug cartel."[65]

It is no wonder that normalistas continue to fiercely defend their institutions. Even in the dramatically different context of a predominantly urban nation in the twenty-first century, they evoke the schools' historic legacy. Their rationale is simple: "As long as there is poverty, rural normales have a reason to exist." So reads the legend inscribed at the bottom of a crude reproduction of Rivera's *La maestra rural* in the normal of Amilcingo, Morelos.

2

A New Kind of School,
a New Kind of Teacher

THE ARTIST JOSÉ HERNÁNDEZ DELGADILLO, who attended the short-lived (1938–43) rural normal of Soltepec, Tlaxcala, said of his experience there, "I met many children of campesinos who influenced me a lot, including their 'uncouth habits' like going around without shoes, clean but neglected.... When I returned home during the normal's vacation, my parents were alarmed, because I was barefoot and my clothes were unkempt. Perhaps they had heard that those normales were communist—it's true, there was that influence. The chapel of that old hacienda of Soltepec, now converted into an auditorium, preserved all the characteristics of a little, feudal European castle. It was completely decorated with frescos, figurative paintings... with hammers and sickles, red flags everywhere." Delgadillo, the son of a middle-class rural family, first went to Soltepec on the recommendation of his elementary school principal, a rural normal graduate and a communist. Troubled by his "normalista demeanor," Delgadillo's parents did not let him return. His murals, which would adorn the walls of numerous educational institutions, however, would contain many of the same motifs he first observed at the rural normal, leading one art critic to refer to him as Mexico's artist-agitator.[1]

Delgadillo's description of Soltepec, its seigneurial architecture now decked out with the symbols and colors of a proletarian revolution and inhabited by campesinos with not-yet-so-reformed ways, provides a telling glimpse into the early life of rural normales, the institutions that would form a new cadre of teachers. This chapter hones in on their early period to examine how their original goals and principles laid a lasting foundation to nurture political radicalism. Specifically, in the context of revolutionary consolidation, the progressive tendencies within state policy during the 1930s—especially socialist education—and the active participation of students in all aspects of institutional life fostered an environment in which radical social actors emerged and later flourished. Politicized by an institution that, on the one hand, cultivated hope for redistributive justice and, on the other, activated reactionary violence against those pushing for such transformation, rural teachers became crucial agents of social change. The agrarian nature of Mexico's revolution, moreover, marked education policy with a distinctly rural, holistic community framework; this framework's abandonment beginning in the 1940s set the stage for the profound inequalities that characterized the rest of the century. Just as enduring, however, was the legacy of the 1920s and 1930s revolutionary project and the teachers trained within it. That project and the experience of this first generation of rural teachers are essential to understanding the resistance that marked the countryside in decades to come.

TRAINING RURAL TEACHERS

In the early 1920s, the countryside's technical and social development was the affair of three institutions: the cultural missions, the rural normal schools, and the central agricultural schools. Originally composed of volunteers, the cultural missions relied on individuals who believed in the power of education to create a new society.[2] They were José Vasconcelos's modern apostles, whom he charged with transforming the countryside. Staffed by teachers trained in art, reading, writing, arithmetic, physical education, and agriculture, the cultural missions visited different communities, imparting two-month courses to local instructors. The teams often brought with them pedagogical materials and medical supplies, as well as agricultural and woodworking tools to augment local schools' meager supplies.[3] Between 1923 and 1930, the number of cultural missions increased from six to fourteen, and their initial focus on teacher training expanded to include work with the entire community. With modest personnel and equipment, they nonetheless had ambitious goals. They sought to establish the basic infrastructure for rural education and to generate an enthusiasm for social change among the local

population. By emphasizing the significance of campesino political participation and valuing indigenous culture, the cultural missions helped shape an
important cadre of local radical leadership.[4] Their direct exposure to rural
communities, in turn, convinced them of the need for structural reform, a
vision that contrasted with that of those confined to the urban world.[5]

If the cultural missions represented the initiation of a federal academic
program, the central agricultural schools linked that program to small-scale
farming. Created in 1926, these agricultural schools reflected the ideology of
President Plutarco Elías Calles (1924–28), who favored technical assistance
and infrastructural projects over systemic reform; his goal was increased
agricultural production rather than land distribution.[6] Taking the United
States as a model, like his nineteenth-century liberal counterparts, Calles envisioned a countryside inhabited by individual small farmers.[7] Constructed
in old haciendas and equipped with modern machinery, agricultural schools
were designed as cooperatives whose three-year program would train agrarian technicians. Duly equipped, graduates would return to their communities of origin to instruct campesinos on better production methods. While
the agricultural schools were supposed to be self-sufficient and stimulate regional development, they were plagued from the start by problems. Rather
than undermining the power of exploitative landowners and caciques, they
actually promoted a clientelistic relationship with the state. Moreover, their
agricultural production undermined or competed with that of local *ejidatarios* (communal farmers).[8] Likewise, instead of being the children of campesinos, a high percentage of the students came from the families of merchants or
middle-income groups.[9] The lax entrance requirements reflected the institutions' difficulties in recruiting students. Finally, few of their graduates undertook the expected advisory roles in remote communities, instead preferring
urban centers. With all their shortcomings, however, the central agricultural
schools attempted to tailor farming to the needs of popular sectors and to
integrate agricultural engineers into the politics of education. They constituted a basis on which to link rural schools and agricultural production.[10]

Rural teachers would be trained at the rural normal schools. Established
under the purview of the Office of Cultural Missions, in keeping with the
countryside's urgent need of teachers, the rural normales began as two-year
boarding schools and initially housed between twenty and thirty students.
They included family-style farms, light machinery, and woodworking and
hide-tanning workshops (figure 2.1). Students engaged in teaching practice
in nearby elementary schools, themselves often built along with the normal.
To be eligible for a normal education, students had to have finished most or

all of elementary school, express a desire to teach, show good behavior, and be in good health. While in their early years the rural normales educated some students from well-to-do families, they increasingly recruited students from impoverished rural dwellings, providing them with modest scholarships to undertake their education. The rural normales' early design sought to mimic family life by promoting the principal and his wife as parent figures who would tend "to students as they would their own children."[11] Teachers, in turn, constituted the older siblings whose deeds and actions were to set a good example. This family structure aimed in part to assuage parents' fears about sending their children, especially girls, to live far from home. The guidelines of the Ministry of Public Education (SEP) emphasized that relationships in the normales not be overly rigid and that life unfold "just as naturally as it does in the home."[12] While the principal was still a paternalistic figure, students and teachers had a say in running the schools, a process that cultivated a democratic spirit and contrasted with nineteenth-century positivist norms that emphasized order and obedience.[13]

By 1932 eight central agricultural schools, seventeen rural normales, and fourteen cultural missions had been established throughout the country.[14] While progress was made in training rural teachers, there were some serious institutional problems, especially with the agricultural schools, many of which reproduced some of the very exploitative structures they were meant to address. Likewise, many of the rural normales were located in or close to urban centers, while the cultural missions' accomplishments were hampered by their transitory nature. The SEP attempted to reform the system by creating regional campesino schools. These institutions fused the central agricultural schools with the rural normales and cultural missions.[15] At the regional campesino schools, students undertook two years of agricultural and technical training, after which they received land and equipment in their home region, where they could either work the land or become agricultural advisers. Those wanting to become teachers received pedagogical training for two additional years.[16] Ultimately, these institutions were far more successful in graduating teachers than agricultural technicians. Partly owing to a lack of personnel with pedagogical expertise in agriculture, this limitation also reflected the higher status of the teaching profession.

The regional campesino schools manifested the more progressive tendencies emerging in the SEP during the 1930s and further emphasized the social responsibility of their graduates, who were to constitute "the rural organizer, the multifaceted figure who advised ejidatarios, the accountant in the Agricultural Credit Bank, the agronomist's assistant, and the 'right hand man'

FIGURE 2.1 Hide-tanning workshop at the rural normal of Matamoros, Puebla (n.d.). Archivo General de la Nación, Photographic Archive, Normales Rurales, C1, Sobre 49.

of the cultural missions' directors."[17] To make sure the regional campesino schools served primarily the poor, admission required proof that students came from humble backgrounds. Thanks to such measures and active recruitment, by 1936 the proportion of students from campesino households grew to almost 70 percent.[18] During this time, the majority of students were between sixteen and nineteen years old, and half of them had studied through fourth grade. They were less successful in attracting indigenous students; only 7 percent of pupils spoke a language other than Spanish.[19] While historically the teaching profession had been socially acceptable for women, at this point normal regulations still capped female entrants at 25 percent, an indication of how much the teacher as community leader was envisioned as male. The low female rates also reflected parents' hesitancy to send their daughters to coeducational boarding schools, especially as these schools grew beyond the small, family-structured institutions of the 1920s. When

FIGURE 2.2 Students cultivating the fields of what would become the women's rural normal of Palmira, Morelos, 1945. Archivo General de la Nación, Photographic Archive, Normales Rurales, C6, Sobre 26.

the SEP divided the rural normales by gender in 1943, the number of female students increased (figure 2.2).[20]

The regional campesino schools, which later became rural normal schools, were the clearest expression of the Cardenista fusion of agrarian and educational reforms. These institutions signaled the central place of rural teachers in the Cardenista project. As governor of Michoacán from 1928 to 1932, Lázaro Cárdenas had witnessed the important role teachers played in organizing the state's labor and peasant unions, some of communist affiliation.[21] Radicalized by the church and landlords' opposition to education, teachers joined campesinos and helped organize them to secure land and schools, demands to which Cárdenas was responsive. As the national government headed by President Calles took an increasingly conservative path, in Michoacán Governor Cárdenas distributed 400,000 hectares of land and opened a hundred new schools.[22] As he concluded his term as governor, Cárdenas was clear about the important role teachers might play at the national level, upholding them as brave guides of popular struggle. They were to "penetrate the fields of the organized campesinos and the workshop of the strengthened unionized worker." There they would hone in on the economic conditions and "defend the interests and aspirations of each."[23]

In some sense, Michoacán represented the cradle of rural normalismo since, on the state's initiative, that is where the first rural normales were built during Francisco Mújica's short stint as governor from 1920 to 1921. With half of the state budget devoted to education, Mújica oversaw the construction of four rural normales, some of whose directors became prominent progressive figures in the state and later in the nation's education movement.[24] These teacher-training institutions, moreover, served as models for the first federally controlled rural normales, one of which was built in Tacámbaro, Michoacán, in 1922.[25] Accounts of its early dynamics vividly reflect the challenges rural normales faced: high dropout rates, interruption of activities owing to lack of funds, church hostility, harassment of female students, and the death of one of its first and youngest graduates at the hands of Cristeros (Catholic rebels).[26] Across the country, early directors reported similar challenges. To face these obstacles, teachers devised numerous strategies, which would later constitute part of the heroic lore of these early institutions. Teachers and students themselves built the school's furnishings; educators contributed their personal funds for school material; the normal spearheaded community projects and invited the local population to attend school events and use its workshops; and classes were held with open windows to assuage fears provoked by coeducation.[27] The spartan nature of these institutions, moreover, reinforced their association with a humble student body who virtuously withstood such conditions. Campesinos were, according to one school director, the only ones who possessed the "spirit of sacrifice and love necessary for anyone wanting to be a rural teacher, qualities hardly compatible with the customs of rich youth."[28]

During Cárdenas's tenure as president, the number of rural normales nationwide increased to thirty-five (map 2.1). It was the only branch of education that met, and indeed surpassed, the goals of Cárdenas's Plan Sexenal (six-year plan).[29] Not only did Cárdenas take the greatest interest in rural education and channel the necessary resources for its development, but his land redistribution went hand in hand with educational reform, providing the necessary structural transformation for schools to have a more transcendent impact. While slow to take root, the reforms represented a dramatic improvement in rural education and would create a lasting legacy, especially with his implementation of socialist education.

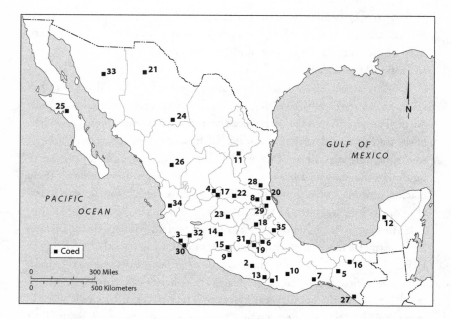

MAP 2.1 Regional Campesino Schools, 1936

1	Amuzgos, Oaxaca	19	Oaxtepec, Morelos
2	Ayotzinapa, Guerrero	20	Ozuluama, Veracruz
3	La Báscula, Colima	21	Ricardo Flores Magón, Chihuahua
4	Bimbaletes, Zacatecas	22	Río Verde, San Luis Potosí
5	La Chacona, Chiapas	23	Roque, Guanajuato
6	Champusco, Puebla	24	Salaices, Chihuahua
7	Comitancillo, Oaxaca	25	San Ignacio, Baja California
8	Coxcatlán, San Luis Potosí	26	Santa Lucía, Durango
9	Coyuca de Catalán, Guerrero	27	Soconusco, Chiapas
10	Cuilapan, Oaxaca	28	Tamatán, Tamaulipas
11	Galeana, Nuevo León	29	Tantoyuca, Veracruz
12	Hecelchakán, Campeche	30	Tecomán, Colima
13	Huajintepec, Guerrero	31	Tenería, Mexico State
14	La Huerta, Michoacán	32	Tuxpan, Jalisco
15	Huetamo, Michoacán	33	Ures, Sonora
16	Jalapa de Méndez, Tabasco	34	Xalisco, Nayarit
17	Lagos de Moreno, Jalisco	35	Xochiapulco, Puebla
18	El Mexe, Hidalgo		

Source: Civera Cerecedo, *Escuela como opción de vida*, 143–45; and Secretaría de Educación Pública, *Educación pública en México*, 117–21.

Note: This map should be taken with a degree of caution since most documentation contains errors or inconsistencies. Especially during the first two decades of their founding, regional campesino schools (which later became rural normales) had short life spans and/or frequently changed location.

DAUGHTERS OF THE REVOLUTION

The writings students produced at rural normales illustrate the way in which they understood, or at least reproduced, SEP directives. Focusing on themes that included the importance of play in learning, the benefits of sports, adult education, and the role of schools in the community, the papers of graduating teachers lauded nature over books, workshops over academic lessons, and loose discipline and a flexible schedule over hierarchical, regimented instruction. But given that theirs was a civilizing mission, they often ignored the knowledge rural dwellers already possessed or simply characterized it as retrograde. As pioneers, teachers were to inculcate new values, new ways of doing things, and a new culture.

"Rural schools are daughters of the revolution" was a consistent refrain in teachers' writing, and three broad tropes marked their academic work in the early 1930s, before the SEP's adoption of socialist education: rural schools as sites of a new modernity, the campesino and indigenous population as a dormant mass with great potential, and teachers as the agents who would awaken and direct campesinos' liberating instinct. Their triumphalist tone mirrored the revolutionary state's official rhetoric, which framed teachers as central actors in the consolidation of a new order. For example, one normalista wrote, "The teacher, emerging from the small and obscure classroom, draws back the curtain of an antiquated past to reveal a picturesque landscape: nature, life."[30] The new order was modern in its justice and allowed life to unfold naturally—an illustration of how nineteenth-century positivist notions persisted in postrevolutionary conceptions. Significantly, decades later, justice and modernity would become competing tropes as normalistas defended their schools based on the revolutionary project while the state dismissed them as relics of the past. In the 1920s and 1930s, however, these concepts were complementary. Wrote another student, "The only faith that gives life and breath to the country has been deposited not in palaces, factories, or skyscrapers but within the humble wings of the rural school."[31] In this new origin story, the meager and rustic classroom would birth a new modern order.

This preoccupation with modernity led early SEP officials to focus on cultural practices rather than structural inequalities. The rural normalistas followed suit and expressed that much needed to be done to "awaken [campesino] ambition and love of progress [by eliminating] pessimism, egoism and vice."[32] In her description of adult education, for example, one teacher wrote that the school's "socializing work transforms individual sentiments and isolated thoughts[; it] keeps alive the collective spirit of justice that the Mexican

Revolution brought about. . . . It converts selfish structures into ones that edify a universal fraternity."[33] The campesino condition, wrote another, is much like that of a "caterpillar that carries within it a butterfly . . . that will take swift flight."[34] While local communities would temper such conceit, it is a good indicator of teachers' self-conscious participation in a larger transformative project, one that in later decades transcended state directives.

The sense of superiority this missionary duty encompassed extended to teachers' conceptions of ethnicity and gender. While educators tended to make little distinction between the campesino and indigenous population—often using the terms interchangeably—they carried with them the logic of assimilation inherent in the SEP's approach to nation building. In an obvious allusion to Vasconcelos's notion of the cosmic race, one normalista wrote, "The mestizo is a positive force in the social betterment of the campesino. With the union of two cultures, the resulting one is better prepared. This is why the mestizo has more clarity about community problems and seeks solutions with more interest than the Indian."[35] His words likewise reflected the view of other educators like Rafael Ramírez, a chief architect of the cultural missions and director of the Department of Rural Education, who had admonished, "You need to be very careful that your pupils not only learn the Spanish language but that they acquire our customs and ways of life, which are undoubtedly superior to theirs."[36] The transformation began with the normalistas themselves, a process the boarding-school structure made easier because, according to one director, it separated students from the "depressing influence of their homes."[37] Or, as another put it, "The timid Indians that a year ago arrived at this institution . . . now see their town's life from a different angle."[38] Students at the normales reproduced this view, often articulating a noble-savage framework. "The ease with which the Indian joins civilization," wrote one graduate, "is eloquent proof that the beating strengths, the racial fortitude, pristine in our Indian, are still alive."[39]

A similar vision framed the approach to women, of whom the SEP held a contradictory view. As victims of the previously backward social order, they were in need of redemption. But they were also key figures in consolidating a new modernity. Teachers' writings reflect this view as they emphasized that with their help, women would emerge from the long lethargy imposed by both male selfishness and female cowardice. Educational projects would harness women's moral strength and natural kindness to construct the new society. Once women received the same education as men, they would cease to be a burden on society and instead constitute "a veritable factor in economic, moral and intellectual progress."[40]

Despite the SEP's paternalistic views on both ethnicity and gender, its project denaturalized many aspects of the previous racial, gendered, and class hierarchies. While the teaching profession had long been accessible to women, the revolutionary government's charge that they organize women's leagues and champion women's rights provided new opportunities for female political participation.[41] Predominantly indigenous communities that might have initially resisted the SEP's attempt to transform their cultural practices and traditions over the long run "pursued their dialogue with teachers and educational authorities in order to bend the school to serve local interests and culture."[42] Moreover, because so many rural teachers themselves came from a campesino-indigenous background, they exemplified the possibilities of a more flexible social structure. Finally, the very contradictions, limitations, and resistance that teachers faced in carrying out their charge tempered their self-righteousness. They instead became conduits by which diverse communities could have a say in the process of state formation. Rather than being the state's missionaries, they facilitated revolutionary citizenship, one that did not always conform to the state's vision.[43]

Overall, student term papers reveal the SEP's changing ideology, from one originally emphasizing social redemption and action pedagogy to one that addressed structures of exploitation and collective organizing. Graduates reproduced educational discourse and mandates, with early 1930s assignments reflecting spiritual or liberal ideals and those toward the latter part of the decade demonstrating a more materialist perspective. "And if the previous apostles of Christianity built churches," wrote a graduate in 1933, "today the advanced soldiers of the revolution create schools. And if the former substituted idolatry with the gospel, the latter replace agony with joy."[44] If teachers were the new protagonists in this narrative of conquest, priests were the new villains. For example, in an essay entitled "The Teacher as the True Social Leader in the Communities," a graduate from the rural normal of Ayotzinapa devoted much of his essay to contrasting the teacher's noble community work to the self-interested actions of the priest. Rather than eschewing Christian doctrine, however, he hailed teachers as its true adherents. They, "filled with faith and love," heeded the revolution's call and "took on the noble crusade of liberating the people."[45]

The grand charge assigned to students at rural normales instilled in young teachers a sense of their own importance. Rather than being corporatist institutions that fostered passivity or compliance, these schools based their whole philosophy on the idea that their graduates should promote community change. Moreover, SEP publications such as *El Maestro Rural* would become venues to denounce the misery of the countryside, foment a campesino and indigenous identity based on collective rights and action, expand on the possibilities of justice offered by noncapitalist modes of organization, and prepare the terrain for socialist education.[46] The magazine also published the writings of rural teachers themselves, thus creating an intellectual community that enriched their experience, encouraged their laboring commitment in the face of constant challenges, and reinforced their key role in Mexico's progressive transformation.

CHURCH, STATE, AND THE BATTLE OVER EDUCATION

The state's educational project had an obvious antagonist in the Catholic Church. The 1917 Constitution contained several anticlerical provisions, including a mandate for secular education. In the latter part of the 1920s, when President Calles implemented laws compelling religious figures to register with civil authorities, prevented the church from making political declarations, and prohibited public religious processions, the Catholic Church and its faithful mounted a powerful rebellion. Concentrated primarily in the central-western states of Mexico, the Cristiada, as the religious revolt became known, involved tens of thousands of campesinos who often targeted teachers, the most visible symbols of the new order. In retaliation for the government converting churches into stables, Cristeros burned schools and tortured teachers. Cutting off their ears and leaving their bodies wrapped in banners reading "Long Live Christ the King" became a signature Cristero mark.

The dynamics behind the Cristero rebellion were complex and involved both elite and popular strains. The former, constituted by the church and large landowners, saw their interests threatened by the new revolutionary order and reacted violently to teachers' efforts to organize peasant and workers' unions. Hacendados, caciques, and mine and plantation owners sponsored armed bands to target teachers, while priests delivered impassioned sermons threatening to excommunicate parishioners who sent their children to school. Previously liberal partisans who had benefited from the Porfirian legislation against indigenous collective landholding recruited Cristeros to preserve order against those they characterized as immoral *agraristas* (proponents of land distribution).[47] In the northeastern region of Michoacán, the US-owned lumber company had their workers sign a pledge promising not to send their children to the newly built school. In several places priests urged community members to run off teachers.[48]

But it would be wrong to characterize all Cristeros as pawns of priests and landlords. The movement also reflected a deep-seated religiosity and defense of local autonomy threatened by the revolutionary state.[49] Many campesinos challenged the legitimacy of property arrangements, citizenship, authority, and cultural identities promoted by the new set of liberal elites.[50] While the vast majority of Mexico's campesinos were Catholic, their varying levels of commitment, practice, and identity structured their religious culture and often determined their reaction to schools, agrarian reform, and anticlerical legislation.[51]

The state defeated the first Cristero revolt in 1929, though more outbursts followed in the 1930s with the implementation of socialist education. Under minister of education Narciso Bassols (1931–34), the SEP moved increasingly leftward, further activating the ire of conservatives and even moderates. A Marxist, Bassols promoted the "essentially economic aspect" of rural education as a way to modify systems of production, distribution, and access to wealth.[52] Operating under the assumption that rural dwellers could not be well educated until they were well fed, the minister promoted agrarian reform as a principal component of rural education. Collectivist approaches to farming, he believed, could remedy campesino poverty, while indigenous culture harbored virtues that far surpassed capitalist tenets.[53]

Under Bassols's leadership, the SEP made headway in secularizing education and creating institutions for teacher professionalization. Bassols promoted coeducation and supported the Mexican Eugenics Society's recommendation that sex education be taught in schools. This latter position rallied conservative sectors of the population already angered by the imminent adoption of socialist education. The National Parents Union and the church mounted alarmist allegations that were eagerly published by newspapers like *Excélsior*. Rumors thus flourished that the study of sexual reproduction constituted basic pornography, that lessons involved kids disrobing, and that teachers would rape young girls.[54] The campaign soon targeted Bassols specifically, in part because of his radical politics. Like socialist education, the right saw sex education as an example of a more general affront to religious and private control of schools, not to mention an attack on the patriarchal order.

As a way to temper the campaign against the government, Bassols resigned as minister of education in May 1934, seven months before President Cárdenas took office and socialist education saw its strongest push forward. His resignation may have alleviated tensions, but the state was about to embark on an experiment with socialist education, which in many parts of

Mexico provided the ideological glue for some of Cárdenas's most ambitious collectivization projects.[55]

THE IMPLEMENTATION OF SOCIALIST EDUCATION

Predating Bassols, the socialist school had its precursors in the early part of the twentieth century, when pedagogues such as José de la Luz Mena promoted the idea of rationalist education. Implemented as official policy in the states of Yucatán and Tabasco by progressive governors Felipe Carrillo Puerto (1922–24) and Garrido Canabal (1920–24, 1931–34) in the early years after the revolution, the rationalist school was scientific and antireligious, upholding respect for individual difference as a way to create a more humane and just society. Eschewing intellectualism, authoritarianism, and single-sex education, it valued manual labor and advocated the active role of the teacher in family and community life.[56] John Dewey's philosophy bridged the rationalist and socialist schools—action pedagogy became practical lessons, and historical materialism's emphasis on the truth replaced the previous focus on real life as the basis for pedagogical inspiration.[57]

As a matter of policy, the directors of the cultural missions first discussed socialist education in a 1932 conference. In debating the type of instruction best suited for the countryside, the attendees agreed it should be one that "satisfied the economic needs of the rural class . . . tending to transform systems of production and distribution of wealth, with a frank collectivist aim."[58] When Mexico's recently consolidated National Revolutionary Party (which later became the Institutional Revolutionary Party, PRI) held its convention in 1933 and outlined its six-year plan, a faction within the educational commission advocated the adoption of socialist education. While this group failed, during the following year, socialist education obtained support from certain branches of the teachers' union.[59] Significantly, it received an unlikely boost from Calles, who, while no longer president, was the *jefe máximo*, Mexico's most powerful political figure. Hardly a partisan of progressive reform, Calles's contempt for the Catholic Church led him to promote socialist education, which to him and many others simply meant secular, anti-Catholic schooling.

When socialist education was approved by Congress in October 1934, few could agree on the meaning of *socialism*. Interpretations ranged from a need to achieve broad-based unity in a country with profound social and ethnic differences, to the creation of schools as instruments of social change, to a necessary step in the path toward a modern society, to an actual stage in socializing the means of production. Ultimately, the adoption of socialist education reflected the popular concerns of the revolution, the severe crisis of capitalism triggered by the Great Depression, the presence of progressives within the SEP, and the link so many reformers saw between education and the creation of a more egalitarian society. While both the left and the right criticized the fact that socialism was not clearly defined, its ambiguity in some respects facilitated its implementation.

Socialist education had its greatest impact in the countryside, where it reinforced notions of the teacher as a community leader whose sympathies lay with the poor. Those who were already politicized took it as a mandate to continue their organizing work. For example, teachers from the rural normal of Oaxtepec in Morelos issued a manifesto to campesinos and workers, stating, "We happily assume the vanguard position that has been given to us and will direct the crystallization of your ideals as a battle of hope."[60] Socialist education thus heightened the link between schools and the need for structural transformation of the economy, in which teachers were to be central protagonists. Where agricultural workers, campesinos, and teachers were already mobilized, it had the most enthusiastic support. In the northern region of La Laguna, long marked by social unrest, the new educational mandate reinforced unionization efforts, ejido formation, and cooperatives, often placing the schoolhouse as the organizing center and teachers as leaders.[61]

In training teachers on its implementation, SEP publications stated that socialism was at its core "a system to enable socioeconomic justice." In contrast to the bourgeois school, which emphasized individual success and the accumulation of wealth—"the only and major goal of capitalism"—the socialist school resolved one's needs by harmonizing them with collective justice. Indeed, the socialist school was but one more institution born of the revolution and should be "the select child of the union, the ejido, the cooperative, and the government, of all the active products of the revolution."[62] At a microlevel, socialist education was to address home dynamics, improving the household's economic, spiritual, and moral organization. Teachers would guide inhabitants on proper dress and food habits, battle superstition and religious fanaticism, instruct on proper hygiene habits, and combat alcoholism and gambling.[63]

At rural normales the use of Marxist language was more explicit. For example, instructions on one exam asked students to complete the exercise shown in figure 2.3 by drawing a line that connected the appropriate categories in the column on the left with the groups of people on the right. The correct answer placed peons and workers under the Exploited category while the rest were Exploiters. Next was a three-part question asking whose labor was used to extract raw materials, who produced commodities, and who obtained the illegitimate profit in this process.[64]

Normalistas were also tested in socialism's political, economic, social, rationalist, and cultural function. When one student answered that its political nature meant campesinos should gain judicial authority, it was corrected to "power in general." Its economic nature, expressed the student, meant a campesino should "struggle to acquire a plot of land to . . . sustain his family." But the evaluator noted that the student missed "a lot of what this aspect entailed."[65] Indeed, socialist lessons often involved the broad principles that explained school as an ideological tool of the revolution, the need to eliminate the vestiges of capitalism, the expropriation of private property, and the eventual rule of the proletariat. Upon graduation, normalistas were thus to teach a materialist conception of history and the universe, explain that class struggle drove human progress, and influence the middle class to think of themselves as proletarians.[66] Such lessons reinforced class consciousness and legitimized an agenda of social justice by explaining basic power dynamics that teachers, in turn, espoused in the communities where they taught.

Normalistas reproduced such analytical frameworks in their graduating term papers. One normalista, for example, expressed the need to build a new future, one "in which current class divisions, those where exploiters own all the wealth and the exploited work, are replaced by an egalitarian society in which wealth is distributed equally."[67] After articulating the power relations between rich and poor and explaining the nature of class conflict in Marxist terms, another paper characterized the rural school as a product of each particular historical stage. In the past there had been convents and seminaries, religious and lay schools. The moment was now ripe for the socialist

Students were asked to draw lines connecting the groups
on the right with the appropriate categories on the left.

Exploiters   Peons
                                    Estate owners
                                    Businessmen
                                    Capitalists
                                    Clergy
Exploited   Workers

FIGURE 2.3 Categorization exercise on a January 1940 entrance exam for the rural normal of Tenería, Mexico State.

school. The opposition to it merely reflected the class conflict at play in the formation of an egalitarian society.[68]

In their communities teachers espoused such messages in whole or in part. Some reported that socialism simply gave a name to what they already did; others used it to encourage community initiatives or social agency, and others to denounce church corruption.[69] But some took the doctrine literally. Seemingly alluding to the Marxist slogan "From each according to his ability, to each according to his need," one teacher reported trying to make the kids understand that "joint work, equally distributed according to ability, was more productive."[70] More broadly, another teacher stated that she taught "in accordance with the interests of the revolutionary proletariat who fight to transform capitalist Mexico into socialist Mexico."[71] These were of course the normalistas' words to the SEP. As Mary Kay Vaughan has shown, in communities they softened state rhetoric that would conflict with long-standing local traditions.[72]

Still, church and hacendado hostility appears as a constant and early challenge to rural educators. Priests circulated flyers warning families that children would now be taught to obey the state, not their parents. "This same socialist school," one flyer elaborated, had "already been implemented in Russia where kids have lost respect and love for their parents, not hesitating to denounce them. . . . Their poor, elderly parents had been jailed, beaten, and humiliated to the great satisfaction of their very own offspring."[73] Newspapers publicized complaints that "rural communist teachers" prompted otherwise compliant campesinos to take over hacienda land and resources.[74] The Cristero movement saw renewed episodes, and teachers continued to be principal targets. They were threatened, their homes and schoolhouses burned; many were mutilated, lynched, or killed, often in quite a gruesome manner. In 1936, for example, in the municipality of Tabasco, Zacatecas, a band of armed men killed and dismembered the young educator María Murillo and then exhibited her breasts as a warning of what happened to communist teachers. The following morning the priest held mass and absolved those responsible.[75]

The constant violence against or assassination of teachers—223 documented cases between 1931 and 1940, though there were likely many more—created an environment in which Cristero actions became etched in normalista memory and formed a constituting element of their origin story.[76] Even before socialist education, teachers faced the hostility of the countryside's power holders, whose violence radicalized them and increased their loyalty to the government's socialist education.[77] The class nature of the violence against teachers is evident from the numerous attacks they faced in states with no Cristero movement, such as Chiapas, where plantation owners, local officials, and hired gunmen regularly targeted teachers.[78] For subsequent generations, the battle between church and state, between progress and reactionary forces, encompassed part of the legacy that made theirs a noble and brave profession. Moreover, as discussed in the next chapter, socialist education provided a powerful analytical framework by which future generations moved beyond the church-state dichotomy in the battle over education.

RURAL NORMALES AND STUDENT GOVERNANCE

The educational philosophy born of the revolution created an environment in which students acquired an important say within rural normales. The initial space for student voices came with the early organizational model meant to mirror family relations, one that emphasized respect, caring, and a decision-making process that benefited all participants. Moreover, as previously discussed, action pedagogy undermined nineteenth-century philosophies that held that teaching should be regimented, hierarchical, and authoritarian. In their early reports, rural normal directors continuously emphasized their schools' "democratic organization," their encouragement that normalistas form student associations, their adoption of a discipline system based on the "students' active collaboration" in its enforcement and "the most freedom possible."[79] Graduates would, in turn, reproduce these tendencies in the communities where they taught and thus would distinguish themselves from previous generations whose practices were encapsulated by the philosophy *la letra con sangre entra* (spare the rod, spoil the child). Pedagogical methods taught at normales increasingly valued children's "freedom, independence, and spontaneity as the first step in the educational process" and emphasized that discipline and good conduct should come from within rather than be imposed by the teacher's authority.[80]

The undercurrent of progressivism that long characterized rank-and-file teachers also contributed to a strong student say in the rural normales. In addition to liberal teachers who promoted student participation as an act of democracy in the 1920s, cultural missionaries who witnessed the problems in poor communities emphasized collective action as a means to resolve them. Likewise, teachers and agricultural technicians who were members or sympathizers of the Mexican Communist Party fought for a voice in institutional decisions. As educators pushed for unionization, they transmitted political lessons to their students, many of whom linked social reforms to change at their normal.[81] Thus, even before the SEP formally sanctioned it in the 1930s, student participation in normales' government had been a de facto practice. As students created their own organizations and demanded a say in how their schools were run, they appropriated and often reframed state goals. In the process, their vision became radicalized and formed the basis for a revolutionary ideology they maintained for generations (figure 2.4).

As the rural normales grew in both size and number during the 1930s, the family model gave way to a cooperativist framework, one that emphasized the needs of the collective over those of the individual (figure 2.5). Indeed, as SEP officials spoke increasingly of fomenting leadership qualities in future

FIGURE 2.4 Mural at the rural normal of Ayotzinapa, Guerrero, which reads, "For a socialist revolution, long live worker-campesino-student unity." The mural's style suggests it was done by José Hernández Delgadillo, whose anecdote opened this chapter. Photograph by author.

rural teachers, student participation in the normales' governing structure became a logical place to promote assertive behavior and to undo what Ignacio García Téllez, head of the SEP from 1934 to 1935, characterized as the "conformist mentality of the exploited."[82] In its 1937 action plan, the Department of Agricultural Instruction and Rural Normal, the office within the SEP then in charge of secondary rural education, emphasized that rural normales had been "created essentially to make the children of poor campesinos . . . youngsters with a class consciousness capable of transforming our rural population." To cultivate "organizing skills, a sense of responsibility, and ability to promote class interests," student councils would assume the school's leadership with no "inferiority complex" and in this way participate in "the country's destiny."[83]

The biggest impulse for students' say in rural normales came with socialist education. This legislation provided a framework by which top-down goals intersected with the undercurrent of popular mobilization spearheaded by teachers' unions and the Mexican Communist Party. At the rural normales, this process crystallized with the formation of the Mexican Federation of Socialist Campesino Students (FECSM). Seeking to combat the bourgeois ideology of traditional student organizations, the FECSM traces its origin to 1934, when a normalista delegation from Tamatán, Tamaulipas, attended a statewide student conference in which they were brushed aside by "university students who had no inkling that students from the campesino class existed." The majority of the students at the conference, continued the FECSM manifesto, were of urban, bourgeois origin. How could they even understand the campesino condition when "the city and the countryside have been eternal rivals[?] . . . The city houses the accumulation of wealth and well-being, while in the countryside there is misery, wanton exposure, and unceasingly brutal work."[84] Such statements exemplify the type of political consciousness that would take shape in the rural normales, one in which students identified as members not only of the exploited class but of the *rural* exploited class. In some ways, the FECSM is representative of the popular organizations that emerged under Cárdenas: it united a newly constituted sector of society in a broad national association; its socialist outlook was acceptable to a government that had legalized the Communist Party and encouraged a critique of capitalist exploitation; and it politicized rural normalistas' understanding of themselves and their institutions. "One belonged to the FECSM," recalled Mariano Orozco Álvarez, who studied at the rural normal of Huetamo, Michoacán, from 1938 to 1941. "That's how I began to learn the theory of scientific socialism."[85] The FECSM thus provided a noninstitutional venue

FIGURE 2.5 Rural normal of Galeana, Nuevo León, 1934. Archivo General de la Nación, Photographic Archive, Normales Rurales, c2, Sobre 9.

to reproduce Marxist discourse, one that was not eliminated with the overturning of socialist education in the 1940s.

The FECSM's early language bears the great sense of possibility that characterized the 1930s, when the crisis of capitalism created expectations of profound social reorganization that would finally meet the needs of the poor. "We are living a transcendent historical moment," opened the 1934 call to form the federation, "witnessing the rise of a humanity unknown until now. Today it rises with previously undreamed longings and with desires and hopes that even a few years ago would have been characterized as utopias." This context had produced "millions of young campesinos anxious to learn but, above all, to struggle for the betterment of their class."[86]

The FECSM's constituting congress took place in 1935 in the rural normal of El Roque, in the state of Guanajuato. In their conference resolutions, the rural normalistas declared themselves in "frank opposition to capitalism, the bourgeoisie, the clergy, and political demagoguery."[87] Their demands included an increase in the number of rural normales (as promised by the government's six-year plan), a call for training teachers specifically for their schools (to mitigate the situation in which most of the teachers hailed from urban normales), the right of the FECSM to report on teachers and administrators who shirked their responsibilities or acted counter to the revolutionary ideology, and a say in disciplinary procedures.[88]

Early FECSM proclamations that saw the possibilities offered by the historical moment soon acknowledged the great obstacles standing in the way of their utopias. A 1937 congress call, for example, stated that, against the backdrop of tragedies like the Spanish Civil War and Japan's invasion of China, "our country, under the rightful progressive politics of General Cárdenas, advances the Revolution's purpose, fighting against the imperialism that oppresses us and destroying latifundismo's [landed estates'] hold."[89] More than any other student group, rural normalistas identified with the Cardenista project, both because they came from campesino origins and because, being on the front line of Cárdenas's reforms, they experienced firsthand the challenges of its implementation. The rural normales' early history involved fending off Cristeros, battling rumors that theirs were schools of the devil, and carrying out community projects. Through direct experience, classroom lessons, or the right's persecution, rural normalistas identified closely with the cause of the oppressed, those whose interests Cárdenas championed. The distinct dynamic at the rural normales did not go unnoticed within the broader community of educators. Alberto Morales Jiménez, a student at Mexico City's National Teachers' School, wrote about his visit to a national congress of rural normalistas at El Roque, Guanajuato, "President Cárdenas had [in the rural normales] a true, loyal, and firm right hand. These youths stood arm in arm with rural teachers and in agrarian communities, towns, and villages withstood the attacks of white guards, hacienda owners, and the fanatics at the service of the political priests. . . . If the university youth had opposed the Cardenista government, there, standing firm, was the rural youth to defend him!"[90] Referring here to the university community's opposition to socialist education, Morales captures an important quality inherent in normalista politicization: a juxtaposition of city and countryside, the former a place of privilege and the latter a site of marginality. As the FECSM manifesto put it, until Cárdenas, the government had neglected the countryside or overseen policies that funneled the countryside's wealth to the cities.[91]

While the SEP initially sanctioned and even promoted student participation in the normales' governing structure, the student federation ultimately threatened official control over these institutions. The SEP thus engaged in a series of strategies to guide student voices through channels that excluded the FECSM. In 1936 the SEP's Rural Educational Council designed statutes that gave students a voice in institutional governance but did so through a framework linking that voice to the goals of the institution. The question of who would define the institution's ultimate project was momentarily tempered by the adoption of socialist education, which provided a sufficiently radical rationale to forefront issues of class. Still, the SEP's trepidation is evident in its language: "Students are not called upon to participate in the school's government to decree rights or prerogatives but to study the school's problems and to help realize the social ends of the institution. The school is not organized against students but in their favor. And they, for their part, should organize in favor, not against, the school. They should do so not as a separate entity but as integrative elements of the school community."[92] An attempt to bring student leaders into the institutional fold, such assertions also reflected an effort to outline a clear hierarchy. The SEP officials emphasized that students would be consulted but could not legislate policy and underscored that the normal's director was the institutional authority ultimately accountable to the SEP. But the normales' philosophy that the school constituted a community gave students ample justification to assert their voice. Normal statutes, for example, read, "The whole notion of what is official or hierarchical within the school needs to be shed in favor of a sense of solidarity and responsibility, one in which everyone confronts the necessary work."[93] This was more than rhetoric: the SEP formalized a design that gave students a role in virtually every aspect of the school's inner workings. This took place through the Student-Teacher Council, a body composed of the school's director, teachers, and elected student representatives. Charged with linking socialist ideas with life at the normal and the education of its students, the council examined technical, economic, and administrative matters related to its daily functions and relationship to the community; considered SEP resolutions pertaining to student life, material resources, and specific school problems; and organized concrete committees dealing with agriculture, sports, social life, work, academic achievement, school desertion, coordination with alumni, and discipline.[94]

Despite the SEP's declarations that the Student-Teacher Council was a consultative rather than an executive body, in most rural normales it acquired substantial say in shaping, and in some cases even determining, internal policy. The tradition of teacher mobilization, the FECSM's resolve to organize students across the normales, and a change in SEP personnel that by 1936 had implemented socialist education all contributed to giving students an unusually important role in their school's governing structure.[95] Additionally, participation in school government provided the perfect opportunity for students to both develop leadership skills and acquire the civic principles necessary to any democracy.

Early concerns about democratic values focused on student discipline. José Santos Valdés, director of several rural normales in the 1930s and 1940s and later the SEP's regional inspector of normal education, was a key figure in designing the disciplinary code adopted at most rural normales. "Discipline," held Santos Valdés, "cannot be the product of theoretical speculations. It has to be the outcome of daily life and experience, of the interaction among children, between children and teachers, and between children and the environment."[96] For this reason, the disciplinary code needed the input of all community members, including students. Only in this way could they understand its logic and the implications of breaking the rules. Adopting such practices required that teachers give up old privileges, specifically those emanating from their position as authority figures, which, Santos Valdés argued, came from the state and rendered them untouchable or subject only to the judgment of their colleagues or superiors.[97] Instead, the logic of the collective, agreed upon, understood, and enforced by all, should frame the question of discipline. Violating the rules would thus challenge not a single teacher or administrator but the school community. This structure, according to Santos Valdés, represented a key difference between a school that prepared students for "enslavement and a life of servitude, and the school that educated for democracy."[98]

These ideals were put into practice through a code of conduct that emphasized student rights and responsibilities, measured through a point system: if students neglected their responsibilities or defied school regulations, they lost points. They began with 100 points, and reaching 40 merited expulsion. While the school director determined the value assigned to each violation, students had a role in enforcing school conventions, especially in ensuring student participation in work commissions, often considered more important than academic performance.[99]

The Committee of Honor and Justice, the committee charged with matters of student discipline, became one of the clearest expressions of student voice in the rural normales. Composed of the school director and selected teachers and students, this council determined the type of punishment for those who violated the code of conduct. The meetings took place before the entire student body and involved group debates that often went on for hours. The cases brought before these councils included neglecting assigned duties, engaging in amorous relationships, stealing, and getting in physical fights, often involving weapons.[100] These open meetings created an environment of public debate, student participation, and individual accountability to the collective. For example, José Ángel Fabre Baños documented a case at the rural normal of Galeana in which a male student was expelled for striking a female peer. In that decision the general assembly issued the following statement: "The socialist school attempts to defend women; we want to make it clear to the entire world that we give women all the consideration they deserve and that we will severely judge all that is unjustly done against their interests whether she is a student or not of our school."[101] In keeping with broader revolutionary tropes that women should be rescued from men's abusive clutches, such declarations still treated women as passive subjects. But Fabre Baños's account shows how open debate linked broad ideological philosophies such as socialism to concrete incidents on the school grounds. In these discussions, students learned how to articulate a grievance, mount a defense, weigh potential punishments, and make a case to the school authorities—exactly the type of skills expected of community leaders.

THE EDUCATIONAL ARCHITECTS of the 1920s and 1930s set out to create a new kind of school with a new kind of teacher. While Mexico's early twentieth-century educational project was one of state consolidation, the revolutionary struggle that produced the Mexican state imbued it with a progressive current that found expression in radical politics such as socialist education. And even before the socialist curriculum, early experimentation with action pedagogy, collectivism, and agricultural education and the emphasis on teachers as community leaders structured rural normales as institutions uniquely poised to preserve the popular undercurrent of the revolutionary struggle. While the state would soon halt these progressive forces, the goals that had previously been articulated were not easily set aside. A whole generation of teachers trained in socialist education would continue to espouse radical principles through their three decades of professional service. Many, moreover, became teachers at the rural normales, effectively continuing socialist education even as the state abandoned it. Students, for their part, conscious of the invaluable opportunity a career in teaching represented, would be increasingly active in the defense of rural normales in the face of a government that in the 1940s turned its attention to the cities at the expense of the countryside. This created an institutional context in which the original progressive philosophies were not only preserved but furthered.

3

"And That's When the Main Blow Came"

FELIPE CORTÉS MARTÍNEZ, who in the 1950s studied and later taught at the rural normal of El Mexe, located in the central state of Hidalgo, considers the first attacks on these schools to have come in 1940: "It's not the same to have [Ávila] Camacho as president as it was to have Cárdenas. And that's when the main blow came, when they took away socialist education."[1] Indeed, the presidency of Manuel Ávila Camacho, who took office in December 1940, signaled a rightward shift in the course of Mexico's revolutionary project. Social reforms had already slowed significantly after 1938, the year President Lázaro Cárdenas nationalized Mexico's oil industry, an act considered the culmination of his progressive policies. Still, President Ávila Camacho's conservative direction had important repercussions for Mexico's educational system as his administration implemented a series of changes that privileged urban over rural schools, transformed the character of the countryside's teachers, ended coeducation in boarding schools, and overturned socialist education.

The international context precipitated by World War II facilitated a change in the Mexican government's rhetoric from emphasizing social justice to privileging national unity. This shift had important policy implications as subsequent regimes replaced wealth redistribution with urban infrastructural development. The battles between church and state of the 1920s and 1930s drew to a close as President Ávila Camacho publicly declared himself a "believer," marking a stark departure from earlier regimes that held strictly secular positions. In this way, the president initiated a modus vivendi with the Catholic Church, which soon found common cause with a state whose discourse became increasingly anticommunist. In addition to openly proclaiming his Catholic faith, Ávila Camacho declared shortly before taking office that he was a democrat, not a socialist. In his government there would be no communists.[2] His successor, President Miguel Alemán (1946–52), went even further. His administration actively persecuted communists, a label that, under the Cold War framework, was broadly applied to popular leaders, dissidents, or critics. Soon after taking office, Alemán created the Federal Security Directorate, an agency modeled after the US Federal Bureau of Investigation and ostensibly charged with protecting national security. Instead, it infiltrated, spied on, and repressed campesinos, workers, students, and even official organizations.[3] The country's major newspapers, such as *El Universal* and *Excélsior*, whose owners had held a fierce anticommunist line since the 1920s, likewise drew few distinctions among Mexico's diverse leftist groups, labeling most forms of popular organizing communist. These newspapers operated with close ties to the ruling inner circle, and their editorial lines, paid advertisements, and numerous articles—some written in the United States—uncritically reproduced the Cold War's bellicose language and magnified the supposed communist threat.[4]

The education system, too, began to undergo a series of changes. Under a framework of modernization and professionalization, the Ministry of Public Education (SEP) implemented curricular reforms to make rural normales more like their urban counterparts. This meant emphasizing academic instruction over community development, farming expertise, and the basic set of trade skills the institutions had previously prioritized. Funding for rural normales was itself jeopardized. No longer the regime's priority, the number of schools decreased. Those that remained increasingly needed student mobilization to preserve what was already a precarious existence. Whereas rural teachers had previously held a special place in the educational system, the SEP reformulated the pay and benefits structure to reward professional training over years of service.[5] This new system relegated rural teachers—who either had little formal training or took their jobs before attaining their degree, or whose remote location hampered their ability to enroll in professional development courses—to the bottom rung of the pay scale. Accompanying these changes was a deliberate transformation in rural teachers' prescribed role. Their social leadership, so touted by the early educational architects, became civic duty: rather than advocating for the working class or rural communities, teachers were to limit their role to the classroom and emphasize self-realization over political militancy.[6]

But the fervor of the previous two decades, especially in the countryside during the Cárdenas years, had created an imprint that was difficult to erase. While discourse and policy at the top changed, the state could not easily transform the ideals and dynamics of educators working on the ground. Despite a changing context in which national unity replaced social justice as the official operative discourse, the rural normales preserved the more radical ideals of the revolution, making them bulwarks of Cardenismo, socialism, and justice for the poor. This process took place, this chapter argues, for three interrelated reasons. First, socialist education had grown deep roots in these institutions as it provided an explanation for the existence of poverty, emphasized its unjust nature, and charged its graduates with changing the conditions that produced it. Moreover, socialism offered a language to challenge the state's narrow definition of modernity, which assumed that support for industry would produce social equity. Second, student participation as a mainstay of institutional reproduction at rural normales reinforced a collectivist logic that normalistas soon internalized as a strategy of struggle. Appeals for students to identify with their school's integrity worked, though not necessarily as the SEP intended. Directives that students be mindful of the institutional reputation and thus adhere to the discipline the authorities demanded clashed with the need to preserve the normales' very existence. The schools' woeful underfunding led students to mobilize for basic improvements with tactics such as strikes that inherently challenged authority and drew attention to the normalistas as unruly subjects. Third, and finally, in the course of such struggles, the Mexican Federation of Socialist Campesino Students (FECSM), the rural normales' student federation, increasingly consolidated its power, holding steadfastly to a socialist framework even as the SEP purged communists from the administrative ranks. The FECSM gradually translated the say students had in quotidian school norms into political power and increasingly prioritized ideological formation. As the political context became more hostile to the poor's vindications—first because national unity to confront the fascists demanded restraint and then because the Cold War rendered the poor's demands subversive—rural normalistas blazed a path that increasingly diverged from that set by the SEP. In so doing, the rural normales developed a unique political culture in which student action, socialist discourse, and justice for the countryside became inextricably linked.

"THE GREAT CALAMITY"

The retreat from the progressive policies of the 1930s took various forms. Toward the end of his term, Cárdenas's reforms had already slowed as capital flexed its muscle, making evident the limits of state autonomy.[7] Cárdenas's conciliatory policies included the choice of Ávila Camacho as his successor. Upon taking office, the new president emphasized that national unity would structure policy and would be the path to "honor and bolster the high moral values of the Mexican family."[8] Class struggle as an analytical framework and popular vindication as a collective goal were no longer officially sanctioned ideas. Whereas Cardenista reforms had challenged the sacred right to private property and asserted Mexico's economic nationalism, Ávila Camacho sought a closer relationship to the business sector and to the United States, appealing to a continental unity that would create a "nobler and more just Christian international order."[9] *Modernization* became the new buzzword and signaled a systematic abandonment of the countryside.

These changes affected the SEP almost immediately. This agency had come to house numerous socialists, who saw in the doctrine an opportunity to address the countryside's historical inequality. Luis Sánchez Pontón, for example, who came from the Cardenista tradition and headed the SEP as President Ávila Camacho began his term in office, defended socialist education and attempted to clarify, if tone down, its meaning. He upheld an educational philosophy committed to collective over individual rights, one that strengthened the "ideals of justice, fraternity, and equitable distribution of wealth" and based itself on the progressive notions of science.[10] Sánchez Pontón reiterated the ideals of the revolutionary school as linked to work and democracy and counterposed it to the "school of indifference," which, he declared, produced "erudite, pompous individuals who fancied themselves geniuses."[11] Despite a language that framed allusions to socialism within the Mexican context and denied it was a foreign-inspired doctrine, right-wing protestations, emboldened by the new president's moderate stance, saw a new light. That an incident at a rural normal led Minister Sánchez Pontón to resign exemplifies the central place of these institutions in the battle against radical education.

In 1941 students from the rural normal of Ayotzinapa in the coastal state of Guerrero initiated a strike demanding the resignation of the school's principal, Carlos Pérez Guerrero, whom they characterized as authoritarian and accused of violating numerous regulations set forth in the normales' governing statutes. According to the students, Pérez Guerrero lived in the neighboring town of Tixtla rather than at the school as required, did not offer the obligatory number of classes, and made decisions with utter disregard for the normal's governing council.[12] In response to the strike, the director circulated rumors—which the national press eagerly published—that students at Ayotzinapa had acted in a blatantly unpatriotic manner against the national insignia. In the version published by newspapers, the normalistas had taken the Mexican flag, stomped on it, burned it, and in its place flown the anarcho-syndicalist red-and-black flag. Protest letters poured into the president's office denouncing the school's adherence to a "Muscovite doctrine" and its invasion by communist cells.[13]

There was never any proof that these events transpired in this way. The story's origins lay in a ceremony held the previous school year in Mexico City, where President Cárdenas gifted students the nation's flag to fly on the school grounds. Awaiting the local ceremony to deliver that flag to Ayotzinapa's principal—which owing to the school's vacation and later its strike, never took place—the student who received the flag folded it up and kept it with his personal belongings. Under Mexican law, this represented an offense to the national symbol, but it in no way approached the gravity of the charges levied in the press. Still, seven teachers and two staff members were fired, and six students were expelled. All were jailed.[14] When their peers protested their detention by mounting a strike, the state governor sent the local army battalion to dislodge the students from the school. Thorough in his job, the commanding coronel ordered additional detentions, including, according to a former school director, seizing the portrait of Karl Marx that hung on the cafeteria's wall. "The Russian communist leader" would be dealt with in Iguala's military headquarters.[15]

Various organizations as well as student associations from other rural normales wrote to the president declaring solidarity with the jailed students, staff, and teachers. Student statements emphasized their loyalty to the government, and a few stated that they had even campaigned in favor of President Ávila Camacho.[16] It was the school director, declared the "Ricardo Flores Magón" student association of Ayotzinapa, who was a traitor to the nation, for he had often spoken against Mexico's oil expropriation.[17] Moreover, they continued, Pérez Guerrero had expressed nothing but contempt for their normal, maligning it as a center of prostitution, a characterization consistent with the right's propaganda that rural normales were immoral, communist hubs replete with sordid sexual practices.[18]

The National Parents Union, an organization of private-school parents that had long fought socialist and secular education, in concert with Mexico's major newspapers (whose owners opposed the leftist tenets of the revolution), blamed Ayotzinapa's conflict on the minister of education himself. The attacks reached a crescendo when Minister Sánchez Pontón was called to answer before congress. Soon after, he resigned. The brigadier general Octavio Véjar Vázquez, who had no experience in education, replaced him. Supported by the right-wing National Action Party, the National Parents Union, and other right-wing groups such as the Freedom and Private Initiative Defense League, Véjar Vázquez immediately made explicit his goals: the elimination of socialist education and the mending of relations with the Catholic Church.[19] The press welcomed him as a "young and dynamic professional." Reports in the national newspaper *Excélsior* expressed that just a few days after taking office, the new minister had established unity among the left, the right, and the private sector and highlighted his declaration to oversee "a school of love, not hate, one that will unify rather than divide us and promote a school that will affirm our nationality."[20]

To normalistas, the removal of Sánchez Pontón was one in a series of public attacks against the rural normales. Writing on the subject two decades later, Hipólito Cárdenas Deloya, Ayotzinapa's former director, termed the incident "the great calamity." Not mincing words, he charged the "mercenary, whorish, and venal press" with representing the interests of those seeking to "outlaw the Communist Party! Elicit the confidence of Yanqui imperialism! . . . Use Ayotzinapa to punish teachers nationally! . . . And veer the Mexican Revolution off course."[21] In his memoir—like in many others written by normalistas—Cárdenas Deloya, incensed by the claim that students had acted in an unpatriotic manner, details the virtues of the rural normales, defends their mission, and situates socialist education as the secret to their ability to serve the poor.

Even during its heyday, socialist education had been controversial. Liberals had attacked it based on the principle of academic freedom, while the right relied on a campaign of moral panic to incite opposition. The National Action Party, the National Parents Union, and Véjar Vázquez himself promoted an association between Marxists—long supporters of coeducation—and immorality. What, other than engage in improprieties, would the two sexes do in such close proximity? Under the communist watch, these groups argued, rural normales constituted centers of loose sexual mores where students cavorted with one another, pregnancies abounded, teachers raped their pupils, and spurned lovers committed suicide or had abortions. Based on rumors of the most extreme kind—for example, that the grounds surrounding the rural normal of Tenería in Mexico State were littered with aborted fetuses—the right propagated the idea that young women, whether as temptresses or victims, did not belong in the same institutions as men.[22]

While instances of unauthorized relationships, sexual harassment, and rape no doubt took place at rural normales, there is no evidence that these were more frequent than in the society at large. In fact, given the strict policing and students' ability to collectively mount a case against offending staff or teachers, such abuses were likely less common than at other institutions or workplaces. To the extent that it did occur, gender-based violence was a product not of rural normal culture but of the general subordination of women, which the socialists were, however imperfectly, committed to addressing. In fact, this was their whole argument for coeducation: equal instruction might help mitigate and eventually do away with "the inequality that has persisted across time and made women the slaves of men."[23] Significantly, some advocates of socialist education went even further. Not only should female students be trained in tasks traditionally considered men's realm—farming and small industry—but male students should take home economics courses.[24]

Still, as is evident from Ayotzinapa director Cárdenas Deloya's characterization of the press as whorish, misogynist proclivities were not the exclusive domain of the right. Socialists responded to critiques of moral transgression with requests for more funding to better police student behavior (little was said about controlling abusive teachers, though engaging in a relationship with a student constituted grounds for faculty expulsion).[25] As it was, interactions between male and female students were strictly guarded, relationships were prohibited, and school medics were charged with monitoring female students' periods.[26] Significantly, when the right won the battle against coeducation, its allegations of immorality did not cease. Instead, they reappeared as campaigns against homosexuality, which supposedly abounded at rural normales. Students and teachers, for their part, rebuked such allegations based on heteronormative values and again demanded resources to prevent or police such relationships. For example, one director's request for more beds stated that the shortage meant students slept two to a bed, a practice that "elicited sexual vices."[27]

The division of normales by gender in 1943 eased some parents' anxieties about sending their daughters to coeducational boarding schools, but it ultimately undermined women's structural equality: once the schools were separated, female students were sent to smaller schools, and the better-equipped, larger institutions were reserved for male normalistas.[28] Tellingly, in their justification for ending coeducation, some school authorities proposed what amounted to female students subsidizing the reduced system-wide spending. Women's schools would not need cooks, washerwomen, or cleaning staff as the young girls were themselves equipped for such tasks, reasoned one report.[29]

The campaign against coeducation and socialist pedagogy went hand in hand with the right's attempt to roll back Cardenismo. More broadly, the right fought the activist teacher, a figure, detractors maintained, who sowed a divisive dogma and substituted political agitation for learning. Such attacks set the stage for critiques of rural education itself. It was in the countryside that the most radical teachers taught and had been given the explicit charge to mobilize the poor. Because of socialist education, stated a 1942 *Novedades* article, "the Mexican government now had to contend with the sinister figure of a teacher saturated with doctrines of hate, engendered by the fetid Marx-Lenin-Stalin trilogy and transmitted to them by the virulent commies of the rural normales." The generation of teachers who graduated between 1937 and 1942, continued the piece, "carried within them the seeds of communism, poisoned consciences, and went on to destroy our valuable Mexican ideals."[30] The critique extended to the very conception of teachers as community leaders, a mainstay of the rural educational system. Since rural schools were political projects, reported another piece, "anyone with the desire to engage in demagogical practices could become a teacher." Or, rather, declared an official sardonically, they "could disguise themselves as a teacher" since their mandates "were not to teach but to do social work."[31]

It would take Ávila Camacho's entire *sexenio* (six-year term) to eliminate socialist education from national policy altogether. During his first state-of-the-union address, the president declared that Article 3's socialist provision needed a clearer definition. To this end, his education minister, Véjar Vázquez, announced a consultation with various sectors of the population, including state governments, university rectors, school principals, and parent associations. The minister of education said nothing about input from teachers, whose increasingly powerful unions distrusted a minister whose designs also sought to undermine their collective bargaining. Notably, rural educators were the most radical among a generally militant membership. In the 1930s one out of every eight teachers belonged to the Communist Party. And, as scholar David Raby reminds us, for every member of the Communist Party, there were three or four sympathizers.[32] In places like Guerrero, 90 percent of rural teachers were members of the Communist Party as well as four out of every six federal inspectors.[33]

At a time when the official party sought to unite Mexico's educators under one union as a means of consolidating its control over them, Véjar Vázquez's battle against communists exacerbated preexisting differences among the various teachers' unions. The minister's intransigence—his hostility was directed not only against communists but against the unions themselves—ultimately led to his replacement in 1943. Before he stepped down, however, a December 1941 congressional reform of Article 3—undertaken without the consultation of the promised groups—replaced previous allusions to scientific socialism with *Mexican revolutionary socialism*, a term defined as a commitment to reduce social and economic inequality.[34]

The right, unabashed in its disdain for materialist-based social critiques, celebrated an official SEP announcement that ordered the burning of a million textbooks, an act that would relegate this "demagogic educational material" to the past.[35] Such praise came from the very sector promoting national unity to fight the fascists, themselves also engaged in book burning. The church, for its part, offered Catholicism as the cultural element capable of bonding the country's classes in a common history and purpose. As would become more explicit once President Alemán took office in 1946, the government recognized Catholicism as a central component of the national identity whose focus on the family and social order coincided with the anticommunist rhetoric of the Cold War. Pope Pius XI's 1937 *Divini Redemptoris*, which expressed specific concern for Russia and Mexico "where Communism has been able to assert its power" and "striven by every possible means . . . to destroy Christian civilization," would see renewed circulation.[36]

In the meantime, the new education minister, Jaime Torres Bodet (1943–46), continued to roll back socialist education but in a subtler manner, with the political finesse his predecessor lacked. Unlike Véjar Vázquez, the new secretary had a background in education. A writer and diplomat, Torres Bodet had also worked closely with Vasconcelos during the latter's time as rector of the National Autonomous University of Mexico and had been in charge of the Library Department at the SEP. His relationship with Vasconcelos notwithstanding, Torres Bodet deemphasized teachers' community action and appealed instead to civic duty.[37] Ending socialist education also meant abandoning the community empowerment approach that had previously characterized the SEP's policy toward the countryside. Teachers' social responsibility would be to care about and support the needy, not to mobilize the masses. But, above all, the teaching corps required professionalization. As the SEP sought to temper teachers' broad social role, it moved to reform their training programs, attempting to make rural normales more like urban ones. Not all references to socialism were immediately eliminated from Article 3 of the Mexican Constitution, but this shift paved the way for the final removal of any such language in 1946.[38]

"A THOROUGH HOUSECLEANING"

While the SEP's leadership reflected the regime's rightward shift, consolidating the doctrine of national unity in an agency that housed so many communists would take time. A considerable number of teachers, especially rural ones, opposed the abandonment of socialist education. Their own humble background, the large proportion who belonged to or sympathized with the Communist Party, and the extent to which socialism provided a lens to understand educational shortcomings not as technical problems but as social ones motivated many in its defense.[39] Thus, even as the SEP handed down directives such as the 1945 reform that unified the curriculum at rural and urban normales, at national conferences, rural teacher delegates reaffirmed their training institutions as socialist, coeducational, regional, and agrarian.[40] The contradiction of declaring rural normales to be coeducational two years after their students had been separated by gender, and of affirming socialist education when such pedagogy had been all but eliminated, reveals the lack of consensus about Ávila Camacho's educational project.

Indeed, the president's own administration proceeded in a contradictory fashion. Education Minister Torres Bodet emphasized the need to professionalize the teaching body, yet he and other officials increasingly called on educators' sense of duty to compensate for the system's lack of resources. The hardship entailed by long hours, large classrooms, remote communities, and little pay should be counterbalanced by teachers' satisfaction at serving their fellow citizens. Through a labor of love, teachers were thus to subsidize a system it was the state's responsibility to maintain.

At rural normales, where, "against the basic principle of labor rights," pointed out one director, "we have always been asked to give all our time to the school," the 1945 urban-rural curricular unification spread teachers increasing thin by expanding the years of study from four to six and bringing a greater number of students to each institution.[41] More and more educators found themselves teaching subjects for which they had no training or acting as dorm monitors or night and weekend guards even as they were paid only for their classroom hours.[42] Torres Bodet did worry about the conditions under which rural normales languished. "The dorms have no supplies. The shelves have no books. And what can we say about the laboratories and workshops that we are so often unable to equip with agricultural tools or farm animals?" he lamented. Such conditions would not only fail to produce the professional teachers the minister longed for but, more ominously in his mind, "intensify the resentment that invades the soul of the dispossessed."[43] Subsequent SEP reports echoed this sentiment, noting that if youth were by nature rebellious, poor normalistas were especially so since "the immediate situation of misery in which they live makes them more sensitive . . . accentuating a great social resentment and increasing the general impulse to rebel."[44] And yet the increased funding that Torres Bodet procured as education minister went predominantly to urban normales, even though the rural ones educated two-thirds of the country's teachers.[45]

As the years wore on, students demanded that SEP authorities increase the funding, their sense of indignation fueled by administrations that, despite presiding over unprecedented levels of economic growth, demanded austerity of rural normalistas. If President Ávila Camacho had slowed the precious revolutionary gains, his successor, Miguel Alemán, attacked them outright. His administration oversaw a policy that purged labor unions of their leftist leadership, surveilled and repressed activists, and applied the law of social dissolution—implemented during World War II to target Axis activity in Mexico—to criminalize leftist protest. Notoriously corrupt— amassing a personal fortune that led him to figure among the world's richest men—Alemán reduced educational expenditures to 7.1 percent of the budget, the lowest since 1925.[46] If he expressed concern for education, it was only to better satisfy the country's industrial needs.[47] Manuel Gual Vidal, Alemán's education minister, whom a US consular report characterized as "the most conservative of recent incumbents in the position," placed the very existence of rural normales in question.[48] The number of schools was already depleted—of the twenty-six that existed in 1940, only nineteen survived in 1948—and Gual Vidal also reduced the number of scholarships by 10 percent in 1950 (map 3.1).[49] When students responded with a strike, rather than negotiating with them, the minister closed the rural normales "in order to study and rehabilitate" them. Little interested in the FECSM's proposals for ways to raise educational funds—taxing alcoholic beverages or instituting lottery sales—in a private meeting Gual Vidal declared that "a student on strike ceases to be a student and as a consequence is not in possession of his rights thereby." He further threatened the movement leadership

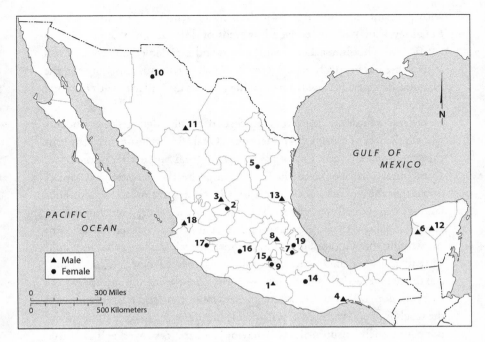

MAP 3.1 Rural Normal Schools, 1948–1949

1	Ayotzinapa, Guerrero	11	Salaices, Chihuahua
2	Cañada Honda, Aguascalientes	12	San Diego Tekax, Yucatán
3	Colonia Matías Ramos, Zacatecas	13	Tamatán, Tamaulipas
4	Comitancillo, Oaxaca	14	Tamazulapan, Oaxaca
5	Galeana, Nuevo León	15	Tenería, Mexico State
6	Hecelchakán, Campeche	16	Tiripetío, Michoacán
7	Huamantla, Tlaxcala	17	Tuxcueca, Jalisco
8	El Mexe, Hidalgo	18	Xalisco, Nayarit
9	Palmira, Morelos	19	Xochiapulco, Puebla
10	Ricardo Flores Magón, Chihuahua		

Source: Meneses Morales, *Tendencias educativas oficiales,* 3:377; and Secretaría de Educación Pública, *Memoria, 1949–1950,* 160–63.

Note: This map should be taken with a degree of caution since most documentation contains errors or inconsistencies.

with permanently shutting down the striking schools.[50] While at the national level the FECSM received hundreds of declarations of support from a variety of schools, teacher organizations, and agrarian communities, Gual Vidal's threats effectively deterred the National Polytechnic Institute and the National Teachers School from launching strikes in solidarity with the rural normales.[51]

Federal education inspectors proceeded to dislodge striking students whose takeover of the schools undermined Gual Vidal's closure mandate. But the SEP inspectors' task was hampered by the local support for normalistas. At the rural normal of Hecelchakán in Campeche, the education authorities noted that the parents association frustrated efforts to close the school since families maintained the cafeteria through their own food contributions. In Atequiza, Jalisco, the municipal president staunchly advocated on behalf of the striking students and, in an impassioned speech, declared that he would "take up arms to defend" them.[52] While in places like Palmira, Morelos, official threats succeeded in having the majority of the student body oppose the strike, in Tamazulapan, Oaxaca, students would not "listen to reason," and the teaching staff exhibited a "remarkable indifference" to controlling them. Reporting such "insubordinate behavior" to parents proved equally futile since, even if they did not support their children's actions, families held little moral sway over them. In this context, lamented one school director, "one person could do little against the strike actions of all the students."[53]

Such support for the normalista strike was not surprising; the schools' precarious conditions were obvious to anyone who looked. The SEP's general director of normal education, various school principals, and "neutral student circles" (presumably those not supporting the strike) agreed that the normalista demands—an increase in daily rations, building repairs, and better school equipment—were just.[54] However, on systemic issues—the reinstatement of coeducation, equalization of the pay structure between graduates of rural normales and those of the National Teachers School, and reinstatement of the scholarships Gual Vidal had cut, SEP authorities were unyielding.[55] After thirty-three days, the FECSM was ultimately forced to call off its strike. Despite the minister of education's refusal to negotiate, the SEP did respond to student pressure by implementing a slight increase in food rations and authorizing new funds for building repairs.[56]

But true to his conservative reputation, Gual Vidal moved to identify and oust teachers and staff who had supported the normalista mobilization.[57] With national newspapers calling for "a thorough housecleaning," the president's office followed up with a broader campaign to counteract socialist influence by creating the Institute of Youth, an organization that would "instill patriotism and democratic tradition in young people."[58] The new organization was meant to undermine the Confederation of Mexican Youth, a national student coordinating body of which the FECSM was a part and which was affiliated with the International Union of Students and the World Federation of Democratic Youth.[59] The press greeted the initiative with great enthusiasm. An *Excélsior* editorial, for example, celebrated President Alemán's directives as liberal measures that contrasted with "the totalitarian efforts that just a few years ago in Mexico sought to tie youth to the heavy shackles of Marxist dogma."[60]

The purging of leftists from the SEP continued under President Adolfo Ruiz Cortines (1952–58) and his education minister, José Ángel Ceniceros, who, wrote the US ambassador to Mexico, "without any fuss or fanfare is weeding out and separating the Communist from the teaching force of the schools. He is not putting it on the grounds of Communism but merely as an administrative matter."[61] These measures affected high-ranking members such as the undersecretary of the SEP, José Gómez Robleda, who had reportedly been appointed to the position on the recommendation of former president Cárdenas. Robleda was condemned by reactionaries for his "communist plan" to adopt "intense propaganda among rural teachers" and disseminate "pedagogical principles that would predispose children to Marxist doctrine," and Ceniceros scored a victory with his ouster.[62]

José Santos Valdés, who in the 1940s and 1950s served as director at five different rural normales and in the 1960s was the SEP's inspector and later supervisor of these institutions, wrote of socialist education, "We knew it was an insurmountable contradiction to carry out socialist education in a country with a system based on private property. But it offered a magnificent opportunity for the necessary creation of a consciousness that, among children and youth, would facilitate the change that Mexico's revolutionaries longed for. The bourgeoisie understood this, and that's why it mounted such fierce opposition."[63] Indeed, despite the 1946 elimination of socialist education from Article 3 of the constitution, the right's hostility to an education system emanating from the revolution continued. Significantly, this hostility now came from within the state itself as the SEP leadership sought to align policy with Cold War tenets that deemed most forms of leftist popular organizing communist. Given the education system's centrality as a tool of social reproduction, the battle to define its parameters continued. So did the language of socialism. And here the rural normalistas experienced what elites called Marxist dogma in profoundly liberating ways.

A SPACE TO PERSIST

The common tropes in normalista narratives show how, before socialism functioned as an explanatory ideology for their own class position or the country's pervasive poverty, it served as a felt experience that helped make sense of their families' generations-long exploitation, the persistent obstacles in their quest for an education, and the possibility of collective action among a peer group whose common denominator was poverty. Here the FECSM served as a structuring and mobilizing body. Made up of representatives from the student association at each rural normal, the FECSM constituted the principal venue by which to channel normalista voices into a formal national organization recognized by the SEP. The student federation continued to uphold the Cardenista notion that rural schools were on the side of the poor and that as such the teacher had to be politicized.

Like other popular unions formed during the 1930s, the FECSM had officialist affiliations. As part of the Confederation of Mexican Youth, the counterpart to the Confederation of Mexican Workers and the National Campesino Confederation, organizations operating under the official party umbrella to harness and channel popular support for the Institutional Revolutionary Party (PRI), the FECSM counted on state financial assistance for its annual conferences, which were frequently inaugurated by state governors, SEP officials, or municipal presidents. The FECSM leadership, moreover, had the right to miss class, schedule makeup exams, or spend a substantial amount of time at normales other than their own for the purposes of running the federation. Despite such measures, unlike the Confederation of Mexican Workers or the National Campesino Confederation, the FECSM did not develop into a clientelistic network delivering wholesale support for the PRI. While some of its leadership did go on to become state officials, the dynamics, ideology, and organizing strategies of the FECSM were so combative that in 1969 the government ceased to recognize it.

As discussed in chapter 2, the FECSM began as an organization advocating for the rights of campesino students. During Cárdenas's presidency this meant securing the newfound gains that enabled poor youth to access a teaching career. It also meant spreading the revolution's ideals of social justice, whose collectivist principles were frequently framed or understood as socialist. As the more conservative regimes of the 1940s and 1950s changed course, the FECSM sought to defend previous gains, combat attacks on Cardenismo, and maintain the rural normales' viability amid an increasingly hostile political climate. Because securing an education required continuous student action, the process produced a dialectic in which students both cherished the invaluable opportunity to study and refused to accept its unsettlingly precarious nature.

On the one hand, rural normales offered them conditions that, however modest, were for most an improvement on their home life.[64] This condition awakened in the youngsters a sense of possibility as they accessed spaces from which their families had historically been barred. Receiving a modest stipend and uniforms and being assured a meal three times a day gave them a glimpse of what it might mean to organize society along the logic of shared wealth. On the other hand, given the bare-bones character of rural normales, there was always a pressing need to improve their tenuous situation. This created a long-standing dynamic in which the FECSM mobilized to assure the schools' basic function and maintenance. Upon arrival, normalistas quickly learned—sometimes intuitively, sometimes as the deliberate result of FECSM organizing—that the chance to escape poverty lay in collective action. The FECSM's lessons in class struggle and revolutionary justice were hardly abstract; the students had but to examine their own family history. That history helps explain socialism's staying power at rural normales.

The memory troves of rural normalistas who studied from the 1930s through the 1960s include their families' experience in the late Porfiriato, the revolution, or the effervescence of Cardenismo. "I still experienced the cattle hacienda regime," recalled Mariano Orozco Álvarez, who was born in 1921 and spent his childhood on the Hacienda de Ojo de Agua in Michoacán's *tierra caliente* (hot, low-lying region), which, as he tells it, was replete with estates whose land grants dated to the colonial period. In 1938 Orozco attended the rural normal (then known as a regional campesino school) of Huetamo, which, he remembered, "the federal government [had] established on an expropriated parish. . . . Lázaro Cárdenas founded it for both men and women."[65] The location was replete with symbolism given the church's long history of siding with the landed oligarchy. That the government set up many other rural normales on expropriated haciendas further reinforced a sense of poetic justice. In the spaces that had previously exploited their ancestors, campesino youth would now receive an education.

Even for those who did not personally witness the hacienda system, their families' history provided a vivid foundation for their own experience. For example, José Ángel Aguirre Romero, who attended the rural normal of Salaices in the 1950s, related his story starting with his family's arrival in Nuevas Delicias, land they and other hacienda workers received after the revolution. To hear the detail with which Aguirre recounts the 1923 settling of a community founded fourteen years before his birth, one would think he had witnessed it himself. Those who came to Nuevas Delicias previously "didn't own the land, they had to share everything they farmed with the boss, and generally they didn't have enough to survive, not even to eat. They lived in crowded rooms, shacks, on top of one another." To get to their new land, "men, women, and children walked; they walked and walked, for three days, until they got to a prairie, an inhospitable place. . . . The people were all poor; some managed to bring a cow or two, spurring them along. Others not even that. Some came with those metal carts that have two wheels and are pulled by a burro, a mule, or a horse, not carrying people but where they put the few things they had: a sack of corn, a sack of beans, a bench."[66] To such epic stories, others add their families' legacies of struggle. José Luis Aguayo Álvarez, who studied at Salaices a few years after Aguirre, shared his family's legacy of exploitation and battles for justice: "My grandparents were agraristas at the end of the nineteenth century. They were also slaves in the southern haciendas. I learned of the subhuman conditions in which they lived and worked. That was the environment in which I grew up. My uncles had long waged agrarian battles. When I was young, they taught me about that struggle. And I listened: I had breakfast, lunch, and dinner with the agrarian code."[67] That the normalistas convey their life stories in a way that so clearly corresponds to episodes in the country's revolutionary history—colonialism, Porfirian exploitation, and revolutionary upheaval—also reflects the type of education they received at rural normales, one the FECSM reinforced in its meetings and study groups.

The obstacles campesinos continued to face in gaining an education after the revolution enhanced socialism's appeal. Not only was there a dearth of schools in the countryside, but family labor needs made it difficult for children to attend elementary schools even when these did exist in their communities. An elementary school education was required to enter the normal, but many attended grade school irregularly, began when they were quite advanced in age, or took excessively long to complete a basic education.[68] Othón Salazar, an indigenous normalista from the coastal state of Guerrero, for example, attended elementary school sporadically. "I'd register for two months and then out I went to work my land parcel or any other thing that could help sustain my family," he related.[69] Manuel Arias Delgado, who came from a mining family in the northern state of Chihuahua, vividly recalled the harsh conditions under which his father and grandfather labored in an American-owned mine. Black lung disease, mining accidents, and wages that hardly supported a family of nine children marked Arias's early life. As a young boy, he did "anything my mom could think up": he shined shoes and sold bread, tamales, and popcorn on the street. His other duties bordered on the macabre. Arias's mother, a seamstress, "made everything from the wedding dress for the neighborhood bride, to the tunic for the young child who died." When Arias was nine, he related, "My mother would send me, tape measure in hand, to record the *angelito*'s—the dead child's—dimensions. I was really scared, but I had to do it: to measure from head to foot, and then from shoulder to shoulder. It was the first time I touched dead flesh. It made quite an impression on me. And since I was from one of the poorest neighborhoods, there were many dead children. There was no running water, no drainage system, and very little food. So child mortality was high." Arias, whose mother birthed fourteen children but had only nine survive, was no stranger to infant deaths.[70]

The stories of Salazar, Aguayo, Aguirre, and Arias—experiences shared by many others—made normalistas keenly aware of the extent to which injustice still structured their lives. Though few understood it as such until they participated in the FECSM's mandatory assemblies, for many, the difficult road to that institution already provided telling political signposts. Priests, for example, continued to appear as foes in normalista narratives, even as church-state relations improved. Felipe Cortés Martínez, whose words opened this chapter, described how, having lost his father at a young age, he faced special hardship when he wanted to attend the rural normal of El Mexe. He was twelve and did not even have enough money for the transportation to take the school's entrance exam. So he went to his godfather, a priest who lived about a day's walk from his town. "What I didn't know is that priests will not share a cent with anyone. They will receive money from everyone, will bless you, give you advice and affection." But when Cortés explained why he needed the money, the priest replied, "El Mexe is where our enemies reside, so I cannot help you. Here is a scapular, and this rosary, and God will help you." Cortés thanked the priest for his help but did not take the tokens. "I returned to my house in tears. It was another day's walk home."[71]

Such experiences gave normalistas clarity on where the church's allegiance lay. Their dire material needs, moreover, often rendered priestly warnings of eternal damnation ineffective. For example, Reynaldo Jiménez, who attended the rural normal of La Huerta, Michoacán, in 1956, related how the town priest tried to dissuade his father from sending him there. "He said I'd become a Bolshevik, a communist. . . . [But] my parents, who were very poor fishermen and farmers, didn't want me to inherit their misery."[72] Normalista narratives reflect a context that placed their schools on the dark side in the Cold War's battle between good and evil. But as they and their families navigated the realm between need and fear, the former often won out. Their misery, the hand-to-mouth existence that marked the home life of so many normalistas, intensified their experience at the normales, where food and shelter were secure.

Tellingly, most remember in far greater detail the type of food they ate than the subjects they studied. For their main meal, stated Cortés, "We had three tortillas, a bit of watered-down soup with a few kernels of rice or pasta morsels floating in it, a tiny piece of meat and beans. That was it. And yet if you only knew how happy those of us who came from the countryside were, because at least we ate—half-ate—three times a day. What did many eat in the outskirts? One or two tortillas. Those who ate beans were the rich ones."[73] In a similar vein, Aguirre stated, "When I studied at Salaices, we had to do without a lot. The food was meager. I was placed in a dorm where there was no bed, nothing. I had only the pair of sheets we were asked to bring, and we all slept on the floor. Of the four dormitories in the school, two had no beds, and those were for the newly arrived. So we slept on the floor, on a bit of cardboard, and it was very cold." But, continues Aguirre, "would you believe it? I was in heaven! Because even if the food was meager, it was at least assured, and where I was from, sometimes we had nothing to eat."[74]

As 1940s and 1950s regimes rolled back the more progressive aspects of the revolution, including support for rural normales, the FECSM stepped up its demands to address school needs. And those were many. Directors' own reports emphasized the dire conditions. "Our poor school buildings . . . are so deteriorated they are close to collapsing," and food allocations were "insufficient by any definable measure," reported the principal of San Marcos, Zacatecas.[75] Rosalva Pantoja Guerrero, who attended the rural normal in Tamazulapan, Oaxaca, in the 1950s, remembers that it took them three years of organizing to finally have their school's central building constructed. "It was like that in all the normales," she related. But thanks to a prolonged strike, "it was built, and our [food] rations were increased. Since then the political struggle has continued strong because all the normales came together under the [FECSM's] organization."[76] Similarly, Graciela Cásares, from the rural normal of Atequiza, Jalisco, recalled that after a strike in 1953, "We finally got some relief and ate a little better. We began drinking milk. Before that, there was no milk; everything was made in water."[77]

That the FECSM acted as the organizing structure most capable of attaining basic needs codified it as the most important venue for normalista politicization, a role it deliberately reproduced with each incoming class.

It organized mandatory student assemblies, implemented initiation rituals for first-year students, and instituted the Political and Ideological Orientation Committee, an organization dedicated to reading Marxist texts, inviting speakers, and training students in oratory skills.[78] While during the 1960s the FECSM would become an increasingly important venue to discuss international events such as the Cuban Revolution and the possibilities of bringing about a socialist revolution in Mexico, during the 1940s and 1950s, the federation more often conflated socialism with Cardenismo. The words of Vicente Estrada, who studied in Ayotzinapa in the 1950s, are a good example of this tendency: Cárdenas "was of the mind that Mexico could be a socialist country. . . . In fact, it was during his government that the normales and their youth saw their biggest boom in the sense that they even had to learn 'The Internationale.' That is part of history. And he had the idea that the rural normales would forge the teachers who'd carry the political catechism throughout the country."[79] The FECSM, moreover, constituted the primary vehicle by which the idea of socialism—however vague—persisted at rural normales long after it was eliminated from Article 3 of the Mexican Constitution. Felipe Cortés Martínez, for example, stated that while socialism was not part of the formal curriculum when he studied at El Mexe, Hidalgo, in the 1950s, "in practice it was, because a socialist mentality is not the same as a capitalist one. In a capitalist mentality, the individual comes first, second, and third, *time is money*. In a socialist one, the idea is to help one another mutually. To say '*Compañero* [comrade/brother], what's wrong? How can I assist you?' Not to say, 'Oh, you're dying, well die.' We graduated with that mentality, to help the needy."[80]

As Cortés's words reveal, many normalistas conflated the socialist tenets of collectivism with the spirit of service that the SEP also sought to inculcate in them. While, for the most politicized student sector, the notion of justice inherent in the revolutionary process clashed with the spirit of national service demanded by an increasingly conservative state, for others the notions complemented one another. As Luciano Vela Gálvez, also a 1950s student from El Mexe, asserted, "Since the FECSM sustained the philosophical principles of the Mexican Revolution, it helped imbue students' spirit with that humanist sense of service to society. . . . What's more, we learned that the principles of the collective come before those of the individual."[81] The officially designed pedagogical doctrine linking socialism to education that existed in the 1930s had created a remarkable legacy that rural normalistas used to express their feelings about the experience of being part of a collective, the discipline that regimented their study, and the consciousness it awakened.

Socialism became the central mediating concept, and it had liberating effects on normalistas, marking their education not as social reproduction but as consciousness. This political awakening was fueled by students' experience of poverty, nurtured through collective institutional norms, deepened by a sense of indignation as the government neglected their schools, and channeled into action by the FECSM.

That normalista youth lived, studied, and worked together further led many to conflate social solidarity with interpersonal concerns. As Aguirre put it, "We reached the conclusion that socialism was better because it is an altruistic system, the opposite of selfishness, and capitalism meant the exploitation of man by man. That's what we carried within us and understood in our treatment of one another, the respect we owed to each other, to the teachers, other students, the leaders and the led. It was a fraternal relationship that I would call socialist but a somewhat utopian socialism."[82] To characterize even interpersonal relationships as socialist demonstrates the extent to which students internalized their ideological position. To acknowledge it as utopian shows an awareness of the context, the structural limitations—no doubt brought into relief by hindsight—of socialist experiments in capitalist Mexico.

Rural normales opened up a world of possibilities for youngsters who lived and studied with their peers from different parts of Mexico and, aside from their regular course load, engaged in sports tournaments, music and dance recitals, and field trips that took them throughout the country. Many saw the nation's capital or the ocean for the first time. In school deliberations, students had their voices heard and noticed that their opinion mattered. Just as significantly, by living far from their parents, they escaped domestic patriarchal constraints, a dynamic that, as discussed in chapter 6, was especially significant for female students. In this process, the day-to-day experience had as much effect as the political dimension offered by the FECSM.

"SCHOOLS THAT EDUCATE FOR DEMOCRACY"

Spending day and night together while conducting myriad different group activities no doubt primed student receptivity to collectivist political principles. The institution's very design reinforced this logic. To a remarkable extent, students participated in the maintenance, reproduction, and enforcement of school norms in institutions that by the 1950s had evolved from small, family-style boardinghouses with a couple dozen students to bustling centers of activity where two hundred to three hundred youth lived, studied, and worked. The SEP's rationale for incorporating students into all aspects of the institutional fabric was threefold: to train them in the skills they would need as rural teachers, to connect classroom learning to daily practices, and to reduce administrative corruption. While the SEP's intent with such involvement differed from the FECSM's logic of student power, in practice, it reinforced many of the federation's own collectivist principles. Concerned with student discipline, institutional integrity, and the need for graduates to teach in remote areas, the SEP continuously emphasized that normalistas be invested in the well-being of their school and the fulfillment of their mission. To that end, students had a say in creating and enforcing regulatory norms of comportment "so they could understand how to govern themselves and participate in the leadership of the community they will eventually be a part of."[83] School officials sought to inculcate "a collective ideal that satisfies the mind, that moves the spirit, and that captures student interests and fantasies."[84] Faculty members were to help normalistas "understand and feel that human beings owed not to themselves but to the social group to which they belonged. Rural teachers should commit themselves to the people and their race, whose interests they are to serve."[85] While such directives could have positivist implications, and the state's language of service conflicted with normalistas' notions of justice, the message that they were to do right by the country's poor majority was emphasized by student and institutional leadership alike.

Depending on the type of school in their home communities, youngsters could be anywhere from eleven to sixteen years old when they began studying at a rural normal. Worried about adolescents' restless nature, the education authorities designed days tightly packed with activities.[86] "Seen from above," reflected a former student, rural normales "must have looked like beehives with teachers and students all engaged in multiple activities."[87] The rigorous schedule began at 5:30 a.m., when a military-style band sounded the wakeup call. Five minutes later, students were in the school's courtyard for roll call. Once that was completed, they had twenty minutes to wash up and make their beds. Their first class began at 6 a.m. An hour later, students were to clean their assigned areas: yards, gardens, or classrooms. Breakfast was at 8 a.m., and classes resumed an hour later and lasted until 1 p.m. Normalistas then had their main meal and could rest until 3 p.m., when a diverse set of activities began anew. These included tending to the school's farm animals and crops or participating in workshops such as carpentry or metalwork. This was also the time for students to rehearse dance, music, and poetry for their Friday social gatherings, for sports teams to practice, and for commissions, clubs, and committees to undertake their duties. At 7 p.m. students had a light meal and at 8 p.m. a mandatory hour of studying. A no-noise call was issued at 10 p.m., when roll was again taken to ensure that each student was in bed. Students had lighter days on Saturdays, with morning classes and either physical education or agricultural practices in the early afternoon. Sundays they had off and could take care of personal matters or visit nearby towns.[88] Given the distance from their home communities, most students stayed in the normales throughout the school year and many through the summer. Some went years without seeing their families.

In 1945 the SEP increased the years of study from four to six, the first three secundaria (junior high school), the latter three professional teacher training. Rural normales also had two complementary years of study corresponding to fifth and sixth grade since most elementary schools in the countryside went only through fourth grade. Except for the farming activities, the curriculum of the complementary and secundaria years corresponded to that of other schools. Students studied math, science, geography, and literature. As their foreign language, they could opt—in theory—for either English or an indigenous language. In practice, the latter was rarely, if ever, offered. Students also enrolled in a series of workshops in agriculture, animal husbandry, industry, woodworking, and metalworking, as well as home economics. Their extracurricular activities included expressive media (art and painting), education aesthetics (song, music, and dance), pedagogy and its psychology, physical education, and civics. Students also had elective clubs and directed studies.[89]

The last three years of the normal were specifically devoted to pedagogical training. Each semester students took courses on teaching methods and pedagogical theory where they produced didactic material. For example, with the assistance of their physics teacher, they constructed laboratories with basic equipment for experimentation with general laws of motion. The first year, they made tools to teach pupils how to measure; the second, they constructed audiovisual material; and in the third year, they focused on building simple devices for experimentation and proof.[90] Their workshops operated under the assumption that they would be pioneers of sorts. For example, in their woodworking class, they learned everything from the types of trees native to particular regions to the construction of doors, windows, and simple furniture for both schools and homes. They also took courses in metalwork, beginning with sheet metal the first year, blacksmithing skills the second, and the application of these techniques to mechanical classes during their third.[91] Students also made periodic visits to surrounding communities, the same places where they undertook their teaching practices. Such activities linked the normal to the local population, a design dating back to the 1920s and meant to connect the school and home environments and to coordinate health, sanitation, or infrastructural policy from government and, at times, private agencies.

The SEP sought to link academic lessons to practical knowledge through various school committees composed of students, faculty, and staff. The Nutrition and Rations Committee, for example, worked with the cafeteria staff to improve students' food and figure out the best use for school crops. In this committee they learned how to construct budgets for weekly student menus, check the market prices for meal ingredients, and find ways to secure discounts, whether though planning in advance or buying in bulk. The Agricultural and Industrial Promotion Committee was to make farming practices and workshops compatible with the surrounding region's local production, while the Social Action Committee organized literacy and hygiene campaigns as well as civic activities in neighboring communities.[92] Moreover, teachers were expected to develop class lessons around committee duties. They could, for example, use math class to close out the monthly budget, track warehouse expenses, and develop a cost-of-living index. In biology, students might determine the number of calories needed for different types of labor and assess the nutritional values of their own food and the vitamins contained in each ingredient.[93]

Most significantly, these student committees had the capacity to enforce norms. The Committee of Honor and Justice upheld disciplinary rules, handled conflicts, and meted out sanctions or commendations. The Hygiene and Material Improvement Committee, which promoted student health, made sure the school grounds remained clean, assessed infrastructural needs, and reported individuals neglecting their duties. The Library Committee, which worked to improve access to research material, ensured that students properly used the study hours, and the Nutrition and Rations Committee had access to spending ledgers to reduce the tendency of "teachers and administrative staff to siphon off food or other supplies."[94] In future years, under this same logic, normalistas would fight for membership in their school's admissions committee and a presence in grading entrance exams to ensure that students were accepted based on need and merit rather than political favors.

A disciplinary code made up of a point system existed at most normales. The Office of Normal Education handed down guidelines, but each school developed its own disciplinary code, which applied to students, faculty, and staff. Each member of the school community began with a hundred points, and points were deducted based on the severity of the infraction. At some schools, reaching fifty points constituted a basis for expulsion; at others, it was not until students reached zero (though in the latter case the same type of violation would result in a larger deduction). Leaving the school without permission, going to bars, or selling equipment that belonged to the institution constituted the largest deduction of points, eight to fifteen; fights, smoking, or disrespect to staff or visitors would lead to a deduction of four to five points; less serious infractions, corresponding to deductions of one to three points, included littering, lack of proper hygiene, disrespect for the flag, damaging of school property, failure to participate in an assigned commission, or use of profanity. For staff and faculty, the larger infractions stemmed from sustaining a relationship with a student (a hundred points), "agitating" the student body (fifty points), or defaming colleagues (a hundred points). Disobeying the director or being intoxicated on school grounds or in adjacent communities led to a twenty-five-point deduction; lying, fighting, smoking in class, or dancing more than one song in a row with a student would lead to the loss of between ten and fifteen points; improper language, tardiness, failure to hand in reports, or neglect of the assigned work or commission would lead to a deduction of between one and four points.[95]

Students cite this point system, which applied to all members of the school community and in whose elaboration and enforcement they participated, as creating a truly democratic environment.[96] José Santos Valdés, who in the 1940s and 1950s served as director at five different rural normales and was one of the main proponents of active student involvement in all aspects of school governance, asserted that their say in disciplinary matters constituted "the fundamental difference between the school that educates for enslavement and servitude and that which educates for democracy."[97] Not all agreed. High-level SEP officials constantly tried to rein in student power and reminded school directors that they constituted the maximum authority.[98] While the goal was to form students who were "neither submissive nor timid," normalistas also needed to be well mannered, attentive, respectful, and mindful of the proper ways of interacting with authority figures.[99] Some officials were outright hostile and characterized student participation in rule making as communist, equivalent to a soldier who debated a sergeant's order.[100]

Proper student comportment could of course conflict with normalista political actions, and as the years wore on, the authorities increasingly conflated their mobilizations with bad behavior, insubordination, unchecked student power, and damage to the school's reputation. The principal and vice principal of the rural normal of Comitancillo, Oaxaca, painted one such picture. So bellicose was the students' nature in this account that it is hard to discern where legitimate concern for the school's integrity ends and contempt for normalista empowerment begins. By the director's account, the school had been in a state of chaos since 1948, after the SEP made a series of concessions to students that resulted in the constant departure of school directors (seven in eleven years) since students would either oust those too strict or take advantage of those too lenient. Other student abuses included disregarding the academic calendar, leaving campus as they pleased, ignoring their work commissions, rebelling against dictates they did not like, and destroying or selling school property "in some cases to satisfy their recreational desires and in others to gratify vices they had acquired." Their "instinct to gain power" had transformed their school "into an institution at their exclusive service," while their disobedience and "indecorous attitudes to employees of both sexes undermined any principle of authority." Such unbridled student power all took place under the direction of "communist shock brigades" sponsored by the FECSM and the Confederation of Mexican Youth. To "guarantee a greater stability in the educational order," the director proposed turning Comitancillo into a women's normal.[101] Such proposals ignored female students' active participation in rural normal strikes; while far less visible in the leadership, they constituted a vital piece of overall normalista resistance.

While it is likely that, on occasion, students unjustifiably sought the ouster of teachers, directors, or staff, not to mention demanded the transfer of individual students opposed to strikes, far more pervasive were blanket portrayals by the SEP, the press, and the government that described rural normales as institutions that housed immoral behavior, gave cover to those unwilling to study, bred subversion, and were of low academic quality, all characterizations harnessed against legitimate student grievances. As with the allegation that Ayotzinapa students had burned the Mexican flag, the press ran with, and the authorities acted on, demonstrably false information.[102] Indeed, as subsequent chapters show, the black legend that to this day characterizes rural normales has long been cultivated through such rumors, falsehoods, and misinformation.

But the demonization of rural normales also reflected larger social anxieties about the poor's potential to challenge their place in the class hierarchy. As already discussed, SEP authorities saw in the dispossessed an inherent social resentment that produced restless behavior. As education minister Torres Bodet put it, given their social condition, normalistas could "accumulate a dark rancor that, once transmitted to the population, will end up representing tragically fermented discord."[103] Empowerment of the sort that poor, indigenous, or female youth experienced at rural normales—for example, the ability to collectively remove authority figures—stoked larger fears of popular defiance. The institutional culture, social relations, and pervasive nature of socialism as an operative framework denaturalized poverty by showing its historically material basis and undermined hierarchy through collectivist principles, and patriarchy by promoting women's participation in heretofore exclusionary spaces. For the authorities, wrote Santos Valdés, a staunch advocate of student participation in school governance, "it is a form of communism that students, with their inferior status, demand to review the budget and expenditures of the administrators—their superiors."[104] In the decades to come, the SEP would increasingly wield educational reform measures to combat this student power.

"A CRISIS IN EDUCATION"

By the 1950s it had become increasingly common to speak of a crisis in education, especially rural education. The crisis resulted, declared SEP officials, from "a lack of centralized planning, direction, and programs that are adapted to the country's changing conditions," and its manifestations were many: the countryside's disproportionately high level of school-age children—about half—who had not set foot in a classroom; teachers' propensity to migrate to the cities; the high attrition rates at the country's normales, especially rural ones; ineffective or antiquated pedagogical methods at teacher-training schools; and the low quality of their graduates.[105] To address this situation, the SEP convened a conference on rural education in 1953, followed, a year later, by one on the teacher-training system. The deliberations from the heads of various SEP departments, technical bodies, zone inspectors, and normal directors provide a glimpse into how the state would frame teacher training over the next two decades.

Notably, the SEP's approach was contradictory. On the one hand, there was a general consensus about the need to professionalize the teaching ranks since too many instructors taught with either no, incomplete, or woefully deficient training. Partly reflecting the need for more teacher-training institutions, this condition also dated back to the 1920s and 1930s when, urgently in need of instructors, the authorities showed a great deal of flexibility about their qualifications. In 1950 the majority of elementary schoolteachers—forty-three thousand out of sixty-five thousand—did not possess a diploma from a normal.[106] On the other hand, conference delegates consistently lamented the loss of an "educational mystique," that quality inherent in the early generation of teachers who, deficient in training but generous in spirit, gave themselves to community instruction while asking for little compensation.[107] Current teachers, bemoaned education officials, too easily turned their back on their fellow citizens by migrating to the cities in search of individual prosperity.

Ironically, the SEP's approach to teacher professionalization had contributed to their migration. Based on the framework of national unity, urban modernity, and the logic that since urban teachers were of better quality, rural ones should be trained in their image, in 1945 the SEP had adopted a uniform teacher-training curriculum that facilitated rural normalistas' ability to transfer to urban normales, especially Mexico City's National Teachers School. In the 1954 conference on normal education, SEP officials recognized the mistake of this measure and soon prohibited such transfers. Furthermore, rural normalistas were to pledge that, upon graduation, they would teach wherever the ministry sent them.[108] Parents, too, had to sign letters indicating that their sons and daughters would continue at the rural normal past their secundaria years.[109] At national conferences, delegates increasingly proposed using the entrance exam as a metric to assess who possessed a true teaching vocation.[110] While in the coming years attrition rates did slow and more rural normales were established, the long-term movement to the cities continued.[111] With few secondary schools in the countryside, students turned to rural normales not only to become teachers but to access other professions. For those who remained in education, a move to the cities still made sense since teaching in urban schools entitled them to higher wages, not to mention better living conditions.

Such migration was part of a larger pattern of urbanization, which the SEP assigned the schoolhouse the impossible task of containing. "We must reestablish the rural school's role in linking people to the land and preventing campesino migration to the cities and abroad," declared Education Minister Ceniceros in his closing remarks at the 1953 conference on rural education.[112] To that end, the agrarian component of teacher training received renewed attention. It revealed a grim reality. Rural normales did not have agriculturalists with proper pedagogical training; even when they did, they lacked a clear vision about their role. In the absence of well-articulated goals about the relationship between agricultural skills and education, this component could not fully take root. "Was the aim to produce qualified agricultural technicians, candidates for higher-learning agricultural schools, aspiring state bureaucrats, or educators truly qualified to teach in the countryside?"

asked one evaluation. Each path, it concluded, demanded a different level, depth, and scope of preparation. Additionally, agricultural cooperatives at the rural normales needed more attention and resources in order to better equip teachers in rural community development.[113]

Santos Valdés, then director of the rural normal of San Marcos, Zacatecas, argued that if the SEP wanted to reduce attrition rates at rural normales, it needed to improve the basic conditions, making them at least on par with Mexico City's National Teachers School. The SEP, he urged, should fortify their physical infrastructure, double the allocation for food rations, provide a basic set of clothing twice a year, and have full teaching personnel so students could actually take the courses they needed to graduate. If the goal was to keep teachers in the countryside, given the challenges that working in impoverished rural areas imposed, they should be paid more, not less, than their urban counterparts.[114] Progressive officials within the SEP also pointed out how teachers' meager pay contributed to low teaching morale. "The living conditions of rural teachers," declared the ministry's general inspector, Luis Álvarez Barret, "are unquestionably inferior to those they had twenty years ago. Their nominal salaries are, of course, much higher, but money's lower purchasing power and the high living cost reduce it to such an extent that their salaries are now half what they were twenty and likely thirty years ago."[115] This situation caused absenteeism since low pay led teachers to seek supplemental income, thus limiting the time and attention they devoted to communities.[116]

And yet, despite teachers' material reality, education officials continued to bemoan their loss of a service ethic, educational mystique, and genuine teaching vocation. Proposed solutions reflected this logic. The following is a good example:

> The teachers who created a rural Mexican school with an international profile did so because of the atmosphere created by the Mexican Revolution: as long as the state that orients and directs the educational policy does not create a new fervor, a new educational mystique, a new humanistic current in which man can be the friend of man, in which collective interests are placed above those of the individual, the plans and programs will serve to prepare teachers technically and professionally but in and of themselves will not achieve the model of an individual identified with the needs of the people.[117]

Recognizing the extent to which the revolution had spurred a laudable education project, officials invoked a return to those principles. But they reduced the state's role to creating a new fervor, a mystique or humanistic current by which teachers' dedication made up for the state's commitment to industry. Absent was the national wealth redistribution that marked the earlier revolutionary project. Despite the enormous economic windfall brought about by the Mexican miracle, the proportion of federal spending devoted to education went from 12.6 percent in 1935 to 8.2 percent twenty years later.[118] The regime would no longer put the interests of the majorities above those of elites nor satisfy popular material needs if it meant sacrificing business or industry profits. The much-celebrated levels of economic growth that from 1940 to 1970 hovered at 6.5 percent did little to address unemployment, rural poverty, and wealth inequality. On the contrary, the inequality increased. Between 1950 and 1963, 10 percent of the population controlled half the national income.[119] Mexico's Gini coefficient, a measure of national inequality and wealth distribution, was the highest in the hemisphere, trailing only Honduras and Brazil. Globally, it was comparable to countries in sub-Saharan Africa.[120]

The crisis in rural education reflected the larger crisis of campesino livelihood in the wake of diminishing state support. During the 1950s and 1960s, Mexican agriculture saw a fiscal policy that taxed more than it invested, a banking system that garnered more in profits than it extended in credit, and a price structure unfavorable to farm products, all of which ensured substantial transfer of wealth from the countryside to the cities.[121] The public and private resources that flowed to the countryside increasingly went to export-oriented agricultural products. As the government declared large-scale agribusiness producing winter fruit and vegetables and the cattle industry immune from redistribution, provided subsidies, sponsored irrigation projects, and focused the Green Revolution's technical innovations on large farming ventures, the ejido and small-scale campesino production floundered.[122]

Within the confines of this model, SEP efforts to build more schools, train more teachers, and reform the curriculum could only fall short. Even if the SEP addressed systemic issues—teachers' low pay, deficiencies in the agricultural training, a general dearth of schoolhouses and instructors—the wider state policy that privileged cities, agribusiness, and industry pushed people to migrate. Even reports from the official teachers' union, which generally acted in alliance with the PRI, pointed out that "the roads, the expensive and ostentatious buildings, the large dams do not in themselves have the magic power to modify the standards and ways of life of the people."[123] While some officials acknowledged that the dismal education rates in the countryside reflected rural poverty, most ignored the extent to which the state's project of modernity displaced the rural population and was itself antithetical to the small-scale community development that the schoolhouse was supposed to spearhead.

THE END OF Cárdenas's presidency saw a halt of the most radical revolutionary principles and a rise in urban and industrial development. The process led to large-scale rural-to-urban migration that by the 1960s had tipped the population scales in the cities' favor. Increasingly, that is where the state concentrated its social infrastructure and where the middle class grew from about 16 percent of the population in 1940 to about 22 percent in 1960.[124] Against this backdrop, the country's poor majorities—urban and rural—fought for their share of the national wealth. These decades saw some of the century's strongest labor movements, with teachers and rail, oil, and telephone workers rebelling against the PRI's domination of their unions, a control that demanded labor discipline and kept industry profits high. Rural inhabitants, too, fought for a decent way of life in the countryside, with rural unrest taking shape through electoral challenges to the PRI, sporadic armed struggle, land takeovers, and battles against *caciquismo* (local bossism).[125]

These struggles seeped into rural normalista consciousness, and students increasingly framed their educational demands in light of this broad social injustice. The FECSM would soon prioritize solidarity with campesino mobilizations, and rural teachers stood as visible figures in the countryside's unrest. At the same time, rural normalistas were caught in the forces of urban migration, and their radical tendencies did not cease when they arrived in the cities. That two of the most militant confrontations the SEP faced in Mexico City—one by elementary schoolteachers and the other by students at the National Teachers School—were led by former Ayotzinapa students is hardly coincidental. Such challenges caused the SEP to reevaluate its approach to rural education and to again modify the teacher-training curriculum. Just as significantly, Jaime Torres Bodet, who returned to head the SEP in 1958, reconsidered the boarding-school structure because its very design facilitated student power.

4

Education
at a Crossroads

OTHÓN SALAZAR, who in the 1950s would lead one of Mexico's most important teacher mobilizations, was born in 1924 to a Mixtec family in Alcozauca, Guerrero. Longing for the type of respect elicited by the village priest, Salazar wanted to master the art of public speaking and, at an early age, sought to join the seminary. Upon hearing of this plan, his elementary schoolteacher presented an alternative: "Wouldn't you rather be a lawyer like don Benito Juárez?"—Mexico's indigenous mid-nineteenth-century president credited for holding the nation together during the Reform War and the subsequent French invasion. Salazar would become neither. Like for other poor youths with professional aspirations, his most viable option was teaching. In 1941 Salazar enrolled in the rural normal of Oaxtepec, Morelos. "I was 17 years old when I first left Alcozauca, and my consciousness was filled with faith. When I returned, after a year in Oaxtepec, I was itching for a fight with the church." Salazar thus expressed his politicization at the rural normal, where, he remembered, "there was not one teacher who didn't invoke the revolution." But it was in Ayotzinapa, where Salazar soon transferred, that "I began to lose the fear and timidity from which I had always suffered. My practices in oratory began to bear fruit." A year later, Salazar transferred again, this time to Mexico City. "The teachers from the normal of Ayotzinapa were graduates of the National Teachers School, and I wanted to be like them," stated Salazar as one of the reasons for this change.[1]

The stream of students who started at rural normales and ended up in Mexico City's National Teachers School was so great that in the mid-1950s, the Ministry of Public Education (SEP) began to prohibit their enrollment there.[2] By then, their large numbers had translated into a high concentration of teachers in the capital. Grouped in Section IX of the state-controlled National Union of Education Workers (SNTE), such numbers gave them leverage, which the Revolutionary Teachers Movement (Movimiento Revolucionario del Magisterio, MRM) used to fight for better wages, benefits, and working conditions. Headed by Salazar and joined by massive numbers of dissident teachers, the MRM fought a corrupt union leadership whose corporatist logic delivered votes to the Institutional Revolutionary Party (PRI) more than it protected its members' labor rights. The SNTE's creation in 1943 had marked a state victory over more militant and independent teachers' unions, and in the following decades, it played a central role in an education system whose continued expansion added ever more members to the union ranks. Through patronage networks and control over hiring, promotion, and seniority rights, the SNTE rivaled the SEP's power. Any federal education reforms required negotiation with the union leadership, which could mobilize its base in support of or opposition to such measures. But like their counterparts in other *charro* (state-allied) unions, the leaders occupied such positions thanks to the support of PRI officials and were rewarded with government offices if they proved to be successful political operatives. This corporatist structure was a cornerstone of PRI rule—one, however, that did not go unchallenged.

In the 1950s oil and telegraph workers took to the streets, rejecting official union appointees and demanding the right to freely elect their own representatives. Most militantly, rail workers rebelled throughout 1958 and 1959, gaining bread-and-butter concessions, but were defeated when it came to union democratization. The government halted such demands by using the army to force strikers back to work. Charged with social dissolution, the movement's leaders were jailed. Many languished there for years. Other important mobilizations marked the capital during this period, including the 1956 student strike at the National Polytechnic Institute, for which the government also deployed the army. Against these movements, the state wielded the Cold War's ideological tool kit and had in the press a powerful means to define the narrative: popular-movement leaders were subversives, agents of foreign governments intent on bringing communism to Mexico.[3] Only the PRI, went the state rhetoric, could safeguard the revolution from such enemies.

Education, too, became a major battlefront. The 1956–58 teachers' strike, of which Salazar became the principal figurehead, sought the democratization of the teachers' union and labor concessions its leadership had been loath to make. If during the 1940s the doctrine of national unity constituted the primary framework by which to tame the radical principles that in the 1930s had linked rural education to land redistribution and conceived of teachers as promoters of social justice, in the 1950s the battle against communism served as the justification to contain those who mobilized for labor rights and free elections for union leadership. To draw out this context, this chapter opens with an account of Mexico City's teachers' movement in 1956–58. That their leader came from a rural normal was not merely an example of these schools' radical legacy but a product of an economic context that channeled the population toward urban centers. And it was the SEP's attempt to reverse the concentration of educators in the capital that embroiled the ministry in an additional battle, this time with students from Mexico City's National Teachers School, which for years had received hundreds of pupils transferring from rural normales.[4] Here, too, an Ayotzinapa transfer student led the normalista challenge to SEP minister Jaime Torres Bodet (1943–46, 1958–64). The far-reaching nature of teachers' militancy, I argue, led the SEP to step up its efforts to depoliticize their training.

The events this chapter details unfolded largely in the context of the Eleven-Year Plan, a state initiative to expand school access in part by providing free government-issued textbooks as part of a larger educational overhaul that also included curricular changes at normales. The church, industrialists, and wealthy families seized on this textbook initiative to make up for the ground they had lost as a result of revolutionary reforms. In a vivid example of the Cold War as counterrevolution, they, too, employed the threat of communism to fight for old privileges long buttressed by family, religion, property, and a minimal state.[5] Accusing the government of impinging on families' religious prerogatives and teachers' freedom of speech, organizations such as the church-affiliated National Parents Union, whose members' children studied in private schools now compelled to adopt government-issued textbooks, characterized this measure as a clear path to communist totalitarianism. Likewise, business groups presented it as a socialist decree whose inevitable next step would be greater government control of industry. Most loudly, the Catholic Church mobilized its faithful, seeking to recover its lost say in education, which Article 3 of the Mexican constitution deemed the state's responsibility.

In this context, popular sectors sought to preserve the crucial link between political and economic rights enshrined in institutions like unions, the ejido, and boarding schools. Rural normalistas, for example, fought to preserve the material integrity of their institutions as the SEP promoted curricular reforms in teacher-training schools and increasingly propagated a model that dispensed with boardinghouses. While the government's Eleven-Year Plan, a project to eliminate illiteracy, necessitated an increase in the number of teachers, the SEP—rather than better funding rural normales, building more of them, or expanding their capacity, as their students demanded—created a new type of institution, the Regional Normal Teaching Centers (Centros Regionales de Enseñanza Normal, CRENs). Built in peripheral cities like Ciudad Guzmán in the state of Jalisco and in Iguala, Guerrero, these schools would train teachers in semiurban areas. Like rural normal students, their graduates were explicitly charged with teaching in the countryside. But unlike the rural normales, the CRENs deliberately moved away from the boarding-school model; their students instead received a stipend to cover their room and board. According to Education Minister Torres Bodet, this would help avoid "so many of the problems at the National Teachers School that had diminished the moral and professional quality of their graduates."[6]

Rural normalistas recognized the political nature of the SEP's approach and in the wake of labor's defeat at the end of the 1950s sought to move beyond bread-and-butter demands. They did so more in theory than in practice. Their strikes continued to focus on food rations, living conditions, learning supplies, and school infrastructure. But their organizing process constituted part of the very foundation for their radical challenge in subsequent decades. As the PRI hollowed out concepts of democracy by attacking political action and branding basic economic rights as communist, the socialist legacy at rural normales anchored educational demands in material sustenance. This link the state was unable to break.

"A FRONTAL BATTLE AGAINST OUR CONDITION AS APOSTLES"

"Those of us from Guerrero were one of the largest groups," stated Plutarco Emilio García Jiménez, who, like Salazar, initially studied at Ayotzinapa and in 1954 transferred to Mexico City's National Teachers School. "The majority were from Mexico City, but we had the second largest number. . . . And we were organized in groups, and there were several groups from different parts of Guerrero, all very politicized."[7] The state-by-state student breakdown at the National Teachers School is difficult to verify. Guerrero, along with Oaxaca and Chiapas, was among Mexico's poorest states and relatively close to the capital. The presence of a prominent *guerrerense* contingent—which, if not the largest, was certainly significant—facilitated more transfers from the state, despite the SEP's attempt to prohibit them. Vicente Estrada, another 1950s Ayotzinapa student, recalled his arrival at the school: "Some of my compañeros went to the National Teachers School. Once there, they sent word that I should come to Mexico City, that it was better there, and that I really should be with them—inseparable as we were in everything, including the struggle. So I came to Mexico [City] with the intent of registering, but that was a whole other fight since they wouldn't just let us in. It took me half a year to enroll."[8]

This flow from Guerrero was perhaps distinct from the larger process of urbanization; however, it mirrored it insofar as it stemmed from the better professional opportunities offered in the capital.[9] High transfer rates made for an unwieldy situation at the National Teachers School, which had 7,000 day pupils, 5,000 evening students, and an additional 1,200 normalistas who lived in the school's boardinghouse, whose capacity was 600. In contrast to the situation at the Higher Normal School of Mexico, which trained postprimary educators, the majority of students at the National Teachers School came from a poor background. Day students residing in Mexico City received a modest meal stipend, factory and domestic workers seeking a better-paying job constituted the evening student body, and students from outside the capital resided in the overcrowded dorms. A 1953 strike led by the boarding-school contingent succeeded in improving some basic sanitation and dining facilities but failed to gain concessions on, to quote a U.S. embassy report, "points of considerable importance." These included a new dorm and auditorium, 250,000 pesos to fund teaching practicums in schools outside Mexico City, and the reinstatement of the Cárdenas-era coeducation structure at the National Teachers School.[10]

Upon graduation, most teachers sought work in the capital, where they became members of the SNTE's Section IX. Membership in the official teachers' union—long a PRI stronghold—had grown in concert with an expanding educational system. Not only did its leadership hold tremendous power, but it became notoriously corrupt, a situation that its base increasingly refused to tolerate. Like the rail workers, Mexico City teachers first demanded improved wages and benefits, and this then evolved into a struggle for union democracy—independence from government-vetted leaders who served to limit labor's demands. In July 1956, when the state-appointed leadership accepted a raise of less than half the amount demanded by the rank and file, a strike broke out.[11] Over the next two years, Section IX teachers, calling themselves the MRM, convened mass demonstrations in the capital and received widespread public support despite police repression and a relentlessly hostile media campaign. The official union leadership depicted the independent union struggle as a mere power grab by teachers interested only in the well-being of Mexico City's educators. The conflict came to a head in May 1958 when, in response to Education Minister José Ángel Ceniceros's (1952–58) refusal to meet with them, the MRM occupied the SEP. Ten days later, the government agreed to begin negotiations. But while these were taking place, President Adolfo Ruiz Cortines (1952–58), accompanied by the SNTE's general secretary and its two previous leaders, announced a raise for teachers throughout the country.[12] This move sidelined the negotiating process with the MRM and gave the official union credit for the pay increase. Headed by Salazar, the MRM leadership refused to accept a raise clearly meant to break their unity, nor would they relinquish their hold on the SEP offices. To return to work, Salazar demanded a meeting with the president. At stake was the recognition of the MRM as the rightful representative of the official union's Section IX teachers. As it stood, not only had the SNTE taken credit for the raise, but it was now accusing the striking teachers of insubordination and threatening their dismissal if they did not return to work. At this juncture, the government leveled charges of social dissolution based on a World War II law created to persecute agents of foreign governments but for years used almost exclusively against political activists.[13]

Hoping to end its battle from a position of strength, the MRM decided to call off its strike. Despite the efforts to present the raise as the work of the SNTE, the wage hikes in fact revealed the lies behind government claims that higher pay was a budgetary impossibility. Having achieved this material victory, the MRM sought to continue the battle for union democracy. In August 1958, when the SNTE held a convention to renew its local leadership, MRM teachers held a parallel meeting, electing Salazar as the representative of Mexico City's Section IX. The contested convention meant that the Labor Ministry would now determine the union's representative. To win a favorable outcome, the MRM stepped up its mobilization efforts.[14]

The government may have acquiesced to bread-and-butter issues, but union independence was intolerable. The SNTE, alongside state and SEP representatives, openly attacked Salazar. President Ruiz Cortines threatened to violently disband the movement, declaring in his final state-of-the-union address, in September 1958, that "if force was necessary to maintain the rule of law, the government would be obliged to use it." A week later, police forcibly dissolved an MRM demonstration, surrounded its office headquarters, and arrested its leaders—including Salazar—charging them, among other crimes, with social dissolution.[15] "They barged into my house in spite of my nine-month-old baby, tied me up, blindfolded me, and took me to the district's garbage dump," recalled Salazar. "At three in the morning, with a gun to my head, they asked how many rubles the Soviet Union sent me."[16]

While the arrests were a major blow, the independent teachers had cause for optimism. In response to the MRM's battle to represent Section IX educators, the labor tribunal ordered new union elections. The imprisonment of Salazar and the other leaders, however, made them ineligible to run. The MRM proposed new candidates, and when union elections took place on October 30, the independent candidates scored a crushing victory of 9,805 to 37 against the charro (official) leaders.[17] Shortly after assuming office in December 1958, President Adolfo López Mateos ordered the release of the jailed MRM leadership, and the SEP announced that the long-demanded raises would go into effect the following month. Through their mobilization, the dissident teachers had scored a powerful victory. In control of Section IX, the SNTE's most numerous union local, the MRM then sought to extend its movement to other parts of the country.[18]

From the beginning of its struggle for teacher rights, the MRM had proclaimed "a frontal battle against our condition as apostles that surrenders us each day to hunger and misery."[19] The declaration constituted a direct challenge to the idea that it was educators' role to sacrifice. Born of the twentieth-century state-consolidation narrative, official discourse long celebrated teachers' role in implementing constitutional reforms. Likening them to colonial missionaries, the revolutionary state's origin story emphasized how early twentieth-century educators had traveled to the country's most remote corners, endured poverty and isolation, erected schools, and been martyred by Cristeros. Their commitment in the face of a perilous situation was a badge of honor. Many teachers accepted this narrative—indeed, many had lived it. Rural normalistas especially deployed it in defense of their institutions, the schools designed to assure a steady flow of educators to the countryside. In their condition as laborers, however, such a narrative justified exploitation, and the revolution had not demanded perpetual sacrifice but imposed justice.

But the SEP held steadfastly to the notion that it was teachers' duty to endure hardship for the good of the nation. It added, however, another, almost antithetical dimension, that of professionalism: the acquisition of specific training norms, disciplined comportment, systematized knowledge, and standardized teaching styles. The contradiction of demanding a professionalized workforce while appealing to apostolic values and offering wages and working conditions corresponding to a volunteer endeavor was lost on the SEP. As the new minister Torres Bodet took office at the close of the turbulent 1958 labor year, he implored the press, "I ask for your help in convincing the country of what, to my mind, is an essential point and an immutable premise: teachers' and students' sense of civic duty and their loyalty to the Republic's destiny."[20] Perhaps he anticipated protest against the directive he would issue a month later to channel teachers out of the capital. And that fury did come, in the form of a strike from Mexico City's National Teachers School. Plutarco Emilio García Jiménez, introduced earlier as one of the student transfers from Ayotzinapa, led this latest revolt in the nation's largest normal school.[21]

"MORE DISCIPLINE, MORE COMPETENCE, AND STRONGER MISSIONARY FERVOR"

President López Mateos's 1958 appointee to head the SEP was not new to the post. Torres Bodet had held this office from 1943 to 1946, overseeing the end of socialist education and the unification of the urban and rural normal curriculum. A disciple of José Vasconcelos, a poet, an essayist, and a diplomat, Torres Bodet now sought an ambitious project for the nation's education system, one that included a "spiritual renovation" of rural normales to produce "active, capable, loyal, and responsible" educators.[22] Assessing Mexico's dramatic educational shortcomings, the minister wondered what had happened in the years since he first occupied the post. "Neither did our 1944 programs bear the fruits we had hoped for, nor did the new normal graduates want to hear anything of 'apostles' or 'missions,'" he lamented.[23] The minister wrote of a transformed teaching body that lacked the "humble and virile frankness" that characterized 1940s educators and instead "invoke[d] the respectability of their profession to demand raises and benefits."[24] These reflections, written about his first twenty-four hours back as minister, did not consider that since 1925 teachers' salaries had not kept pace with inflation. Indeed, not until 1965—and thanks largely to the MRM's 1950s struggle—did instructors' monthly earnings recover their 1925 real wage value.[25]

Torres Bodet moved to reduce the concentration of teachers in the capital. To that end, he announced a "social service" requirement in early 1959 that, effective immediately, assigned graduates of the National Teachers School to a one- or three-year position in a location determined by the SEP.[26] Proposed as a measure to address the lack of teachers in the countryside, the decree generated strong opposition among students in Mexico City's National Teachers School. Graduates there objected to its abrupt nature, the lower pay scale to which it would subject them, and the lack of relocation funds. A significant proportion of the students at the school had moved to the capital expressly because of the professional opportunities offered there. In Mexico City normalistas could continue their studies at the Higher Normal School of Mexico (which trained secondary teachers as well as those for normales) or other institutions of higher learning, the proximity to the SEP headquarters eased the burden of the constant paperwork, and the capital provided greater job options, be they in teaching or in other professions.[27]

With an appeal to social responsibility and the stroke of a pen, Torres Bodet sought to combat the centripetal force created by two decades of economic policy that had focused on urban development at the cost of the countryside. Moreover, argued normalistas, Mexico City schools still needed educators. Why were these positions, they protested, increasingly allotted to teachers from private normales?[28] The new requirement was also irresponsible, they argued, since, as an urban normal, the National Teachers School did not prepare normalistas for the exigencies of rural elementary schools, most of which were *escuelas unitarias*, one-classroom learning centers composed of multiple grades.[29] Torres Bodet responded that by its very nature the *National* Teachers School trained them to work throughout the country, an argument that would have had greater weight had previous SEP minister Ceniceros heeded earlier student requests to fund practicums in rural areas. Needless to say, the objections of graduating teachers—which they subsequently expressed as a strike—only confirmed Torres Bodet's view of an entitled generation with no commitment to the nation.

The strike at the National Teachers School began on March 2, 1959. Normalistas received strong support from Mexico City's Section IX members, who, under independent leadership since 1958, continued to fight for fair wages, an increase in their yearly bonus, and the prompt payment of raises owed to them since January (many teachers had not received the mandated increases, and, amid bureaucratic confusion, a number had obtained no pay at all). Other grievances included violations to their seniority system since the SEP frequently appointed outsiders over career teachers to administrative posts. Their demands merged with those of the normalistas, a natural alliance given that National Teachers School graduates went on to populate the Section IX ranks.

The press quickly branded the normalista movement a communist conspiracy. *Excélsior* editorials labeled it the work of a "red commando," while reactionary sectors took it as proof of what they had long proclaimed: the National Teachers School was a "communist seedbed."[30] Joining the chorus, the SNTE characterized the strike as "sterile agitation" over "artificial issues" and chastised normalistas' lack of patriotism, for which it blamed the MRM.[31] The independent Section IX leadership denied involvement, but MRM teachers did join the normalistas on their March 24 march from the National Teachers School to SEP headquarters.[32] The authorities, taking advantage of the small contingent left guarding the school, retook the campus, where the SWAT team, plainclothes police, and two companies of military troops charged the school, arrested sixty students, and temporarily detained 350 others.[33] The military occupation spurred great protest. Angered by the government's show of force, students from the National Autonomous University of Mexico and its various affiliated high schools, previously reluctant to join the normalista strike, now marched alongside them. Labor and normalista demands expanded to calls for individual rights; social guarantees; freedom for political prisoners; an end to worker, student, and teacher persecution; and a call for the authorities to respect the nation's constitution.[34]

Torres Bodet expressed contempt for the protestors. About a negotiating commission that visited his office, he wrote, "Never had I been surrounded by so many dirty jackets, so many shirts in need of ties, so many dirty fingernails, and hair so long and unkempt it symbolized the ideas of those who proudly waved it." The minister's solution was to close the dormitories of the National Teachers School, "for it was the dorms that gave refuge to the most aggressive troublemakers," he wrote. "Never again would we make the mistake of funding boarding schools that serve violent youth."[35]

This decision was telling. The government had responded similarly to the 1956 student strike at the National Polytechnic Institute, and this increasingly became a matter of policy. From the perspective of the state, teachers had to be incentivized and controlled. For example, the SEP later reported about the National Teachers School: "Until 1959 this campus offered room and board, which caused academic and discipline problems. This administration replaced it with a system of scholarships increasingly perfected so that today these funds—issued by the nation—not only constitute help for low-income students but are a real incentive to study."[36] Rather than a right, access to education became conditional; scholarships were not a matter of justice but depended on student behavior. By this logic, boardinghouses—as spaces where youth congregated, organized, and discussed political matters—had the noxious effect of disengaging students from their patriotic duties.

While the social-service requirement triggered this latest conflict, at stake were larger principles for those who labored in education. By invoking the missionary fervor of an earlier generation, the state expected abnegation. The rewards endowed by a noble profession were to compensate for meager material well-being. This flew in the face of labor rights. That students who had received a scholarship had to commit to three years of social service, as opposed to the single year required of those who paid their own way, further undermined notions of a right to an education.

"Confronted with the demand that we pay back our scholarships or comply with the social service," remembered García, one of the strike leaders, "we replied that a teacher's service is always social and that the scholarships came from the people, so why would we have to return the money?"[37] It was a delicate line to walk. If teachers characterized their job as a social service funded by the people, then their duties were indeed subject to public need. As laborers, however, teachers sought some protection from an employer—the state—that demanded, on the one hand, the selfless commitment of apostles and, on the other, an objective professionalism in which they performed their assigned classroom duties and dispensed with the social leadership of yesteryear. The state demanded all this while it paid a salary that offended the dignity of the profession and eliminated the cherished infrastructural support that boardinghouses represented.

The problems originated from the countryside's vast poverty—as the government's own study on school dropout rates recognized.[38] Teachers opposed paying the price for a state project that left the countryside to languish. They refused to conform to the model President López Mateos invoked in his inauguration speech, which demanded of teachers "greater efforts, more discipline, more competence, and stronger missionary fervor."[39] For this refusal Torres Bodet thought them absurdly entitled. He, like other SEP officials, blamed part of the countryside's educational problems on teachers' unwillingness to live and work in remote areas. "It was precisely the capital," expressed the minister, "that turned the youth (the majority of whom were born hundreds of kilometers away from Mexico City) into boastful maniacs, accustomed to demand what others would have been ashamed to solicit: to settle, with their backs turned to the republic, in the middle of the city that insulates so many men and women from the excruciating pain of our people."[40] The minister did not reflect that such an assessment applied to the government's own policy, which focused resources and infrastructure on the cities and kept agricultural prices low to satisfy urban consumption. Not only teachers were seeking a better life in the cities; most sectors of the countryside were also migrating. With no attention to its root causes, migration would continue unabated.

That the labor mobilizations were a reaction to an economic model that extracted ever more profits from labor is perhaps most evident in the extent to which Cardenismo still acted as a reference for the revolutionary project. The real material gains that workers and campesinos had attained with Lázaro Cárdenas's expropriations—themselves achieved through their mobilization—haunted the right and inspired the left. According to sources close to the U.S. embassy, the government repressed the teacher and normalista movement because it would have otherwise "marked the beginning of a long series of extremist disturbances." Allegedly, the former president Cárdenas sought to force "the present regime to adopt a more leftist and nationalistic approach to economic problems such as labor and foreign investors." Such interpretations—that Cárdenas himself was pulling the strings—were, in the words of the reporting officer, "vague and poorly substantiated and the Embassy has virtually no information which supports them."[41] Indeed, the labor unrest resulted not from the machinations of the former president but from the deliberate abandonment of a revolutionary project rooted in social justice programs and nationalist principles. To attribute the popular mobilizations to a single man was to deny the social violence caused as the state charted a new course, not to mention the tenacity of peasants, workers, and students in resisting that project.

For the left, the Cárdenas years symbolized the possibility of building a progressive social structure. For teachers especially, the former president held immense appeal even as, arguably, his regime had demanded greater sacrifice of them, embroiled as they were in battles with Cristeros and caciques during his term in office. A critical difference, however, lay in the palpable social gains Cárdenas's policies had engendered, which reinforced notions of justice. Tellingly, the 1959 graduates of the National Teachers School chose Lázaro Cárdenas as their class name, "because we were leftists and Don Lázaro was at the time a figurehead of the left," stated García, the student president.[42]

Invoking Cárdenas as an inspiration reveals how much teacher and normalista battles were still about the course of the revolution and, ultimately, Mexico's twentieth-century national project. This dynamic would become painfully clear as right-wing protest emerged in response to the SEP's free-textbook program. First initiated by groups long hostile to the revolutionary state—the National Action Party (Partido Acción Nacional, PAN), the National Parents Union, and the Catholic church hierarchy—the movement gained traction as it mobilized its religious base and invoked the communist menace. These groups became a decided threat when business potentates assumed the mantle, signaling their hostility to even modest tilts to the left.[43]

THE TEXTBOOK CONTROVERSY

The free-textbook program proved to be the most controversial aspect of President López Mateos's Eleven-Year Plan. While the state fought teachers' democratic union representation and closed boarding schools because they facilitated student collective action, it spent millions of pesos ensuring all primary schoolchildren had access to textbooks. The dedication of such resources speaks volumes about the logic of the PRI, a party that in the mid-twentieth century was less averse to public spending than to independent popular organizing. The free-textbook programs, moreover, could strengthen the state by better allowing it to shape the national narrative kids learned in school. The right saw the initiative as an opportunity to recover ground lost after the revolution. The PRI thus found itself on the receiving end of the very right-wing hysteria it had marshaled against teachers and increasingly wielded against rural normales.

Before 1959, private companies, with state subsidies, had produced school texts, which parents were responsible for purchasing. This market-based system meant that only 25 percent of students—mostly in private and urban schools—had access to schoolbooks.[44] Understanding poverty as one of the causes of the high dropout rates, the SEP hoped that free access to learning materials would help extend school coverage. To that end, the SEP took over the textbook production and distribution process, and President López Mateos appointed the prominent liberal writer Martín Luis Guzmán to head a committee that would select and write new history, language, geography, math, science, and civics texts for elementary schools. In keeping with the SEP's policy that education be a source of national unity, the new books would emphasize solidarity, civic virtues, and love of country and—in an implicit critique of socialist education—dispense with "views that might incite rancor or hate, prejudices, or sterile controversies."[45] National integration was the guiding principle, and the SEP instructed history-book writers to structure the narrative around a pantheon of Mexican heroes. Their actions, rather than social processes, were history's driving force.[46] Textbooks, moreover, underscored the significance of mestizaje and treated the colonial period as one of "gestation and development of the Mexican people."[47] When it came to religion, the government's texts were quite moderate. They exalted missionaries for learning indigenous languages, acculturating the native population, and protecting them against conquerors' abuses. They were, however, critical of the church, which, they pointed out, had sided with Spain and excommunicated independence leaders. Civics texts pointed to the democratic character of Mexican institutions, whose origins lay in the nineteenth-century liberal republic, a framework that placed the revolution not as a break but as a restoration of those values.[48]

In almost every aspect, the books differed little from the privately produced ones already in circulation. Their vision was in fact consistent with ideals dating back to Justo Sierra, the education minister under dictator Porfirio Díaz.[49] Indeed, as with previous measures to *forjar patria* (forge a nation), current efforts had as their premise a strong, centralizing state that would establish a uniform national identity. In that logic the state made the books mandatory—all private, state, and municipal schools were to adopt them. If teachers wanted to assign additional texts, those had to be optional; students could not be required to purchase them.[50]

The outcry from the right was not long in coming and soon developed into a powerful storm. Former textbook authors and the companies employing them were among the first to object. Bringing the writing and production process under state control stymied a profitable venture, and publishing houses argued that such a monopoly doomed the books' quality by undermining competition. Their mandatory nature elicited critiques that the books were pedagogically constraining and ignited debates over academic freedom, state authoritarianism, and a family's right to determine the nature of their child's education. The Catholic Church, through lay groups such as the National Parents Union, which in the 1930s had staunchly opposed socialist education, quickly protested the measure and mobilized broad sectors against the state's control of education.

The religious hierarchy, which still resented the constitutional curtailment of its power, saw the government's textbook initiative as an opportunity to test the political waters. It once again challenged the legitimacy of Article 3, claiming it gave the state a dual monopoly over education since, in addition to curricular oversight, the government controlled the teachers' union.[51] In the Cold War context of the late 1950s—which the Mexican government intensified by constantly invoking communism to repress labor—religious allegations that the public education system harbored Marxists found new echoes. Indeed, under their "Bolshevik" leader, Othón Salazar, teachers had taken to the streets for almost half the decade.[52] In sermons and publications and through lay groups, the church warned that the normales were breeding grounds of a renewed communist threat. One article contained the following calculus: "Annually, about a thousand teachers finish their studies. If each one of them educates sixty children a year, do the math. . . . A people will think as instructed by their teachers, just as the teachers think in accordance with what they learn at the normal. Mexico will be what the normal is. That's where the communist lair is."[53] Warnings became ever direr with the 1959 triumph of the Cuban Revolution, as conservatives propagated rumors that the Mexican government would follow suit and nationalize private schools. In this context, the church positioned itself as a defender of religion, family, and nation against a government whose education policy would, like the apocryphal stories about Cuba, end with children in the Soviet Union.[54]

The National Parents Union denounced Mexico's textbook program as Soviet and Nazi inspired and demanded reforms to Article 3 that would return to parents "the individual education liberties that had been stripped from them for over half a century."[55] The organization criticized the "materialist and atheist" perspective of the new texts based not so much on the books' content as on their sin of omission: the books' spiritual emptiness and ignorance of religion, which was detrimental to children's relationship with God.[56] Yet more was at stake than religion. Beyond threatening parents' worldviews, the texts undermined carefully guarded class privileges.[57] Elites had long distrusted the quality of public education. With more resources and a lower teacher-student ratio, private schools avoided many of the problems that plagued public ones. Private-school parents, moreover, could purchase learning instruments, texts, and workbooks above and beyond what the state made accessible to all. Why should their children now be constrained by new national standards?

As members of upper-class families, business leaders sought to protect the economic model from which they had benefited handily during the previous two decades. The constant labor mobilizations during the late 1950s threatened a social breakdown. Despite President López Mateos's willingness to restore order though force, some of his policies and declarations made him suspect—such as when he famously stated that, while staying within the constitutional rule, his government was to the extreme left.[58] The Cuban Revolution and the president's apparent support of it disturbed powerful interest groups, which used the textbook controversy to register their criticism.

In cities like Monterrey, Guadalajara, Morelia, and Puebla, business leaders took unprecedented measures. In November 1960, for example, three of Mexico's most powerful business groups published a declaration in the national newspaper *Excélsior* entitled "Which Path Mr. President?" stating their disapproval of recent state actions such as the nationalization of the electric company. The text ended with a question: "Are we headed toward state socialism?" More alarming than the letter itself was the group's decision to voice such discontent publicly. Traditionally, these matters had been resolved through private channels.[59]

The controversy also strengthened the right-wing PAN, which received the support of the disgruntled Textbook Authors Association, the National Parents Union, and the recently created Christian Family Movement. A longtime ally of the Catholic Church and an opponent of broad social spending, the PAN criticized the textbook program as yet another manifestation of government despotism. Adolfo Christlieb Ibarrola, the PAN's president, denounced that the texts' free distribution pursued a "uniformity of consciousness under the direction of an authoritarian state."[60] In López Mateos's attempt to define his government as leftist within the confines of the constitution, the PAN saw increased control of industry, state intervention in the private sector, and a preponderantly public workforce as proof that "state capitalism was equivalent to a communist regime."[61]

The communist hysteria—domestically a product of the PRI's own propaganda—fortified the PAN's longtime arguments. In using the red scare to justify its repression of popular mobilizations, the government had cast a net so wide that the right could now characterize the state's own nationalist and liberal policies as dangerous doctrines foreign to Mexico's innately conservative tradition—which the PAN had positioned itself as long upholding. The state's battle against Mexico City's teachers and normalistas, moreover, deprived the government of committed allies, as they had been for Cárdenas in the 1930s. Instead, the official teachers' union, seeking to prevent further divisions within its ranks, made only meek pronouncements in support of the free-textbook initiative.[62] Dissident educators, embroiled in their own battles against the SEP and the official union, were little inclined to close ranks with officialist teachers behind a state that branded them as communists, incarcerated their leaders, and deployed the army against them.

In an environment rife with anticommunism, the campaign against the government textbooks became virulent. Groups in some schools confiscated and burned the SEP-issued texts.[63] In a 1962 parade in Chihuahua celebrating the revolution's anniversary, members of the crowd hurled objects at a float on which children proudly waved the textbooks.[64] As they had in the 1930s, church officials again advised parents against sending their children to school.[65] For rural teachers, this hysteria could not but evoke the Cristero wars when Catholic militants had torched schoolhouses and mutilated teachers in protest of socialist education. The connections were made more palpable as President Cárdenas became an outspoken defender of the Cuban Revolution and criticized the Mexican regime's authoritarian practices.[66]

The crisis came to a head in February 1962, when business groups, the National Parents Union, and the church organized a massive protest in the northern industrial city of Monterrey, Nuevo León. With cries of "Christianity, not Communism!" and "Religion, family, and country are sacred; do not tarnish them," 150,000 people demonstrated against the government textbooks.[67] The march reverberated nationally, forcing the government to act. The SEP sent a negotiating committee to Monterrey and agreed that local organizations could study ways to adapt the national curriculum to the particularities of the state. While government officials continued to insist on the obligatory nature of the textbooks, they allowed the Nuevo León Parents Association to propose and distribute its own pedagogical materials within the state. This strategy portended an informal national arrangement by which private schools would continue to demand other texts under the guise that they were complementary. The SEP proved accommodating and looked the other way when private schools refrained from using books from the official list.[68]

While the government had shown a willingness to negotiate in Nuevo León, it sought to reassert its power by taking a hard line in states like San Luis Potosí and Guanajuato, where it defended the textbook program as a necessary popular reform to benefit the people. It shored up its promotional campaign through the Confederation of Mexican Workers and the National Campesino Confederation, publicizing the extensive support it received from rural school families, ejidos, and unions and showcasing their gratitude for the regime's revolutionary measures.[69] The official teachers' union, too, stepped up what had been timid support and focused its arguments on the defense of Article 3, pointing to private schools as a threat to popular education.[70]

Meanwhile, business leaders, satisfied with the show of force they had displayed in Monterrey, began to withdraw from the issue. Two events at the national level helped mitigate their concern about López Mateos. First, President John F. Kennedy's 1962 visit to Mexico created much fanfare among Catholics and validated the Mexican president's credentials among many right-wing sectors. López Mateos's defense of Cuban self-determination notwithstanding, Kennedy's trip won their confidence in the government's fervent anticommunism. Joint U.S.-Mexican declarations about individual liberties and the condemnation of totalitarian institutions received wide praise from Mexico's business groups and the church hierarchy.[71] Second, the right was further appeased a year later with the unveiling of Gustavo Díaz Ordaz as the PRI's 1964 presidential candidate. The choice of Díaz Ordaz, minister of the interior under López Mateos and a fierce anticommunist, heralded an institutional hard line against popular mobilizations. The new president would not disappoint.

PROFESSIONALIZING TEACHERS

The textbook controversy has long overshadowed other significant aspects of the Eleven-Year Plan. Not since Vasconcelos in the 1920s or Cárdenas in the 1930s had there been such a concerted federal effort to expand schooling.[72] Education Minister Torres Bodet took an active role in defining elementary school study programs and curricular changes at normales, directed their implementation, and used his office as a bully pulpit to harness public support. Having penned the 1946 reform of Article 3 that replaced socialist education with an emphasis on individual human development and patriotism, his second tenure as education minister in the 1960s would further his long-term imprint on the Mexican education system.[73] Sincere in his concern for Mexico's educational plight, as a matter of policy he sought both to increase elementary school coverage and to better prepare the workforce— skilled and semiskilled labor, technical workers, and professionals—for the country's industrial and service sectors.[74] Reluctant to accept Alliance for Progress money and conscious that Mexico's private sector could not be counted on to invest in education—"their reaction to the free-textbook program showed the extent to which their indifference was a mark of disdain," he wrote—Torres Bodet pushed to increase the country's embarrassingly low levels of education spending.[75] To reformers like him, the three million Mexican children who by midcentury still did not attend school represented a dereliction of the state's constitutional responsibility for education.[76]

Torres Bodet conceived of teachers as moral guides whose authority and effectiveness he sought to strengthen through professional development. Aside from increasing their number in the countryside and building more schools, his reforms sought an overhaul of teacher-training programs to eliminate their lackluster quality and modernize their pedagogy. He first turned to the massive number of instructors—58 percent in 1955—who taught without proper credentials.[77] Torres Bodet thus increased the funding and infrastructure of the Federal Institute for Teacher Training. Created in 1945, during his first term as education minister, this institute offered courses to the hundreds of *maestros empíricos*, teachers who taught with little or no formal preparation. By 1958, through correspondence courses, weekend workshops, and summer training, this institute had granted degrees to 15,620 teachers.[78] During Torres Bodet's second term, the SEP increased the institute's capacity and extended its reach by creating twelve regional offices and thirty-eight coordinating agencies. Along with this expansion, the SEP published new manuals and textbooks and broadcast radio lessons.[79] It also organized professional development programs to disseminate the new curriculum and provided additional training for teachers who already had their degrees. The pace of its accreditation increased markedly, and by 1964 it had granted degrees to 17,472 additional teachers.[80]

The second measure to professionalize educators focused on the 53,376 teachers (out of the country's total of 89,932) who had attended a normal and completed their coursework but had not fulfilled the final requirements—through an exam or thesis—to receive their degree.[81] Declaring that "their teaching experience constituted sufficient guarantee of preparation and aptitude," President López Mateos waived the thesis and exam requirements for those teachers who had attended federal normales, had completed their coursework no more than five years prior, and had taught for five consecutive years. To minimize this problem in future decades, his decree also established a two-year limit on the time between finishing coursework and passing the professional exam.[82] A degree not only provided instructors with additional training but also allowed them to benefit from a rank and seniority system otherwise inaccessible to them.[83]

But Mexico did not just need professional teachers; it needed more teachers, especially in the countryside, where the educational infrastructure was significantly inferior to that of the city. In the late 1950s, when Mexico's population was distributed about evenly between urban and rural centers, 81 percent of schools in the countryside did not reach through sixth grade, and the vast majority operated with one teacher who instructed several grades simultaneously. Thus, of the enrolled student population, over half (55 percent) was in first grade, and 91 percent in grades 1 through 3.[84] In 1955 the student-teacher ratio in rural elementary schools was 51 to 1, compared to 43 to 1 in cities and 31 to 1 in private schools.[85]

The López Mateos regime set out to build more schools in rural areas. One SEP program commissioned the mass production of prefabricated schoolhouses through which communities received the building's basic components, which they then assembled and adapted to local climactic conditions. The building sets also included furniture, a small library, didactic equipment, and small living quarters for the teacher, a design the SEP hoped would encourage educators to settle in the communities and reduce the absenteeism caused by a commute from distant urban centers.[86] During his term López Mateos founded 6,760 new schools, and the normal system issued 50,772 teaching degrees.[87]

Still, the problem of staffing persisted. While most of the new schools were built in rural areas, the majority of the new teaching positions went to urban and semiurban population centers.[88] In 1960 the SEP tried to correct this imbalance through a new type of institution, the CRENs, that would train teachers in semiurban areas but dispatch them to the countryside. Unlike the rural normales, however, the CRENs deliberately dispensed with the boarding-school structure and instead provided students with a stipend to cover their room and board. The first two were established in Ciudad Guzmán and Iguala in 1960, and the tone of policy makers conveys the sense that the CRENs held the solution to the problem of entitled and obstreperous teachers.[89] In its assessment of the sexenio's educational accomplishments, a SEP publication stated that the CRENs' first graduating class possessed a "notable professional responsibility, a teaching devotion and a spirit of cooperation and efficiency in their educational duties."[90] When Torres Bodet visited these new schools in 1963, he highlighted the "friendly atmosphere between students and instructors," contrasting these normalistas with those of Mexico City's National Teachers School. "What a difference between the former's patriotic will to help and the selfishness demonstrated by Mexico City's 1960s graduates!" At the CREN, continued Torres Bodet, normalistas "understood what we expected of them. If sent to teach far from the capital, none would have felt exiled in their fatherland."[91] In this way, the minister reiterated the notion of teacher sacrifice and patriotic duty, which he hoped to cultivate in normalistas so it would bear fruit in the subsequent teaching body.

For Torres Bodet, the CRENs represented a fresh start—new institutions that still upheld the countryside as a site for Mexico's spiritual renovation but were not bogged down by the notions of revolutionary justice that produced the entitled teachers he had battled in the capital. After all, increasing the countryside's teachers could have been accomplished by expanding or increasing the numbers at rural normales, as long demanded by their student associations. But by the 1950s the government was loath to fund boarding schools, a point vividly made when, in 1956, it closed the dorms in Mexico City's National Polytechnic Institute and when, three years later, it did the same at the National Teachers School. Despite the right's fear of Cardenismo, a host of such measures demonstrated a state willing to do away with sites of collective empowerment. Rural normalistas would increasingly come forth to object.

THE BATTLES AT RURAL NORMALES

During the 1950s rural normales were not yet considered the repositories of radical student activism. Mexico City's National Teachers School held that distinction. While the 1956 strike at the National Polytechnic Institute showed youths' capacity to mount powerful movements, labor struggles were much more dominant throughout the 1950s. The state's repressive response to labor did not go unnoticed by students at the rural normales. The Mexican Federation of Socialist Campesino Students (FECSM), the federation representing rural normalistas, understood the teachers' and the rail, telegraph, and oil workers' movements as labor's attempt to push forward the revolution's progressive elements. Tragically, they concluded, "reactionary, imperialist, and counterrevolutionary forces" revealed their strength. This context, according to FECSM, made it imperative to design demands that were political in nature rather than limiting their battles to material ends. According to rural normalistas, their schools "represented the realization of the revolutionary movement" and were also under threat as the government and the right "conjured up false claims, damaging maneuvers, and dangerous argumentation" against these institutions.[92] The federation's battlefronts were many: maintaining the basic material integrity of rural normales, combating their schools' reputation as anarchic learning centers, and opposing the PRI-allied union's attempts to control their institutions' inner workings (figure 4.1).

Throughout 1958, rural normalistas had undertaken various walkouts to obtain more scholarships and expanded dorm capacity.[93] In 1959 the FECSM presented the SEP with a list of twenty-two demands to fortify the countryside's rural teacher-training system. Notwithstanding the federation's declaration that their struggle was political, most of their demands were material in nature. Three points, however, stand out for the ideological principles they sustained: a call for greater normalista supervision over the funds their schools received, an appeal for the SEP to assert its dominion in the face of

FIGURE 4.1 Protesting rural normalistas in SEP offices meeting with the director of normal education, 1955. Archivo General de la Nación, Photographic Archive, Normales Rurales, C24, Sobre 106.

private and religious groups that increasingly built their own schools, and a recognition of the boarding-school structure as central to the integrity of rural normales.[94]

Such calls were premised on the notion of education as a right and sought institutional mechanisms by which to preserve the poor's access to a professional career. First, by overseeing funds, students sought not only to prevent school administrators from siphoning off food or other resource expenditures but to assert some power against the state's co-opting mechanisms. In the hands of school administrators (who, like teachers and staff, were members of the official union), funds were subject to co-optative politics, and as discussed below, the SNTE was indeed anxious to increase its power in rural normales. Second, the FECSM's point about religious schools implicitly invoked Article 3 to remind the state of its educational responsibilities and warn of the right's increasing power. Based on the reactionary sectors' opposition to mass education after the revolution, normalistas continued to denounce religious and monied interests as threats to revolutionary gains. That the textbook controversy revived old arguments about Article 3 and united the church, business groups, and the private-school sector demonstrated the prescience of normalista fears. Finally, the FECSM insisted that dormitories were critical. Any restructuring of the rural normal system had to recognize the centrality of their boardinghouses. The material support provided to boarders, after all, made possible an education for the poor. Given the country's demographic growth, dormitory capacity needed to be increased. Here the FECSM used the language of the state to make its case. Boarding schools, it declared, "represented the guarantee of youths' perfect civic formation in accordance with the state's politics and philosophy."[95] This logic linked patriotic duty to a fulfillment of students' material needs, a sign of how students experienced dorm life—it entailed responsibilities and awakened national consciousness owing to their interaction with peers from other parts of the country (figure 4.2).

Ultimately, however, the material demands constituted the bulk of the FECSM's petition. Normalistas sought an overall expansion of the rural normal system through an increase in the number of institutions, two thousand new scholarships, and state and municipal contributions. To improve pedagogical training, the FECSM proposed better methods to select and prepare their teachers, including a call for a Higher Normal School specifically devoted to educating teachers for rural normales. The remaining points addressed very specific improvements, such as construction projects and building repairs at particular schools, electrification, improvement of schools' medical centers, increases in food rations and stipends, and provision of equipment such as film projectors, laboratory tools, typewriters, and books.[96]

In its response, the SEP acknowledged that rural normales needed to be expanded in accordance with the demographic pressure on the existing system. It addressed each of the FECSM's individual points primarily by listing the resources it had already invested and the various projects then underway. The SEP pointed out the recent construction of four rural normales and countered the FECSM's calls for two thousand scholarships with 150, stating that the CRENs under construction would ease the increased demographic pressure. On the FECSM's emphatic point about the centrality of the boarding-school structure, the authorities warned that it would be maintained only if dorm life guaranteed the "civic and ethical edification of future teachers" and constituted a "truly educational venue." With regard to state and municipal funding, the SEP replied that it could make suggestions but

FIGURE 4.2 Dorms at the rural normal of Misantla, Veracruz, 1956. Archivo General de la Nación, Photographic Archive, Normales Rurales, C27, Sobre 14.

had no power to legislate in that matter. On the issue of student oversight of resources, the SEP remained silent. About religious schools, it stated that the constitution already laid out the parameters within which private schools had to comply with official curricular norms. The SEP rejected the call for a new institution specifically designed to train rural normal teachers, since the Higher Normal School of Mexico already offered a program to that end. It referred to a recently instituted hiring structure that paid attention to the educator's area of specialization as a measure to ensure better teachers. The SEP further placed the onus on the normalistas themselves, stating that since most teachers at rural normales hailed from these institutions, elevating their quality depended on improving the normal student body. With regard to material demands, it highlighted the current resource allocation, asserting that concrete assessments needed to be conducted if funds were to go elsewhere (figure 4.3).[97]

Two issues stand out in the SEP's response: its conditioning of boarding schools on student behavior and its reference to CRENs as the institutions that would meet the demands of demographic growth. The student petitioners had carefully framed their appeal in a language of civic duty that might resonate with officials. The SEP took the normalista point about complying with "the state's political and philosophical orientation" as an opportunity to issue a veiled threat. It conditioned new dormitories on their educational purpose and students' moral character and comportment. In appropriating state discourse, normalistas—like teachers—confronted the contradiction of asserting collective rights in a state that demanded compliant citizens. Tellingly, by citing the CRENs, institutions deliberately designed to dispense with dormitories, the SEP declared boarding schools a thing of the past. Education Minister Torres Bodet's experience with Mexico City teachers had shaped his conviction that dorms produced disruptive students who later became entitled teachers.

The official teachers' union, or SNTE, a close state ally, contributed to this view. With its Mexico City members in frank rebellion, it sought other mechanisms to flex its muscle and further ingratiate itself with the state. Rural normales stood as important spaces for it to assert control, not only because official unions were supposed to be instruments of the PRI, but because the SNTE itself faced constant challenges from normalistas, who brought forth grievances against affiliated school administrators, teachers, and staff. In response to such actions, the official union declared that rural normales suffered from a "crisis of moral values . . . since disciplinary, academic, and moral standards grow worse every day." Students' propensity

FIGURE 4.3 The cafeteria at the rural normal of Misantla, Veracruz, 1956. Students referred to the women who cooked for them as *las tías* (the aunts). Archivo General de la Nación, Photographic Archive, Normales Rurales, C27, Sobre 14.

to oust personnel did not constitute a victory, it asserted, but evidenced a system suffering from an "inversion of values."[98] The PRI-affiliated union dismissed student charges of sexual harassment, inhumane actions, or despotic behavior by school officials as fabricated grievances against those who demanded rigorous work or dared to enforce unpopular rules.[99] According to the SNTE, normalistas defended incompetent directors so long as they gave in to student concessions—likewise with teachers, who risked student ire if they handed out low grades. The worst-performing students, asserted the SNTE, spearheaded the ouster of school personnel. In a tone that invoked the state's rhetoric of teacher sacrifice, the union declared that teachers actually preferred to work at rural normales as a matter of idealistic commitment even though at schools with no dorms they had more free time and were "respected, appreciated, and left alone in their private life."[100] Yet it was precisely the ousted directors and teachers, warned the SNTE, who propagated the negative view of the rural normales as they recounted their expulsion. The SNTE chastised the student body for their constant agitation and appealed to the FECSM to stop defending the causes of wayward students who made a career for themselves as political leaders or who harbored personal resentment against particular staff members.[101] The SNTE likewise criticized any teacher or administrator who rallied students and advised staff "not to get involved in student affairs nor to make common cause with them." If teachers were found mobilizing students in their own support or against school directors, "they'd be expelled without discussion."[102] The official union even referenced the language of social justice by affirming that rural normales "stood as material accomplishments of popular longings." But it then shamed students for their demands. With the money the SEP had invested in student housing, asserted the SNTE, it could have improved thousands of elementary schools, indigenous boardinghouses, literacy centers, and cultural missions.[103]

The SNTE's discomfort with student leaders is evident in other appeals it made to the SEP. For example, it warned the SEP about those it assigned to staff classes for the rural normales' "complementary years" (fifth and sixth grades, offered to those who had not finished their elementary school education). The SNTE argued that precisely because of the time normalista leaders devoted to the struggle, they were unqualified teachers who could not meet the challenges of this particular teaching cycle. But the SNTE's appeal revealed another concern: the moral suasion recent graduates could exert over the student body. When conflicts arose that pitted teachers or administrators against normalistas, stated the SNTE, the recent graduates felt more identified with the students. If graduates had to be placed in teaching positions at the rural normal, it should be "once their influence as student leaders had disappeared completely." The SNTE sought further requirements for teachers designated to teach the complementary years: that they be the students with the highest academic achievement, show impeccable discipline, be duly recommended by the school authorities, and pledge loyalty to the administration.[104]

The official teachers' union presented the SEP with suggestions to strengthen the power of school directors. One proposal involved relieving assistant principals of their teaching duties so they could devote more time to disciplinary matters. They would maintain work logs for staff, and discipline and achievement tallies for students, supposedly to apply proper penalties or sanctions. If the SEP agreed to this measure, the SNTE would ensure that those filling the assistant principal positions were drawn from loyal ranks and pledged their utmost collaboration with school directors.[105] Such proposals must have been appealing to the SEP given the constant challenges it faced from student associations that relentlessly invoked the principles of constitutional rights, the ideals of the revolution, and class-based vindications, frameworks often at odds with official calls for sacrifice, discipline, and professionalism. For now, the SEP sought a curricular overhaul at rural normales, which officials presumed would help fulfill these institutions' historical mission of transforming an ailing countryside.

RURAL NORMALES, A CURRICULAR UPDATE

In 1956 the Normal Education Commission proposed to overhaul the teacher-training programs in an effort to transform a curriculum judged pedantic in its content, encyclopedic in its delivery, and overwhelming in its breadth.[106] Proposed reforms acknowledged the error of the 1943 decree that established a uniform curriculum across urban and rural normales. This measure, noted education officials, had contributed to the high transfer rate of students to urban normales or other professional schools and had reduced teachers' overall commitment to the countryside. It had obscured, moreover, the unique mission and social implications of rural education, thus undermining the "educational mystique," that selfless, spiritual commitment to modernize the countryside through education.[107] Accordingly, in 1960 the SEP again turned its attention to the distinct nature of rural education and formally divided the General Directorate of Normal Teaching into urban and rural branches.[108] While rural normales would have the same sequence and curricular structure as urban teacher-training schools, their study plan would include a whole set of pedagogical practices meant specifically for the countryside and, through elective classes, would offer flexibility to tailor activities or research projects to their region.[109] Given their distance from the "restless and impatient city life," declared Minister Torres Bodet in 1962, rural normales were well equipped to provide "active, capable, loyal, and responsible teachers to the suffering Mexican countryside."[110]

Though approved by the SEP in 1960, these changes would not be implemented in rural normales until 1964 after being experimented with in CRENs.[111] The rural normales presented both challenges and possibilities for the reforms. On the one hand, they lacked the basic infrastructure to put new programs into practice. Teachers complained that they could hardly conduct directed readings given their limited book collections and in some cases asked students to buy texts out of their own pockets.[112] The FECSM in fact included in its 1965 petition better-supplied libraries since as they stood, they "lacked the books to comply with the reform's requirements."[113] Teacher staffing, not to mention the retraining needed to adopt the new pedagogy, was another stumbling block. As it was, rural normal instructors often found themselves at the head of a particular class not because it matched their academic background but because that subject needed staffing.[114] Other infrastructural needs included science laboratories, equipment and transportation for fieldwork, and extracurricular activities, resources rural normalistas consistently included in their petitions to the SEP.

On the other hand, even as the spartan nature of rural normales presented extensive challenges to the new mandates, long-standing activities at these schools had at their root two characteristics the new SEP measures sought to emphasize: hands-on learning and community engagement. The latter, believed education officials, was crucial to teachers' commitment to serve in the countryside. Rural normalistas had long organized community festivals, run workshops for the local population, and conducted their teaching practicums in surrounding towns. The national networks of rural normales created additional opportunities for community outreach. The schools had an important tradition of organizing sports tournaments, literary festivals, and music and dance recitals. These activities both showcased normalista accomplishments and provided venues to exchange and develop pedagogical projects.[115] Noteworthy among them was the students' own Political and Ideological Orientation Club, charged, among other things, with instilling in new students the historical significance of the rural normales (figure 4.4).[116] In some schools this club oversaw oratory instruction with the aim of "boosting political activity . . . considering how fundamental public speaking is to politics." Teachers' ability to express themselves powerfully and their command of language, stated one student declaration, were necessary to fulfill "our role as community guides and to prepare us for confronting those who are reactionary or enemies of our schools."[117] In this manner, the SEP's broader goal to professionalize teachers reinforced student notions that theirs was a transformative mission.

The new measures reduced the number of required courses at rural normales, mandated more hands-on training through increased laboratories and workshops, and established seminars and research projects. The reform made its strongest push in the area of agriculture, instituting changes to the farming curriculum, a longtime defining feature of these schools. The farming curriculum was conceived as a measure to both train normalistas in land cultivation (lessons they would subsequently impart to communities) and

FIGURE 4.4 Mosaic on the student association's office at the rural normal of Tamazulapan, Oaxaca. Photograph by author.

provide resources and revenue for institutional sustenance, but in practice the schools routinely fell short of these goals. As one report from the rural normal of Cañada Honda in Aguascalientes noted, "rather than an integral part of the curriculum," agricultural activities "merely train students to be good field hands. . . . The lands that border our schools are better cultivated and more productive and cause campesino incredulity about our good intentions to provide guidance." Like so many problems at rural normales, the shortcomings stemmed from a lack of resources, including a dearth of qualified agricultural instructors.[118] Those imparting farming classes did not have training in agricultural techniques, while bona fide agronomists knew little about proper teaching methods.[119]

To address such shortcomings, the reformed study plan imbued agricultural practices with greater curricular importance, increasing the number of hours of weekly instruction in these areas.[120] New guidelines directed schools in choosing crops appropriate to the area and encouraged production activities linked to the farm animals they already possessed. Normalistas were to engage with nearby ejidos and cattle ranches, and agricultural teachers were to collaborate with geography, biology, and math instructors to develop an overall pedagogical coherence. Instructors, moreover, were urged to better integrate theory and practice by explaining to students the rationale for their specific techniques. Finally, normalistas were given the charge to work with nearby elementary schools to develop gardens, greenhouses, seedbeds, fruit groves, and reforestation projects, as well as to survey surrounding farms and participate in efforts to improve animal husbandry and reduce plagues that destroyed crops or killed farm animals.[121]

Seeking to produce a well-rounded student with the confidence to spearhead community development, the new program set immediate and longterm goals. In the short term, successful agricultural production at the rural normales would enrich student diets by using the grains, fruits, vegetables, meat, eggs, and dairy to stock the schools' cafeterias. Excess goods could be sold and the funds invested in the school. This endeavor, the logic went, might help ameliorate some of the rural normales' chronic economic problems and give students the satisfaction of engaging in remunerative activities.[122]

The long-term goal, emphasized education authorities, was not to produce skilled agronomists but to graduate teachers who could fulfill the principles of rural education: better the living conditions of campesinos by instructing them in the productive use of natural resources, awaken in schoolchildren a love of the land and its flora and fauna, encourage a harmonious relationship between the school and the community, and undertake projects beneficial to the region's inhabitants. Rural teachers would promote land rights as a key tenet of the revolution. Notably, efficiency rather than justice would now be the framing logic, in the belief that only through the "rational cultivation of their plots" would campesinos appreciate the "revolution's principles." Teachers were thus to emphasize modern techniques that made effective use of the region's resources and to encourage links with the agricultural and livestock industry.[123] That the interests of the industrial, agricultural, and livestock groups were at odds with those of small cultivators was not mentioned, a measure of how far the state had traveled from socialist education's class analysis.

The new curriculum would be divided into requirements, electives, and practices. Students could take electives as a way to either improve their skills in core subjects (language, math, science) or cultivate a specialty such as indigenous education, arts and crafts, zoology, or health. This type of curricular restructuring, hoped education officials, would enable a new generation of teachers to recover the devotion of earlier decades. The new study plan also emphasized an active learning process. "Teacher graduates of our normales will not be adequately trained," stated one SEP commission, "if they can only count on theoretical knowledge and don't have the necessary practical experience of distinct activities to complement their training. This is why it is so important to *learn by doing*."[124] Class time was expanded, and teachers were guided to use workbooks rather than impart dictation; they were to incorporate directed research and emphasize class discussion. Students would begin teaching after they completed their six-year course plan but would not receive their degree until they finished a year of instruction. During this teaching year, they would still be under the normal's tutelage and would attend regular seminars but would have the same salary, benefits, and responsibilities as regular teachers. At the year's end, the new teachers would write a report, to be evaluated by their supervising normal.[125]

The grading system was also amended. Rather than giving monthly exams, teachers were to incorporate "exercises, research, quizzes, occasional tests, and extracurricular activities."[126] What mattered was that "the material, rather than a desire for high grades, awaken student motivation."[127] The exams themselves were to assess critical thinking in place of memorization. Traditional courses and electives would still be given numeric marks (between 1 and 10), but workshops, labs, home economics, art, classroom observation, and teaching techniques would be evaluated by simple measures such as "very good," "good," or "bad." The SEP provided guidelines for these formulations that included punctuality, dedication, care, and ability to work in groups. This grading system would "lighten the excessively theoretical load" and cultivate a quality of "maturity . . . difficult to verify through a written exam."[128] Previous mechanisms by which students could make up a course by simply taking an exam were significantly reduced, and certain core subjects could not be replaced by an exam at all.[129] Students who had missed 15 percent or more of classes would not be permitted to take the final exam.[130]

Finally, class time and teaching styles were also to be reformed. Smaller, longer classes would provide the space for greater student-teacher contact. Through seminars, students could take ownership of the material by means of constructive, teacher-guided discussion.[131] "Long gone," explained one directive, "were the days when school was an institution in which the teacher led everything and relegated the student to a passive, submissive, obedient receptacle."[132] Such initiatives represented an important attempt to deepen rural normales' mission as institutions of community development and to cultivate assertive attributes in their students. Duly trained, the logic went, their graduates could aptly address the countryside's problems.

And yet the rural crisis continued. Had they been adequately funded, such curricular reforms could have significantly improved rural normales. But their allocated resources remained sparse. Year after year, the students mobilized to demand pedagogical and material improvements. But rural normales remained underfunded, a telling condition. School precarity was a hallmark of rural Mexico, a country that even in a time of unprecedented economic growth spent proportionately little on education. President López Mateos's education project was significant, but its impressive nature lay partly in how little the previous two administrations had devoted to education. His spending, for example, did not reach the percentage levels under the Cárdenas administration.[133] As a response to rural-urban disparities, moreover, extending primary-education access did little to address the root causes of poverty, migration, and inequality. And, however good their training, rural teachers could not ameliorate the crisis.

"THE EXPANSION of primary education followed a promising path," wrote Torres Bodet in his memoirs. "We multiplied schools even if we did not always feel proud of the teachers we assigned to animate them. We printed and distributed millions of textbook copies, and the campaign against them would not cease."[134] The minister thus expressed his frustration, on the one hand, with teachers who would not willingly go to or stay in the countryside, who demanded better pay and working conditions, and whose academic preparation often faltered and, on the other, with elites who resented an interventionalist state and actively sought to counter revolutionary reforms. Torres Bodet's acerbic critiques of the way power conditioned relations in the international realm—based on his experience as a diplomat and head of UNESCO (the United Nations Educational, Scientific, and Cultural Organization)—are absent in his domestic analysis and conception of education as a liberal endeavor focused on the individual. Nowhere in his vast volume of writing, noted one analyst, is there an understanding of education "as an integrative part of the social system. . . . In vain one searches for indications of some study about the relationship between the school and social processes, its effect on social stratification and mobility, and its contribution to income distribution. . . . The perspective of all the enacted reforms is limited to the direct responsibility of the public education 'branch,' understood as a sector of activities isolated from the rest."[135] Viewed in structural terms, his efforts to combat illiteracy, build more schools, and professionalize the teaching corps, however heroic, did little to mitigate the contradictions of an economic miracle that concentrated wealth in the countryside through land accumulation and in the cities through increased worker control and exploitation. As economic analyses for the 1960s have shown, an increase in the years of education did not correspond to a higher income or reduced unemployment, nor did it substantially improve intergenerational social mobility.[136]

If labor constituted the most visible form of social discontent during the 1950s, in the 1960s students would take its place. In both decades campesino protest was a constant, and, much to the state's dismay, normalistas and their instructors, as well as rural teachers in general, supported, facilitated, and even led this process. Significantly, rather than being narrow protests over academic matters, student struggles consistently had at their core broader economic or political grievances. As with labor, the state would meet student challenges with the army, spurring a cycle of protest and repression throughout the country.[137] In this sequence, the most militant challenge came from rural and state normalistas in Chihuahua, where students and some teachers from Salaices, Saucillo, and Chihuahua City joined campesino land takeovers throughout the decade. In distant sierra communities, teachers spearheaded marches, protests, and appeals for justice given the increasing campesino land dispossession and their murder at the hands of landowners' hired gunmen. In 1965, after years of government inaction, a joint campesino-teacher-normalista group sought justice through armed means and formed a guerrilla group. Thus began the reputation of rural normales as guerrilla seedbeds.

5

"The Infinite Injustice Committed against Our Class Brothers"

IN SEPTEMBER 1964 the rural normal teacher Pablo Gómez wrote to Education Minister Jaime Torres Bodet protesting his transfer from Saucillo, Chihuahua, to Atequiza, Jalisco. Chihuahua's governor, Práxedes Giner, had long sought Gómez's removal, accusing him of taking students to campesino land invasions. Students took action of their own accord, protested Gómez. They, like youth around the globe, were conscious of the world's problems and sought practical solutions. Teachers may have had an influence, but that was only in "accordance with the social implications specified by Article 3." What right, continued Gómez, did state politicians, "enemies of normal education, and of President Adolfo López Mateos's great free textbook program," have to remove him? So hostile had these same authorities been to federal education policy that Saucillo's municipal president had suggested storming public schools to burn the government-issued textbooks.[1]

As Gómez pointed out, those now objecting to the free textbooks were the same groups long hostile to public schoolteachers and demeaning of the institutions that trained them. Not only had Article 3 of the Mexican Constitution undermined the church's historic dominion over schooling, but in its expansive definition of the educator's role—to aid in land distribution, organize unions, and publicize agrarian rights—the revolutionary state had birthed political agents. Notwithstanding later efforts to transform teachers' role to one more akin to social work, rural normales preserved the Cardenista tenets of socialist education. Justice for the countryside remained a constituting element of their institutional culture, one continuously infused by students' family histories of exploitation and by promises of revolutionary reform, not to mention normalistas' own coming of age amid a socioeconomic order that, in several regions of the country, eerily resembled Porfirian times. This presence of campesino consciousness made rural normales particularly radical educational sites.

By showcasing the nature of rural normalistas' participation in northern Mexico's agrarian struggles of the early 1960s, this chapter highlights how student protest marked Mexico's periphery before the widely recognized 1968 movement in the capital. Hidden in plain sight, normalista mobilizations in Chihuahua challenge the notion of student movements as a uniquely urban phenomenon. In the country's periphery, students from the rural normales of Salaices and Saucillo participated in land takeovers alongside campesinos, dramatizing the country's increasing land concentration and the violence that undergirded it. In this struggle, teachers like Pablo Gómez and Arturo Gámiz acted as leaders, advisers, organic intellectuals, and links with organizations at the national level. They were the visible incarnation of the socially committed, politically militant teachers the revolutionary state had once held as models.

Emerging from the ranks of the Popular Socialist Party (Partido Popular Socialista, PPS) and the independent General Union of Mexican Workers and Campesinos (Unión General de Obreros y Campesinos de México, UGOCM), Mexico's agrarian struggle of the 1950s and early 1960s reinforced the progressive ideology on which rural normales were founded. Internationally, the 1959 triumph of the Cuban Revolution expanded the spectrum of possibilities and stoked their imagination. Normalista frameworks of justice increasingly pushed Cardenista notions beyond campesino empowerment to a state controlled by workers and campesinos. When the hardening repression and ever more elusive reforms produced a local guerrilla group in 1965, its actions crystallized the broad-based association between rural normales and the radical protest of their students.

CHIHUAHUA: *LATIFUNDISMO* AND ITS DISCONTENTS

Chihuahua has long been a source of wealth for foreign investors, Mexican business owners, and local caciques. During the early twentieth century, thanks to Porfirio Díaz's business-friendly policies, families like the Terrazas and Creels built empires that rivaled those of U.S. magnates of the time.[2] Their monopoly over land, cattle, banking, manufacturing, and mining was so great that, unlike in other northern states, no dissident elite emerged to challenge them during the revolution. Instead, the middle class, peasants, and workers allied against them and forced reform over the years of fierce fighting.[3] But Chihuahua's persistent oligarchs, to use Mark Wasserman's term, proved adept at navigating the new order. While the northern revolutionaries Francisco Villa and Álvaro Obregón expropriated much of the Terrazas-Creel land for redistribution during the 1920s and 1930s, the relatives of the large landowners repurchased it, often with the very money obtained as compensation for previous expropriations. Their postrevolutionary holdings represented but 20 percent of their previous possessions; however, it was some of the state's best land and nearly matched the total acreage redistributed by the government during the 1930s. Other magnates arose from the ruins of the Terrazas-Creel estates. Families like the Vallinas, Almeidas, Quevedos, and Borundas—pervasive names in campesino grievances—purchased many of their previous holdings.[4] Chihuahua's mining, cattle, agriculture, and lumber sectors provided seemingly endless possibilities for wealth. Exemption decrees, which deemed certain businesses key to the national economy, aided the process by shielding the great cattle and agro-export industry from expropriation. As had been the case during the Porfiriato, political connections helped protect and grow investment. The new elite formed banking associations, cattlemen's organizations, and a chamber of commerce, interest groups that wielded immense power regionally and nationally. While no single family achieved the previous Terrazas-Creel power, by midcentury the Vallinas—in partnership with Terrazas descendants—came close.[5]

Bosques de Chihuahua is a good example of the process by which new elites built fortunes on the remnants of Porfirian-era enterprises. In 1946 Eloy Vallina, a prominent banker, and Carlos Trouyet, a powerful entrepreneur, acquired half a million hectares of land held by Northwestern Railway, a company founded in 1909 that, under foreign ownership, consolidated Chihuahua's rail and timber industries. Bosques de Chihuahua's success came in no small measure thanks to President Miguel Alemán, who would become a silent partner in the venture.[6] Before leaving office, Alemán issued a presidential decree wherein the Mexican state bought the railway lines now under Bosques' control; this business deal helped provide Vallina and Trouyet with funds to expand the company's timber industry.[7] More important, in 1952 President Alemán granted Bosques a fifty-year concession of half a million acres on which the company would supply raw materials to three key paper and lumber businesses.[8] For generations prior, small-scale ranchers had inhabited this land as well as the 260,000 hectares Bosques bought from Northwestern Railway and now proceeded to enclose, partition, and sell. Arguing that the company constituted a latifundio, residents petitioned the government for ownership rights. Thus began a years-long struggle against an enterprise whose investing partners, in addition to the former president, included some of Chihuahua's most powerful men: Antonio Guerrero, a former military commander; Teófilo Borunda, the state's governor from 1956 to 1962; Tomás Valle, a businessman and state senator; and members of the Terrazas and Almeida families.[9]

If, on the one hand, Bosques de Chihuahua exemplified the crony capitalism that in Mexico lay at the heart of huge fortunes during the latter part of the twentieth century, on the other, the Ibarra family, who bought portions of the land and forcibly removed its occupants, epitomized the violence that undergirded this process.[10] Newspapers and federal agents reported a growing list of victims murdered by the Ibarras, whose terror methods also included rape. So common was their sexual violence against women that José Ibarra produced a noticeable crop of unacknowledged offspring.[11] The murders of prominent local activists at his hands would be an important catalyst of Chihuahua's popular unrest.

In 1949 organizations disenchanted with the government-controlled National Campesino Confederation formed the UGOCM and channeled that unrest into direct action. In the subsequent two decades, the UGOCM spearheaded three principal forms of struggle: local and federal elections; a defense of collective rights, especially as related to the ejido; and demands for the breakup of latifundios and distribution of land. The UGOCM was affiliated with the Popular Party (Partido Popular, PP), formed in 1948 by Vicente Lombardo Toledano, which grouped communists, reformists, and critics of the increasing reactionary tendencies of the Institutional Revolutionary Party (PRI) under President Alemán; members of the union's executive council also belonged to the party's national board. Prominent among them was Jacinto López, the UGOCM's secretary general, who in 1949 ran for governor of Sonora under the PP banner.[12] The party's and union's organizational structure provided networks that crisscrossed Mexico's northern states and frequently passed through Mexico City. The PP's focus on electoral strategy, however, would be a source of tension, as local leaders and rank-and-file members pushed for direct action. Some UGOCM members and teachers like Pablo Gómez and Arturo Gámiz, who ran for local office under the party's banner, would eventually become radicalized and ultimately insist on armed struggle.

Rural normales and other educational centers serving Chihuahua's poor became important hubs of party support. In 1960 the PP became the PPS, which together with its affiliate, the Popular Socialist Youth, enjoyed substantial teacher and student support.[13] Party literature and organizational strategy encouraged student involvement in campesino struggles.[14] But the PPS also found fertile ground because the teachers and students saw their own family history reflected in campesino battles for land. In addition to the rural normalistas from Saucillo and Salaices, students in Chihuahua City who attended the State Normal School, the Arts and Trade School, the Ladies' Industrial School, and the various Normal Night Schools became important participants in the mounting agrarian battle.[15] If students' poor background imbued them with a sensitivity to campesino grievances, boarding schools provided the space, and student associations the vehicle, for them to act on this sentiment. While Chihuahua's State Normal School lacked the institution-wide boarding-school component of the federal rural normales, it provided living quarters for low-income students who came from outside the capital. These dormitories were located in the same building as those for the Arts and Trade School and the Ladies' Industrial School.[16] In 1962 students from these three schools as well as the rural normales and numerous junior high schools formed the Chihuahua Student Federation. A portent of what was to come, their inaugural meeting was attended by three thousand delegates.[17]

"BOSQUES DE CHIHUAHUA, ASSASSINS"

The November 29, 1959, murder of Francisco Luján Adame, a rural teacher from Madera, triggered the unrest that shook Chihuahua for the following half decade. Killed in his home by a man later identified as Encarnación García, Luján Adame had been a regional secretary of the UGOCM and long assisted Madera's campesinos who sought ejido expansions. Madera residents never accepted the knife-wielding assailant as the lone murderer; they pointed instead to José Ibarra as the crime's intellectual author. Luján Adame traveled frequently to Mexico City to carry out paperwork on behalf of campesinos and denounced Bosques de Chihuahua agents who constantly harassed rural dwellers into vacating their lands.[18] His death drew the largest funeral procession in Madera's history, reported one state newspaper, as mourners emptied "the community in silent protest of the macabre act."[19] In the months that followed, demands for Bosques' expropriation merged with calls for justice over Luján Adame's murder.[20]

Before the assassination of Luján Adame, the region's campesinos had already faced a series of murders, many at the hands of the Ibarra brothers. For example, Ibarra henchmen had killed Anselmo Enríquez Quintana, a campesino who refused to give up his land. For this murder José Ibarra was indicted but never arrested. On September 4, 1959, his nephew, Rubén Ibarra, killed another teacher, Luis Mendoza. Six months later, Rubén's father, Florentino Ibarra, shot and killed Carlos Ríos, a Pima indigenous activist. Despite receiving an eight-year prison sentence, Florentino spent only three days in jail. José Ibarra, the most notorious of the family, had a murder record that dated back to at least 1942.[21] Despite this—or perhaps because of it—the state authorities let him command the military and state police, who terrorized the population by hanging campesinos from trees. Instead of a noose, Ibarra's men used a knot that would strangle but not kill their victims, referred to as *cordadas*. Federal intelligence agents reported such abuses, the support the Ibarras had from both state and federal forces, and their success in forcing many campesinos off their land.[22]

"Bosques de Chihuahua, Assassins," soon became a rallying cry as protests spread to the state capital.[23] There students, especially normalistas, held rallies in support of the sierra's campesinos. The youth articulated a clear connection to the agrarian struggle: they were the sons and daughters of campesinos, who were the land's "legitimate owners."[24] Arturo Gámiz, then a student at the Chihuahua State Normal School, delivered a moving speech. Offering a damning analysis of the country's situation, he ended with an impassioned plea: "The youth cannot allow their teachers to be murdered. On the contrary, the youth, as part of the people, must actively fight against injustice. Even though we are young, we worry about the fatherland's problems. We students are poor; we are the children of campesinos and workers. That's why we are here, asking the people to raise their voice in protest, demanding justice."[25] In asserting both their campesino origin and their status as youth "worr[ied] about the fatherland's problems," Chihuahua's students insisted on the link between the fate of campesinos and that of the nation. Normalistas especially positioned themselves as natural advocates of the rural poor. Such a responsibility resonated profoundly as a rallying cry for Chihuahua's students during the first half of the 1960s and would push many of them to the sort of decisions their grandparents had made during the revolution.

At the one-year anniversary of Luján Adame's murder, when the UGOCM organized a nine-day march from Madera to Chihuahua City, students were among the first to join campesino calls for land and justice. Designed to co-incide with López Mateos's visit to the state capital, the UGOCM protest led delegates to meet with the president and demand he expropriate Bosques' land and address the impunity behind Luján Adame's murder.[26] The president was unsympathetic. He criticized the marchers for their "unnecessary agitation" and inability to recognize that Bosques de Chihuahua was an "industry that benefited the nation" and dismissed calls to prosecute José Ibarra when the material perpetrator had already been imprisoned.[27]

"We have been subjected to all sorts of abuse," wrote Leonel Luján, son of the slain teacher, shortly afterward. In a public letter to Chihuahua governor Teófilo Borunda, Luján detailed the long history of abuse in Chihuahua's sierra, "not only assassinations . . . but the burning of our humble homes and eviction from land we possessed for more than fifty years."[28] Where President López Mateos saw agitation, normalistas saw the dignity of their families; where the president saw a prosperous company, normalistas saw an insult to the letter and spirit of agrarian legislation; and where the president saw a just criminal court system, normalistas saw another murdered activist. What kind of a future did such a system hold for poor youth?

Thus, the murder of Luján Adame, a rural teacher who had long denounced repression and fought for campesino rights, became a catalyst that drew normalistas into the center of a storm. For half a decade, together with campesinos and rural educators, they forged a movement bonded by a common origin and shared—almost sacred—constitutional rights: land and education. In the context of the 1960s, these twin principles increasingly provided the basis for a radical trajectory, one that reverberated with particular intensity at the rural normales, where the link between agrarian justice in the present and education's hope for the future constituted a founding principle.

ARTURO GÁMIZ AND PABLO GÓMEZ

Few figures personify the revolutionary essence of the committed rural teacher better than Arturo Gámiz and Pablo Gómez, even if they themselves were not schooled at rural normales. It was partly because of their charismatic leadership that hundreds of normalistas joined Chihuahua's agrarian struggle. Their legacy, like that of Genaro Vázquez and Lucio Cabañas in Guerrero, would become intimately linked to the narrative—both official and popular—of the rural normales. Gámiz's and Gómez's personal histories and political leadership gave them a strong presence among a cross section of Chihuahua's aggrieved population. Both came from a humble background in northern Mexico, both studied for a time in Mexico City, both became involved in the PPS, and both returned to Chihuahua. There they delivered their lives to agrarian justice.

Gómez and Gámiz were not the sole leaders of Chihuahua's 1960s agrarian struggle. Just as significant were campesinos like Álvaro Ríos and Salvador Gaytán, with whom Gómez and Gámiz shared similar life experiences.[29] The two teachers planned actions in concert with Ríos and Gaytán, and these campesino leaders profoundly shaped their ideology. Their relationship is an example of the dialectical nature of political consciousness. As much as the government and the media portrayed the agrarian unrest as stemming from teachers and normalistas who agitated the campesinos, poor rural folks were just as responsible for developing educators' consciousness. The attention to Gómez's and Gámiz's leadership here stems from my focus on rural normalismo. Partly because of these two teachers, who waged a struggle that bridged classroom and field, Chihuahua's normalistas could imagine and follow a revolutionary path. Their biographies are thus worth exploring. Each life is a measure of the dynamics that produced movement leaders in the context of broader social processes—migration, urbanization, schooling—taking place in midcentury Mexico.

Born in Durango in 1940, Gámiz came from a humble background, and there were several rural teachers in his extended family, who also had a tradition of involvement in local struggles.[30] Gámiz spent his early youth in Mexico City, where his family moved in 1950. There he attended the National Polytechnic Institute (Instituto Politécnico Nacional, IPN) and was active in the youth section of the PP. In 1956 IPN students went on strike demanding greater participation in school governance; the resignation of the director, whom they charged with being corrupt and autocratic; and increased funding for scholarships and school infrastructure. The movement reverberated nationally as schools across Mexico—including the rural normales—joined their strike.[31] As a student at the IPN, Gámiz participated in the mobilizations and distinguished himself as a skilled orator and sophisticated thinker.[32] The government ultimately responded to this strike with repression. In a prelude to Chihuahua governor Giner's attack on the state's normales, the army occupied IPN dormitories on September 23, 1956, forcibly removing students in the early morning hours.[33] Targeting dormitories was an effective strategy since these living quarters were important spaces of political organizing.

Soon after, Gámiz moved to Chihuahua and worked as a teacher in the municipality of Guerrero. He remained there for two years and in 1959 applied to Chihuahua's State Normal School, where he studied for two additional years.[34]

At the normal, Gámiz participated in student mobilizations, especially those in support of campesino struggles, including a November 1960 caravan from Madera to Chihuahua City. Gámiz's charisma, his political activism, and his passion for agrarian justice quickly made him an inspiration to other students, who followed his footsteps and joined campesino mobilizations. Tellingly, the agrarian leader Salvador Gaytán referred to him as "the young man who always brings a lot of students to the campesino marches."[35]

In 1962 Gámiz moved to Mineral de Dolores, a community on Chihuahua's border with Sonora. There he joined Gaytán, whom the community had elected as their representative. In a town that had not had a teacher in twenty-eight years—caciques were using the school as a stable—Gámiz set up a makeshift classroom in the town plaza, where he taught sixty-five children. Once he and Gaytán recovered and rebuilt the schoolhouse, they named it the Escuela Primaria Prof. Francisco Luján Adame, after the Madera teacher slain in 1959.[36] Mineral de Dolores had once been a prosperous town, but the foreign-owned mines had halted activities twenty years earlier, "taking with them all the wealth, leaving nothing but ruins, bare mountains, and nostalgia," wrote Gámiz. But the region's economic depression, he continued, "is not only due to the end of mining; there is another important reason: the formation and entrenchment of a *cacicazgo*, an empire of assassins."[37] Gámiz's work in Dolores followed a script straight out of the 1930s: build a school, teach the children, assess the community's needs, make them aware of their rights, and organize them to attain these rights. But, thirty years later, the SEP (Ministry of Public Education) wanted instructors whose work stayed within the classroom walls. Lázaro Cárdenas's stewards of social justice had little place in Cold War Mexico.

Two years later, jailed, Gámiz recounted his experience to Salvador del Toro Rosales, an agent from the attorney general's office whom the federal government sent to investigate the state's increasing protest and violence: "I am an unemployed normalista teacher. They took my job away long ago," Gámiz told Toro Rosales.

> How do I survive? Well, thanks to the help of campesinos. I teach their kids how to read and write, and in return they give me some food; and when they see I have no shoes, well, they buy me some; sometimes they give me the clothes they no longer wear. That's how I get by. . . . Living among rural folks, I learned of their fatigue and misery, and, as paradoxical as it may seem, authorities deny them the right to the soil they walk on, even though their parents and grandparents are the legitimate owners

of the roads, forests, and ranchos in the state of Chihuahua. . . . As soon as it became known that I helped campesinos, I was blacklisted and labeled a communist agitator.[38]

Reproduced years later by Toro Rosales, Gámiz's words may say as much about the young teacher as they do about Toro Rosales's reflection of the situation he was sent to investigate. Either way, Toro Rosales was clearly moved by Gámiz. If he had this effect on those from the establishment, it is no wonder he galvanized the students and campesinos around him.

Fourteen years his senior, Pablo Gómez was another important protagonist in the state's mobilization. Born in 1926 "to an agrarista campesino family," as his daughter Alma put it, his early life was one of poverty. In a region where temperatures can drop below freezing during the winter months, with no heating at home and few warm clothes, Gómez would take refuge in local cantinas, where he would sleep curled up atop a billiard table "until the bar closed," said his daughter. Like Gámiz, Gómez prepared for a teaching career at Chihuahua's State Normal School, where he met his wife, Alma Caballero, who also studied there. But Gómez's dream was to become a doctor, a career he would pursue in the early 1950s at the National Autonomous University of Mexico in the country's capital. Three of his five children were born during this time. To support his family, Gómez taught elementary school by day and attended medical school by night. After obtaining his medical degree, he chose to practice medicine in Flores Magón, a town in the northwestern part of Chihuahua where he knew several teachers at the rural normal. Unable to sustain a medical practice because he consistently treated poor patients for free, he supported his family by teaching at the rural normal.[39] In Flores Magón and later in Saucillo, where the rural normal moved in 1962, Gómez was always active in local campesino struggles and became a member of the PPS and a UGOCM delegate.[40] "During that whole process of campesino mobilizations, he, his brother, and other leaders faced repression," recalled Alma, who witnessed the new wounds that continually appeared on her father's body as his involvement intensified. "He had a scar from an attack with a glass bottle; his nose was broken; he had a stab wound in his back. He was detained several times. It was an environment of both generalized and selective repression. . . . His last time being jailed, I remember he told my mother, 'I prefer to die than to live under this repression.'"[41] Aside from the physical aggression Gómez suffered as state and federal forces dislodged him and other campesinos from land takeovers, Governor Giner, and eventually the SEP authorities, sought his transfer out of the state. Accusing him of inciting Saucillo's normalistas to participate in land invasions, the SEP reassigned him to Atequiza, Jalisco, in 1964.[42] Gómez quit rather than accept this transfer. He sought instead to move to Cuba with his family, but this plan was reportedly blocked by the upper echelons of the PPS.[43]

Alma described her home environment as liberal. "Four of the five of us [siblings] were baptized but only because my father liked having *compadres*. But we never went to church. We did not have a religious upbringing." As the years wore on and Alma's father became more involved in local land struggles, her home environment went from liberal to radical. The triumph of the Cuban Revolution in 1959 provided a framework of hope in a local context where striking injustice was punctuated by popular and dramatic acts of resistance. From a very young age, Alma remembered her father glued to their shortwave radio. "Every day, very early in the morning when I woke up, I'd hear my dad listening to Radio Habana. We'd hear speeches by Fidel and Che, all that." It was an atypical household, a situation Alma realized early on through the constant harassment she and her siblings suffered, especially when they moved from Flores Magón to Buenaventura, a town about forty-five miles away where Alma's father wanted to practice in the clinic of a surgeon he admired. "In spite of everything, the situation in Flores Magón was different because of the environment created by the normal. But in the Buenaventura valley, there was no counterweight; it was an incredibly reactionary town. We lived there for a year, and it was a very difficult time for us. My brother Pablo and I often had to take a taxi to school because on the streets they'd hound and throw stones at us for being communist." Alma searched for ways to fit in and thought church could be a venue: "I went to mass every Sunday, and on one Sunday, in his sermon, the priest began to explain that when, in an apple orchard, there is a rotten apple, if it's not removed in time, it will rot and contaminate the rest. Same with tomatoes, and I don't remember what other examples he used. Then he said: 'That's what happens in society. Sometimes there are people who can contaminate and ruin the rest of society. And these people need to be eliminated. In the case of this community, it is Pablo Gómez.'" Alma felt as if the earth had parted beneath her. "I felt afraid, anxious, and angry, but I didn't want to worry my parents, so I didn't say anything." But news travels fast in small towns. Before Alma even got home, her parents knew. Her father was furious and prohibited her from ever going back to church. "I was eleven. . . . That's when my religious life ended."[44]

In 1962, after a year of living in Buenaventura, the Gómez family again moved, this time to Delicias. Her father continued to teach at the rural normal, which had relocated from Flores Magón to Saucillo. There Alma began her studies in 1963. "I don't remember the moment nor the circumstances in which I decided to become a teacher. I think it was a very natural process. Since my childhood I had been close to the normal. My father was a teacher there. I would often stay in the dorms with the girls [*muchachas*]. . . . So I had a really close relationship with the normal. . . . I never even asked myself if I wanted to be a teacher; I just went straight to the normal." Alma Gómez, like her father, would be an important activist in Saucillo and in the 1970s joined a guerrilla movement.[45]

Gámiz's and Gómez's humble beginnings, travel to urbanized centers, social mobility through education, struggle for an elusive agrarian justice, and state persecution exemplify the broader social experience of many rural normalistas. That students from Salaices and Saucillo became important protagonists in their struggles intertwined these teachers' legacies with that of the rural normales. In the pantheon of unofficial heroes, Gómez and Gámiz stand alongside figures like Rubén Jaramillo, Valentín Campa, Demetrio Vallejo, Othón Salazar, Lucio Cabañas, Genaro Vázquez, and Ramón Danzós Palomino—popular figures who fought the PRI's authoritarianism and paid a heavy price. Gómez and Gámiz are ignored by official history—except to illustrate that rural normales have a subversive tradition. From below, however, that tradition looks more like dignified resistance to a long history of injustice.

FAMILY HISTORIES, LEGACIES OF RESISTANCE, AND PATHS OF STRUGGLE

Chihuahua's 1960s agrarian struggle, with its appeals to campesino rights, its direct action, and a leadership that invoked the Cuban Revolution, provided rural normalistas ample opportunities to act. Education officials might no longer have advocated for an activist teacher, but in places like Chihuahua, the UGOCM's struggle did. Those who heeded such calls came to understand the struggle through ideology as much as through their family's history and poverty. For example, José Luis Aguayo Álvarez, who studied at the rural normal of Salaices and in 1965 became head of the school's student association, recalled his early political awakening: "Our family was very poor. . . . Early on I perceived the social division, we were not all the same. And since my uncles were active in the struggle—they were agraristas—they'd emphasize to us, to their kids, that one had to be committed to the people."[46] Such personal memories could grow deep roots at the rural normales, institutions whose founding logic was to improve the campesino condition. As José Ángel Agu-irre Romero, also from Salaices, stated, "We were educated to give ourselves wholeheartedly to the campesino causes. And in that time [the 1950s] there was a lot of caciquismo in the state; there were huge latifundios here. One latifundio, Bosques de Chihuahua, made up almost half the state. So land-petition groups began to emerge, and we couldn't be detached from such causes."[47] Aguirre, whose family had received land in 1923 as a result of the revolution, described in painstaking detail the hardship his family endured even with such reform:

> The conditions were almost worse [than in the hacienda where they pre-viously worked] because they got land but no protection. That land had been expropriated from another hacienda. . . . They did not even have a plow to farm and had to break the land with a pick and shovel and culti-vate small plots of corn, beans, squash, whatever they could. But the yield was quite small; some had to go work in a nearby town at the hacienda of El Sauz, where a few got jobs. But the majority went to the nearby sierra to cut wood and collect it in little carts. Then they sold it in Chihuahua City. It would take four days to go, fill a little cart, come back, and sell it. They'd receive six pesos, six pesos they would use to buy some corn or beans; there was no hope of buying meat or anything like that.[48]

Bosques de Chihuahua would later enclose the forested lands, which many of Chihuahua's inhabitants used to supplement their household income. And like Aguayo, Aguirre would also become head of Salaices's student federa-tion, the Mexican Federation of Socialist Campesino Students (FECSM), an experience that likely reinforced and politicized the memories of his family history.

From a different social sector but with a similar story, Manuel Arias Delgado, who came from a Chihuahua mining family, vividly recalled the harsh conditions under which his father and his grandfather labored in a U.S.-owned mine. Black lung disease, mining accidents, and wages that hardly supported a family of nine children marked Arias's early life. To help sup-port his family, Arias worked various odd jobs, including as a gardener in a U.S. neighborhood in Chihuahua. "That neighborhood was straight out of a postcard: there was grass, pools, fine-bred dogs. . . . The *gringitos* looked like they were from a Gerber commercial. . . . My toy was a metal wheel that I would push around with a hanger. And they had bicycles they left lying on the grass. They had grass! Here we had rocks. There they had a pool; here we didn't even have drinking water. And I thought, 'Why such inequality?' I was the example of poverty in the middle of an insulting abundance." In that abundance Arias found the explanation of his own poverty: "They have what I lack. And why do they have this money? Well, because they took it from my father and his compañeros. That's it, an unequal distribution." It is no surprise to hear Arias articulate this Marxist labor theory of value. Indeed, he characterized the rural normales as "centers of socialist ideological formation." Students had a mobile revolutionary library: "That's where we became acquainted with Marx, Engels, and Lenin. It was a mobile dynamic library. These were books whose pages were all loose because of so much use."[49]

Out of a student body with this background, figures like Gámiz and Gómez engaged in the state's agrarian movement. And while such personal histories alone would not spur political struggle, the rural normales' own radical culture, the 1960s political effervescence (especially among youth), and the inspiration of the 1959 Cuban Revolution created a propitious context for rural normalistas to act on their institutions' long-proclaimed ideals. Doing so enhanced an already radical tradition. It also aggravated the authorities, who saw the alliance among teachers, campesinos, and students as proof that social unrest was the work of agitators rather than the result of unfulfilled or betrayed revolutionary promises. As normalistas invoked the Cuban example, they joined youth throughout Latin America who were hungry for alternative political projects and expanded the notion of the possible. U.S. aggression against the island served to confirm the righteous nature of the Cuban road.

Across the rural normales, organizations like the FECSM circulated images of bearded revolutionaries constructing a new society with agrarian and educational reforms at the center. The island's revolution itself offered new material for political study circles. Silvina Rodríguez, a student from the rural normal of Saucillo, for example, recalled, "We'd have meetings on Fridays, and at those meetings Prof. Pablo Gómez would bring a map and explain to us how the Cuban Revolution was going, who had advanced in what moment and on what day. So Fridays we'd hear how events had unfolded for the week."[50] Her classmate, Alma Gómez Caballero, likewise remembered, "On May 23, 'Students' Day,' there were a series of activities, among them a parade with various floats. And there is a picture that must have been taken in 1961, where on one of those floats the girls are dressed with beards and in olive green clothing. That was the influence of the Cuban Revolution, and how it came all the way over here."[51] A few years later, the 1967 graduating class at this normal voted to call itself the "Castro Ruz Class," a name they wanted printed on their diplomas.[52]

The enthusiasm for the Cuban Revolution, moreover, provided additional opportunities for alliances between students from different schools. As was the case throughout Mexico, Chihuahua's students protested the Bay of Pigs invasion, and on April 24, 1961, Chihuahua's State Normal School and Cuba's Friendship Society organized a demonstration condemning the U.S. aggression. Hundreds gathered in the state capital. The event turned violent when a fight broke out between demonstrators and members of the Catholic Youth Association, who, according to the student protesters, threw tear gas bombs into the crowd. *El Heraldo*, a newspaper long disparaging of social protest, reported that the "pseudo students" in a "commie romp" had instigated the violence, unprovoked, by beating an innocent bystander who later died from his injuries. In a premeditated act, continued the piece, demonstrators then vandalized the newspaper's headquarters. In a tone characteristic of the official press's portrayal of rural normalistas, the newspaper asserted that the demonstration's organizers, "in cahoots with the teachers of the rural normales of Salaices and Flores Magón [later Saucillo], nests of permanent agitation, brought irresponsible students to this city with instructions to deface *El Heraldo*'s building."[53] Normalista participants insisted that the right-wing youth had provoked the violence. An agent provocateur, they maintained, threw a Molotov cocktail into the crowd. The reported death, according to one normalista, had not taken place but was made-up government propaganda.[54] The magazine *Política* later reported that the bishop, Monseigneur Espino Porras, had mobilized Sinarquistas (an ultranationalist Catholic organization founded in the late 1930s) and members of the right-wing National Action Party to attack the demonstrators.[55] Regardless of who triggered the violence, the skirmish illustrates how high passions ran when it came to Cuba. Just as it inspired the left, it created fear among the right. It also provided a convenient new phantom that the church used to relaunch its critique of secular education.[56]

"All were brought from the rural normal of Salaices," *El Heraldo* headlined its article on the six students arrested during the day's events.[57] That those apprehended were all from Salaices was likely a coincidence. A group from this rural normal had parked their truck by the newspaper offices, and police nabbed them as they returned to their vehicle.[58] But *El Heraldo*'s reference to the rural normales as "nests of permanent agitation" and allegations that their students were brought to the city—implying they were willing troublemakers—are telling examples of the long-standing vilification of these schools. This narrative demonized rural normalistas, but it did not demobilize them. On the contrary, the arrests galvanized Chihuahua's students, who in the following weeks vigorously protested the students' detention and ultimately gained their release.[59]

"Nothing has infused the oppressed of the Americas with the same hope and trust in the future as the Cuban Revolution," proclaimed Arturo Gámiz.[60] Rural normalistas still preserved socialist education as an ethos to articulate notions of justice, but to it they added another layer. Normalistas mounted increasingly radical critiques of the Mexican government, which had little tolerance for socialist appeals at home, its defense of Cuban self-determination notwithstanding. The Cuban Revolution had an influence in the rural normales, a Salaices graduate would later write. "Leftists groups that went beyond the liberal Cardenista politics characteristic of the boarding schools began to proliferate."[61] This was not an uncontested process. While persistent, the notion of the politicized teacher carried with it certain contradictions. There was an inherent tension between the prospects of upward mobility a teaching career afforded the poor and the charge to serve the people. For teachers in training, moreover, the political mobilizations themselves triggered a range of debates—many of them contentious—about goals and strategies. As Arias put it, "We had everything: from the honest radicals to the radical demagogues. . . . And from there the indifferent ones: 'I came to study, and when I graduate, I'll be a teacher, locked inside my little school. I'll have my family, and the world can turn as it may.' Between these two perspectives, there was a broad spectrum of different character profiles."[62]

As with any politicized sector, rural normalistas were usually divided. In the context of 1960s Chihuahua, these divisions manifested themselves in two ways. First, some students thought that at the rural normal, their responsibility was to complete their teaching preparation and *then*, degree in hand, aid and participate alongside campesinos. To that end, they thought political participation should be confined to issues involving resources needed to complete their studies. A second source of contention was the form that political participation itself should take. Some advocated peaceful and legal mobilizations, while others sought more dramatic actions, ones capable of precipitating a revolutionary uprising.

Gámiz himself addressed the matter and rejected the notion that normalistas best served the cause by first obtaining their degree. "If the goal is to serve the people," he wrote, "it is necessary to participate in their struggle, and here a degree has no relevance. One does not serve the people as a professional, one serves them as a revolutionary, and no university provides a degree for this cause." To mount separate struggles, argued Gámiz, to think that it should be "students alongside students, campesinos alongside campesinos, workers alongside workers, and men alongside men, is to raise a Great Wall of China between one another. That benefits only the oligarchy." Wanting a career was not in itself negative, Gámiz clarified; "collective interests could combine with family and personal ones. The danger, the real betrayal, is the pretext it gives to abandon the ranks of the proletariat, the group [whose taxes and labor] fund the professional schools."[63]

Gámiz made such declarations as he reflected on the First Gathering of the Sierra, an event he, along with other teachers like Pablo Gómez and his brother Raúl, as well as the campesino leaders Álvaro Ríos and Salvador Gaytán, organized in an effort to broaden and define Chihuahua's agrarian movement. It was held on October 7–12, 1963, in Cebadilla de Dolores in the municipality of Madera, and the organizers invited campesinos, students, and workers to discuss "the youths' role in resolving the general problems of the people."[64] The attendees were housed by the area's campesinos or camped in the community's elementary school. The meeting's chosen location was itself significant. First, it signaled to the sierra's caciques that land-hungry campesinos were not alone in their struggle.[65] Indeed, with representatives from eighty-five different associations in attendance, organizers hoped to expand the movement beyond Chihuahua.[66] Second, for students from the state capital, this was a chance to venture beyond the urban areas that had predominated as protest sites. Indeed, the ten-hour walk to the Cebadilla ejido was in itself a test of will, a small taste of the physically demanding nature of radical action.

According to government informants, about seventy-five people journeyed to Cebadilla de Dolores, where they were received by sixty-four ejidatarios.[67] The delegates discussed an array of topics ranging from the forging of closer connections with countries of the socialist block, to a condemnation of U.S. imperialism, to the role they should play in Mexico's upcoming presidential elections. Shortly after the First Gathering of the Sierra, Gámiz issued his own theoretical piece discussing students' revolutionary potential. Published in the weekly magazine *Índice*, Gámiz's text alluded to a point of contention within the Salaices student delegation.[68] The students of this rural normal, he maintained, held the "curious and idealistic view that before making the revolution and taking power, they must teach the masses ethics." As would be expected, continued Gámiz, other students as well as the campesinos, themselves schooled by years of struggle, rejected this notion. If students wanted to be the vanguard, asserted Gámiz, they had to act deliberately and with abnegation, "not with absurd notions that the student movement was pure and untainted."[69]

The discussions held at the First Gathering of the Sierra reflected wider debates over strategy. While figures like Gámiz, Gómez, and Gaytán recognized the need for electoral struggle—indeed, they were members of the PPS and had run for local office—they increasingly clashed with the national leadership. State leaders like Jacinto López and national ones like Vicente Lombardo Toledano demanded moderation and, in certain instances, opposed grassroots direct action, yet the rank and file grew impatient. In fact, this meeting may well have marked a point of divergence between the radicals and those they regarded as reformist.[70]

"RURAL *PROFESORCILLOS* RILING UP THE HENHOUSE"

In the months after the First Gathering of the Sierra, Chihuahua witnessed a significant number of campesino land invasions. Coordinated and led by the UGOCM and with the heavy participation of rural normalistas, these actions were meant to dramatize Mexico's land concentration and to pressure the agrarian authorities to resolve pending distribution petitions. Hundreds of campesino families occupied vacant land—sometimes simultaneously, sometimes in relay fashion—until the authorities removed them. While for the urban marches and demonstrations the press and government agents cited the participation of the student bodies from several professional schools, in the land invasions the authorities dwelled on the involvement or leadership of students from the rural normales. This dynamic solidified the reputation of rural normales as particularly radical. After all, rural teachers—the official narrative went—were agitating the otherwise quiescent population of the countryside. Based on this logic, rather than addressing campesino demands for land, the state sought to contain student-teacher involvement, a tactic that, to the more radically inclined, confirmed the need for armed struggle.

The 1964 land takeovers thus paved the road to armed struggle. Campesinos from the northwestern municipality of Janos marked the New Year by occupying the property of the cattle rancher Hilario Gabilondo. They remained there for twenty days until the military violently removed them.[71] Denouncing the army's unrestrained cruelty, in which soldiers beat women and children with their bayonets and rifle butts, UGOCM leaders stated that if "those responsible were not punished, the campesinos and the people would mete out justice by their own hand."[72] Deaf to such warnings, Governor Giner declared that future invasions would be "repressed with no [special] considerations and the full rigor of the law."[73] Meant to instill fear and deter future land takeovers, such threats had little effect, and February marked a particularly intense month of land invasions. Chihuahua appeared like a game of checkers, with normalistas and campesinos invading lands and the army removing them, while new invasions took place in other parts of the state. On February 19 alone, the state witnessed at least eight simultaneous land takeovers. In the municipalities of Saucillo, Delicias, Lázaro Cárdenas, and Meoqui, reported intelligence agents, students from the rural normales led or advised the invaders. "Young ladies from Saucillo dressed as men interspersed themselves among campesino ranks," read one such report.[74] Reacting to the ubiquity of rural normalistas in these actions, Benjamín Fuentes, assistant director of teacher-training education, personally visited Saucillo, urging the students to end their "agitating and disorienting actions."[75] Officials from the SEP tried again and again to dissuade Saucillo students from participating and advised educators to use "moral suasion and take advantage of the affection the students had for their teachers in order to orient and control them."[76] Some were harsher, instructing all rural normal directors to prevent students from joining political acts by threatening them with sanctions.[77] Teachers at these schools, many themselves sympathetic to the campesino struggle, countered by citing students' commonsense notions of justice, "an ideology that leads them to act in favor of the humble classes. . . . While they listen respectfully, they had an agreed-upon course of action to which they were intractably committed."[78] The decision on whether to expel those who chose to act on their commitment soon passed into the hands of Education Minister Torres Bodet.[79]

As SEP officials sought to control normalistas through institutional reprimands, state authorities jailed campesino leaders. Neither strategy worked. On the contrary, the state's heavy hand gave them further reason to mobilize. In Saucillo, for example, rural normalistas congregated outside the municipal jail where the authorities had detained and charged several UGOCM leaders with property dispossession and criminal association. The students remained there until late in the night and the following day organized a demonstration in Saucillo's town plaza. Intelligence agents reported 1,500 people in attendance.[80]

Protests soon extended to the state capital. On February 22, students from several normales and one junior high school gathered in Chihuahua City's central plaza demanding the freedom of jailed UGOCM leaders and the resolution of the state's agrarian problems. As the event unfolded, a group of between two hundred and three hundred students made their way to the agrarian offices, with about fifty of them forcing their way into the building. There they demanded that the administrator phone national headquarters.

The agent instead called security forces. When the students refused to vacate the agrarian offices, the SWAT team forced them out with tear gas. The authorities detained thirty-five students and hauled them off to the nearby government offices for processing. In a city center now guarded by municipal police, the secret service, and the SWAT team, students gathered in the city plaza demanding the release of their peers. By then, their numbers had swelled, perhaps the result of reinforcements from "outside normales," noted one newspaper. After the students refused to heed General Manuel Mendoza's orders to disperse, the police fired some thirty tear gas canisters, leading to a prolonged skirmish instead of the desired quiescence.[81] And here the general was acting with restraint: "If it were a different time," he later boasted to a federal agent, he would have beat up these "insolent and disrespectful youngsters. . . . There would be none of this nonsense that because they are students we can't touch them."[82]

While the general decried the protection afforded by student status, students themselves invoked their campesino identity. As they were corralled and detained, they shouted, "We are sons and daughters of campesinos and won't remain indifferent to the injustices in the countryside."[83] The students, almost all under the age of eighteen, insisted they had no leaders and had taken action of mutual accord. The authorities later released thirty of the detained but charged the older participants with inciting the younger students. Among the five people accused of forced entry, attack on the general communication lines, injury, and armed assault was Carlos Herrera, a teacher from Ciudad Juárez and a former student of the rural normal of Salaices.[84] Herrera declared that "he defended the interest of the campesino class that, with no real advocates, had in desperation turned to the student youth."[85] The student-campesino link thus resulted not only from family connections but from students' social responsibility, which they emphasized to show how badly the revolution had failed the countryside.

With a maddening disregard for reality, Governor Giner declared that in Chihuahua there were no latifundios. The increasing unrest was the work of "rural *profesorcillos* [no-good teachers] riling up the henhouse." Accordingly, he moved to treat the symptom, not the disease: he requested that the SEP close Chihuahua's rural normales "because they are veritable serpents' nests, complete communist nests." If their closure were approved, boasted Giner, he would "turn them into pig farms and oust all the lazy students; those who want to work can raise pigs."[86] State authorities were especially disparaging of female normalistas. In an explicitly gendered critique of Saucillo students, one agent described how they "slept in the fields alongside campesinos with no regard to the honor lady students should preserve."[87] Mendoza, the same military general who lamented that he could not beat students in the ways of yesteryear, declared about female participants, "They are like those lowlife women from the streets. . . . What are those girls doing with campesinos out in the hamlets? . . . What are they doing far from home at night, at dawn?"[88] Not to be outdone, the governor mocked the female students when they protested his attempts to close their normal: "Why do they want boarding schools if they like to sleep with campesinos in the field[?]" he declared.[89] So pervasive were these attacks on female normalistas' morals that the UGOCM felt compelled to protest—if paternalistically—against the numerous allegations. "Regarding the female students who have supported us," read an UGOCM statement, "we see them not as *soldaderas* [women who fought in the revolution] but as our daughters, and as such we have offered them what is at our disposal: our sincerity and, above all else, our profound respect and admiration."[90]

Federal authorities, for their part, were increasingly alarmed by rural normalista participation. Schools like Saucillo and Salaices, one intelligence report stated, "are graduating teachers who, deforming their educational and social function, constitute real problems when they start teaching in their assigned communities. Their attitudes are ones of anarchy and cause confusion and disorientation, especially among campesino groups."[91] Two months after the SEP's assistant director had visited the schools, a SEP commission returned, this time headed by the normales' general director himself. The director scolded students and their instructors, stating that their actions were detrimental not only to the profession but to the nation. He had believed earlier claims about their political participation to be exaggerations but now proposed assigning Salaices and Saucillo graduates to positions outside Chihuahua. Within the state, he asserted, they had too many ideological links with "communist cells and extremist groups," code words for campesinos demanding land restitution.[92]

Everywhere in Chihuahua, it seemed, teachers and normalistas were at the center of campesino unrest. Their storming of the agrarian offices in the state's capital represented the final straw after months of protest, declared Governor Giner. He vowed no more tolerance and promised to "energetically repress all acts that encouraged the violation of our laws."[93] Before he could make good on such threats, the federal government stepped in. The state's unrest had reached such levels that in late February 1964 the attorney general's office sent two officers to Chihuahua. To take stock of the situation, the lead investigator, Salvador del Toro Rosales, met with state authorities as well as students. His memoirs reveal a dismay with Giner and his cabinet, whom he characterized as ignorant and crass. For Gámiz—brought from jail to meet with Toro Rosales—he conveyed admiration. Less sympathetic to Gómez, whom he portrayed as manipulating campesinos, Toro Rosales recognized the unjust nature of the situation, though not the critical level it had reached.[94] In a press conference, he soon announced the liberation of the detained students, teachers, and campesinos and declared that the federal government would dispatch a team of agronomists to study the disputed lands. Careful not to legitimate popular protest, he emphasized that campesino petitions would be processed as a measure of justice, not as a response to their "agitation."[95] For a certain group of teachers and campesinos, this was too little too late.

A DEEPENING CRISIS

The first signs of guerrilla activity came at the end of February 1964. With Gámiz in jail, a group close to him burned a bridge along Bosques de Chihuahua's industrial road. Calling themselves the Popular Guerrilla Group (Grupo Popular Guerrillero, GPG), atop the rubble they left a message reading, "We burned this bridge to demand the freedom of campesinos and students and the resolution of the agrarian problem."[96] A few days later, GPG members killed the cacique Florentino Ibarra to avenge the murder of the campesino leader Carlos Ríos, whom Ibarra had shot in cold blood because of Ríos's refusal to abandon his land.[97] On April 12, in Dolores, the group detonated homemade bombs on the Ibarras' property, destroying the family's radio transmitter. This site, which state authorities used as a command center, would again come under guerrilla attack on July 15, 1964, when the GPG surprised the very group charged with tracking them down. There the guerrilla members captured the five state agents led by Rito Caldera Zamudio, a former Ibarra family henchman. After a prolonged discussion, the guerrillas decided to spare the state agents' lives, taking only their arms and ammunition.[98] In response, Governor Giner commissioned the army to join in pursuing the guerrillas. He also advised José Ibarra, the brother of the slain Florentino, to leave the state for his own safety.[99]

In the state capital, the political tension also intensified. In early April 1964, violence broke out in Chihuahua City at an election rally for Gustavo Díaz Ordaz. After the presidential candidate spoke before a crowd that, according to intelligence agents, numbered thirty thousand people, the normalista José Mariñelarena stormed the stage and began an impassioned speech enumerating student and campesino grievances. As security agents moved to cut the microphone, many in the crowd chanted, "Let him speak." Audience members, including campesinos sitting in the front row, fought to hear the student. They threw their folding chairs at security agents, forcing Mariñelarena's release. The normalista then led the crowd to Díaz Ordaz's hotel—located a block from the plaza. There the unrest continued as rocks, sticks, and wood pieces flew from all sides, one striking Díaz Ordaz himself. Not long after, as protesters and Díaz Ordaz supporters battled it out, someone set the stage ablaze. The adjacent Municipal Palace also caught fire. Eventually, a military dispatch arrived, emptied the plaza, and "took control of a large swath of the city."[100]

Students from Salaices and Saucillo "planned the events that took place during Gustavo Díaz Ordaz's campaign visit to the city of Chihuahua," an intelligence agent later reported.[101] Governor Giner, too, blamed the rural normales, though he charged the shiftless teachers with equal culpability.[102] The day's events initiated a hardening of the government's position as Giner sent the army to occupy the Salaices and Saucillo campuses, where, according to students, soldiers had orders to beat or jail anyone attempting to leave. The governor cordoned off an additional area, instructing the state's public transit not to allow students to board. The situation, the students declared, evoked Porfirian times.[103]

The government's understanding of such unrest—as conveyed through intelligence sources—was simplistic at best. Reports dwell on what leaders, political organizations, or subversive ideology led teachers, students, and campesinos to protest. Some reports pointed to José Santos Valdés, the supervisor of Mexico's northern rural normales, as the one pulling the strings. From his residence in Torreón, Coahuila, he reportedly controlled the directors of Saucillo and Salaices and teachers like Pablo Gómez. Since Santos Valdés oversaw student stipends in the amount of 1.5 to 2 million pesos, he used this money, implied one agent, to support political activity. Rural normal directors and their teachers, the majority of whom sympathized with the PPS, according to intelligence agents, influenced the political ideology of the students, inciting or allowing them to participate in land invasions.[104] The composite picture is an upward spiral of blame: older students brainwashed younger ones; teachers brainwashed their normalista pupils; together they manipulated campesinos into protest. This all occurred under the aegis of an old socialist guard of normal teachers and directors, the most prominent of whom was Santos Valdés.

As tensions mounted, rumors circulated that the next president would close twenty of the country's rural normales. As it turned out, these accounts were not that far off the mark, but for now the SEP feared that closing the institutions would provoke too much resistance.[105] Governor Giner was less apprehensive and closed normales and dormitories under his jurisdiction. In the cities of Ojinaga, Parral, Juárez, Saucillo, and Chihuahua, the governor closed the Normal Night Schools, arguing they had served their purpose. In a state with an excess of teachers, reported an article announcing the closure, there was no reason to maintain these schools.[106] Curiously, the same front page of *El Heraldo* that explained the closure by citing an overabundance of educators included—two columns over—an article about the number of un-filled teaching positions the state faced when the federal government failed to send the teachers it promised.[107] Holding that dormitories constituted sites of promiscuity and homosexuality and inhibited learning, the governor also closed the dormitories of the State Normal School of Chihuahua and those of the Arts and Trade School and the Ladies' Industrial School.[108]

Youth did not accept these measures without a fight: the State Normal School quickly declared a strike. Seeking to prevent the rural normales from joining, the local authorities postponed the start of classes, arguing that the buildings had to be repaired, a lie that students did not let pass uncon-tested. Once classes started, the assistant director of the rural normales again traveled to Saucillo and Salaices, urging students not to support the strike, declaring that the leaders' intent was to create "a climate of agi-tation that would harm their studies."[109] When the rural normal of Saucillo planned consecutive work stoppages and invited campesinos from the re-gion to attend their demonstrations, the police inspector general ordered the interception of any vehicles carrying campesinos to Saucillo.[110] The teachers' union joined its voice to the protest. They criticized Governor Giner for un-dermining the revolution's principles and pointed out that while the govern-ment closed institutions serving the poor, the number of private schools was rising.[111]

The student protest did not succeed in preserving the Normal Night Schools, nor in saving the dormitories of the Chihuahua State Normal School, the Arts and Trade School, and the Ladies' Industrial School. Nonetheless, students ended their strike in December 1964 when the state government agreed to fund alternative student housing, subsidize rent, ex-pand medical care, provide scholarships for the students of the closed eve-ning normales so they could attend private schools, and refrain from retal-iation against students, teachers, and families who supported the strike.[112]

By the year's end, the state of Chihuahua faced a critical situation. Blinded by their focus on teacher and student culpability, state authorities had fueled the growing unrest. In the sierra, a teacher-campesino contingent had taken justice into their own hands; the state capital was the scene of constant demonstrations, some with violent outcomes; and the normales were either on strike or under military occupation. While the federal government seemed poised to implement some reform, the choice of presidential candidate augured the ominous times ahead.

THE MADERA ATTACKS

In April 1965 Miguel Quiñónez, a graduate from the rural normal of Salaices who now taught in the Sierra Tarahumara, sent a letter to Javier Flores, also a rural teacher and Salaices graduate. The missive invited Flores to a series of talks, scheduled for later that year and taking place in either Saucillo or Salaices. Flores was to exercise extreme caution in the matter and share the information only with compañeros in whom he had the utmost trust since "it regarded illegal methods of struggle."[113] In his two years as a teacher, Quiñónez had undertaken an economic survey of the region, documented community needs, organized a cooperative, and fought alongside the ejidatarios of Ariseáchic in defense of their land. The portion of his salary that he did not send to his parents he used to finance trips to Mexico City's agrarian offices, where he and other community members sought federal intervention in the region's pressing land problems.[114] "Miguel's drive was palpable," recalled Flores, his fellow teacher. "Rumors reached us about the conflicts throughout the state, particularly in the Sierra. We knew of the problems besieging the normal of Saucillo. Campesinos continued to fight for land, and normalistas stood alongside them. Miguel had already expressed the need to take a position, to change the situations of the ejidos, especially the poorest ones. We had beautiful discussions, ones that illustrated and helped me understand the state of the world, the country, the region."[115]

Quiñónez was born in Durango, the fifth of nine children in a campesino family. He had long been a good student, scoring at the top of the eight hundred applicants who took the Salaices entrance exam in 1957. Possessing great discipline and a calm temperament, he continued to stand out academically and socially at the normal, where he headed several student groups, including the school's FECSM. "He was radical in his thoughts and actions," wrote Santos Valdés, "and even though he was happy and cordial and displayed a sense of camaraderie, when it came to ideological issues or political theory, he was stubborn, tenacious, persistent. If it concerned what he believed was a just political view, he willingly sacrificed a long friendship." Quiñónez had participated in Chihuahua's numerous mobilizations and hoped the state's leftist groups could form a unified coalition, one strong enough to effect change.[116] Instead, the latter part of 1964 witnessed a slowdown in the land mobilizations with which the year had begun. State repression was indeed having an effect. In January 1965 Quiñónez and three other rural normalistas addressed a manifesto to "students of the rural normales, their alumni and parents association, and to all worker, campesino, and student revolutionary organizations." Mexico, declared the text, was dominated by *latifundistas* and despite repeated petitions that often took twenty years to process, campesinos remained empty-handed. In light of this situation, the writers declared their commitment to revolutionary struggle and appealed to the students, whom they urged to join the workers and campesinos in a movement against the bourgeoisie. "It has been the youth, students," noted the manifesto, "who in one way or another have bravely initiated the great liberation movements in the world." The declaration addressed rural normalistas specifically, urging them to reflect on this assessment "and, whether you agree or not, pursue the complete liberation of our class, without giving up, much less betraying it."[117]

The text was an example of the type of radicalization taking hold within a small group of students, teachers, and campesinos who had participated in Chihuahua's land struggle. Alluding to the reformist view that Salaices delegates expressed during the sierra's First Gathering, the declaration condemned that position, characterizing it as "diametrically opposed to the principles and revolutionary traditions that rural normalistas had always been proud of." Such an attitude, continued the text, resulted from the influence of previously progressive SEP authorities—including Santos Valdés—who had sown fear among the student body, warning that continued agitation alongside campesinos would deliver "a death sentence to the rural normales."[118]

Previous ideological divides became tactical ones as the small guerrilla group sought to lay the groundwork for armed insurrection. The resolutions of the Second Gathering that took place on Durango's northern border with Chihuahua are a good example of this radicalization. Organizers chose this location partly as a show of solidarity with the six hundred families of that region who had been fighting for the redistribution of the latifundio of Torreón de Cañas.[119] Intelligence agents reported seven hundred people there, "all campesinos along with some students from the rural normales of Chihuahua and Durango."[120] The organizers' own resolutions listed twelve different student, campesino, indigenous, normalista, and teacher organizations in attendance.[121] If, two years earlier, the First Gathering's resolutions expressed a frustration with peaceful means, the Second Gathering's

Five Resolutions foregrounded the path of armed struggle. From a Marxist perspective, the text discussed imperialism, Third World liberation struggles, Mexican history, the failures of its 1910 revolution, and campesinos' revolutionary potential. In a clear allusion to Ernesto "Che" Guevara's writings on guerrilla warfare, this last resolution, entitled "The Only Path Forward," made clear that the conditions for revolution could be created, even if by only fifteen or twenty guerrillas. "The struggle will be very long, one counted not in years but in decades. That's why it's necessary to begin at once, while young, to gain the qualities that only come from years of action," outlined the document.[122] The guerrilla group would indeed remain small. As became increasingly clear, the teacher, student, and campesino participants in Chihuahua's agrarian struggle were sympathetic to those in arms, but few were ready to make the revolutionary leap themselves.

Graduates of Saucillo and Salaices provided pivotal support networks that sustained the guerrillas in the Sierra Tarahumara, a striking vertical landscape with jutting canyons in a mountain range whose peaks climb to over nine thousand feet. In fact, a whole network of rural teachers coalesced in this sierra.[123] Javier Flores, who taught in the municipality of Guerrero after graduating from Salaices, remembers the specific task Quiñónez assigned him: "I was to go to all the communities near Heredia y Anexas, whether on horseback, by foot—however I could. I would speak with the ejidatarios, the campesinos, the region's indigenous people, asking them to shelter the guerrillas and provide them cover if they needed to quickly escape, found themselves isolated, or needed any other kind of help. Everyone offered food for one or two people, one or two horses, and, of course, hiding places in the sierra's caves."[124] José Ángel Aguirre Romero, another Salaices graduate who taught in the region, remembered that people he did not even know sought him out on the recommendation of Gómez or Gámiz. Aguirre helped with logistical matters and provided additional contacts. "I never got involved directly but [when they left], knowing that they never had any money, we'd reach into our pockets and take out twenty pesos; that was a lot in those days." Aguirre would further offer, "You don't have a place to stay? You can sleep here." Asked to participate in the attack on Madera, Aguirre rejected the invitation. He remembered telling Quiñónez, "Look at the conditions! You're asking me to come along, and I never even knew I was part of the plan. I've never even handled a weapon. If that's the state of everyone else, think about it, they will kill you all."[125] That was the last time Aguirre saw Quiñónez, who left angry, frustrated by his friend's refusal to join the planned attack on Madera.

Because of its dramatic nature, the September 23, 1965, guerrilla attack on Madera's military barracks has received a great degree of attention, often obscuring the long and widespread mobilizations from which it emerged.[126] It was indeed a daring, if suicidal, undertaking. Conceived by teachers and campesino leaders who had been key figures in Chihuahua's land struggle since 1959, the assault followed the logic of the guerrillas' previous clandestine actions, especially the successful July 1964 ambush in Mineral de Dolores. The planned Madera assault was to involve between thirty and forty participants, twenty of whom had received military training from a former army captain in Mexico City.[127] Madera's choice was both strategic and symbolic. The town lay at the heart of the region's long struggle against caciques, the guerrillas had the population's sympathy, and the region's mountainous terrain afforded good cover. The plan was straightforward: overpower the military barracks, expropriate the local bank's funds, and issue a radio proclamation publicizing their revolutionary principles. Their success would motivate groups throughout the region to take similar actions.[128]

Confident they could overtake a military installation that, by their estimations, housed two dozen soldiers, the guerrillas expected losses but not the carnage they suffered. What is startling about their attack is not the plan itself but the refusal to call it off when key components fell apart: two of the three armed contingents did not make it to Madera by the agreed-upon date. One was lost in the sierra, and the other, which had the military materiel (obtained during the previous attack in the Mineral de Dolores), could not traverse the raging rivers left by days of heavy rain. The Madera barracks, moreover, housed not the two dozen soldiers the group had calculated but over a hundred, prompting Gómez and a few others to propose postponing the attack. But Gámiz remained adamant, and his view prevailed.[129]

Predictably, the thirteen guerrilla members were no match for the soldiers, whose rain of bullets killed eight of the attackers, including Gámiz and Gómez. Five soldiers reportedly died. Five of the guerrilla attackers managed to escape.[130] That they were not captured by the heavy military detachment ordered to comb the sierra bespeaks the support participants had among the local population, one cultivated by members of the group but also resulting from the population's resentment against the authorities' long-standing harassment and brutal counterinsurgency campaign, which included hanging people from helicopters and dangling them along the jutting rocks.[131]

While the core of the GPG was eliminated, this hardly represented the end of guerrilla struggle in Chihuahua, much less in Mexico. An armed clandestine organization calling itself the Arturo Gámiz Popular Guerrilla Group continued to operate in the Sierra Tarahumara. Indeed, Mexico's Cold War guerrillas were nourished by a tradition of rural insurrection that had emerged almost immediately after Cárdenas left office.[132] In addition to the previous agrarista component, students, teachers, and graduates from Mexico's rural normales helped fuel the socialist ideals of the 1960s radical left.

"WE WERE ALL THERE"

At the time of the attack, Pablo Gómez's daughter, Alma, was fifteen years old and a third-year student at the rural normal of Saucillo. Alma's cousin brought her the news of her father's death. "In that moment I didn't feel anything—obviously confusion," she related, "but I didn't have a reaction." After talking to her cousin, Alma made her way back to the dorms, where she passed a group of "compañeras that had participated in the campesino marches and adored my father. They also protected and took care of me. . . . I must have had a tormented expression because they asked me, 'Alma, what happened?' 'They killed my father,' I answered. That's when I broke down in tears."[133]

Of the eight participants who died in the attack, only Gómez, Alma's father, was over twenty-five. He was also the only one married with children—five of them. "So everyone is awed," pointed out his daughter, "that a man with kids made a decision like that. All the others were young and single. To make that kind of a decision is a very important act. . . . But I believe that a key factor in this difficult choice was his compañera [partner/wife], a woman who was a rebel, a leftist, intelligent, daring. He knew he was not simply abandoning us to a difficult situation. It is obviously not easy to bring up five kids, but he wasn't leaving us in total misery. He knew that my mother would see us through. And she did."[134]

Alma's point is more than a personal vindication of her mother. Her statement concerns the broader mobilization that produced the now-mythical Madera attacks. Women's participation in those mobilizations—which intelligence agents had noted with alarm, state authorities had disparaged with misogyny, and UGOCM leaders had minimized with paternalism—was central. "We were all there," stated Alma. "Yes, while we didn't go [to Madera], the assault was a process in which campesina women, students from the normales, we all participated. It was not just a man's fight."[135] Indeed, had it not been for guerrilla members' views that women needed to be protected rather than treated as fighters in their own right, some normalistas from Saucillo might have joined the attack itself.[136]

The teacher-campesino contingent that attacked Madera did not propel the revolution forward, but it did puncture the narrative that armed groups did not exist in Mexico. Threatened by the broader struggle that produced them, the authorities would not forgive such a bold transgression. Governor Giner issued explicit orders preventing family members from retrieving their loved ones' bodies. Instead, after the mangled, bullet-ridden corpses had been paraded around Madera, the governor had them thrown in a mass grave. In a play on the word *tierra*, which in Spanish means both "land" and "dirt," Giner declared, "They wanted tierra, give it to them until they've had their fill."[137] While publicly dismissing the guerrilla attack as the work of a small group of agitators, the federal and state authorities responded with a massive show of force. Governor Giner characterized the action as insignificant, "a crazy adventure at the orders of Pablo Gómez." He was, after all, continued the governor, "a poisoner of the minds of inexperienced youth."[138]

Just two weeks after the attacks, government agents reported the arrival in Chihuahua of rural normalistas from various parts of country.[139] For normalistas who knew the participants and had struggled alongside them in marches, demonstrations, and land takeovers, and for the teachers who provided the underground infrastructure that sustained the small cadre, Madera was to be celebrated. Within days of the attacks, normalistas issued pamphlets, visited the graves, and mobilized local support. One manifesto issued by the rural normales of Chihuahua praised the rebels who had placed themselves "at the service of the humble and oppressed class and whose bodies had been destroyed, riddled, and thrown in a common grave like animals." As state and federal authorities sought to contain news of the attack, normalistas publicized the event, deposited wreaths at the guerrillas' mass grave, and issued declarations urging "the continuation of the revolutionary movement begun in Madera."[140]

The local population's reaction was more measured, with many residents hesitant to celebrate the event. One demonstration planned by the FECSM had to be canceled because teachers—graduates of the state's normal school—opposed it, fearing it could turn the people of Chihuahua against them.[141] At a town council meeting in Madera, participants expressed varying views on the attack. Taking note of such divisions, the municipal president planned to issue a statement reading in part, "The inhabitants of Madera are lovers of peace and work and had nothing to do with guerrilla movements nor with the planned visit to the grave of those who fell on September 23rd."

Nonetheless, noted the government spy reporting on this meeting, the majority sympathized with the slain guerrillas, "a consequence of the grave abuses and arbitrary harassment the military dispatch committed against the inhabitants of the sierra's hamlets and in the town of Madera itself."[142] Other reports also noted this abuse, describing how, in its investigation, the army mistreated, humiliated, and taunted the local population. In fact, because of the vulgar manner in which the military inspected trains, conductors refused to lend their services in Madera. Aware of such abuses, the military general in charge considered them "lamentable but necessary" in the efforts to locate the escaped guerrillas.[143]

A year later, state authorities remained intolerant of public commemorations of Madera, detaining normalistas from Saucillo for handing out flyers.[144] Aguirre, the Salaices graduate who had declined Quiñónez's invitation to participate in the attack, remembers the enduring climate of fear. Even though he disagreed with the guerrilla actions, he wanted to pay homage to the fallen participants. Traveling throughout Chihuahua as the teachers' union representative, he recalled the anxiety he encountered. "Everywhere I'd go, I'd find a great deal of fear. Anything having to do with organizing had to be done clandestinely. Flyers were made clandestinely and handed out quietly. The fear lasted a long time, especially in Madera. The first time I went there, I held a meeting with the teachers of the whole region. There were about 150 teachers. . . . As soon as I gave my presentation, I honored the fallen compañeros. I remember that as we were leaving the meeting, the teachers tried desperately to hide me. 'They're going to kill you.' They did not kill me; nothing happened. But that's how much panic there was."[145]

THAT RURAL NORMALISTAS DREW such inspiration from the Madera attacks is one of the many manifestations of the radical student culture brewing within their walls. But it was also part of a more general student tendency that marked the global 1960s, a decade on which youth protest left a lasting imprint. What normalista actions show is how this student protest took shape outside Mexico City. At rural normales, where the campesino world was ever present through familial ties, agricultural pedagogy, and teacher commitment and was a constituting element of the FECSM's ideology, agrarian movements had a powerful resonance. Indeed, the revolution's campesino struggle had produced these institutions, and it was a struggle many normalistas sought to further. To the campesino consciousness that permeated the schools, the 1960s added an international repertoire of struggle inspired by the Cuban Revolution, the worldwide student movements, and the decolonization struggles. In this context, rural normalistas would increasingly posit their vanguard role. As one 1966 FECSM proclamation put it, "It is up to us, the youth, especially the campesino youth educated in the glorious rural normales, to bring about the fourth stage of our history: socialism, to achieve a nation that has fewer poor people and fewer rich people. This is how we, the students of the rural normales, think—we who come from the countryside and observe the infinite injustices committed against our class brothers and our very families."[146]

As the decade wore on, the country's rural normales would come to house powerful elements of old- and new-left politics. The economic rights that Cardenismo had extended to the poor during the 1930s increasingly comingled with youths' awareness of themselves as political actors and the idea that a revolution could be made through deliberate and willful action in which students played a vanguard role. This combination—along with the hardening of the federal government—continued to pave the way for radical struggle. Far from an anomaly, the Madera attack inaugurated two decades of guerrilla movements that in other parts of the country would likewise be linked to rural normales.

6

Learning in
the Barricades

ON MARCH 18, 1965, the director of normal education, Alfonso Sierra Partida, held a meeting with teachers and staff from Palmira, Morelos, an all-women rural normal. At the meeting, convened in the offices of the National Union of Education Workers (SNTE), the state-allied teachers' union, Sierra Partida discussed strategies to address the most recent unrest at the school. Palmira students had accused the director and four other teachers of corrupt practices, drunken behavior, and sexual impropriety. Having stoned the principal's home and held a demonstration in the state capital, Cuernavaca, Palmira students vowed to continue mobilizing until the offending teachers and director were dismissed. This protest came in the midst of a nationwide conflict between Mexico's twenty-nine rural normales and the Ministry of Public Education (SEP). In February the Mexican Federation of Socialist Campesino Students (FECSM), the normalistas' student federation, had issued a petition soliciting, among other things, improved school infrastructure and teaching personnel, a rise in per-student funding, and an increase in the admission age. With the FECSM threatening a strike if these demands were not met, Sierra Partida showed frustration at the new dimension the Palmira conflict introduced. In need of drastic measures to confront what the SEP considered "focal points of agitation," Sierra Partida sought the official union's collaboration to close or restructure these schools. The general secretary of the SNTE's state branch agreed, characterizing rural normalistas as subversives and an affront to President Gustavo Díaz Ordaz (1964–70).[1]

With specific attention to students' lived experience, this chapter telescopes outward from the previous focus on Chihuahua to examine rural normalistas' politicization during the 1960s. As their twenty-nine schools languished in precarious material conditions, normalistas ever more vocally demanded resources from the SEP. Their organizing process fostered expansive notions of democracy that combined political and economic rights. While their boarding schools nominally met their basic needs, the precarity of the system itself led students to a constant confrontation with the state, most often in the form of school strikes. During these mobilizations for better food, decent shelter, appropriate learning infrastructure, and protection from abusive teachers, students both honed their organizing skills and tasted the freedom of upending hierarchies. Despite the specific constraints female normalistas faced, rural normales were sources of newfound freedom for them especially. While they faced stricter vigilance from school authorities and their mobilizations were often structured through a gendered division of labor, such patriarchal limitations were counterbalanced by the initiative women developed in their collective defiance. Access to a teaching career, moreover, gave them the economic stability that allowed them to make long-term choices with a degree of individual freedom lacking for those who were economically dependent.

Still, unlike other student sectors, who, as scholars have argued, represented harbingers of modernity, rural normalistas mobilized with an eye to the fulfillment of past projects and came of age within an institutional framework structured by the principles of the old left.[2] The FECSM operated through a hierarchical structure, the logic of class struggle, and the primacy of the group over the individual. Cardenismo constituted the most consistent reference, the Communist Party was a close ally, and democracy was conceived as access to public goods rather than political freedom. The FECSM, moreover, subsumed gender and ethnicity within the logic of class struggle. But the analytical tools afforded by Marxism, the organizing process needed to pull off a school strike, and the interaction normalistas had—before, during, and after their studies—with popular sectors awakened many to the way racism, sexism, and the education system itself structured their subjugation.

Like most poor youth, rural normalistas grew up fast. Doing so far from their families, in institutions that assigned them a leadership role in the national project, and amid a peer group whose organizational body emphasized the collective, contributed to an "understanding of themselves as politically consequential individuals," a tendency Greg Grandin identified throughout Latin America where institutions of the old left afforded the dispossessed a chance to have a say in their destiny.[3] For rural normalistas, who during the turbulent decade of the 1960s continued to populate the barricades, this dynamic played out in a militant culture whose emphasis on economic rights distilled other forms of consciousness, including race and gender.

"I WENT THERE BECAUSE I HAD NO OTHER ALTERNATIVE"

When asked if he enjoyed his time at the normal, Ramiro Arciga, who first studied in Tiripetío, Michoacán, and later transferred to Ayotzinapa, Guerrero, replied, "I'll be honest, it is an extreme situation. I went there because I had no other alternative." To study engineering, which is what he really wanted, "cost money, and I was an orphan with no support. My studies would have ended in junior high school, so I had to accept a career in teaching. It's harder when one doesn't have that calling. But as time passed, the interaction with my compañeros, living together, and working in groups with compañeros who had certain similar ideals gave me a path. It helped me.... We even organized field trips; the biggest one at Ayotzinapa was for those who graduated, and I had the opportunity to go to Isla Mujeres. It was the first time I traveled by boat, from Puerto Juárez to Isla Mujeres."[4] Arciga, whose statement invokes his professional aspirations, political organizing alongside his peers, and the personal awe he experienced through travel, is a telling example of how rural normales fused insurgent individuality and social solidarity, intensely political experiences that harmonized self-interest and the common good.[5] Like Arciga, most other normalistas recount an early life of poverty; a challenging exam in which hundreds of applicants competed for a few dozen spots; the joy of securing a scholarship that entitled them to room, board, and a modest stipend; and the wonder of living among a peer group that, while similar in socioeconomic background, brought a diversity of family, ethnic, and geographic experiences. But despite the nostalgia that tinges most accounts, normalistas also relate the difficulties of adjusting to life away from home. "I must say, for those first few days, there were moments in which I temporarily hated my mother [for sending me there]," stated César Navarro about his early days at the rural normal of San Marcos, Zacatecas.[6] Others cried most nights during the first month; their relative material security compared to their home life—an individual bed, three meals a day, a new set of clothes— could not make up for the separation from their families (map 6.1).

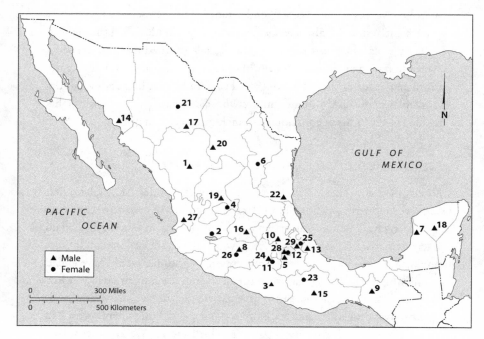

MAP 6.1 Rural Normales, 1968–1969

	SCHOOL	OFFICIAL NAME		SCHOOL	OFFICIAL NAME
1	Aguilera, Durango	J. Guadalupe Aguilera	14	El Quinto, Sonora	Plutarco Elias Calles
2	Atequiza, Jalisco	Miguel Hidalgo	15	Reyes Mantecón, Oaxaca	Moisés Sáenz
3	Ayotzinapa, Guerrero	Prof. Raúl Isidro Burgos	16	Roque, Guanajuato	Lic. Gabriel Ramos Millán
4	Cañada Honda, Aguascalientes	Justo Sierra Méndez	17	Salaices, Chihuahua	Abraham González
			18	San Diego Tekax, Yucatán	Gregorio Torres Quintero
5	Champusco, Puebla	Emiliano Zapata	19	San Marcos, Zacatecas	General Matías Ramos
6	Galeana, Nuevo León	Gral. Mariano Escobedo	20	Santa Teresa, Coahuila	Prof. Rafael Ramírez
7	Hecelchakán, Campeche	Justo Sierra Méndez	21	Saucillo, Chihuahua	Ricardo Flores Magón
8	La Huerta, Michoacán	Miguel Ángel de Quevedo	22	Tamatán, Tamaulipas	Lauro Aguirre
9	Mactumactzá, Chiapas	Pantaleón Domínguez	23	Tamazulapan, Oaxaca	Vanguardia
10	El Mexe, Hidalgo	Luis Villarreal	24	Tenería, Mexico State	Lázaro Cárdenas
11	Palmira, Morelos	Gral. Lázaro Cárdenas	25	Teteles, Puebla	Carmen Serdán
12	Panotla, Tlaxcala	Lic. Benito Juárez	26	Tiripetío, Michoacán	Vasco de Quiroga
13	Perote, Veracruz	Gral. Enrique Rodríguez Cano	27	Xalisco, Nayarit	Emiliano Zapata
			28	Xocuyucan, Tlaxcala	Lázaro Cárdenas
			29	Zaragoza, Puebla	Basilio Vadillo

Source: "Escuelas Normales Rurales," February 20, 1968, Archivo General de la Nación, Dirección Federal de Seguridad 63-19, Leg.3, H75–76.

Note: This map should be taken with a degree of caution since most documentation contains errors or inconsistencies.

But this physical separation also contributed to the intensity of their bonds with peers and the development and reproduction of a politicized culture. At rural normales, students operated under a two-tiered set of norms and regulations, one set by the SEP and overseen by the school's administration, staff, and teachers and the second directed by the student governing council. The latter's power, through both its say in institutional norms and its ability to organize student collective action, often rivaled that of school authorities. As one student put it, "In Reyes Mantecón attending the political orientation classes was more obligatory than the academic ones. The internal sanctions among us were harsher."[7]

Normalistas also had deliberate initiation rituals known as *novatadas*, whose logic signaled a break with the past, an integration into the institution, and an allegiance to the collective student body. Most common at male normales was shaving incoming students' heads and assigning them nicknames. Other activities included sweeping and mopping the halls, cleaning bathrooms, or performing specific tasks for older students. Many involved pranks such as locking entire groups in the basements "because they'd say we were ugly and our presence would scare people," recounted one student from La Huerta, Michoacán.[8] Proceso Díaz, from El Mexe, remembered how "they'd throw us into the canal, which had sewer water," a tradition that made him cry.[9] Such practices seem to have been exclusive to male normales and are thus noteworthy as a public display of masculinity.[10] In these rituals, older students could demonstrate their power and leadership, while the younger cohort's ability to withstand the humiliation indicated their strength and resilience, qualities necessary to navigate life in the normales and in the poverty-stricken communities where they would teach after graduation.

Decades later, former normalistas reflected on such practices in different ways. For some, they represented harmless youthful pranks; others remembered the glee when it was their turn to shave the heads of incoming class members; for a few students, they sat uncomfortably as a form of bullying.[11] Others emphasized that normalista novatadas were mild compared to those practiced at Mexico City's National Polytechnic Institute, the National Autonomous University of Mexico, or their American football teams, where, as Jaime Pensado has described, students held yearly parades on the streets of Mexico City that "featured humiliating and ridiculous displays, such as shaving of young novatos' heads in public, forcing them to dress in diapers or other outlandish outfits, making them crawl like animals, or forcing them to ride a tricycle sucking a pacifier or drinking from a gigantic baby bottle."[12]

In contrast to the novatadas or the difficulty youngsters had in adjusting to a new environment, many speak of how older students provided protection and comfort. Proceso Díaz, who above recounted his painful memories of being pushed into El Mexe's water canal, said he soon found someone from his hometown to shield him from student pranks, to which the incoming class was especially vulnerable. Likewise, Aristarco Aquino Solís from Reyes Mantecón, Oaxaca, remembered, "Fellow students at the normal who were from my same community shielded me from the traditional actions that students did to the new ones, to the *pelones* [those with shaved heads]. They'd protect me."[13] Older students also afforded comfort and affection, often acting as a surrogate family. Herminia Gómez Carrasco, from Saucillo, for example, described it thus: "There was a way in which the students from the higher grades would adopt and teach us. . . . I was placed on the committee in charge of food. 'Why me?' They said I was too skinny, and they wanted to see if that would help me gain weight."[14] When asked if there were novatadas at women's normales, students—male and female—responded with an emphatic no. On the contrary, women emphasized how affectionate and protective their older peers were. "It was an environment of total sisterhood," responded Elsa Guzmán; "it never would have crossed our minds to engage in such practices."[15] More than notions of sisterhood—the counterpart of which also existed at male normales—traditional gender norms mitigated such rituals at women's schools. Indeed, shaving female students' heads was unthinkable largely because it challenged traditional notions of femininity. "It's not like the compañeras were going to act like the allied forces did when they liberated France," stated a normalista from San Marcos, alluding to the practice by which crowds publicly shaved the heads of suspected female Nazi collaborators—often because they had born children of German soldiers.[16]

With both its conflict and its camaraderie, group living offered the time and space to fortify collective bonds. In fact, some youngsters secured a spot in the rural normales thanks to support from older students. As Isidro Rodríguez from the rural normal of La Huerta, Michoacán, remembered,

> I took the exam but did not score high enough to get a scholarship. There were so many who took the test, and so few who gained entrance. . . . We did not have a right to food, dorms, or classes. But we could stay thanks to the aid of some friends who had scholarships, who supported us, who helped us find a little space in the dorms. Sometimes we'd sneak into the cafeteria and there wasn't a problem, but other times they were closely

guarded and we couldn't get in. So our friends would sneak us out a bread roll with beans, a piece of meat, a little cup of milk or coffee.[17]

Augusto Carrasco Orozco, who also arrived at Reyes Mantecón in Oaxaca thanks to this arrangement, stated, "They'd call us pups; we were the pups of those in the fifth or sixth year at the normal, they were the ones who'd protect us." But such arrangements made for a precarious existence. "There were some sad moments," continued Carrasco, "because sometimes you were about to eat breakfast—you'd be there like any student who did have a scholarship—and all of a sudden a teacher would show up and take your food portion away."[18] These students faced a similar situation in the classroom. As Rodríguez recalled, "Some teachers would make us leave class; others were more flexible and would let us stay. And so we'd struggle. I fought alongside ten of my peers for six months until we got the news that we could be regular students and have a scholarship. We still had to pass the exams. If we did, we could stay; otherwise, we'd have to leave."[19] For such students, the experience of collective struggle began even before they formally enrolled in the normal.

If the transition to their boarding schools was difficult for most youngsters, it was doubly so for those from indigenous communities. Aristarco Aquino Solís, an indigenous Zapotec from Yalalag, Oaxaca, who arrived at Reyes Mantecón in 1967, stated, "It was a shock, first because life in a boarding school is not easy. Second, because of my limited knowledge of Spanish.... I got there without really knowing that I would have to abandon my way of dress. I still wore sandals."[20] In a similar vein, Carrasco, who attended the same normal in the 1960s, stated, "About 60 percent of us were indigenous and openly spoke Mixteco or Zapoteco—those were the predominant ethnicities. Our problem was not speaking Spanish, and even among ourselves we'd make fun of one another.... And those 30 or 40 percent who did not speak an indigenous language and spoke Spanish would reprimand or insult us about speaking our own language. 'Speak Christian' [a colonial way of referring to Spanish], they'd tell us. 'Speak the correct way!'"[21] While such an acculturation process was painful, indigenous students were also aware that learning Spanish could be a tool of empowerment. As Aquino himself explained in detail:

> An aspiration of both teachers and our parents was that we learn Spanish ... not just Spanish but *good* Spanish. Because they knew, or they intuited, that it was a resource against what the PRI [the Institutional Revolutionary Party] did to us. When we were adolescents, we'd feel powerless as we heard of, saw, or got wind of the humiliation of those who fought against

injustice, against impositions from the capital and for our people's right to decide through assembly and through consensus. All this made us restless and started opening our eyes. I say this because to confront those who are in charge, who impose everything, you must know Spanish; otherwise, you'll be at a disadvantage. The other side of this was that we didn't take sufficient care to preserve the Zapoteco language.[22]

From the outset, Mexico's education project had been a state effort to forge a mestizo nation. Indigenous languages, dress, and practices were to be abandoned or subsumed within a campesino class identity. However, rather than supplanting indigenous culture and history, at rural normales being campesino—ever expansive as a category—meant many things, including being indigenous, despite a curriculum, student culture, and general framework that reinforced the logic of mestizaje. Many indigenous normalistas who in the 1960s studied in the rural normales of Oaxaca and Chiapas went on to become prominent members in the 1970s movement for union independence and democratic representation. In the decades to come, they would increasingly demand a curriculum based on indigenous language, culture, and practice.[23] Without forgetting the discriminatory practices of their teachers and peers, indigenous students cited the political awakening they experienced at rural normales, a basis for how they later understood exploitation of indigenous people—and resistance to it. For this they credit the FECSM.

"THAT'S WHERE I FIRST HEARD
THE SECOND DECLARATION OF HAVANA"

"One of the first activities that caught my attention," related Aristarco Aquino Solís, "was when [older students] gathered us to tell us we'd initially be attending weekly talks on political and ideological orientation. That's where we learned of the existence of the FECSM, about the rationale for participating in their struggle."[24] The FECSM had long assumed the responsibility for strengthening student power as a way of shielding rural normales from policies that chipped away at the revolutionary gains. By the 1960s, FECSM committees constituted a mainstay of the rural normal system with a powerful hold on school life. Student associations, which in each school were affiliated with the FECSM, prioritized political education, had a say in institutional matters, and consistently promoted involvement with popular struggles outside campus walls. In their meetings and initiation activities, the FECSM exposed students—most arriving when they were barely adolescents—

to a politicized world before they understood the meaning of political involvement. Students as young as eleven piled into crowded cafeterias that
doubled as assembly halls. There "we'd discuss anything from trivial matters
related to daily life in the dorms, to the advances of international socialism,
to the growing development of proletarian class consciousness in the world
and the country," detailed a student from the rural normal of Mactumactzá, Chiapas.[25] It was at these assemblies that many students first heard of
revolutionary teachers like Arturo Gámiz, Pablo Gómez, Genaro Vázquez,
or Lucio Cabañas, who would become icons of rural normalismo. As one
student recounted, "I was too young to be interested in politics. But at the
assemblies I'd see others debating, reading letters from Lucio Cabañas—
Cabañas would send us letters when we had mobilizations, encouraging us
[in the struggle]."[26] Aside from their missives, these figures often made personal appearances, thus serving as an early marker in the process of political
awakening. As César Navarro stated, "Having met Arturo [Gámiz] and then
hearing that he'd died in such an incredible, astonishing act [in Madera],
then hearing about Lucio and his struggle with other compañeros, it makes
you ask, 'What is happening here?'" International events also provided early
political signposts. Continued Navarro, "I remember that one of the agenda
items was to play a record; . . . that's where I first heard the Second Declaration of Havana. I assure you, I did not understand a thing! I was too young."
But students treasured that record, stated Navarro, who felt proud when his
turn came to guard it.[27]

As venues where students took charge, made plans, and had a voice, the
student-organized assemblies were as significant as the content of their
discussion. After impassioned speeches and contentious debates, normalistas voted on resolutions involving school strikes or solidarity with mobilized
popular sectors or discussed motions to redress matters related to staff, teachers, or school administrators. On a practical level, too, it "was a formative
process. After five or six years attending such assemblies, you're bound to
pick up *something*, even how to organize a meeting, how to put an agenda
together, how to come to an agreement. We would vote and then end by sing-
ing the federation's anthem, the anthem of the International Student Union,
whose headquarters were in Prague, and we would always close with 'The
Internationale.'"[28] For many, this experience was remarkable and evoked
collective processes in their home communities. "Until then," described
one student, "I had never witnessed, much less participated in, the type
of a situation my family, as campesinos, and my father, as an ejidatario, had
lived."[29] The practice fed an important dialectic that provided an opportunity

for individual expression but could be articulated only through collective action. Like the ejido that the revolution bequeathed to campesinos, students came to understand rural normales as a matter of justice encompassing collective rights and responsibilities.

Not all, of course, were interested in politics. Those who were not remembered sports, cultural events, or recreational activities as their primary pastime. Belén Cuevas, who studied at Saucillo, Chihuahua, for example, explained that she "was never really aware of politics. . . . I was sociable. I was always on the social events or recreational committee, organizing tributes to the flag." Pedro Martínez Noriega, from Reyes Mantecón, Oaxaca, likewise stated, "I was never passionate [about politics]. I never seriously got involved. . . . We were fourteen or fifteen, so at that age some of us were indifferent to marches or philosophical theories." And yet in the next breath both normalistas invoked the politicized environment around them. Continued Martínez, "We were drawn to Castro Ruz and 'Che' Guevara, because they were our idols of the time. There wasn't much about China, . . . but Cuba and Russia were our inspiration." Cuevas, for her part, remembered, "In those times we were filled with the ideas of Fidel Castro, which we would hear very clandestinely; . . . sometimes on one of our teachers' radios, we would listen to Radio Havana. So we were filled with socialist ideas of protest."[30] Such accounts speak to the broader culture of rural normales, an indication not that every student was politicized but that all were exposed to an environment in which socialism, however vague, was a pervasive reference point.

Still there were doubtless students who, by surreptitious means, undermined collective organizing. A good portion of the information in government intelligence reports likely came from student informants. And, by normalistas' own accounts, there were plenty of cynics and opportunists. "Radical demagogues," one graduate from Salaices termed them, "those who advocated armed revolution from within our school as if we as youngsters had the logistics or the military discipline to carry that out. Those were the ones who ended up selling themselves out completely. They are today the worst persecutors of teachers, the most charro leaders."[31] Indeed, normalistas commented that student leaders were especially attractive as targets of co-optation by those in power as their organizing skills could be useful to the PRI. At a more general level, another student put it as follows: "There is plenty of talk about students who were socialists, but once they participated in civic life, they became conservative and even reactionary. Of that type there are plenty of examples throughout history, not just in this country, in any country."[32]

Students thus engaged with the FECSM to varying degrees. But all were exposed to it, and all had to reckon with the hold it had on school life. Even for those students antithetical to political activity, collective action was the surest way to preserve their spot, graduate, and secure a teaching position. Peer pressure, too, operated as a motivating force during strikes. Some teachers "tried to draw us back to class, and it was up to you if you went. But no one did because they did not want to be singled out as betraying the movement," recalled a student from Atequiza, Jalisco.[33] Or, as another student put it, "Some [participated] out of tradition rather than conviction."[34] Those not interested in political struggle thus made calculated choices. "We participated in what we had to," stated Catalina Calderón. "I was involved but only within the school, in the roles I had to assume. But nothing outside campus. . . . I liked to read, to do my homework and prepare for class. That was my focus."[35]

That the FECSM concerned itself as much with broad political ideals such as socialism and anti-imperialism as it did with school maintenance, food rations, and enrollments naturalized its existence for students who may not have otherwise been drawn to political struggle. Unlike in any other educational institution in Mexico, the FECSM held a powerful hold on institutional life. It ran parallel educational activities in the form of political organizing, enforced a disciplinary comportment in accordance with collective action, and tied both processes to the betterment of the rural normal system. "Democracy, as a critical, personal judgment, was not in and of itself a goal at our normal," synthesized one student. "We dispensed with such simplistic and basic notions. . . . Self-governance was the democratic means to participate; the end goal was to improve ourselves by improving our school."[36] Improving their school usually meant mobilizing, since, as Alma Gómez put it, "Unless we organized a strike, our petitions would never be addressed."[37] Indeed, the FECSM's petitions—always ambitious—met with piecemeal concessions. And even the few concessions the SEP did make were often implemented only after student strikes. The survival of the rural normal system thus became premised on student actions, a dynamic that helps explain the FECSM's enduring centrality.

"TALKS THAT WENT NOWHERE"

If the FECSM's political assemblies provided normalistas' ideological education, strikes imbued them with practical experience in collective action. And rural normalistas went on strike almost continuously during the turbulent 1960s, a necessity, as they saw it, against a regime that had condemned their schools to a slow death. The government, the FECSM pointed out, devoted more money to food rations for military horses than to normalistas.[38] Indeed, as the dramatic events of 1968 unfolded in the country's capital, the FECSM was in the midst of negotiating a long list of demands with the SEP. For some, this dynamic constitutes evidence of their narrowly material concerns compared to Mexico City's university students, who put forth political grievances.[39] And yet the framework rural normalistas employed, rooted in the poor's right to an education, was grounded in expansive notions of democracy where political and economic rights went hand in hand. The strikes, in turn, helped forge a culture of militancy because, in their fight, students transgressed institutional norms to fashion the necessary building blocks of struggle. They created cross-campus alliances, appealed to surrounding communities for support, used their stipends to sustain the movement, and held an ideological vision that linked student grievances to those of campesinos. In these practices the state saw anarchy and selected elements of student organizing strategies to malign the rural normales, constructing a narrative it would later invoke to justify their closing.

The length of FECSM petitions from the 1960s—with demands that replicated points made a decade and a half earlier—reveals the degree to which students were the primary advocates for their own education. Aside from increases in students' food, medicine, stipends, and uniform allocation, normalistas sought infrastructural repairs for water and electricity in some schools and the construction of dorms, cafeterias, classrooms, and sports facilities in others. The FECSM also petitioned for laboratories, workshops, library books, movie projectors, and musical instruments—the tools to develop the basic skills the SEP demanded of them as teachers. In a similar fashion, students sought trucks for their agricultural work, transportation to their practicums, funds for community festivals, and typing and stenography courses to better complete their culminating projects, such as theses and field reports, or to elaborate didactic material.[40]

Normalistas also made staffing and administrative demands. Some simply sought teachers for required subjects. Others, however, aimed specifically at diminishing corruption and, partly to that end, sought a greater student role in institutional governance. The FECSM's 1963 petition, for example, requested personnel to oversee food distribution and mitigate administrators' tendencies to siphon off supplies.[41] To preserve the integrity of the admissions process, prevent the sale of enrollment spots, and ensure their schools remained "strictly for working-class and campesino families," in 1965 the FECSM demanded a student presence in the committee that graded entrance exams. It also critiqued the exam itself, stating that it measured intelligence based on theory rather than knowledge, a quality that privileged urban applicants.[42] Because the countryside's students usually started elementary school at a later age than their urban counterparts and took longer to finish, the federation called for an increase in the age limit for admission (set at fifteen years for those starting secundaria and nineteen for the professional course cycle). As they stood, argued the federation, the age limits made it especially difficult for indigenous students to qualify given the poverty, family labor needs, and lack of schools in their communities. This 1965 petition also objected to the SEP's school-zone demarcations, geographic restrictions that limited to which rural normales students could apply. Such rules, argued the FECSM, stifled the otherwise-enriching dorm life engendered when it grouped students from a wide number of states.[43]

In the 1960s strikes, the FECSM also called for an expansion of the rural normal system itself. Normalistas' 1963 petition, for example, sought three thousand more scholarships.[44] In 1965 they demanded that in every admissions cycle, schools accept an additional 4 percent, students who would become eligible for scholarships as spots opened up.[45] As it was, each normal had between 80 and 120 students (about 30 percent of the student body) who lived in dorms and attended classes but had no funding. As described above, they stayed at the school thanks to the initiative of individual students or to informal agreements between directors and student leaders who collected and contributed stipend money to sustain them.[46] The status of these students was a constant source of tension. When schools took too hard a line, as at La Huerta, where a new director expelled eighty of them, students went on strike, appealing to other normales to join them.[47]

While the SEP conceded little in relation to the FECSM's long and detailed list of demands, the students' relentless struggle achieved some favorable arrangements. For example, the SEP agreed to implement formal procedures by which nonfunded students could enroll. If they scored well enough on their final exam, they would be eligible to occupy the spots vacated by those who deserted or were expelled. But concessions were limited. In fact, this was the SEP's counter to the FECSM's 1963 demand for three thousand new spots.[48] And yet, while the SEP explicitly stated that this was a one-time arrangement, by 1965—based on renewed petitions—SEP officials formally adopted a policy by which rural normales accepted 4 percent more students than there were spots available.[49]

For the most part, however, the SEP only promised to study normalista requests. Any measures it did agree to, it implemented at a snail's pace—so much so that students frequently engaged in follow-up strikes, not because they had new demands, but because the SEP had failed to comply with signed agreements. Little seems to have come, for example, from the FECSM's 1963 petition. During the latter part of the year, normalistas pressured the authorities through a series of rolling strikes. By 1964 they threatened actions at SEP headquarters in Mexico City. But Sierra Partida, director of normal education, dissuaded them from such an escalation and convinced the leaders to instead present a revised petition.[50] The FECSM had already withdrawn its demand for three thousand additional scholarships, heeding Sierra Partida's assertion that such a concession would produce too many teachers and thus hurt their job prospects.[51]

The following year, on March 8, 1965, the FECSM once more presented the SEP with a twenty-two-point list of demands, mostly a reiteration of those issued in 1963. Faced again only with a promise to consider their list, on March 26, students in all but two of the rural normales—Tenería, Mexico State, and Xocoyucan, Tlaxcala—began rolling walkouts.[52] Agustín Yáñez, head of the SEP from 1964 to 1970, warned that his office would not begin talks until students desisted from what he characterized as blackmail. Responding that their demands dated back to 1963, the FECSM declared they were "tired of initiating talks that went nowhere" and would escalate their actions until their calls received attention.[53] On April 2, 1965, they began a general strike that stretched across the country.[54]

At that juncture, the FECSM's system-wide mobilization merged with the local grievances at the rural normal of Palmira, where students demanded the removal of four teachers and the school director for drunken behavior and sexual harassment.[55] The SEP had created two commissions to investigate the charges, both of which had cleared the faculty and director of any wrongdoing. The students dismissed that outcome as the foregone conclusion given that the commission was headed by a PRI loyalist. The parents association at the school also rejected the findings.[56]

It was not uncommon for male teachers to proposition, harass, or engage in relationships with female students, although this appears sparingly in the documentation. The FECSM's 1965 petition, for example, demanded the firing of a male teacher from the women's normal of Atequiza, Jalisco, for seducing students.[57] Charges at other women's normales dated back to the 1950s, such as in Cañada Honda, Aguascalientes, where the head of the student council denounced a teacher for having sexual relations with two different students.[58] Rosalva Pantoja Guerrero, a 1950s student and later a teacher at the rural normal of Tamazulapan, remembered a case of a teacher who was forced to retire after several instances of exchanging grades for sexual favors. "But that was thanks to the intervention of the parents association," stated Pantoja, who wished that, as students, they had protested earlier and more vociferously. "It was sad, humiliating, that for a grade we'd have to stoop to that level. . . . For crying out loud, [respect] was why we came [to school]!"[59]

The case at Palmira, with which this chapter opened, was one of the few that produced a school-wide movement against the offending teachers. Tellingly, however, the federation did not prioritize the case among its demands, and the SEP and the SNTE, the PRI-allied union, closed ranks to dismiss the young women's charges. Likewise, from the outset, the SEP sought to contain Palmira's normalistas. Hoping to reduce the critical mass necessary to sustain the protest, Sierra Partida sent letters to parents instructing them to withdraw their daughters until the conflict passed. The SNTE, in turn, ordered school personnel to abandon the campus. Cafeteria services were closed.[60] But Palmira students and their parents garnered support from the surrounding community, and local shop owners donated supplies.[61] National FECSM representatives as well as delegates from the National Central of Democratic Students (a communist student organization) traveled to Palmira and there joined strategizing meetings, a move the Morelos governor condemned as outside interference.[62] The SNTE was especially passionate in defending its accused members. It demanded their full restitution and a faculty vote of confidence and declared that "to avoid this type of future disorders, the entire rural normal system needed to be restructured."[63] Unabashedly, Mario Aguilera Dorantes, a high-ranking SEP minister, declared to the Palmira students, "I will not take on the entirety of the country's teachers just to punish the five instructors you accuse."[64]

Despite the high stakes at Palmira, the case became subsumed within the larger system-wide normal strike. If the national strike could be addressed, asserted intelligence agents, the SEP could quietly resolve matters at Palmira by simply replacing the school director.[65] Indeed, Palmira students joined the national mobilization that by the end of April 1965 had received some concessions, the most significant of which involved changes to the admissions process. The SEP agreed to expand age limits for eligibility by eight months. It also accepted student participation in the admissions process. Moreover, 33 percent of admissions would be reserved for indigenous students, whose own communities would recruit and select them. The SEP likewise affirmed a continued policy of accepting a 4 percent excess of applicants, who could occupy spots as they became available. As for material demands, the ministry approved an increase in funds for food, medical attention, and transportation as well as library books and lab supplies.[66]

When the FECSM first presented its 1965 demand list, the SEP stated that it would take 38 million pesos to meet it and instead countered with concessions that would total 2 million.[67] The FECSM accepted, much to the chagrin of some students who saw the decision as bowing to the ministry's will.[68] But even that amount was not provided. A year later, the normalistas complained that they had received barely 287,000 pesos toward their petition.[69] When the FECSM convened in 1966 to renew its executive committee, students again discussed a list of unmet demands.[70] By 1968 they had drafted a new petition that included appeals made since 1963: increased funds for food, medicine, uniforms, pedagogical material, and library books as well as building repairs; an increase in the age limit for admission and the staffing of needed positions; and more scholarships—six hundred specifically for women—to be distributed throughout the female schools or through the creation of a new women's rural normal.[71]

The SEP issued its standard response. It agreed to a few demands, pointed to existing policies that addressed others, and promised to take most of them into consideration. Ramón Bonfil, the new head of normal education, praised students' willingness to dialogue and assured them there would be "no need for combative behaviors" since his office shared the "goal of improving conditions in all the schools in the rural normal system." Demands would be fulfilled if a SEP commission determined there was need and if the ministry could budget the funds (figure 6.1). Bonfil also reiterated an invitation to FECSM representatives to accompany him as he toured the schools to identify specific needs. Unconvinced by this response, in February 1968 all but three of the rural normales began strikes.[72]

A week later, the SEP made additional concessions that addressed just over half of normalistas' demands. But it also warned that "if the problems went beyond the school realm," it would no longer be the ministry that mediated the conflict.[73] The FECSM, still dissatisfied, further resented what it saw as a veiled threat. Education authorities in the meantime sought to bypass the FECSM leadership by appealing directly to the student body, instructing the school directors and state governors to convene meetings that would publicize the ministry's concession. The SEP also instructed local school authorities to issue a warning: strikes counted as absences, and too many would make students ineligible to take the final exam, requiring them to repeat the year.[74] Additionally, to temper teacher support for students, the

SEP appealed to the SNTE to control its members: none should aid or abet striking students.[75]

The SEP, moreover, enlisted the PRI-controlled National Campesino Confederation to publicize the ministry's spending and portray student leaders as deceitful to their base. The confederation sponsored radio advertisements urging normalistas to return to class and published declarations that the money spent on rural normales could be better utilized aiding peasant production.[76] Students thus denounced "the press, radio, and other media outlets that, for a few pesos, published a false version of events to confuse people . . . to distort our good intentions."[77] Other PRI-affiliated organizations also mobilized against normalistas. Most alarmingly, the Confederation of Mexican Youth (the PRI's youth branch) called for eliminating the country's rural normales altogether. In the national newspaper *El Universal*,

FIGURE 6.1 Representatives from rural normal parent and student associations meeting with Ramón Bonfil, director of normal education, 1968. Archivo General de la Nación, Photographic Archive, Normales Rurales, c79, Sobre 44.

it declared that these schools were foci of agitation and parasitic institutions with an overwhelmingly lazy student body.[78] In the rural normal of Cañada Honda, Aguascalientes, the parents association protested the government's lies that claimed normalistas had rejected a resolution meeting 80 percent of their demands. "Only a fool would believe that students would reject a victory of that nature," pointed out school parents.[79] This type of media campaign was, in the end, one of the most effective tools against normalistas, limiting popular support and contributing to a perpetual black legend about their schools. Reactionary forces had effectively used this publicity tool kit since the 1930s, at the time against government reforms; now the state wielded it in an attempt to contain and roll back revolutionary gains.

Despite such odds, sustained normalista pressure again succeeded in extracting some concessions. In early March 1968, the ministry agreed to pending demands—an increase in food, clothing, and medical supplies. When the student leadership brought the SEP's offer to a system-wide vote, 70 percent of the school delegates approved it. But the mobilization had taken its toll and created some internal conflict. At various points during the approximately two-week strike, some schools had refused to participate (Tenería, Galeana, El Quinto, and Reyes Mantecón), while others (Champusco, La Huerta, and Palmira) joined despite strong internal opposition. In Tamatán the government's propaganda was effective, leading students to believe their leaders had deceived them. Finally, not all were happy with the outcome. When voting on the SEP's third offer, Mactumactzá delegates expressed dismay that not all demands were met. Moreover, once the FECSM voted to end the strike, five schools (Tekax, La Huerta, Tiripetío, Tamazulapan, and Mactumactzá) refused to heed the decision, possibly jeopardizing the SEP's concessions, delegates worried. Two months later, during the FECSM's May 1968 national congress, delegates complained that the SEP had not met the agreed-upon demands. By October there was discussion of another strike.[80]

"THERE IS NO AUTHORITY TO STOP THEM"

More than their assemblies, the logistical tasks that students undertook to resolve quotidian matters as they paralyzed their schools fortified a long-lasting, politically militant normalista culture. The tactics necessary to pull off a strike involved local, regional, and national coordination. Since the authorities would end cafeteria service, normalistas sought donations from surrounding communities.[81] To finance the negotiating committee's stay in

Mexico City, they pooled portions of their scholarships.[82] To fortify their takeovers, students traveled to each other's schools. Gómez provided a view from the barricades: "Our compañeros from Salaices would send reinforcements [because] we'd close access to the school. We'd stand guard at night so no one could enter. During my time there wasn't repression, though had there been, our compañeros wouldn't have been much use in stopping it. Still, they were there as reinforcement."[83] This accompaniment, which Gómez recognized would have been futile in the face of state forces, was nonetheless more than symbolic. It fed strategies of collective action, instilled commonsense notions of resistance, and imbued students with the experience of challenging authority and confronting state repression.

Normalistas consistently organized along gendered lines. As male students from Salaices reinforced the guard at the women's normal of Saucillo, female students from Palmira traveled to El Mexe and Ayotzinapa to prepare meals for the male student body there.[84] Despite the conservative notions such a gendered division of labor reinforced, overall the strikes created a disruption that, by force of circumstance, broke down other social constraints. In the words of one intelligence agent, "Disorder reigns in the rural normal of Palmira, only four days after the strike at all the country's rural normales began; the students come and go as they please, and there is no authority to stop them."[85] The report's alarm stemmed from the fact that not only were Palmira's students moving freely on and off campus, in the absence of the school staff, but law students from the state university of Morelos had come to the normal to confer with them, creating the potential for broader alliances.[86]

But most troubling from the state's point of view were student alliances with campesino groups. These were also the actions that most deeply challenged patriarchal structures. Female normalistas, whom teachers and staff subjected to far stricter vigilance than their male counterparts, defied the school authorities and in so doing revealed the extent to which purported school safety measures were actually about controlling young women. As Belén Cuevas remembered, "The teachers followed our steps. . . . They'd give us twenty minutes to go to the stores in town, to buy soap, toothpaste, what we needed. . . . On Sundays we'd get a half hour; some had their boyfriends in town, and so we'd have to be careful not to arrive late or we'd be written up, and you'd have points deducted. So that's how it was, you'd have to run back to your gilded cage as we used to say. Though that cage certainly wasn't gilded."[87] Another student, also from the rural normal of Saucillo, Chihuahua, who was expelled for her political activities, commented on the hypocritical nature of such control: "There was such strict discipline, specifically because we were girls. For example, when vacation started, they'd send letters to our families to make sure we could be released. So how is it possible that [when they expelled us] they just threw us out on the street? 'Here are ten pesos, and go who knows where with those ten pesos!'"[88]

School authorities reported such activities to parents, often in vain.[89] One student, for example, spoke of how the school director at Saucillo sent her parents and others a letter that read, "'Your daughter Herminia Gómez participated in a march from Parral with 120 workers from this date to that date.'" She continued, "Our parents were furious, thinking we had gone and spent the night with the workers. . . . But once we explained to them that we came and went and didn't sleep there [in the factory], the situation calmed down."[90] Similarly, Silvina Rodríguez, also from Saucillo, recalled that if they did not receive permission to leave the school, "We'd take off anyway." In Rodríguez's case, her father ignored the first notice he received about his daughter's political activities. But when a second one arrived, he began to worry. "So he came to the normal, to the principal's office, to talk to him. Then my father came to me—I don't think the director had really convinced him of anything! My father was a campesino and operated under a different logic. In his mind, what I was doing was magnificent."[91] The reaction of Rodríguez's father was likely not the norm; in fact, many parents were alarmed to learn their daughters had left the school's watchful eye. But this case exemplifies how student-campesino alliances could stretch traditional gender constraints. Rather than ordering his daughter to remain under the school's guard, Rodríguez's father was heartened by her defense of their family's class interests.

The authorities worked the public-opinion angle by spreading rumors of sexual promiscuity and asserting that older students exerted undue influence on younger ones.[92] The types of charges differed by gender. At male schools, education authorities charged, dorms fomented homosexuality as older students seduced younger ones.[93] The coexistence of "students of different ages, tendencies, and interests," argued one official, "led to abuses, deviation, and disorder."[94] Ultimately, this would be one of the justifications for separating the junior high school cycle from the three years of professional training.[95] The FECSM understood charges of immorality as specifically directed against the normales' dorm structure and pointed to their ridiculous nature by taking such accusations to their logical conclusion. If boarding schools were indeed breeding grounds for immorality, UNESCO (the United Nations Educational, Scientific, and Cultural Organization) itself should call for dismantling all boarding schools, including those in the United States, the Soviet Union, England, and France.[96] Army barracks should also not be exempt from that logic.[97] Normalistas further argued that if education authorities were genuinely concerned about student well-being, their attention should be directed against *porros*, agents provocateurs that infiltrated campuses and were especially ubiquitous in Mexico City's universities.[98]

Indeed, had the authorities been sincerely troubled about impropriety or sexual abuse, they could have taken seriously the charges female normalistas levied against their male teachers who accosted them. And yet, as the case of Palmira demonstrates, in such instances the SEP and the official union closed ranks, ensuring the power structure remained intact. No wonder that, even despite normalistas' organizational logic that sent male students to reinforce their compañeras' barricades and female normalistas to cook, women experienced their political mobilizations as a source of empowerment. While a teaching career offered the possibility of economic independence, it was "above all the political formation," emphasized one normalista, "that developed our critical ability to challenge injustice."[99]

"OTHERS ENJOY THE FRUIT OF OUR PARENTS' LABOR"

Amid one of the many strikes rural normalistas organized during the 1960s, judicial police arrested three students from Salaices and Saucillo who were handing out leaflets. "Go to Salaices," read their flyer, "find out how students live, how they sleep on hay and withstand the intense cold." Lawmakers, the text elaborated, oblivious to injustice, made only empty promises and maligned the institutions that stood as "the last stronghold of the 1910 armed movement." "We demand what is ours," it then asserted, since "others enjoy the fruit of our parents' labor."[100] The justice owed to the countryside as a result of the revolution continued to provide a structuring framework for normalista demands. Through their agricultural training, which sought to ground students' identification with the countryside as members of institutions built for the descendants of campesinos, the state had itself created rural normales under the logic of revolutionary justice.

And along with these rights came responsibilities, which the FECSM articulated through involvement in campesino struggles. At the FECSM's national conferences, where delegates from the twenty-nine rural normales met to elect their leadership, they also reported on local school matters; discussed regional, national, and international struggles; and formulated strategies of action. A 1965 congress in Aguilera, Durango, provides a vivid picture. There students from the rural normal of San Diego Tekax in Yucatán gave a presentation about labor conditions, reporting that campesinos who worked for the henequen company Cordemex "worked from sunup to sundown, earning five pesos daily while living in subhuman conditions"—this in a company "whose influence was so great it imposed or removed authorities at will." Students from Nayarit similarly reported that the Anderson and Clayton Company "condemned its workers to poverty" and was but one of the many examples of the worldwide ramifications of "Yanqui imperialism."[101] The national leadership assigned delegates to study relevant problems and to produce assessments about the causes, nature, and potential for normalista involvement. Such conferences frequently included visits from labor and campesino leaders. On this occasion, for example, Othón Salazar, the head of the Revolutionary Teachers Movement, spoke about workers' rights, the criminalization of protest, and the country's numerous political prisoners.[102] International solidarity, too, was an ever-present theme at FECSM conferences. Students condemned U.S. intervention in countries like Vietnam and the Dominican Republic and expressed support for the guerrilla struggle in Guatemala.[103]

In addition to its own conventions, the federation took advantage of the annual system-wide cultural and sports gatherings to exchange impressions and strategize for upcoming struggles.[104] While athletic competitions might be devoid of politics—in fact, students who excelled as athletes had the reputation of being less political—other activities at these festivals provided ample opportunity to display militancy. At a 1965 system-wide oratory contest, for example, students delivered speeches highlighting campesinos' historic participation in Mexico's struggles, denounced foreign companies' exploitative practices, and highlighted the systemic poverty of the countryside. Different orators asserted the need for students and teachers to devote themselves to achieving justice, condemned the limits of the 1910 revolutionary process, and urged future struggle—even through armed means.[105]

Most significantly, normalistas participated in popular mobilizations involving workers and campesinos. While sporadic, their involvement, when it took place, had important ripple effects that both challenged conventional norms of student comportment and created alliances across social groups. From land takeovers in Durango, Sonora, and Chihuahua, to support for the indigenous Ajijic community in Chapala, Jalisco, to accompaniment of workers at lumber and bottle-making factories in Chihuahua, normalistas consistently displayed a presence in struggles outside their school walls; they joined marches, publicized worker and campesino grievances, and supplied dissidents with food from school warehouses. Students did this despite the authorities' threats, detentions, and checkpoints meant to prevent them from traveling to conflict sites.[106] Such acts of solidarity were important to campesinos and students alike. As the agrarian leader Álvaro Ríos expressed to the five hundred normalistas who joined a campesino march from Durango to Mexico City, "You are to us the closest and most notable compañeros; you are the sons and daughters of campesinos, and together we can reach new heights. . . . This meeting between campesinos and students marks the beginning of a renewed Mexican revolution to defeat capitalism and install socialism."[107]

The potential for such alliances led some students to conceive of themselves—often problematically—as the revolutionary vanguard. While normalistas cited their own humble origin as a natural source of allegiance with campesinos, their student status marked them as a group apart. For example, at a 1966 campesino-student caravan, one student declared, "We want to remove the blindfolds of the humble classes, and that's how we can initiate unity between students and campesinos." Such language positioned normalistas as agents of redemption and echoed the vision of the state intelligentsia who conceived of the educational process as a civilizing mission—one that would redeem and assimilate backward rural folk. It also reveals a larger contradiction: while a culture of political militancy existed at rural normales, upon graduation this militancy did not always persist, a dynamic not lost on campesinos. One woman at this rally thus urged the students to "continue being as revolutionary as you are now, since once you become professionals and start earning money, you forget about the people."[108] Her words bespeak the extent to which it was campesino notions of justice that infused rural normales with their particular militancy. The class transformation students underwent once they graduated militated against long-term radical action. Looking back, most rural normalistas themselves recognized this dynamic. This is partly why lifelong militant teachers like Othón Salazar or those like Lucio Cabañas, Pablo Gómez, Arturo Gámiz, and Genaro Vázquez, who lost their lives in the course of the struggle, made such an impression on them.

THERE IS SOMETHING UNIQUE, scholars have noted, about the way people remember revolutionary times or instances of collective action. Latent sensations and previously passive or unsettled observations come into sharp relief and have long-lasting effects on past and subsequent experiences. This sense "of accelerated time (or timelessness)," in which individuals become aware of societal structures, partly accounts for the outsized role political participation plays in normalistas' memories. Reflecting on their youth, most do so with nostalgia and ascribe meaning to their lives by highlighting instances in which they were part of something bigger than themselves.[109] At the same time, the deliberate political education undertaken by the FECSM— itself part of the institutional structure—ensured student exposure to an ideological world of radical politics that interwove the schools' very existence with a history of justice for the dispossessed. For campesino and indigenous students, hailing from a life of poverty, such justice was hardly abstract. An education, free room and board, and a teaching job after graduation represented the palpable material evidence. That the state had created a dynamic in which students had to petition, strike, and mobilize to preserve the institutions giving them a chance at a better life placed individual advancement squarely within the framework of collective action.

Such action took many forms. While it mostly focused on securing the continuation of the rural normal system, the FECSM's broader ideology also led to participation in agrarian and worker mobilizations, a sector with whom normalistas professed to have a natural allegiance. This interaction reinforced a revolutionary ethos already widespread among youth during the 1960s. As incubators of resistance, rural normales thus constituted both a building block for a larger repertoire of struggle and a component of the 1960s groundswell of youth action. Not surprisingly, as general student unrest grew during the 1960s, the authorities increasingly worried that normalista grievances would merge with those of other student coalitions.[110]

Like their counterparts around the globe, elites in Mexico searched for ways to control a generation intent on challenging established norms. Turning their attention to rural normales, the education authorities saw a system in crisis, sites where "instability and anarchy" reigned.[111] In their eyes, student power had remained unchecked for too long. In 1967 the SEP thus convened a national conference where it proposed to study the rural normales to implement changes that would at once update the system and restore what, in the eyes of the state, were its original principles. Tellingly, in his opening remarks education minister Yáñez declared, "Normal is derived from norm. Norm is the rule that leads to order, that which is indispensable to the proposed achievements."[112] Needless to say, the achievements proposed by the SEP and the student body differed markedly.

7

"A Crisis
of Authority"

IN MAY 1967 the Ministry of Public Education (SEP) summoned supervisors, directors, teachers, and students to a national meeting on rural normales, to be held later that summer in Mexico City. Participants would evaluate the problems affecting the countryside's teacher-training system and propose solutions. In the meeting's inaugural remarks, Education Minister Agustín Yáñez described the rural normales as "an innovation of the revolutionary regime" and praised the schools that had once produced committed teachers whose spirit of service led to a "heroic period" of education in the countryside. The narrative—a celebration of a revolutionary project whose attention to the countryside had proved transformative—was a familiar one, long repeated by officials, teachers, and students alike. But if the normalistas invoked earlier regimes, especially that of Lázaro Cárdenas, for their commitment to the countryside, SEP officials did so to highlight teachers' abnegation in service of the nation. Yáñez's speech proceeded in this latter tradition. Only through "authentic patriotism," he emphasized, could Mexico relive the achievements of the 1920s and 1930s.[1]

Front and center in both the opening remarks and the conference proceedings was the issue of student comportment. Yáñez lamented normalistas' tendency to approach issues "emotionally rather than thoughtfully." This conference, he stated, would offer a chance to mediate that passion with the knowledge of experts. And yet he then proceeded with more of a reprimand than a sage mediation. Students needed to understand, declared the minister, that the social justice they demanded was a quid pro quo: "If you freely accept the benefits of an education that is conditioned to a specific goal, this goal must be fulfilled." Normalistas should be treating their schools "not as a gold mine of personal privileges but as sites made for work and for the privilege of serving Mexico." Yáñez specifically criticized collective action for promoting "misguided solidarity" and stifling "genuine liberty"—in this case the individual rights of younger students, whom he charged older ones with manipulating. He concluded with a warning typical of the official characterization of dissent: "The Mexican teacher must be an agent of Mexico, not of foreign interests or, worse, of interests that go against Mexico."[2] The undersecretary of normal education, Federico Berrueto Ramón, who followed Yáñez, went even further. Normalista demands actually "conspired against Mexico" for, in such a poor country, their myriad petitions detracted attention from the educational needs of others. Declaring accusations of blame useless, Berrueto Ramón—with no apparent sense of irony—proceeded to fault the teachers at rural normales for the system's shortcomings. "I've often asked myself," he stated, "if the pervasive agitation in our normales results partly from poor teacher leadership."[3]

Yáñez's and Berrueto Ramón's words reflect a common trope regarding state authority vis-à-vis an unruly populace, all the more characteristic of a decade marked by youth mobilization. But there is an additional layer to their critique, one discernible in their disbelief that campesino students were not simply grateful for the chance to attend school and in turn eager to serve the state that had granted them this opportunity. That normalistas demanded school improvements demonstrated a sense of privilege unbecoming of their social class. Since they were unappreciative and, as the authorities saw it, unresponsive to their corresponding duties to study diligently and serve eagerly, the state would do better to channel its resources to the millions of other poor campesinos.

Normalistas, however, did not see school funding as a zero-sum game, at least not one to be played out against members of their own social class. They did not dispute the critical state of rural education, but the causes they identified and the solutions they proposed differed markedly from the SEP's. While the authorities attributed educational shortcomings to demographic growth, teachers' lack of commitment, and educators' poor training, rural normalistas understood them as symptoms of structural problems, including insufficient spending, educational goals that did not challenge systemic exploitation, and an unequal distribution of wealth.[4] In this conception, social justice measures were not a quid pro quo but necessary policy to right historic wrongs.

This chapter examines these two visions of education. Turning first to the 1967 conference proceedings, it shows education authorities' preoccupation with student-body discipline. While official assessments also addressed matters related to resources, academic programs, and faculty labor conditions, the pervasive attention to students' perceived power at once reveals their persistent activism and the degree to which their actions disturbed the authorities. Concerned about the teacher-training system more broadly, in the spring of 1969, the authorities met again to discuss reform measures. By fall they had implemented a broad set of changes that included increased course requirements, an additional year of study, the separation of normales from their affiliated junior high schools, and new pedagogical methods. Framed as a measure of professional efficiency and meant for all normales, the reform had a particularly drastic effect on rural ones, first because these were the normales that had affiliated junior high schools and, second, because the reform converted fourteen of the twenty-nine into technical agricultural schools.[5] The institutions that once constituted the backbone of rural education were now reduced by half.

That this initiative came on the heels of a decade marked by widespread youthful unrest signaled to rural normalistas an effort to tame their power. Unique among Mexico's student body, campesino students had generally inserted themselves into the terrain of struggle through the framework of justice owed to the countryside. But the latter part of the 1960s had brought them closer to their urban peers, and in concert with them, they organized national actions and experienced state repression. This interaction added an additional dimension to their struggle, one in which they began to consider educational content as a matter of capitalist reproduction. They did not go far with the implications of this analysis. The 1968 student movement and its repression soon overwhelmed their momentum and initiatives. The army's massacre of civilians peacefully demonstrating at Tlatelolco had ripple effects throughout the rural normales. Significantly, these were less related to normalista participation in the events leading up to the massacre or to the fact that state repression moved many to more radical action in the years thereafter. What most connected normalistas to Tlatelolco was the 1969 restructuring of their schools, a measure they experienced as retribution for their generation's crime of rebelling.

The 1967 National Assembly on Rural Normal Education, the first of its kind, is best understood within the context of a renewed plan for education reform. The last major restructuring, the 1959 Eleven-Year Plan, had increased elementary school coverage, expanded general education requirements in junior high and high school, and created more technical training opportunities. Ending illiteracy, having a culturally informed citizenry, and preparing a labor force better equipped for the country's modernizing development had been the SEP's key goals with such changes. "Well intentioned," as one analyst characterized them, the measures focused on the education system as if it operated in isolation from the broader social structure, which rendered them "simple improvisations."[6] Aggravating the problem was the SEP's haste in implementing new reforms, the product of changing presidential administrations, each more concerned with differentiating their own approach from their predecessor's than with productively engaging past ones. Moreover, successful educational overhauls meant retooling teachers—including at normales, where those instructing future teachers would also have to be retrained. "The changes proposed to the 1960–1964 study plan were profound," explained one study, "and even though they were supposed to be implemented in a gradual and progressive manner . . . their content was never applied, both because of lack of time to evaluate the results, and because of a lack of the specific preparation and retraining of teachers at normales. There the 1964 graduating class would have been the first trained in the new approach, and yet by 1969 the decision had been made to once again radically change the 1960–1964 study plan."[7]

At rural normales, these earlier changes had involved reducing the number of academic requirements while increasing agricultural activities, conceiving the curriculum through long-term holistic goals rather than a laundry list of mandated subjects, and improving pedagogical methods through more discussion-based classes and holistic evaluation rather than a numerical grade. The 1967 National Assembly on Rural Normal Education would evaluate these reforms along with six other aspects of the teacher-training project: school governance, institutional supervision, postelementary school restructuring, the academic calendar, professional training, and schools' material needs. An assessment of each of these seven topics was precirculated among the rural normales and would constitute the basis for each panel discussion. Significantly, in a sign of how much student activism had become characteristic of the schools, these evaluations turned continually to normalistas' political involvement. Characterized as a disregard for hierarchy, excessive power, and an overblown sense of rights, student mobilizations, stated the evaluation, had created a crisis of authority. One assessment made a particularly drastic proposal to address these issues: dorms should be eliminated, and students should instead receive scholarships to find room and board in private homes. All twenty-nine rural normales should be converted into technical agricultural schools for junior high school students. In their stead, six new rural normales—each with the capacity for a thousand students—should be created. Establishing technical agricultural schools, proponents of this measure reasoned, would help curtail migration to the cities by educating students in rural development strategies. Moreover, eliminating the boarding-school component of rural normales would end many of the problems inherent in these institutions, including the wide range in pupils' age (some as young as twelve with older ones in their early twenties), the lack of academic correlation between secundaria and the three years of professional training, and the insufficient number of teachers and service personnel—doctors, psychologists, social workers—to provide support for "the psychobiological changes all adolescents go through."[8]

Such proposals stoked normalistas' worst fears. "Any policy involving the closure of boarding schools is reactionary," protested the Mexican Federation of Socialist Campesino Students (FECSM). "Only the enemies of public education who dream of turning the teaching profession into a right-wing tool repeatedly focus their attack on our schools."[9] While creating career paths other than teaching for the children of campesinos was indeed laudable, intelligence documents also speak to the political motivation for eliminating dorms. "Political-ideological control could be applied to scholarships and enrollments, thus ending conflicts such as strikes or work stoppages," reported Fernando Gutiérrez Barrios, then head of Mexico's Federal Security Directorate. This arrangement, he continued, would end the pervasive mobilizations around food rations and dorm conditions.[10]

Invited to attend the 1967 conference, the FECSM understood its presence as a mere formality in a meeting meant to approve rather than debate changes to the system. "A select group of PhDs in pedagogy have summoned us to Mexico City, where we'll be informed that our normales can no longer exist," declared one normalista flyer protesting the conference.[11] They were not opposed to reform, "but educational experiments take time to bear fruit; until then, we consider it neither just nor revolutionary to mutilate rural normales."[12] Students' outrage gave the authorities pause, and the SEP soon eliminated the point about restructuring the secundaria years from the conference proceedings.[13] And yet the students were not mistaken in their alarm. Two years later, the SEP implemented a version of this very measure when it converted half of the rural normales into technical agricultural schools.

In the meantime, the meeting proceeded with a discussion of the other six topics. Despite the range of issues, at almost every turn, school officials identified student agitation as a major problem. For example, the first discussion point, school governance, while recognizing the importance of student voices, critiqued their political involvement, frequent and direct appeals to the SEP offices in Mexico City, and repeated moves to oust teachers, staff, or administrators. Recommendations thus sought to channel normalista energies through the proper school governing council, strengthen the director's authority, and handle problematic staff through labor law and union structures rather than in response to student mobilizations.[14] This latter proposition was reasonable, except that it was student protest that brought staff and faculty transgressions to the attention of the relevant authorities. The National Union of Education Workers (SNTE), Mexico's official teachers' union, not only was a longtime ally of the state but wielded immense power within the SEP itself. When it came to inept, authoritarian, or abusive teachers, the SNTE shielded them from normalista protest.

If the first working group sought to strengthen the institutional hierarchy within rural normales, the second, on school supervision, emphasized system-wide hierarchies, namely, SEP oversight of each normal. Rural normales were "disorganized and anarchic" because ministry supervisors had insufficient funding and little reach to gauge pedagogical outcomes. No one evaluated how classes were structured, how students learned, and how instructors taught. As a result, rural normales produced bad teachers. The solution lay in making the system more legible by better delineating supervision and assigning oversight. Recommendations included creating ten regional zones, assigning each to a supervisor who would conduct extensive visits and have the authority to determine and implement changes.[15]

The third commission, charged with evaluating the decade's earlier reforms, produced a bleak assessment. Not only had the new educational norms not been properly applied at rural normales, but to the extent that they had, they were counterproductive. The reforms had generally been conceived for urban institutions, had been precipitously implemented, or could not be applied owing to a lack of staff and resources. Meaningful research or transcendent school projects could hardly be conducted in the outdated labs, bare libraries, and dilapidated workshops of the rural normales. Moreover, agricultural training was so lackluster that it was problematically similar to hacienda peonage. Students tilled or weeded assigned plots but had no corresponding vision for the land. When it came to teachers, stated the assessment, "student political interests, sectarian politics, as well as personal and union rivalries," hindered the constructive work of the system's few effective instructors.[16] As boarding schools, rural normales required greater devotion, and yet teachers were otherwise engaged, since low pay forced them to seek supplemental jobs. Better campus housing, full-time teaching positions, and updated professional training could help ameliorate this problem. Students, for their part, should receive instruction more tailored to the pedagogical reality they would face as teachers, including preparing them for *escuelas unitarias*, the multigrade, single-classroom schools that predominated in the countryside.[17]

The state of the academic calendar, the subject of the fifth working group, was, according to the assessment, another cause of the "anarchy that deformed the character of future teachers."[18] Again the evaluation posited student power as a major source of the problem. The students, stated the precirculated assessment, pressured teachers to cancel classes for noncivic holidays like the Day of the Dead, Holy Week, Mother's Day, or regional festivals. Other class disruptions included field trips, school festivities, or anniversary commemorations. Finally, too many students missed class owing to their involvement in the student council, the FECSM's Committee of Political and Ideological Orientation, or political activities in general. These disruptions were a prime example of the inordinate student power "since student leaders made demands in the name of the entire student body, assuming they'll automatically gain authorities' approval."[19] Some of the blame, continued the evaluation, lay with the teachers and staff, who either coaxed students to request class cancellations or—fearing retribution if they did not succumb to student wishes—were quick to grant requests for unauthorized holidays. To help ameliorate the problem, the commission outlined regulations on scheduled activities, recommended national-level approval for any changes, and advised sanctions for teachers who "incited" students to demand additional holidays. Interestingly, while the precirculated assessment advocated punitive measures for students who violated attendance policies, the conference recommendations focused more on institutional practices and the teachers who enabled them. "Good professional preparation itself inspired youth" to remain in class, the conference proceedings concluded.[20]

The sixth commission assessed teachers' and students' professional quality. Instructors, it stated, had high turnover rates, were disillusioned or conformist, and tended to evade their responsibility, while pupils were uncultured, displayed a general disregard for authority, and acted irresponsibly in support of student leaders with unchecked prerogatives. Solutions included purging bad instructors, offering ongoing professional development, and better screening those hired. A similar logic applied to students: officials needed to pay closer attention to the pupils they admitted and to exert greater control over student organizations. Significantly, the committee did note the need for improved facilities such as libraries, laboratories, and workshops so that teachers could have instructional resources.[21]

"The designated amount is never enough," began the final point, devoted to an economic analysis of life at rural normales. It was not enough for "student services; not enough teachers and staff; not enough to run the agricultural and workshop production of the schools."[22] These problems, continued the assessment, had existed from the outset because the SEP had never done adequate research and planning. Instead, it had formulated an idealized view of what could be done with the assigned funds—budgets that had not been reassessed in decades. Rather than adjusting plans to fit the funds actually assigned, directors—under student pressure—solicited more money from the SEP. Rural normales had thus developed a paternalistic culture, constantly petitioning the SEP for more rather than taking the initiative to solve their own needs. The committee proposed solutions that fit into three broad categories: a SEP commitment to meet basic student and infrastructural needs, realistic budgets conceived with schools' input, and teacher-student proposals to better rely on their own productive capacities.[23]

The 1967 conference proceedings reveal much about rural normales, about the SEP's conception of the problems therein, and about official strategies to address them. Mainly, they should be understood within the framework of modernizing development, in which education served to ease but not transform structural inequality. Despite variations from administration to administration, the SEP's general approach since the 1940s had focused on modernizing pedagogical techniques, increasing school access, and professionalizing the teaching body. There was indeed an official consensus that the lack of resources affected the academic quality of rural normales as well as a recognition that earlier reforms seeking to make them more like urban normales had been detrimental. Their condition of scarcity, however, was aggravated by teachers' inability or unwillingness to adhere to the latest pedagogical mandates. With insufficient school inspectors, the SEP could not enforce compliance. Exacerbating these deficiencies, according to the authorities, was the unbridled student power; students' political commitment, insistence on celebrating folk holidays, and tendency to resort to federal rather than school authorities undermined the institutional hierarchy and the very resourcefulness that could help address the situation. This latter dynamic especially bewildered SEP officials, who, given the pervasive rural poverty, held that ideal students should "be cognizant of their unbridled privilege, given the living reality of millions of young campesinos . . . and understand their training is made possible through the sacrifice of the people."[24]

The conference proceedings do not make evident the nature of student participation, though, judging from the more tempered quality of the published recommendations as compared to the precirculated assessments, their presence had an effect. Significantly, their earlier protest had managed to exclude the proposal to restructure rural normales and eliminate their dorms. The extent to which the FECSM's vision contrasted with that of the education authorities is evident in their discussions and in the proclamation they issued in the two years following the SEP's 1967 meeting. The Atequiza Declaration, named after the rural normal in Jalisco where students met to discuss the future of their schools, for example, reveals the fundamentally different premise under which the normalistas operated. First, student representatives did not accept the argument that the country had limited resources for education that simply could not keep up with demographic growth. They pointed to the United Nations' 1963 Conference on Education and National Social Development, which recommended that countries dedicate at least 4 percent of the gross domestic product to education.[25] Mexico's spending ranged from 1.94 to 3 percent in the latter part of the 1960s.[26] Second, the FECSM objected to the derisive class perspective that framed schooling for the poor as a privilege rather than a right. The resources they sought, asserted one of their declarations, constituted part of "workers,' campesinos,' and youths' historic struggle to achieve structural, social, and economic change for the country."[27] Finally, the FECSM's underlying logic was that structural reform was both necessary and possible, an assumption that contrasted with the SEP's reformist or modernizing approach. This conception of education reform was rooted in the radical example of the 1930s and the renewed sense of possibilities brought about with the 1959 triumph of the Cuban Revolution.

In a new approach, normalistas vowed to begin to "*challenge* the content and orientation of the education" they received.[28] For decades the federation had emphasized material demands and had rarely included course content. This transition meant understanding education as a mode of capitalist reproduction. While the FECSM did not develop subsequent proposals in this regard—likely because the SEP's elimination of half of their schools in 1969 forced them into a defensive struggle for survival—the call speaks to a broadening ideological vision and an increasing disjuncture between students' lived experience and their classroom lessons. Here their interaction with Mexico's broader student movement, especially the National Central of Democratic Students (Central Nacional de Estudiantes Demócratico, CNED), helps explain this evolution.

A SCIENTIFIC, DEMOCRATIC, AND POPULAR EDUCATION

If normalista participation in the early 1960s agrarian struggles of Chihuahua (chapter 5) represented the clearest manifestation of their links to campesinos, their alliance with the CNED exemplified their relationship to the broader student movement. This national organization was short-lived, dominated mainly by youth affiliated with the Mexican Communist Party, and represented an attempt to unite diverse student organizations, harness radical activism, and challenge the hold of the Institutional Revolutionary Party (PRI) on worker and peasant unions. With this in mind, the organizers convened their first meeting in Morelia, Michoacán, in 1963. Two hundred and fifty delegates, reportedly representing 100,000 students, gathered at this first congress. Participants began their convention with a minute of silence honoring campesino leader Rubén Jaramillo and rail union activist Román Guerra Montemayor, both recently dead at the hands of the army. Students then invoked the names of prominent political prisoners. This act at once vocalized their solidarity with popular struggles and condemned the PRI's repressive apparatus. To articulate their vision, CNED leaders drew up the Morelia Declaration, a document setting forth three goals: a student alliance with the masses; a demand for popular, scientific education; and the creation of an independent, democratic, and revolutionary student movement.[29]

Their goals speak volumes about the nature of student grievances and the context of the 1960s. In their evaluation of the terrain of struggle, labor's defeat in late 1950s loomed large as the PRI managed to stymie teachers' and rail workers' struggle for independent unions. Schools, ablaze with protest, had picked up the baton. In Guerrero, Puebla, Michoacán, Sinaloa, Durango, and Mexico City, students had mobilized for university autonomy, ousted corrupt or authoritarian state governors, and organized protests against U.S. imperial aggression.[30] An especially significant struggle took place, at the University of Michoacán San Nicolás de Hidalgo (popularly known as Nicolaita), which became a battleground where both the national government and local right-wing forces sought to contain Cardenismo, which had most recently manifested itself through the former president's outspoken defense of Cuban self-determination specifically and Latin American liberation— from foreign and oligarchic domination—more generally.[31]

While ultimately overwhelmed by the 1968 student movement in Mexico City, the CNED constituted an important attempt to harness radical student activism, unite diverse campus groups, and challenge the Confederation of Mexican Youth, the PRI's youth association. In the five years after its creation, the CNED held two other congresses, organized a National Day of Action in 1967, and in February 1968 convened a march from Dolores Hidalgo in the state of Guanajuato to Morelia, the capital of Michoacán, demanding freedom for political prisoners. The impact of these actions on the power structure was less significant than the individual experience of those who participated in them, many of whom internalized the goals of solidarity with nonstudent sectors or acquired organizing skills they employed long after the CNED dissolved.[32]

For rural normalistas, CNED actions became opportunities to expose the precarious nature of their situation, seek broad student support, and establish connections with schools outside the teacher-training system.[33] The central's articulated goals fit almost naturally with rural normalistas' grievances, which consistently dramatized the condition of schools meant to serve the poor. Normalistas' rural background and propensity to act alongside campesinos, moreover, represented a vivid manifestation of CNED ideals that linked students to popular organizing. In the next few years, the CNED consistently invoked rural normalista rights, defended their schools' dorm structure, and insisted on the poor's right to a professional education.[34]

In April 1967 the CNED programmed a series of nationally coordinated actions specifically calling for the democratization of education, the improvement of student services (dorms, cafeterias, medical care, and scholarships), and freedom for political prisoners. According to *La Voz de México*, the Communist Party newspaper, up to 150,000 students throughout the country, including at all the rural normales, participated in this event through strikes and demonstrations.[35] Other national CNED events involved the February 1968 March for Liberty demanding freedom for political prisoners.[36] Starting out from Dolores Hidalgo, the cradle of Mexico's 1810 war of independence, the organizers evoked Mexico's historic struggles for liberation. Tellingly, the Justice Ministry ordered local agencies to prevent activities associated with the march, and the SEP instructed school directors to expel students who participated.[37] As it had long done, the government conflated the student problem with communist infiltration, thus fanning hysteria against youth. Rural normalistas who participated speak of the hostilities they endured and their effort to mitigate violent attacks by placing female students at the head of the march, hoping crowds would be less likely to attack women.[38] "There was a whole media campaign saying, 'Here come the communist students who eat children,'" remembered Alma Gómez Caballero, who, along with a contingent from the normal of Saucillo, participated in the march.[39] Indeed, in several places reactionary groups like the Sinarquistas, or PRI-affiliated unions like the National Campesino Confederation, jeered the marchers.[40] With cries of "Long live Christ the King," "Down with the reds," "Go back to Cuba," or "Go back to Russia," people threw stones, tomatoes, and eggs at the students.[41]

The little tolerance the government showed for the CNED is a testament to its significance. In Valle de Santiago, fifty-five miles from their destination, the military intercepted the 1,800 marchers. Using a train derailment to construct further propaganda against the students, the press reported the incident as student sabotage. The army soon surrounded the marchers, "returning us prisoners," as one normalista from Roque, Guanajuato, put it, "to the very towns and cities we had just traveled through."[42]

Since its inception, intelligence agents had characterized the CNED as an extreme leftist group and sent "special inspectors" to its events with instructions to "weaken the association and prevent the organizers from achieving success."[43] Indeed, the CNED encouraged the formation of regional student federations, which emerged in Chihuahua, Morelos, Puebla, and Guerrero, thus facilitating coordinated action by students from different types of educational institutions.[44] The CNED, moreover, showed a consistent presence in local normalista struggles, including Palmira's 1965 effort to oust teachers accused of sexual harassment and that year's system-wide rural normal strike.[45] Because of such actions, intelligence agents warned, the CNED was poised to take over the leadership at both rural and urban normales, leading to "a total politicization of future teachers, an unfortunate communist fanaticism."[46]

What intelligence agents painted as communist fanaticism normalista participants saw as a "program of democratic renewal," as one student leader from Saucillo put it. "We wanted a renewal of normalismo, and we participated in the national movement with that intention, alongside university students from the entire country."[47] The CNED contributed to a broader normalista engagement with the student movement by spurring connections with other educational institutions. Its national conferences, days of action, and ambitious mobilizations increased the contact students from different types of schools had with one another and gave rural normalistas an opportunity to compare grievances and establish alliances. The CNED's goals for a scientific, democratic, and popular education echoed many of the FECSM's historic principles. For example, normalistas had long defended secular schooling, identifying the church and the landed elite as the enemies. The CNED updated such notions by pointing to international capitalists as the new power holders in the post-Cardenista order. The confederation's calls for scientific education not only were anticlerical but constituted a vision in which schools created a conscious citizenry rather than a pliant workforce. To be democratic, moreover, educational opportunities ought to not only be expanded but incorporate student voices in their design and execution. Finally, the CNED's call for popular education emphasized connections between the school campus and the factory and the fields. In this latter characteristic especially, it was rural normalistas who could best assist the CNED in putting its ideals into practice. The relationship was thus a two-way street.

Meanwhile, events in Mexico City continued to heat up during the summer of 1968. The escalating state repression generated student fervor and, increasingly, public attention. The growing mobilizations, the students' creative tactics, and the international spotlight on Mexico as it prepared to host the Olympic Games proved too unnerving for President Gustavo Díaz Ordaz, who during his September state-of-the-union address condemned restless youth for violating the rule of law and tarnishing Mexico's image abroad. "We have been tolerant to a fault," declared the president, "but everything has its limits." Ominously, he invoked his powers as commander in chief and lauded the military's role in maintaining order.[48] A month later, on October 2, troops opened fire on student demonstrators in the Tlatelolco Plaza, leaving hundreds of civilians dead.

In the months leading up to the October 2 massacre, the rural normalistas issued statements of solidarity with the students, staged walkouts, and protested the government's mounting repression.[49] Rural normalistas had participated in the mobilizations in Mexico City and had been arrested in the government crackdown.[50] But at the rural normales, the aftershocks of the Tlatelolco massacre were slow and uneven. Proceso Díaz, who began his studies at the rural normal of El Mexe, Hidalgo, that fall, remembered students suspending classes: "I was new to political matters and didn't really understand what was happening. I saw the red-and-black flags, for the strike, to mourn the October 2nd massacre. And so with that I felt that something was happening."[51] At other schools such as La Huerta, Michoacán, activities proceeded normally. "October 3rd was our school anniversary," remembered

José Francisco Casimiro Barrera, "so many didn't even notice [Tlatelolco] because we were busy celebrating."[52]

But a storm was brewing. In November the SEP temporarily closed seventeen normales, in some cases using the army. Those not closed went on strike in protest.[53] When classes resumed later that month, students noticed the absence of some of their peers. "We knew how involved they were in '68 and that their participation continued," recalled Aristarco Aquino Solís from Mactumactzá, Chiapas. "They were expelled since they no longer showed up [to class]. We'd get wind of them occasionally, nothing lengthy nor too precise. . . . I know they ended up in the MAR."[54] The Revolutionary Action Movement (Movimiento de Acción Revolucionaria, MAR), one of the many armed groups that emerged in the aftermath of 1968, would count on the significant involvement of rural normalistas, many propelled by the closure of their normales or by their expulsion.[55]

The government's repression at Tlatelolco confirmed an ideological position many already held: peaceful or reformist calls for change were futile. Rural normalistas had, moreover, an important radicalizing precedent in the 1965 attack on the Madera military barracks in Chihuahua. Despite its failure, students celebrated what they saw as a heroic challenge to an authoritarian state. Even before 1968 some rural normalistas furthered the legacy of the September 23 martyrs, by providing support for the Arturo Gámiz Popular Guerrilla Group, that operated in northern Mexico.[56] In the south, Lucio Cabañas, the former head of the FECSM and a graduate of Ayotzinapa, would soon lead an armed guerrilla movement in the coastal state of Guerrero.

As the 1960s drew to a close, rural normalistas, like other students, had experienced a turbulent decade. The Cuban revolutionary process, especially its resistance to imperial attacks; Mexico's own agrarian mobilizations and the government's assassination of its leaders, so egregiously personified by the army kidnapping and murder of Rubén Jaramillo and his family in broad daylight on May 23, 1962; and the constant string of student battles in universities throughout the country all fomented youthful agitation and compelled many to act. That the student movement sowed panic in the halls of power is most exemplified by the state terror at Tlatelolco on October 2, 1968. But the government would not rely on brute force alone. In the case of the rural normales, the SEP implemented the measure students had long feared, closing half of their schools. Labeled an education reform by the SEP, the closure was experienced by students as a mutilation of the rural normal system, one that dealt a major blow to the FECSM.

"One of the major results of the recent student disturbances," stated a U.S. embassy report from Mexico, "was to give new impetus to the problem of education reform."[57] Despite earlier insistence that communist and other nefarious international forces were responsible for the 1968 student movement, President Díaz Ordaz now expressed that the root cause was an education system in need of profound reform. Accordingly, the president ordered a reassessment of all educational levels with the broad charge to focus on quality over quantity, critical thinking, and the idea that learning was a lifetime endeavor. When it came to Mexico's teacher-training system, the president decried normales for producing improvised teachers who lacked not only sufficient abnegation but also basic knowledge.[58] Thus, in 1969, when education authorities met in Saltillo, Coahuila, to discuss changes to the country's normales, improving teachers' foundational knowledge (*cultura general*) became a principal preoccupation. Broadening cultural knowledge, emphasized Education Minister Yáñez in his opening remarks, would be the foundation on which to render effective the SEP's imminent reform, whose specific measures included increasing course requirements, adding a year of professional training, rewarding the type of training over years of service, and implementing new pedagogical approaches that privileged active learning by students. Well-rounded teachers would transmit knowledge to their students while linking that knowledge to vocational and professional training through modern teaching methods. Cultured teachers would be moral ones. Their civic concerns would translate into a spirit of service that would counter a situation that had made normales "fodder for anarchy against the country's institutional order."[59]

The conference proceedings followed up on some points discussed in the 1967 National Assembly on Rural Normal Education, for example, on the need to draw students specifically interested in becoming teachers rather than those who used the normal as a springboard to other professions. With this in mind, the junior high schools currently linked to normales would be separated, a measure that affected mainly rural normales, whose years of study began with seventh grade. The only other normal with affiliated junior high schools was Mexico City's National Teachers School. In the latter case, the schools' jurisdiction was transferred to the Department of Secondary Education, where they were redesignated as regular secundarias rather than feeding schools for the normal. In the case of the former, the change was more dramatic since it not only separated secundarias and normales but entirely transformed fourteen of the twenty-nine rural normales into technical agricultural schools. This drastic restructuring, according to education officials, was necessary to offer rural youth careers other than teaching. Now under the jurisdiction of the Office of Technological, Industrial, and Commercial Education, these secundarias preserved their dorm structure but would train agricultural technicians, who, it was hoped, would remain in the countryside and use their skills to improve campesino agrarian production.

If the philosophical underpinning of the 1969 education reform was that learning was a lifelong process, the practical one linked critical thinking to technological instruction that would increase economic production. "Learning while doing" and "teaching while producing" became oft-quoted mantras to describe the new pedagogy. While this approach was laudable, stated one independent analysis of the reform, the lack of teacher training for its effective implementation, school facilities with inadequate technology, and the lack of basic equipment for scientific activities continued to render education quality low.[60] Specialists like Pablo Latapí, the founder and head of Mexico's Center for Education Studies and a lifelong researcher of pedagogy and education policy, critiqued the 1969 reform as a disjointed plan that lacked any scientific basis and was inoperable in practice.[61] In private, Latapí was more frank. A U.S. embassy representative related that Latapí did not believe people in the SEP were willing or able to implement real reform. According to the American official, Latapí believed that "'learning while doing' and 'teaching while producing' are empty slogans that are not new and signify no substantial reform of the education system."[62]

Among the measures Latapí critiqued publicly was the assumption that technical agricultural schools—such as those created from previous rural normales—would have any discernible effect on diminishing migration to cities or mitigating unemployment problems in the countryside. For those schools and other rural education measures to be successful, he wrote, resources would need to be channeled to peripheral areas; training would have to target not only youth but adult campesinos; and the rural population would need to be conscious of their rights in order to participate in the political and economic choices that affected them.[63] Other critics pointed out that to truly improve education quality, the state needed more revenue, which could be attained by taxing the rich or implementing fiscal reforms, neither of which would happen under the Díaz Ordaz administration, whose rate of spending on education diminished significantly.[64] Just two years later, in 1971, the new president, Luis Echeverría, would convene a different commission to again overhaul the education system. Many of the 1969 changes would thus go unimplemented and also unstudied. Their main merit, to again quote Latapí, was that "for the first time, there was open critique of the state of national education in which even some public officials recognized its deficiencies."[65]

"THE REACTIONARY FORCES' GRAVEST, MOST CRIMINAL AND ANTIPOPULAR DREAM"

A permanent measure of the 1969 reform, and the one rural normalistas most resented, was the conversion of half of their institutions into technical agricultural schools and the elimination of the secundaria years at the remaining fifteen. This was the biggest transformation the system had seen since the early 1940s, when coeducation and socialist pedagogy were eliminated. Institutions that had previously encompassed up to eight different school grades (three of junior high school, three of normal, and one or two complementary years for those who had not completed elementary school) were now reduced to four. The FECSM saw no merits in the SEP's arguments and interpreted the restructuring as a retaliation for the 1968 student mobilizations in general and a strategy to undermine the federation specifically. Denouncing the restructuring as a move "against all the forces participating in the popular-student movement that began on July 26th," the FECSM claimed that the government harbored special fury toward rural normalistas because of their combative nature. The FECSM did not oppose the creation of technical agricultural schools, but why, leaders protested, did these have to come at the expense of rural normales? With such measures the government had carried out the "reactionary forces' gravest, most criminal and antipopular dream: the elimination of our boarding-school system."[66] If the SEP sought to improve the quality of teacher graduates, why not expand the resources for the three-year professional cycle rather than add an additional year of study? This measure placed undue hardship on poor students, according to the FECSM, since it delayed their salary and thus their ability to support their parents and siblings, who still languished in poverty.[67]

In response to the SEP's argument that the current structure yielded educators who were not motivated by a teaching vocation, the FECSM cited the example of Cuba. The island's government, stated the federation, sought committed teachers not by searching out those with an innate predisposition—the calling that education officials constantly bemoaned that Mexican teachers lacked—but by cultivating it in a "revolutionary environment that is constructing a new society."[68] Indeed, one might see the environment in

Mexico during the 1920s and 1930s—the period the authorities themselves constantly invoked—as heroic, but its structural reforms, such as land redistribution and industry nationalization, had been not only abandoned but actively reversed by the state.

It is difficult to establish the 1968 student movement as the rationale for separating the secundaria from professional training at rural normales. Certainly, the timing does not seem coincidental. But such proposals had been discussed since 1954, and calls for the bachillerato (high school) requirement dated even further back.[69] Moreover, as was evident in the 1967 Mexico City conference on rural normales, education authorities saw students' persistent mobilization as a problem before the dramatic events at Tlatelolco. The SEP would likely have separated the professional cycle from the secundaria and increased it by a year regardless of 1968's events. However, the specific act of transforming half of the rural normales is drastic enough to suggest a strategy of containment, if not directly linked to the student movement in the capital, then at least in response to a decade of youthful unrest. That rural normales existed throughout the country, were interconnected through the FECSM, had recently developed ties to urban students through the CNED, and had a tradition of participating in campesino struggles made them significant organizing nodes, ones Díaz Ordaz's administration was loath to tolerate.

A clear sign that a plan was in the works before the events at Tlatelolco is a February 1968 report commissioned by the Federal Security Directorate. That an intelligence agency rather than an educational one conducted the study bespeaks its political nature. This geostrategic study described the size, cultivation, and political affiliation of the ejidos surrounding each of country's rural normales.[70] Significantly, once the SEP issued the order to transform fourteen of the rural normales into secundarias, it relied heavily on official campesino organizations to counter protest. During the summer months of 1969, in addition to the police, military, and other security forces, campesino members of the PRI-allied League of Agrarian Communities guarded the schools, having been promised that their children would receive spots there.[71] The latter strategy effectively pitted the poor against each other and was a manifestation of earlier declarations that if the normalistas did not appreciate the opportunities they were given, these would be directed to campesinos who did, ones, moreover, who were loyal to the regime. The level of state and federal coordination as well as the number of organizations involved in carrying out the change is striking. In addition to the League of Agrarian Communities, the state relied on other official organizations such as the National Campesino Confederation and the National School Repairs Commission as well as various security forces, including the federal and state police, undercover agents, the military, and the transit police—the latter installed roadblocks to prevent support contingents from reaching individual schools.[72]

In the months leading up to the change, normalistas met to determine how best to resist the restructuring. Aristarco Aquino from Reyes Mantecón, one of the rural normales in Oaxaca that would be transformed into a technical agricultural school, remembered, "We formed brigades; those from the sierra were to make their way to the communities to inform, to explain the blow it represented to communities, and to seek support for the normal's continued existence. We covered the entire state . . . and since there were a lot of teachers [in the communities] who had studied at Reyes Mantecón or Tamazulapan [another rural normal in Oaxaca], they took us in and supported us."[73] Student organizing yielded protest letters from communities throughout the country who argued for the preservation of the twenty-nine rural normales as a matter of revolutionary justice, because they served the "humble classes" and because they are "all that is left of the Mexican Revolution for which Villa and Zapata fought."[74] Letters pointed to the restructuring as hypocritical, noting that what education really needed was more resources and that it made little sense for a government purportedly committed to eliminating ignorance and promoting progress to close teacher-training schools. "Don't make us think we continue to live in the era of Porfirismo," stated a letter signed by twenty-eight campesinos from San Luis Potosí, "a time when only the children of the bourgeoisie received an education."[75] Pointedly, others declared, "Why do we want agricultural technicians? What we need is land."[76]

"Of course they ignored us," stated Aquino. "The decision had already been made."[77] While ultimately unsuccessful in stopping the measure, normalista efforts mobilized significant resistance in several locales. In Palmira, Morelos, students had done such extensive canvassing, noted intelligence agents, that school officials managed to enroll only three pupils for what was now a technical agricultural school, and teachers thus had to cancel classes. In Tiripetío, Michoacán, students opposing the change soon took over the school, preventing all but eleven students from enrolling. In many normales, students occupied the campuses during the summer, a process the SEP fought by ending food services and cutting off the water and electricity.[78] In many schools the parents association protested in support of the students.[79] In some cases, they did so because their kids would be sent to schools farther away, making it harder for parents to visit them. This situation was aggravated for female students, whose families were already reluctant to have them live away from home. In many cases, teachers and staff also opposed the change and supported students by speaking at their demonstrations, finding them lodging, or holding meetings at their homes.[80] Students also found backing among surrounding communities. For example, in Perote, Veracruz, local businesses gave normalistas food and monetary donations; in Tamatán, Tamaulipas, school staff found places for students to stay when the authorities dislodged their school occupations.[81] "We tried so many things," recalled a normalista from Tiripetío, Michoacán. "We'd canvass, we'd denounce, we'd invite communities, knowing [there was little hope]. But we'd do it, not everyone of course, but some. Still, the official propaganda was too strong."[82]

So were the threats. The authorities notified the students that if they did not present themselves at their newly assigned schools by September 6, they would lose their scholarships. Where students occupied normales, police forcibly removed them and threatened the complete closure of their schools.[83] At some institutions the authorities displayed a massive show of force, as one student due to return to Salaices, now transformed into a technical agricultural school, recalled: "What we saw was astonishing. The road to the normal looked like an anthill—it was soldiers who did not allow us to come into the school. They told us our place was now in Aguilera, Durango."[84] Numerous students were detained at military checkpoints or plucked off passenger buses, and the soldiers tormented and harassed them.[85]

The restructuring caused division within many rural normales themselves. While the government's show of force bespeaks the measure's general lack of popularity, not all students opposed the change.[86] As long as their scholarships remained intact, many normalistas were content to change schools. While some administrative and teaching personnel opposed their reassignment, their response was decidedly more mixed than that of the students. In Reyes Mantecón, for example, the staff predominantly originated from the Isthmus of Tehuantepec region, and their transfer to Chiapas actually put them closer to home.[87] In some communities surrounding rural normales, the government's campaign—waged through organizations like the League of Agrarian Communities and the National Campesino Confederation—effectively halted or overturned support for student protests.[88] The hardships entailed in occupying a school with no water, electricity, or food further dissuaded others.

Still, the FECSM continued its resistance and on September 3, 1969, called for a system-wide strike.[89] The minister of normal education, Ramón Bonfil, took it upon himself to visit individual schools to address this resistance. In Ayotzinapa, accompanied by representatives of the SNTE, the state-allied teachers' union, local education officials, public-security members, and the head of the state's judicial police, Bonfil issued students a forceful warning: if they were found agitating, their food would be suspended, and their teachers removed, and their water and electricity would be cut off; those who did not like the reform were invited to leave. If they organized, they would be expelled and blacklisted, preventing them from enrolling in other normales. Before leaving, the minister singled out ten student leaders, pulled them aside, and energetically reiterated the threats to them. He ended with a blanket warning against any type of mobilization, including complaints about food. When Bonfil departed, the uniformed police then guarding the school were removed, leaving in their place three undercover agents disguised as workers.[90]

But even such warnings failed to completely quell protest. After the minister visited Mactumactzá in Chiapas, the students changed their strike to rolling absences with thirty different students abstaining from class every day.[91] Teachers who supported student protests also received threats. In Atequiza, Jalisco, the education authorities reminded instructors that their salaries came from the government and, above all else, their loyalty should lie there. They were to report any student organizing and were warned that the SEP had a list of teachers and staff who had "fomented or encouraged the subversive activity of students."[92] The education minister soon dangled a carrot alongside this stick, promising teachers better benefits if they opposed student organizing.[93]

The FECSM put on a brave fight, but by the end of September, it was clear that they could not stop the restructuring. Its leadership reaffirmed its commitment to the rural normal system, declaring it would remain firm in its fight for educational access, and demanded that the government continue to recognize the federation as an autonomous organization representing rural normal students.[94] But their struggle became a defensive one, reduced now to securing enrollment for those expelled for protesting the reform. Distress—the sense that a major battle, and perhaps the war, had been lost—pervaded the FECSM leadership. To the extent that the 1960s marked the explosion of youth mobilization, this blow to rural normales was even more crushing. Saúl López de la Torre, from the rural normal of Mactumactzá in Chiapas, vividly evoked the leadership's sentiment in the wake of the restructuring: "During the first week of November, I attended what would be the last FECSM convention of that period. The meeting—more like a funeral than a national political assembly—took place in a small establishment in the historic center of Mexico City. No more than twenty of us from different parts of the country came to discuss the path we'd take in light of the new power relations."[95]

What the FECSM lost with the system's restructuring was not teacher training spots. Those numbers would ostensibly remain the same, albeit confined to half as many schools. The true loss, as a FECSM leader explained, was the means to politicize and organize students starting at the junior high school age. "As of 1970, when the reform went into effect, the FECSM had six thousand fewer members and a reserve of only two school years in which to politically prepare students to sustain the national organization. This was without a doubt one of the most intelligent acts that the education authorities could have undertaken. In one fell swoop, they decimated the best-organized forces that the independent and democratic student movement preserved after 1968."[96]

THE 1969 RESTRUCTURING of rural normales stands as a watershed moment in normalista narratives, even for those who did not experience it directly. Time and again, students cited the elimination of fourteen rural normales as official retaliation against a network of schools that produced unruly subjects. Given the 1968 student protest in the capital, their logic goes, President Díaz Ordaz was proactive in stifling those poised to take up its mantle. In their accounts, normalistas rarely, if ever, mention the accompanying academic measures. Even the additional year of study that postponed their receipt of a salary—in the moment a significant grievance—merits scant attention decades later. Such an interpretation, and the outsized role that political action plays in normalista memories in general, reveals both objective and subjective realities. In the case of the former, it shows the extent to which leftist ideological formation constituted a part of school life—a parallel curriculum, as one study termed it.[97] The elimination of half of the country's normales also served to confirm the oft-repeated message of student leaders: post-Cardenista administrations had no interest in preserving these institutions; on the contrary, given the opportunity, they would be eliminated. More broadly, this understanding speaks to the 1960s as a decade of youthful mobilization, which, despite scholars' focus on Mexico City, encompassed the entire country, including rural areas.

With regard to subjective realities, emphasizing Díaz Ordaz's political motivation allows for the possibility that the normalistas, too, were historical protagonists—even if defeated ones. Given the prominence that Tlatelolco has come to occupy in Mexico's recent political narrative, it is not surprising that rural normalistas tie their own mobilizations and the state's response to this event, especially since, until the 2014 attack on Ayotzinapa, rural normalistas remained largely invisible in national histories of student protest. At a personal level, moreover, highlighting their intrepid spirit of resistance helps reconcile a basic contradiction between the ideal and the reality of their education and professional trajectory. While rural normales were to graduate committed teachers whose missionary duty would have them return to the countryside, where they would teach and live among the most vulnerable population, graduates instead gravitated to urban areas where they had greater professional opportunities and a chance at a more comfortable life. Whether or not they continued their political activism, and whether or not they upheld leftist ideological principles, normalistas overwhelmingly emphasize the noble ideal of the rural normal project. No wonder they condemn a measure that curtailed it.

Less evident in their oral histories but pervasive in the documents produced at the time are the fundamentally different assumptions under which the FECSM and the education authorities operated. Both recognized deficiencies in rural normales and the extent to which limited resources aggravated the problem. For students, this financial neglect was representative of the state's larger disregard for campesinos. The problems were structural and demanded radical action, measures that seemed possible based on the Cardenista past and the revolutionary present. In a decade marked by global student movements and anticolonial and anti-imperialist struggles, in which the Cuban Revolution figured prominently as a socialist example, this is hardly surprising. In both universities and normal schools, Marxism, relayed an alarmist U.S. embassy report, was the dominant framework by which students understood their reality.[98]

For the SEP, the shortcomings at rural normales were symptomatic of larger problems within the teacher-training system, to be resolved through updated pedagogical methods, professional efficiency, appeals to self-sacrifice, and better instilling of moral and civic values. While SEP authorities dismissed student calls for structural transformation as based on youthful idealism, their own emphasis that normalistas ought to demonstrate a selfless spirit of service was itself an idealistic appeal, compelling teachers to renounce basic material comforts in the name of patriotic duty. Accepting this condition was the best way to serve a poor nation like Mexico. From this perspective it is easy to see why normalistas' political involvement constituted such an obstacle to professional efficiency. Not only did it give students the ideological tools with which the challenge the state, but it took them away from classes, disrupted the smooth running of institutions, and produced constant obstacles to state dictums. Whether politically motivated or not, halving the rural normal system constituted a means to curtail this challenge.

8

"That's How We'd Meet . . . Clandestinely with the Lights Off"

"WHEN WE ARRIVED at the normal of Tamazulapan, the environment was very hostile," recalled Elsa Guzmán, who began her studies there in 1970. "I think [school] authorities took their task very seriously, and some of the staff thought they had all the power over us." Guzmán spoke of verbal abuse, insults, and general mistreatment—a painful environment that hurt students' self-esteem. "We endured it for two years, until it became intolerable. When I was in my third year, we started meeting in the bathrooms. At first it was just two of us, then three, four. That's how we'd meet . . . clandestinely, with the lights off." When their secret meetings reached twenty people, they decided it was time to call a strike, to lead the rest of the student body in a walkout. "If people joined us, then we'd made it; otherwise, we knew we'd be expelled."[1] Much to their surprise, their peers followed. So began the process of reconstituting the Mexican Federation of Socialist Campesino Students (FECSM).

The 1969 reform that converted fourteen of the twenty-nine rural normales into technical agricultural schools and separated the secundaria from the professional training stands as a traumatic moment in normalista memories. The reform decimated the rural normal system by reducing the number of schools, constraining their geographic reach, and curtailing the years students spent at the institutions (map 8.1). That the Ministry of Public Education (SEP) implemented this transformation in the wake of the 1968 Tlatelolco massacre rendered political a purportedly educational reform. The changes came with a tightened control over the student body—an iron fist, as one intelligence officer characterized it. School administrators prohibited student associations, and officials refused to recognize the FECSM as a mediating body.[2]

This chapter examines the rural normales in the aftermath of the 1969 reform amid the political fallout generated by the Tlatelolco massacre. It traces the process by which the FECSM reconstituted itself and the nature of rural normalistas' political involvement in the 1970s. This decade saw important transformations for the student body. Most significantly, the federation that reemerged was more militant but also more fractured. This quality was itself a product of the contradictory political environment in which it regrouped. President Luis Echeverría (1970–76), eager to repair the beleaguered image of the Institutional Revolutionary Party (PRI), embarked on a series of reforms. Seeking to portray himself as an heir to Lázaro Cárdenas's legacy, Echeverría declared education expansion and land redistribution two cornerstones of his administration. He also touted a democratic opening, lowered the voting age, and freed political prisoners—many of whom had languished in jail since the labor struggles of the 1950s. Echeverría also sought to revive Mexico's revolutionary credentials by providing asylum to those fleeing Augusto Pinochet's Chile and taking a leadership role in Third World politics. This context provided some breathing room for the FECSM and contributed to its ability to regroup and, eventually, regain SEP recognition. Most remarkably, it enabled the construction of a new rural normal in Amilcingo, Morelos.

But the PRI's new face had its limits. Echeverría maintained the state's repressive apparatus—and not only against radicals, a fact vividly demonstrated with the 1971 police and paramilitary attack on student demonstrators in Mexico City. The operation left two dozen dead and more than a hundred injured.[3] In the sierra of Guerrero, the regime that sought to revive Cárdenas's legacy encountered guerrillas led by rural teachers, the very figureheads of 1930s Cardenista policy. Lucio Cabañas, a 1963 Ayotzinapa graduate and former FECSM general secretary, took up arms after a series of government massacres blocked his effort at peaceful protest. In response, the state unleashed its full might, a dirty war that forcibly displaced, killed, tortured, or disappeared hundreds of campesinos.[4]

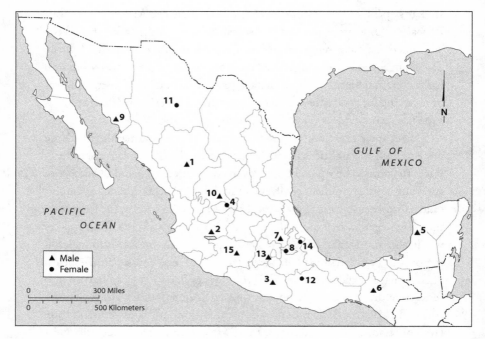

MAP 8.1 Rural Normales, 1969–1970

1	Aguilera, Durango	9	El Quinto, Sonora
2	Atequiza, Jalisco	10	San Marcos, Zacatecas
3	Ayotzinapa, Guerrero	11	Saucillo, Chihuahua
4	Cañada Honda, Aguascalientes	12	Tamazulapan, Oaxaca
5	Hecelchakán, Campeche	13	Tenería, Mexico State
6	Mactumactzá, Chiapas	14	Teteles, Puebla
7	El Mexe, Hidalgo	15	Tiripetío, Michoacán
8	Panotla, Tlaxcala		

Source: "Escuelas Normales Rurales," August 18, 1969, Archivo General de la Nación, Dirección Federal de Seguridad 63-19, Leg.9, H189–91.

Note: This map should be taken with a degree of caution since most documentation contains errors or inconsistencies.

It is not surprising that Echeverría resorted to such brutal force. He had been, after all, part of the inner circle that presided over the Tlatelolco massacre. Nor is it surprising that his populist attempts to reform the economy failed. In this latter effort, he was hampered not only by three decades of economic policy that favored industry, agribusiness, and the urban sector but by elites intent on preventing changes to a system from which they had benefited so handily. As Echeverría came to be besieged by northern industrialists and right-wing elements of the middle class, his administration increasingly tried to characterize normalistas' protest as antirevolutionary.[5] Under the logic that any protest against the president ultimately fortified reactionaries, the SEP painted leftist normalistas as "instruments of a fascist process."[6] These allegations had little staying power. But the official demonization of their schools persisted and, in fact, was cemented during the 1970s. Normalistas' new tactics—which included commandeering buses and setting up roadblocks—made them increasingly visible to an urban public and fed the view of them as disruptive troublemakers whose last priority was to study. That their schools became recruiting grounds for clandestine groups branded rural normales as guerrilla seedbeds, a label that persists to the present. As the 1970s wore on and new educational reforms created a byzantine teacher-training system in which private and state (as opposed to federal) normales increasingly crowded the institutional landscape, rural normales distinguished themselves ever more by the militancy of their students.

"THE REACTION OF THE COMPAÑERAS WAS FIERCE"

The 1969/70 academic year was turbulent at rural normales. Unable to halt their schools' restructuring, normalistas disrupted its implementation. It took some time for the education authorities to gain control of the situation; when they did, it was through draconian disciplinary measures, including the prohibition of student associations. "The crisis was terrible," remembered Marcos José García, who in the fall of 1969 began his studies in Reyes Mantecón, a rural normal in Oaxaca, now turned into a technical agricultural school. The environment left him unsettled. "I got very scared and went home. . . . When I came back a month later, the situation was calmer."[7] Or so it seemed. Tensions bubbled up as collective rage. "When [SEP] officials arrived, there would be war in the cafeteria," recalled Aristarco Aquino Solís, a student from Mactumactzá. "It started slowly, with pieces of bread. One visiting official ended up doused in coffee."[8] Elsa Guzmán spoke of similar moments in Champusco, Puebla, where she was first transferred in the wake of the restructuring. When the general secretary of normal education, Ramón Bonfil, visited the school, "the reaction of the compañeras was fierce. Plates started flying. The man left covered in food. . . . The aggression was strong; they even threatened to close the school because of that action."[9] At San Marcos, Zacatecas, the outbursts at cafeterias went further, with students hurling dishes, overturning tables, and slamming furniture, a mess they were all made to clean up.[10]

The sources of this pent-up resentment were many. Not only did the tightened control elicit authoritarian practice, but it increased graft. With no student associations to oversee them, teachers, administrators, and staff could more easily extract food funds, resources, and boarding-school supplies. Reconstituting the FECSM in this environment was no easy task. The intensity of the 1969 resistance and the normalistas' inability to prevent the system's restructuring exhausted their energies and dampened morale.[11] Some of the most active student leaders had been expelled or had joined guerrilla struggles. Those completing their last year of study were especially hesitant to participate in strikes or to engage in other acts of resistance since doing so jeopardized the timely receipt of their diplomas.[12]

But an undercurrent of discontent persisted. Organizing efforts at individual schools soon overlapped with those of delegates who sought to reconstitute the FECSM nationally. The processes fed off one another. Only if students gathered sufficient organizing capacity at individual schools could federation delegates force the SEP to the negotiating table. In Mexico City, students from various rural normales had been meeting since the summer of 1970. Little came of it until 1972, when they united rural normales behind a set of demands consisting of freedom of association (including facilitating the conditions under which FECSM delegates could travel to national meetings); increased food rations, stipends, scholarships, and teachers; and the resignation of rural education director Lucio López Iriarte for his "despotic, arbitrary, and inept" policies.[13]

Normalista delegates presented this list of demands to the SEP in July 1972, but not until November, when all rural normales went on strike, did the authorities respond, agreeing to raise food amounts and stipends but deferring the other matters to a later date.[14] Still, these two concessions stood as a victory. Rural normales had presented a united front and brought the SEP to the bargaining table. By meeting with FECSM delegates, the SEP had again recognized it as a legitimate representative body. The student group moved quickly to organize a reconstituting congress in December. Seventy-five representatives from the fifteen rural normales attended this meeting at Tenería in Mexico State.[15] The FECSM soon achieved another victory, the removal of López Iriarte, whom they accused of systematically rejecting any petition brought before him.[16]

These nationally coordinated efforts overlapped with a series of mobilizations at individual normales. In Saucillo the normalistas pressured for the readmittance of two students expelled for protesting the 1969 reform; in San Marcos students ousted the director, whose authoritarianism had crossed a line when he struck a student; Mactumactzá and Tiripetío followed, the former running off their director for fund mismanagement and the latter for negligence.[17] Telling with regard to how students experienced the reassertion of their power are the words of Elsa Guzmán, whose story opened this chapter: "We came together to fight for our freedom, our autonomy to again organize ourselves and the normal. . . . It then fell to me to tell the assistant principal who mistreated us and the teacher who groped students that they had twenty-four hours to abandon the school."[18]

The FECSM made headway on both material and political demands. The latter involved a lenient absence policy for delegates, whose duties meant frequent travel and who would otherwise lose their right to take final exams.[19] Normalistas also achieved important concessions in agrarian disputes involving their schools. Significantly, such victories benefited neighboring campesino communities as much as the normales themselves. In 1974, for example, students from Tenería secured the restitution of sixty-three hectares of land that they proposed be cultivated by landless campesinos, alongside whom the students would work to fulfill their agricultural training requirement. The campesinos, in turn, would keep the harvested crops.[20] Likewise, in 1975, in the rural normal of El Mexe, where teachers had appropriated land meant for agricultural training, students mobilized to turn it over to the neighboring campesinos.[21] In other instances, normalistas secured support from rural dwellers to preserve or expand their schools. For example, in Sonora, when the SEP sought to transfer the rural normal of El Quinto to Guesave, Sinaloa, because it did not have enough land, students opposed to the move convinced campesinos in the surrounding area to donate the required acreage in return for compensation by agrarian authorities.[22]

More broadly, the FECSM assessed the national context to formulate a path of struggle beyond school walls. In their 1974 conference in Mactumactzá, 250 normalistas debated strategies for broader popular engagement and named commissions charged with approaching workers, campesinos, and the poor in order to better understand their problems and support their struggles.[23] At individual schools students had already made concerted efforts to participate in popular mobilizations. The list was long. In January 1973 the federation convened a meeting in Tiripetío to determine how best to aid striking sugarcane laborers in Veracruz; the following year, students from El Mexe sent sugar, beans, and coffee to striking cement workers in Tula, Hidalgo, and later joined the workers as they attempted a factory takeover; in northern Mexico, students from Aguilera and Saucillo supported and participated in campesino land takeovers.[24] Mactumactzá students aided mill workers at Maderas de Comitán as they formed an independent union, and those from Tenería supported the workers at the Radio Majestic factory in the nearby state of Tlaxcala when they sought higher wages; in Hecelchakán, Campeche, normalistas mobilized against the hike in bus fares.[25] Telling of such support for workers, one intelligence report—after listing the various agrarian, worker, and civil servants (*burócratas*) struggles in Chiapas—commented, "Of course, all of these movements are spearheaded by students of the state's rural normal."[26] These actions represented a continuation of rural normalistas' engagement with popular struggles and, while sporadic, added elements of praxis to the revolutionary theory they read and discussed in their political study groups.

Internally, the FECSM attempted to make some changes in its organizational structure, though the degree to which it underwent substantive change is unclear. At their 1974 conference in Mactumactzá, Chiapas, delegates discussed proposals for a less hierarchical organization, one in which the national council became a coordinating body and the secretary general a mediator rather than a figurehead charged with decision-making. The position, moreover, would be subject to more frequent rotation. Conference proceedings also indicated the need for more deliberate and systematic study of Marxism-Leninism to best "direct the struggle of the working and lower classes" when conditions were ripe. Finally, during this conference the delegates voted to assume the representation of the technical agricultural schools, the rural normales that had become junior high schools with the 1969 reform.[27] The arrangement was short-lived, partly because of the strong retaliation of the education authorities, who tracked normalista organizers and, after their first joint national strike, expelled close to nine hundred secundaria students.[28] In a volatile environment also characterized by fissures within the FECSM itself, representation of the secundarias proved untenable.

By some measures the FECSM that came together in the early 1970s was more militant but its divisions more salient. Still, if 1969 stands as a moment of defeat, the protest actions of the early 1970s evoke a sense of renewed student power, whose manifestations went from outbursts of rage, to strikes, to solidarity campaigns with workers and campesinos, to direct action in which students commandeered buses or mounted roadblocks. The most radical joined armed movements. In this context, divisions over strategy, ideological debates, and organizational allegiances became more accentuated and drove wedges between militant groups and the general student body. Four factors contributed to this tendency. First, the restructuring of rural normales from six-year institutions that included both secundaria and professional training to four-year teacher-training schools reduced the age span of the student body and shortened the amount of time students spent there. This effectively diminished the FECSM's time frame for recruitment, ideological continuity, and organizational training. Second, for individuals anxious for change, actions such as commandeering buses or collaborating with guerrillas provided an outlet that came at the cost of the slower, piecemeal work involved in consciousness raising and collective organizing. Such activity, in turn, gave the government and media outlets more ammunition with which to demonize the rural normalistas, who were often presented as marauding youth gangs. During the FECSM's 1974 conference in Chiapas, for example, a San Cristóbal de las Casas radio announcer took to the airwaves to warn parents that students from rural normales and a group of indigenous people—whose mobilization in the neighboring town normalistas had supported—planned to attack kindergartens and elementary schools with stones and Molotov cocktails. In response, principals closed the schools as anxious parents picked up their kids. "The report was false," wrote an intelligence officer later. "No students from the rural normales were in the vicinity of the elementary schools, nor were there any incidents there."[29]

Third, the government stepped up its efforts to co-opt students. The Socialist Workers' Party (Partido Socialista de los Trabajadores, PST), which one 1970s normalista characterized as "neither a party, nor socialist, nor of workers," was one vehicle for recruitment into state circles. "They were of a filiation very close to the PRI," explained Marcos José García from Tiripetío, where the PST's efforts were especially strong. "They were practically the left wing of the PRI. They would go to normales to co-opt . . . [and] conjure up conflicts, divisions."[30] In 1975 the FECSM itself denounced government and education authorities for using the party to undermine the federation's long history of struggle.[31] The PST began recruiting members at rural normales and gained strength through its ability to curry favor with high-level SEP officials.[32] In schools like Tiripetío, El Mexe, Hecelchakán, and Mactumactzá, its affiliates soon claimed to have ousted the FECSM as a representative body.[33] In 1976 the PST planned a national constituting conference in El Mexe to wrest control away from the FECSM.[34] While ultimately unsuccessful in supplanting the FECSM at the national level, the PST's actions led to considerable division among the student body.

Finally, despite initial SEP concessions that allowed the FECSM to regroup, the education authorities soon moved forward with stricter regulations on collective action. Any strikes of five continuous days or ten aggregated ones would result in the suspension of classes, declared a 1976 SEP regulation. Students would thus lose credit for the entire semester. Modifications to the school calendar made in previous decades to account for days lost to strikes would now be disallowed, preventing students from making up the time.[35] The only option would be to repeat the year. "Young students, you should stop and think!" declared the head of teacher-training education, "*the schools and universities that the sons and daughters of the rich attend do not miss any days. It is noteworthy that the more the academic indicators in our own schools descend, the better they remain in universities and institutions of higher culture.*" Tinged with class contempt, the statement further asserted that student mobilizations elicited hostility among surrounding populations, undermined institutions emanating from the revolution, and led earnest students to drop out and militant ones to be expelled, thus undermining the teaching profession more generally.[36]

In this way, while the FECSM was able to regroup, SEP authorities also stepped up their efforts to foment a black legend about rural normales. The proliferation of guerrilla groups throughout the country and their connection to rural normales (discussed later in this chapter) further facilitated the criminalization of these students and their schools. That Echeverría provided visible concessions to campesinos and students—such as the recognition of the new rural normal in Amilcingo—reinforced the impression that militant normalistas were being unreasonable.

"AN ACT OF JUSTICE TO MEXICO'S AGRARIAN MOVEMENT"

Remarkably, given the 1969 closing of half of the rural normales, the community of Amilcingo, Morelos, pushed through the creation of a new one in 1974.[37] The population of Amilcingo, located on the state's eastern border with Puebla, consisted mainly of subsistence farmers and seasonal agricultural workers. Spearheaded by Eva Rivera, a local elementary schoolteacher and a 1957 graduate of the rural normal of Palmira, and Vinh Flores, a member of the Youth Communist Party, the initiative brought together actors of various political stripes. Rivera belonged to the local evangelical church and recruited support among its members, including Benedicto Rosales Olivar, the president of the ejido association, and Justo Rivera, a local town council assistant. Other municipal authorities associated with the PRI, like Nabor Barrera, also joined the effort.[38] This small, unlikely group of evangelicals, communists, and priístas (official party members) put together a makeshift teacher-training school whose classes began in Amilcingo's municipal building, where teachers from Rivera's school volunteered their time imparting evening classes. Flores recruited students from nearby communities, many of whom were initially housed by campesinos and, in exchange, helped with farming tasks. Twenty-six students passed through Rivera's home alone. As enrollment increased, the school moved to the town's evangelical temple. Soon the initiative came to the attention of students at other rural normales. Pedagogical material arrived from Tamazulapan, Oaxaca; mattresses from Tenería, Mexico State; and FECSM delegates from El Quinto, Sonora. Calling itself a *normal rural popular*, in its first few months, the school had a constant, if unstable, flow of students.[39]

In the first few months of operation, the school's main challenges were logistical: providing room and board for students, finding adequate classrooms, managing the informal personnel, and retaining a stable student body. Only official SEP recognition would bring the necessary resources to address these matters, not to mention legitimize the graduates' diplomas. The school's federalization thus became the next goal, a battle that the FECSM joined. The federation's involvement strengthened the movement as rural normalistas from across the country traveled to Amilcingo, organized community brigades, and incorporated the school's recognition into the demand list they issued to the SEP.[40] As the mobilizations in favor of the school picked up pace, so did official opposition. On March 21, 1974, for example, normalistas and community members held a joint demonstration in Cuautla, where Eva Rivera figured visibly as a speaker and organizer. In the following days, the local school inspector ordered her transfer from Amilcingo to a remote community in the southern part of the state.[41]

Rivera's removal triggered the first of several fissures in the movement. Some ejidatarios blamed the normalistas for the government's retaliation. Since the students' arrival, the town had begun to see graffiti reading "Long live Lucio Cabañas" and "The guerrillas are the people." Indeed, at a Cuautla demonstration, the normalistas had shouted antigovernment proclamations and handed out leaflets in support of Lucio Cabañas's guerrilla group.[42] Such proclamations made many locals nervous. Undeterred, the FECSM pressed forward, calling a strike of rural normalistas in support of the normal's recognition and the restitution of Flores to her original post.[43] Despite tensions, they planned a joint community-student march from Amilcingo to the SEP's offices in Mexico City on May 5, 1974. Their cause drew support from students at the Autonomous Universities of Guerrero, Zacatecas, Yucatán, and Puebla, as well as the agricultural schools of Chapingo, Delicias, Iguala, and Venecia.[44] Independent campesino organizations also responded to the call for support. When the marchers reached the city of Cuautla, they encountered a commission that included Morelos governor Felipe Rivera Crespo and normal education secretary Víctor Hugo Bolaños. Backed by an army dispatch, the state officials convinced the participants to call off the march and enter into negotiations.[45] By the end of May, the authorities agreed to support the construction of a women's normal—to be named Emiliano Zapata—"an act of justice to Mexico's agrarian movement and its principal proponent."[46] A committee made up of SEP members, students, and campesinos was tasked with obtaining the required fifty hectares on which to build the school. Within less than a month, the ejidatarios had agreed to provide just shy of that amount (49.83 hectares).[47] Campesinos and rural normalistas from various schools cleared and prepared the land for construction, with students forming brigades to procure food donations to sustain the volunteers.[48]

The process was anything but smooth. Not all members of the ejido association had supported their land's expropriation. While the initial disagreements were resolved within the ejidatario council, conflict bubbled up again during the compensation process.[49] Objections were practical as well as political. The land that the agrarian authorities offered in exchange was farther away, and the distance represented a hardship for farmers. Politically, opposition came from those who sympathized with the Popular Socialist Party, opposed as it was to an initiative spearheaded by communists on the one hand (such as Vinh Flores) and priístas (municipal and ejido authorities) on the other. Such conflicts soon turned violent and before the decade's end left all but one of the leaders dead. Benedicto Rosales Olivar, the head of the ejido association and a strong proponent of the school, was the first victim, shot in the back just outside his home on November 12, 1975. A year later, Vinh Flores, the young communist and key protagonist of the initiative, was found dead, killed alongside his uncle in the neighboring region of Puebla.[50] Rumors placed the blame for these murders on local gunmen protected by state authorities.[51] Given official disinterest in pursuing an investigation, three campesinos who had fought alongside Flores took justice into their own hands, killing his alleged murderers. This crime the authorities did pursue, apprehending and torturing those responsible.[52] Two years later, the murders continued with the killing of Nabor Barrera, the president of the newly created municipality of Temoac and an early supporter of the Amilcingo normal initiative.[53] The presumed intellectual and material authors responsible for slaying the school proponents were themselves killed in 1979.[54]

There were other troubling dynamics. Conflicts within the student body developed during its first federally operated school year. Some of the students sought to maintain a close relationship with Amilcingo's community members, while a rival group wanted decisions made under the rubric of institutional autonomy. This conflict stifled future grassroots collaboration between the community and the school, the very solidarity that first gave the initiative strength. As it evolved, the school-community relationship became more functionalist. The normal provided educational opportunities for the daughters of the local population—70 percent of its student body came from Morelos, with the rest hailing from Guerrero, Puebla, and Oaxaca.[55] Moreover, the staffing and administrative positions went to the Amilcingo population, providing a much-needed source of employment. In addition, the normalistas undertook their student teaching in the local elementary schools and organized festivities surrounding civic holidays.[56]

As with other rural normales, Amilcingo developed a strong activist tradition. National FECSM delegates immediately organized a student committee there. Ever determined to ensure a presence in all normales, the FECSM appealed to students by invoking education both as an opportunity for material security and as a popular vindication. Xóchitl García, who began her studies in Amilcingo a year after its founding and was active in the student association, remembered, "Our compañeros helped and at the same time pushed us to learn. They said that it wasn't just about arriving once the table was set, or about just becoming teachers. It was about participating [in the struggle] so that it could be stronger, so that more students could arrive and continue to have professional opportunities, to change the country, to feed their families, and to help the people."[57]

In the Morelos countryside, such messages found fertile ground, and even if the Amilcingo community did not participate in the decision-making structure of the new school, the students who studied there engaged—indeed, often had ties to—local histories of struggle. Xóchitl García is a case in point. The daughter of a prominent Jaramillista—a campesino movement that in preceding decades had fought for agrarian rights through legal and armed struggle—García was no stranger to the state's repressive apparatus. Not only had Rubén Jaramillo, the movement's leader, been massacred by the army alongside his wife and three sons a decade earlier, but García's own father had been the victim of a brutal attack by hired gunmen.[58] To García and the politicized student body of the normal, the fate of activists like Vinh Flores confirmed the repressive nature of the state, not to mention the precious quality of social gains, which more often than not came at the cost of human life. With no formal accountability for the murders of local activists, their fate came to be understood within the pattern of violence meted out to community leaders. As García stated about Flores, "He was a brave man of the countryside who did not get to see the culmination of the normal because he was assassinated. We found out later—because the truth was hidden for a long time—that it was the state government that had him killed. . . . They ambushed him alongside the person he was with. . . . They massacred them out in the fields and left them there like animals."[59] Amilcingo's student committee would take its name from the slain leader, and today a large mural in the school's cafeteria honors him along with Nabor Barrera and Benedicto Rosales Olivar, the two other local leaders who fought for the school's creation and were killed in the ensuing years.[60]

In both its victory and the lives lost to secure it, the rural normal of Amilcingo presents a vivid example of the achievements and sacrifices of resistance movements. The timing of its creation symbolized Echeverría's proclaimed commitment to education and to the countryside. Seen in a long-term context, it displayed the PRI's tried-and-true carrot-and-stick strategy. But Echeverría's populist measures and political reforms could not erase his close association with the Tlatelolco massacre. And if to many 1968 symbolized the point of no return in the move from reformist to armed tactics, the 1969 decimation of the rural normales further reinforced the logic of guerrilla struggle since it signaled a large-scale strategy of containment against student movements. Faced with the opportunity to join or aid clandestine groups, many rural normalistas took it. Some viewed their choice as a moral imperative, others as a logical action since they had been expelled, and yet others as the most effective way to create change. Regardless of the motivation, the rural normales' history, militant tradition, and presence throughout the country would make them both recruiting grounds and hubs of guerrilla support.

"TO CHANGE THE WORLD"

If the 1965 guerrilla attack on the military barracks of Madera, Chihuahua, had already revealed the symbolic and material link between armed struggle and rural normales, the various guerrilla groups that emerged throughout the country in the wake of 1968 solidified this connection. The Revolutionary Action Movement (Movimiento de Acción Revolucionaria, MAR), the 23rd of September Communist League (Liga Comunista 23 de Septiembre), the National Revolutionary Civic Association, and the Party of the Poor—itself led by a graduate of the rural normal of Ayotzinapa—all included rural normalistas as either participants or support networks. The proliferation of guerrilla groups in Mexico was another symptom of the PRI's legitimacy crisis. Even before the 1968 Tlatelolco massacre, state repression had led popular leaders to take up arms. Rubén Jaramillo in Morelos, Arturo Gámiz and Pablo Gómez in Chihuahua, and Genaro Vázquez and Lucio Cabañas in Guerrero had all resorted to armed struggle when the state's targeted persecution and campesino massacres closed other avenues of protest. October 2 uncovered this reality for the urban, middle-class public, leading many university students to pursue a similar route.

For many student insurgents, the international context was equally significant. Since 1959 the Cuban Revolution had inspired hope about the possibilities of socialist revolution. Anticolonial struggles in Asia and Africa vividly showcased Third World actors as protagonists of liberation, while the war in Vietnam laid bare the brutal nature of U.S. imperialism. In Europe, Japan, and the United States, internal protest showed that the First World was hardly the model modernization theorists had long maintained. And in both life and death, Ernesto "Che" Guevara stubbornly stoked the youthful imagination.

During the 1970s there were twenty-nine guerrilla organizations in Mexico, together involving 1,860 participants.[61] The MAR, the 23rd of September Communist League, and the groups led by Vázquez and Cabañas in Guerrero most intersected with the rural normales. Initiated by about a dozen students, most of whom belonged to the Communist Youth Cadre, the MAR dated back to the mid-1960s, spurred in no small measure by the repression at schools outside the capital. In Michoacán many had congregated in the Nicolaita Student House, living quarters for out-of-town university students and the place where rural normalistas from La Huerta and Tiripetío took refuge during their resistance to the 1969 normal restructuring.[62] Some of the MAR's initial participants had studied in the Soviet Union's Patricio Lumumba University and would later receive training in North Korea, which during the 1960s and 1970s supported liberation struggles throughout Asia, Africa, and Latin America. The MAR conceived of itself as the vanguard group that would eventually lead Mexico's socialist revolution.[63] It first sought training in Cuba, but the island's close diplomatic relationship with

Mexico kept it from lending support. North Korea, which then sought to foster a policy of guerrilla internationalism, eagerly took them in and from 1969 to 1970 lent military training to fifty-three MAR members.[64] Upon their return, in conjunction with other armed groups, the MAR saw its task as accelerating the conditions for a popular uprising. By the early 1970s, with almost a hundred members, it had a presence in at least ten states and the Federal District.[65]

From Chihuahua, rural normalistas like Alma Gómez Caballero and Herminia Gómez Carrasco, students from Saucillo and daughters of the activist teachers Pablo Gómez and Raúl Gómez respectively, joined the MAR. Gómez Carrasco's involvement with the MAR began while she was studying at Saucillo. Long active in campesino mobilizations, whose land takeovers she participated in, she was expelled in October 1969 for taking part in a commemoration of the 1968 student massacre. "By then, a compañero from Ayotzinapa, Guerrero, . . . had already recruited us to be part of the Revolutionary Action Movement," she recalled. "We were going to join once we finished at the normal; we weren't going to just grab a gun and leave. But since they expelled me . . . I went to Mexico City and from there to North Korea, where we received military training as part of the MAR. We were there a year and then returned as an armed group—to change the world!"[66]

Individual normalistas' reasons for joining or supporting armed movements varied. Gómez Carrasco's last phrase, a reflection said half in jest, is a common frame. Ushering in a better world seemed within arm's reach, and the normalistas—involved in political action from a young age—wanted to be part of that effort. Such impulses reflect a commonsense devotion to political struggle amplified by radical strains in normalista culture and accentuated by the decade's zeitgeist.[67] Many specifically cite the 1968 Tlatelolco massacre as an event that signaled the close of legal channels. "You're expressing your right to free speech, you're fighting for your constitutional rights, and you're defending simple things like university autonomy, and the government responds with bullets! What message is it sending?!" reflected Alma Gómez Caballero, who joined the MAR.[68] For those moved but not convinced by 1968, the 1969 closure and clampdown at rural normales acted as the final push. Today some think of the decision as naive, while others marvel at the courage it took—a product of youthful temerity, a bravery possible since they were not weighed down by family responsibilities.

To the extent that there is a relationship between youth and audacious acts, it was the 23rd of September Communist League that most capitalized on this propensity. The league, an urban guerrilla group taking its name from the date of the 1965 attack on Chihuahua's military barracks in Madera, also had significant reach in rural normales. Founded in 1973 in Guadalajara, the league was the most radical and largest of the guerrilla groups in Cold War Mexico, made up of a coalition of seven independent guerrilla groups together numbering about 450. Its membership was primarily student based.[69] Ideologically, the league saw universities as institutions integral to the process of capitalist accumulation. By extension, students were proletarians. The group relied on revolutionary expropriations (bank heists) and kidnapping of prominent figures—Eugenio Garza Sada, the powerful Monterrey industrialist; José Guadalupe Zuno, the president's father-in-law; and Terrence G. Leonhardt, the U.S. consul general, were three of their most high-profile abductions. Tactically, the league prioritized political violence over grassroots organizing, and members often found themselves in open confrontation with the police. Despite its urban focus, the group did recruit and gain adherents in rural normales.[70] Elsa Guzmán from Tamazulapan, Oaxaca, remembered her collaboration with this group. "As a security measure, we never asked their names. But there was this one woman whom we called *la maestra*, and she was pregnant. She seemed about to give birth, and she still trained us in how to use a gun." Guzmán characterized that training as a self-defense measure for when she took supplies to guerrillas. At other points, Guzmán remembered bringing league members to the normal to eat at the cafeteria. "They're my aunt and uncle," she would respond to anyone who asked.[71]

But it was Lucio Cabañas's Party of the Poor, a campesino guerrilla group based in Guerrero, that became most associated with the rural normales. Not only was Cabañas an Ayotzinapa graduate, but he had been the head of the FECSM in the early 1960s; his fame resounded throughout the rural normal system, and he himself relied on normalista networks while operating clandestinely.[72] The character of Cabañas's guerrilla group, moreover, was in some ways closer to rural normalista culture than either the MAR or the 23rd of September Communist League. A campesino group based in Guerrero's sierra, Cabañas's Party of the Poor had long defended rural dwellers against cacique violence, and as a teacher in the Atoyac sierra, Cabañas had mobilized for basic reforms for the local population. Cabañas himself traced his early political consciousness to his years at the rural normal. "Those of us from Ayotzinapa, from the rural normal school, would go into all the little towns and everywhere organize demonstrations, bringing the campesinos along. Even when we were leaders in Ayotzinapa, we'd give clothes to the poor campesinos who did not have anything to wear and would approach us at Ayotzinapa." It was at the normal, he later declared, that their consciousness was born.[73]

Genaro Vázquez, another Guerrerense schoolteacher (trained at the National Teachers School), organized a different armed group, the National Revolutionary Civic Association. A longtime defender of Guerrero's campesinos, Vázquez was an early advocate for coffee, coconut, and sesame seed growers; spearheaded land invasions; coordinated struggles for municipal democratization; participated in Mexico City's 1950s Revolutionary Teachers Movement; and mobilized against the repressive Guerrero governor Raúl Caballero Aburto in 1960. His political career shared many characteristics with those of Pablo Gómez and Arturo Gámiz; like them, Vázquez did not study at a rural normal, although Ayotzinapa students claim his legacy, vividly showcasing him along with Cabañas in their murals. Specifically citing the government's decimation of the rural normal system, the flyers of the National Revolutionary Civic Association beckoned normalistas to "participate in the people's struggle and avoid the next blow the government is planning against rural normales."[74]

That rural teachers like Vázquez and Cabañas commanded armed campesinos in Guerrero, inflicted army losses, and, for several years, defied federal operations to capture and subdue them inspired rural normalistas in no small measure because they offered a concrete example of retributive justice, direct action, and a revolutionary path to socialism. These teachers were living incarnations of education as consciousness, of the disquieting attitude that there was more to be done. Still, while many rural normalistas joined guerrilla groups, more commonly students aided them with supplies, provided cover, or facilitated transportation. Such students often acted of their own accord, hiding their deeds not only from school administrators but from the student governing council. Elsa Guzmán, a student from the rural normal of Tamazulapan, for example, recounted how she and another student aided the guerrillas:

> We were in touch with the community of Jamiltepec, the people who had direct contact with Lucio Cabañas. But that was just two of us, and it had to be kept a secret. We filled a truckload with blankets and other stuff, claiming it was for the campesinos of Jamiltepec. We knew their true destination. . . . We later received a strong scolding from the student council when they found out the length to which we had gone, the extent to which we had exposed ourselves, because we had gone to meetings in Jamiltepec and had received a lot of death threats.[75]

Intelligence agents also noted that collaboration was more the purview of individuals or small groups than a school-wide initiative.[76] In fact, while normalistas made constant proclamations in support of the guerrilla cause in Guerrero, they rejected accusations of outright participation. For example, students at the rural normal of Tenería declared, "We may have the same goals and ideals, but our type of struggle is completely different. Prof. Cabañas has chosen an armed movement, and we fight with ideas. In no moment— and this should be clear—have we tried to imitate him. So in our institution and in the rest in our country, there isn't, as some of the regime's authorities would have you believe, armament the guerrillas give us."[77] In a public demonstration in Chiapas, normalistas from Mactumactzá explicitly decried the government branding them guerrillas and rabble-rousers, responding that they were simply students seeking justice for the people.[78] While much of the student connection was indeed at the level of ideals, as the normalistas claimed, it also behooved those linked to clandestine groups to deny any concrete collaboration since it not only elicited repression but bolstered the authorities' portrayals of rural normales as guerrilla seedbeds.

Flyers from the urban guerrilla group the 23rd of September Communist League turned up in the hands of rural normalistas, and on at least two occasions the authorities detained individual normalistas for possession of modest caches of arms.[79] According to a May 1974 intelligence report, Tenería had many participants in the league.[80] But the relationship with this group was at best fraught. At the rural normal of Tiripetío, Michoacán, for example, the student assembly sought to avoid what they characterized as the league's infiltration.[81] No matter the degree of normalista engagement with armed struggle, the government constantly showcased connections and thus dismissed normalista protests as simple cover for violent subversives. The students charged that, in fact, the government sponsored infiltrators to sow chaos by distributing drugs and holding rowdy social gatherings. Aside from painting rural normales in a bad light, such actions, they denounced, disrupted FECSM efforts to cultivate political consciousness.[82] In some cases, the students themselves identified these government agents and sought their expulsion.[83]

For the broad student body, it was the guerrilla symbolism they most engaged with. The heroism of armed struggle provided a significant rallying cry, one normalistas evoked within a framework of heroic masculinity. At one demonstration, for example, students carried a banner reading, "Did my mother breed a man or a castrated being? Let's open new guerrilla fronts."[84] Women normalistas, too, called on their compañeras to adhere to this model of bravery. In a demonstration in San Juan Chamula, Chiapas, held in concert with the FECSM's annual convention, one female orator specifically appealed to women to incorporate themselves into the revolutionary process and join the guerrilla movement in Guerrero.[85]

The mystique behind the guerrilla struggle was compelling. But, overall, the relationship between rural normales and armed movements was unstable. On the one hand, armed groups found in these institutions fertile recruiting grounds as well as spaces of refuge and support. On the other, the fact that groups like the MAR, the 23rd of September Communist League, and other clandestine organizations lacked a substantive popular base, were highly persecuted, and advocated risky, often-sensationalist actions made for a hotly contested and highly contentious relationship between the student body and insurgent members. Even guerrilla leaders like Cabañas cautioned students about the delicate nature of the path of armed struggle.[86] That the authorities used students' relationship to guerrillas as a justification for the military takeover of rural normales showed just how high the stakes ran. In 1976, for example, the army and police forces ended a strike at the rural normal of Atequiza, Jalisco, with a massive show of force. The justification was the school's supposed ties to subversives since one of its graduates had participated in the 1974 kidnapping of the first lady's father.[87] The rural normal of Aguilera, Durango, experienced a similar show of force when, on February 27, 1975, the military surrounded the school while the judicial police forced students out of the dorms—beating one who resisted. In this operation, security forces retrieved the fourteen buses the students had sequestered "but found no armament," reported the intelligence officers, "only leftist propaganda."[88] Throughout the country the authorities circulated lists of the "leaders and negative activists," tracking normalistas so closely they listed their seat numbers on buses they took to attend a FECSM conference.[89] In other instances, the SEP attempted to stymie rural normalistas' contact with "campesinos and the people more generally" by ordering directors to disable schools' agricultural vehicles so students could not use them for transportation. When this action failed, the ministry appealed to transit police to detain all rural normal vehicles and prevent their circulation.[90] In Guerrero the SEP singled out Ayotzinapa normalistas attempting to organize the junior high school students in the neighboring community of Tixtla.[91] The authorities did not stop at surveillance, and throughout the country students denounced the state's repression, including instances of kidnapping, beating, torture, and, in some cases, killing of normalistas.[92]

In Guerrero, governor Rubén Figueroa unleashed an undeclared war against the rural normal of Ayotzinapa, threatening to turn the institution into a tourism school. "Those rabble-rousing teachers and students will pack their bags and get the hell out of Guerrero," he declared.[93] Official disdain for Ayotzinapa continued in the years after Cabañas's death, with Figueroa and the school principal jointly squashing student organizing. Even modest acts of student engagement with the local population ran up against the state's wrath. During the summer of 1978, for example, a group of students sought to undertake a socioeconomic study of the region to better engage with community needs. The school director moved to prevent these efforts by notifying parents to come for their sons, who would otherwise be expelled. If they refused to leave, they would be forcibly removed, and their physical integrity could not be guaranteed. The principal also targeted any organizing links among students, teachers, and staff and decreed that if students missed more than two classes, they would lose the right to take their exams. For students, such measures revealed him to be a mere lackey of the governor. It was Figueroa who ultimately determined students' fate, charged normalistas, a power the governor made clear by constantly sending the army to Ayotzinapa.[94]

Without concrete figures about the number of normalistas who joined the guerrillas compared to students from other educational institutions, it is difficult to know for certain if they joined in greater proportion. No guerrilla group was made up exclusively of rural normalistas, and the MAR and the 23rd of September Communist League counted on numerous university students. However, some characteristics of rural normales, such as their nationwide web and the autonomy students enjoyed by living far from home, rendered them appealing sites for clandestine groups to both recruit and seek refuge. Their radical tradition, moreover, made many of their students receptive to guerrillas' message. Significantly, unlike for other schools, the narrative that links rural normales with guerrillas persisted. The association between these schools and armed struggle was heightened by the fact that they continue to be hubs of protest, are located outside or on the periphery of urban centers, and have a predominantly poor student body that proudly claims the legacy of martyred rural teachers like Pablo Gómez, Arturo Gámiz, Genaro Vázquez, and Lucio Cabañas. While, of them, only Cabañas and Gómez had institutional ties to these schools, both students and the state invoke a connection, albeit in fundamentally different ways. For students, the links to guerrillas stand as a genealogy of resistance: from Pancho

Villa and Emiliano Zapata, whose revolutionary struggle brought land and education to the poor; to Lázaro Cárdenas's socialist teachers, who traveled to remote communities with a book in one arm and a rifle on the other; to the daring 1965 assault on the military barracks in Madera, Chihuahua; to the 1970s armed movement in Guerrero, rural normales represent centers of critical consciousness, the bulwarks of revolution whose restless students are the consequence of a besieged countryside (figure 8.1).

From the perspective of the state, rural normales were once heroic institutions that produced committed educators whose willingness to forgo their own well-being ushered in admirable national achievements. With time, however, they developed a sense of privilege that turned the schools into agitation hubs with students always demanding more than what a poor nation could possibly provide. In the process, normalistas squandered their educational opportunity with disruptive acts of protest, uselessly offered

FIGURE 8.1 Mural at the rural normal of Ayotzinapa, Guerrero. The image of the rural teacher with a rifle over one arm and a book in the other is a common allusion to the generation of teachers of the 1920s and 1930s who had to contend with Cristero violence. Photograph by author.

their energies to workers and campesinos, and collaborated dangerously with subversives. For President Echeverría, who faced business-class ire for his attempts to revive policies of agrarian distribution and social spending, the militancy of these institutions deprived him of support that might shore up his credentials as a leftist reformer. The SEP thus continuously dismissed normalista demands, claiming they served the right's cause against the revolution.

"IT IS IN YOUR HANDS TO SAVE OR DESTROY THE RURAL NORMALES"

As the 1970s wore on, the SEP increasingly sought to wrest from the FECSM the revolutionary mantle with which the student federation had long defended the rural normales. If the FECSM's ability to regroup and the SEP's recognition of a new rural normal in Amilcingo represented a change from Gustavo Díaz Ordaz's clampdown, over the course of Echeverría's administration, policy toward rural normalistas would harden. Initial concessions had not succeeded in taming the FECSM. On the contrary, within its ranks and within the rural normales more generally, guerrilla groups found support as well as fertile recruiting ground. These tendencies the SEP addressed by presenting itself as the agency willing to implement the revolution's mandate of popular education against a student organization that harbored privileged, reckless activists who ultimately, went its logic, served a fascist cause.

The SEP's negotiations with the FECSM show an effort to isolate and portray it as an entity controlled by outside interests, ones intent on corrupting the consciousness of future teachers and endangering the rural normales' very existence.[95] In a March 27, 1976, letter to rural normalistas, their parents, and all education workers, the secretary and undersecretary of rural normal education, together with the principals of sixteen rural normales, attempted to walk back earlier concessions. The declaration honed in on the federation's demand for a flexible absence policy for its national delegates, characterizing it as "exaggerated" and "bourgeois." These types of privileges, stated the letter, would lead students "to forget their class origin and commitment to the people." Pitting the students against the poor communities from which they came, it further asserted that such arrangements took "resources away from campesinos" since low-quality teachers represented a "negation of educational services to the children of indigenous and campesino communities."[96] In the months to come, SEP language acquired a particularly scathing tone. For example, when responding to a FECSM letter demanding compliance with earlier agreements, officials caricatured their petition, declaring, "How is it possible that students from rural normales, *real students*, are okay with a demand list that includes the privilege of leaders not to study and yet receive credit almost as a mere formality? This, when others must comply with all their obligations."[97] It was student organizing, argued school officials over and over, that most threatened and corrupted the existence of rural normales, and neither they nor teachers had "the right to endanger the institutions that are the patrimony of generations of campesino children."[98]

In a specific attack on normalistas' propensity to join popular struggles, the SEP declared that the duty of student revolutionaries was to study. How could they possibly privilege "daily contact with culturally marginalized groups" over book and classroom-based learning? Would such contact enable "a command over mathematics, the fundamental tool of thought and discovery, and the confirmation of nature's laws?" Rather than participate in demonstrations or give speeches that show "a superficial and dogmatic view of revolutionary theory," students should "learn the principles and laws of physics, chemistry, and the natural sciences that will permit a clear vision of the universe, of man, and of how phenomena unfold."[99] What could normalistas possibly learn from the people, chastised another SEP declaration, when it was their job as future teachers to elevate that population's general cultural level?[100]

Education authorities thus expressed their concern for the peasantry, a sector that deserved good teachers, whose commitment to academics would keep them in the classroom and away from disorderly popular mobilizations. For a regime claiming the legacy of Cárdenas, who had vindicated teachers as community leaders, this position was, to say the least, ironic. But officials went even further in their appropriation of the revolutionary mantle. The SEP lumped normalistas with the regime's right-wing foes, accusing them of aiding fascism. Echeverría's attempted international leadership of Third World nations further gave the SEP license to tout its revolutionary credentials as it implored students to adopt "the system of *work and study* that existed in nations that stand at the revolution's vanguard."[101] This position the minister of normal education contrasted with rural normalistas' "ignorance, irresponsibility, and childlike behavior," which would ultimately hurt their schools and was blind to the ways in which fascism had been imposed in many parts of Latin America.[102] "*It is in your hands to save or destroy the rural normales,*" the minister later warned the FECSM. "*Choose one road or the other, but if you select the wrong one and our institutions are abolished, don't blame others; you will be the only ones responsible.*"[103] Despite the new twist, the SEP's narrative was familiar. The deficiencies in rural education were of the normalistas' own making. Their actions generated chaos and anarchy and stymied teacher quality, ignored a service they owed the nation, and demonstrated a disregard of their own privilege given the massively coveted spaces at rural normales.

But the real threat to rural normales was structural. By the 1970s teachers' demographic background—where they were from, where they trained, and where they worked—was increasingly urban. The number of private and state-funded teacher-training institutions had grown since the 1960s, their presence confined almost exclusively to urban areas. These new normales had proliferated in response to an increased demand for teachers as the SEP expanded elementary and secondary education and offered greater opportunities for professional advancement, making teaching a more attractive profession.[104] In the 1970s, especially as the economic crisis unfolded, there was a glut of teachers—everywhere except in the countryside.

"CONSTANT REFORM"

Early on, Echeverría declared that Mexico's revolution demanded "constant reform" and that within that process education "holds a special place."[105] President Díaz Ordaz had already identified education as in need of attention, but Echeverría's approach differed. While Díaz Ordaz had sought to starve universities into submission, his successor courted them through financial largess.[106] Echeverría's administration both increased funding for existing institutions, like the National Autonomous University of Mexico, and created new ones, such as the Autonomous Metropolitan University, a decentralized system with a campus in each of Mexico City's cardinal points. The latter both provided university education for an expanding student body and opened a slew of stable teaching and research positions for intellectuals and scholars.[107] Echeverría also funded new high school–level institutions like the Academy of Sciences and Humanities—schools linked to the National Autonomous University of Mexico whose graduates gained automatic entrance to the university—and the high school academies meant to provide specialized degrees to those entering the workforce rather than the university.

The SEP also undertook changes at other educational levels, although these were less substantive. It rolled out a new elementary school textbook program that updated materials issued by President Adolfo López Mateos a decade earlier. These new texts aligned the curriculum with the regime's democratic opening and emphasized critical thinking, student potential for creativity, and an active learning process.[108] To be meaningful, such changes would have required a concomitant transformation in the normal system that equipped teachers with the tools to appropriately implement the pedagogical shift. But at normales this change took place at best superficially since few instructors there were themselves qualified to teach the new methods.[109] Needless to say, this process reinforced a number of academic deficiencies.

Educational structures, methods, and the system itself, announced Echeverría in his first state-of-the-union address, would undergo a process of permanent renovation.[110] At teacher-training schools, this translated into a series of precipitous curricular changes that often worked at cross-purposes. In 1972, for example, the education authorities turned their attention to the status of a teaching degree, a long-standing question whose resolution had been kicked down the road for three decades. Unlike professional training programs in law, medicine, or engineering that required a bachillerato (a high school diploma), students could enter a normal straight from junior high school.[111] This difference in schooling partly accounted for teachers' lower pay and status. The 1972 reform made it possible for students to receive their bachillerato alongside their teaching degree. To meet such standards, normales increased the number of required subjects, a change that proportionally decreased courses in pedagogy.[112] With this reform, instructors at normales were expected to possess expertise in a particular field or fields (since they often taught more than one discipline) as well as the pedagogical methods of that field. The dust had barely settled on this reform when, in 1975, the SEP implemented an additional change that reduced the number of requirements by consolidating subject areas.[113] Whereas the 1972 legislation emphasized subject knowledge, the SEP now brought the focus back to teaching methods.[114]

These reforms, which, like others, took place without the educators themselves being consulted, generated chaos, especially since they began a mere three years after the 1969 restructuring. The Revolutionary Teachers Movement, a longtime PRI challenger, issued a proclamation that put it best:

> Normal education is in the utmost state of confusion and contradictions: confusion because teachers and students ignore the programmatic content of many of the subjects they are to learn and develop in the coming academic year ... [and] because a good portion of the teaching body does not know with certainty which subject they will impart, if it will be in their area of specialization or a different one. But they will be obliged to im-

part it owing to the continuously touted duty to serve. It is contradictory because two different study plans are being carried out on the same campus, the 1969 and the 1972 restructured one.[115]

This critique highlighted a longtime SEP tendency in which each presidential administration unveiled a new education policy, which, time and again, SEP bureaucrats had elaborated with no input from teachers.[116] No wonder these reforms did not achieve their objectives, condemned a normalista from Tenería: "the grand pedagogues get together ... and decide everything a priori—programs, texts, methods, systems."[117] More often than not, such policies addressed symptoms of larger structural problems, especially in the countryside. "It's like treating cancer with an aspirin," commented an op-ed on the reforms, "the headache will be gone, but the patient will never be cured."[118] Without a profound transformation of the system itself, student teachers experienced the changes as a haphazard reshuffling of class time, one "that takes hours from one subject to give to another, squeezing into three years what should be distributed into eight or nine." From a labor perspective, the reforms were even more problematic since "electronic minds" put it on teachers to resolve the problems of education through "appeals to the spirit of sacrifice and the apostolic nature of teaching."[119] In the meantime, "we are subject to the same market laws as any other worker who sells their labor power," continued the normalista from Tenería, "we sell our intellectual work. We can't be asked for extreme sacrifice for grand endeavors that mask sad realities."[120]

During the 1970s, the SEP's professionalization strategy added academic pedigree but did little in terms of substance. In fact, the logic was often contradictory. One of the justifications for the 1969 separation between secundaria and teacher training had been that, with no obvious relationship between each cycle, an abundance of students enrolled in rural normales not because of a desire to teach but because they sought a junior high school education. Once they completed the secundaria years, rather than continue at the normal, these students transferred to other educational institutions. Rural normales, argued the architects of the 1969 reform, should be the sole domain of those with an inner love for teaching—the much-touted *vocación* or *mística*. And yet the 1972 reform that established the simultaneous normal-bachillerato track held as its logic that those with a calling to teach could pursue other careers requiring a high school degree. Aside from the dizzying curricular back-and-forth these changes implied for normales' curriculum, rather than increasing the prestige of a teaching degree, the change reinforced its inferior status vis-à-vis other professions since it basically equated a teacher-training degree with a high school education. Not only did it not improve the academic quality of normal education, but it triggered a mad rush for *títulos* (degrees), a tendency that did much to raise individual pay but little for teachers' overall collective status and material security.[121] With the bachillerato degree, graduates of normales could pursue a licenciatura—roughly equivalent to a college degree—in education or in other careers. Those opting for the latter could follow it with a master's and a PhD, making them eligible for high-ranking positions at teacher-training schools or in the SEP administration.

With this change, the number of normales increased, especially in urban areas, contributing to an ever-growing sector of educators who were urban in both background and training. Many teachers already in service pursued their advanced degrees at the National Teachers School or the Higher Normal School of Mexico, where 80 percent of the student body were part-time students gaining their specialization during the summer months.[122] With these degrees, teachers could improve their pay and status, an upward mobility that for rural educators meant moving to the cities. The countryside would thus continue to lack teachers.

And yet the rural normal model was increasingly abandoned. Instead, nine Regional Normal Teaching Centers were built, as were thirty Experimental Normal Schools, improvised teacher-training schools that required far fewer resources than formal institutions.[123] Moreover, the agricultural component, one of the curricular aspects that most differentiated rural normalistas from urban ones, decreased amid the changing course requirements implemented by the 1972 and 1975 legislation. This occurred, first, because the new reforms reduced the number of required hours for agricultural classes and made them electives within normalistas' three broad areas of study; and, second, because, after the 1969 restructuring, much of the focus on farming became concentrated in the institutions that had been transformed from rural normales into technical agricultural schools. These schools drew the bulk of agricultural teachers.[124]

The 1969 reform that in rural normales separated the secundaria and professional training added an additional hurdle for students from the poorest, most marginal areas. Given the high demand, gaining a spot at these schools had long been difficult. The 1969 reform raised the bar since applicants now had to finish both elementary and junior high school before applying. In a country where, in 1971, only 9 percent of the children from rural areas finished elementary school (compared to 54 percent in the cities), this was no small feat.[125] The socioeconomic characteristics of the eligible applicant pool likely went up since, for the nation's poorest campesino youth, a junior high school education would remain elusive. Accentuating this trend was the SEP's 1974 cancellation of the *pase automatico* (automatic acceptance) for graduates of technical agricultural schools, one of the few concessions made to the FECSM during the 1969 restructuring. Thus, the fourteen schools meant to provide a secundaria education for the country's rural poor now curtailed the opportunity for upward mobility offered by a teaching career. Moreover, despite previous FECSM efforts to change the nature of the entrance exam, the SEP preserved a single entrance exam for rural and urban normales, a test that privileged abstract over practical or technical knowledge.

The Echeverría administration did adopt a patchwork of programs to address the shortage of teachers in the countryside. The SEP created new incentives for those who taught in the countryside, including salary benefits, housing, farming plots, opportunities for professional development, and promotions for those who devoted more years to rural communities.[126] It also granted some teaching positions to the communities themselves so that the funding would stay with the locality rather than follow the teachers, so many of whom transferred after only a few years in remote communities. In addition, the SEP instituted the position of community promoter, by which youth with a secundaria education could receive intensive course training to then teach in areas too small to build a school. This policy was especially significant for indigenous communities, whose ownership of the position began an ever-slight reversal in the SEP's long-standing acculturation model.[127]

But education policy did little to address the country's grave social problems. The economic crisis of the 1970s accentuated the inequality that had characterized the Mexican miracle, and Echeverría's increased spending improved neither education's quality nor access to it.[128] The benefits continued to accrue to the urban upper and middle class, a tendency reflected in the fact that higher education served only 4 percent of the school-age population but absorbed 20 percent of school spending.[129] President José López Portillo (1976–82) continued Echeverría's policy; during his sexenio, enrollment rates at universities increased 90.6 percent while those at elementary schools grew only 34.4 percent.[130] Between 1970 and 1976, the number of institutions of higher learning went from 400 to 646.[131] By the early 1980s, the poorest rural and indigenous communities invested proportionately greater amounts in their children's education.[132] Overall, education became, as one study put it, "a relatively inexpensive means to compensate for the lack of opportunities of social mobility outside the school."[133]

FOR MANY OBSERVERS, the 1968 state violence at Tlatelolco marked the end of the revolutionary process the PRI had claimed to carry out over the course of four decades. Some went as far as reevaluating the nature of the 1910 revolution itself. Had it indeed marked the end of a dictatorship that ushered in a social justice project? Or had it merely transformed Porfirio Díaz's rule into a single-party dictatorship? As Echeverría sought desperately to convince the population of the former, guerrilla groups acted under the logic of the latter.

Rural normales, which encapsulated the principles of redistributive justice, state consolidation, and upward mobility, complicated this dichotomy. Systemically, they provided an outlet for a besieged rural population by offering campesino youth a chance to study and to eventually receive a stable, if modest, income. That this was a generational improvement in their livelihood made rural normales a tangible revolutionary gain. For most graduates, this process of upward mobility produced a life of political quiescence, and, ironically, constituted a stepping-stone to urban life that fortified the PRI itself. As Arturo Gámiz, the rural teacher-turned-guerrilla, lamented about normalistas' own education, "For every one instructor who imparts revolutionary content, a hundred will teach reactionary lessons."[134]

Subjectively, however, rural normales' uniquely radical genealogy made their pupils' training as much political as academic. The revolutionary regime's original emphasis that teachers graduate as community leaders first had the effect of producing student leaders within the rural normales themselves. The boarding-school structure accentuated this tendency since it provided a context in which it was easier to organize the student body than it would be to mobilize the population in rural communities. Given the constant besieging of rural normales, individual advancement in fact depended on collective struggle to defend the integrity of the institutions. This process itself awakened a radical consciousness in a number significant enough to undermine the politically palliative effects of the state's education project. In the long-term process of state formation, consolidation, and legitimacy, this was an unintended lesson of revolution.

Education, Neoliberalism, and Violence

CREATED IN 1922, Mexico's Ministry of Public Education (SEP) constituted one of the revolutionary government's most important institutions of state consolidation. By building schools, publishing textbooks, and dispatching teachers throughout the country, it helped forge a national identity and established a strong, centralized state. Half a century later, the SEP had grown to such an extent that the government found its bureaucratic morass an obstacle to enacting policy. Moreover, the National Union of Education Workers (SNTE), allied with the Institutional Revolutionary Party (PRI) and including the entirety of workers associated with federal education—from teachers, to museum staff, to janitors, to members of the SEP's own bureaucracy—had become the largest union not only in Mexico but in Latin America. Its power had grown to such an extent that presidents had to contend with a leadership not always in line with their education projects.

In the 1970s President Luis Echeverría sought to temper the SNTE's power through two strategies. He appointed university-trained professionals—economists, lawyers, engineers—over career educators to key SEP positions, and he created new administrative units throughout the country for teachers to process paperwork related to pay, seniority, and benefits.[1] This new structure not only saved time and money that teachers otherwise spent traveling to the capital but also bypassed union representatives, who until then had been the primary vehicles to address such matters. Termed *desconcentración* (deconcentration) by lawmakers, the process grew teeth through the latter part of the decade as President José López Portillo increased the number of technocratic appointees to the SEP and framed educational reforms as a matter of school quality. Tensions with the PRI's longtime union ally were not long in emerging. Previous education policy based on the growth of the school systems had been mutually beneficial—to the government because it could boast of the number of classrooms and schools built and to the SNTE because such expansion grew its membership.[2] But foregrounding quality not only precluded such growth but also entailed establishing mechanisms by which the SEP, not the union, more closely supervised and evaluated teachers.

As Mexico faced a crippling debt crisis in the 1980s, an increasingly technocratic governing class cut social spending, auctioned off state-owned industry, reduced tariffs, and weakened entities—such as unions—that might interfere with market dictums. Transnational corporations would steadily establish their dominance. This decade thus marked the transition of the PRI from a populist state party to a neoliberal one. The shift was dramatic for a party that had historically relied on a corporatist spending structure to exert dominance and mitigate capitalism's most devastating effects. Just as significantly, the shift to neoliberalism marked an affront to the 1917 Constitution, which had established a strong, socially conscious, nationalist state.

Under the framework of efficiency, neoliberal measures began restructuring most state entities. Transforming the education system to conform to this model would take time, but neoliberal doctrine reinforced previous efforts to "deconcentrate" the federal government's hold on schooling. Under the logic of decentralization, President Miguel de la Madrid (1982–88) sought to hand over control of elementary schools and normales to state governments. Such a change threatened the SNTE's very structure for it implied its fracture into state syndicates, a transformation its leadership would not willingly accept. Nor were state governments eager to undertake the political, labor, administrative, and economic responsibilities involved in decentralization.[3] This combined dynamic, together with the democratic teachers' movement that since 1979 had been mobilizing in the country's southern states, stalled de la Madrid's initiative.

But his administration could boast of a different accomplishment, finally making a high school diploma (bachillerato) an entrance requirement for normales. In 1984 rural normales thus became colleges, a condition that, theoretically, gave teachers the same professional status as doctors, lawyers, and engineers. According to its proponents, this would improve education. Its detractors, who cited student-teacher ratios of forty-seven to one and a school system in which 56 percent of the nation's elementary schools were single-classroom, multigrade institutions, saw it as a counterproductive measure in a country still in need of rural teachers.[4] The bachillerato requirement meant it would now take longer and be more expensive to become a teacher, reducing the profession's accessibility to the poor. The results, according to one assessment, were disastrous, first because new courses, subjects, and majors were simply added without the corresponding personnel or instructor training; and, second, because those who could opted to invest the extra four years of study in careers that paid better.[5]

Significantly, though, much of the debate over the bachillerato requirement was subsumed by a larger battle for the SNTE's democratization. During the late 1970s and into the 1980s, rank-and-file teachers from Oaxaca, Chiapas, Guerrero, Hidalgo, Morelos, and Mexico State waged a powerful movement that challenged both the government and the official union. From the former, dissident teachers demanded better pay and benefits; from the latter, they sought the right to freely elect their own representatives. The teachers' revolt slowed down education's decentralization. At a time of economic crisis and presidential transition, the PRI could not afford to systematically antagonize the leadership of its most powerful corporatist organization. Not until the government of Carlos Salinas de Gortari (1988–94) would the SEP's administrative and budgetary decentralization be accomplished.

Graduates of rural normales came to occupy an important role in the democratic teachers' movement. In Chiapas, which along with Oaxaca constituted the bulwark of democratic unionism, the rural normal of Mactumactzá produced a vocal leadership contingent. In central Mexico, Misael Núñez Acosta, a graduate of the rural normal of Tenería, Mexico State, and a longtime organizer of laborers and *colonos* (newly arrived urban dwellers) became one of the movement's most prominent figures. A member of the democratic executive committee in Mexico State, he was assassinated in 1981 as he exited a community meeting. The gunmen killed a parent and wounded a teacher who accompanied him. Later detained, the perpetrators reported that they were hired by a SNTE adviser. This attack was not exceptional. Núñez Acosta was merely the most prominent victim in a movement that officials dealt with through threats, torture, kidnapping, and violent confrontations.[6] His image and those of Lucio Cabañas and Genaro Vázquez are today the insignia of the National Coordinator of Education Workers, which, since its founding in 1979, has waged a battle for union democracy and fought neoliberal reforms to the education system.

In 1992 President Salinas implemented the National Accord for the Modernization of Basic and Normal Education, which formalized in law the system's decentralization. Building on the initiatives of his predecessors and ousting the longtime SNTE leader Carlos Jonguitud Barrios, who opposed the decentralization, Salinas negotiated the terms of the reform with Elba Esther Gordillo, his choice to succeed Jonguitud Barrios. The arrangement let the SNTE preserve its national representation of education workers, while transferring administrative control to the states. The federal government maintained the power to formulate educational plans, programs, and materials; to write and update textbooks; to establish evaluation criteria; and to design and carry out professional development programs. States thus acquired the administrative functions, while the central government preserved the normative ones.[7] Such a division ensured the continuation of a strong, centralized executive with the power to align the education system with its changing political and economic vision. Indeed, the Salinas administration would make this evident in an initiative to rewrite the nation's elementary school textbooks.

By 1992 the narrative of Mexico's history textbooks found itself at odds with a decade of structural reforms that had altered the economy in favor of foreign investment, privatization of state industry, and reduction in public spending. Salinas's neoliberal rhetoric and policies mirrored those of Porfirio Díaz, the dictator whose authoritarianism and liberal economic model had caused the revolution. Salinas's solution was to rewrite history. Along with Ernesto Zedillo, then minister of education (and president from 1994 to 2000), Salinas was closely involved in the writing and production of a new set of books that offered a revised vision of the Porfiriato, Emiliano Zapata, U.S. intervention, Lázaro Cárdenas's presidency, and the Catholic Church. In their texts, Díaz was a modernizer rather than a dictator; Zapata was a military hero rather than an agrarian one; U.S. designs—rather than imperial—were inextricably linked to both nations' progress; Cárdenas's oil nationalization was a necessity of World War I that was met by an understanding U.S. government; and the Catholic Church was treated in an uncharacteristically dispassionate manner.[8] It is not, as one scholar wrote, that previous generations of textbooks "were based on class analysis, economic nationalism or 'Yankee-phobia.' Their celebration of Zapata's revolt and Cárdenas's presidency were mostly lip service from a regime little concerned with their ideals. But the interpretive shift evident in the new texts is sufficient to suggest the influence of a powerful new orthodoxy. Even lip service to the old ideals had become intolerable." Tellingly the church, the private sector, and the National Action Party, groups that had harshly critiqued the López Mateos and Echeverría administrations' texts, not only praised the new books but directed their ire against the leftists who criticized them.[9] Still, the general outcry was so great that Salinas and Zedillo ultimately pulled the texts, demonstrating that the consolidating elements of revolutionary state formation could not easily be written away.

EDUCATION REFORM AND NORMALISTA RESISTANCE

Vicente Fox's 2000 presidential victory unseated the PRI from a position it had held for seventy-one years. Under the historically right-wing National Action Party, President Fox and his successor, Felipe Calderón (2006–12), continued the PRI's neoliberal policies and used the PRI's previous allies to do so. When Calderón implemented an education reform bill mandating universal testing for students and teachers, he did so with the support of the SNTE and its by then notoriously corrupt leader, Elba Esther Gordillo.[10] These new standardized tests would be a principal mechanism for hiring and promotion, thus undermining seniority rights and long-established job guarantees. Gordillo expressed her own contempt for rural normales when in 2010 she declared that they constituted guerrilla seedbeds and that it was necessary to close at least some of them. She had previously suggested they be turned into centers to train workers for the tourist industry.[11] If for most of the twentieth century rural normalistas had been villainized as communists, agitators, and subversives, more recent epithets labeled them vandals, pseudostudents, and troublemakers. In the neoliberal era, normalista fights became increasingly defensive, responding to ever-creeping cuts to resources and scholarships and charges that they had no place in a predominantly urban nation.

Salinas's decentralization shifted the target of normalista grievances from federal authorities to state ones. For the most part out of the public eye, rural normales drew attention when the authorities violently quelled their protests. During these moments the press issued a consistent script: normalistas were more interested in wreaking havoc than in studying. Students' poor and often indigenous background, moreover, evoked racialized dismay that they could not merely be grateful for the opportunity to study. Given that budgets were now in the hands of governors, normalistas increasingly had to petition local authorities for the resources due to them. This further fractured the Mexican Federation of Socialist Campesino Students (FECSM), which during the 1970s and 1980s had already been seriously weakened. While students from sister normales traveled to each other's schools to lend solidarity, the previous dynamic in which the FECSM leadership negotiated with the federal SEP authorities in the name of the entire system was rendered untenable.

Radical in their history and fierce in their protests, normalistas continued to act in ways that led to dramatic episodes (see figure E.1).[12] One of these, at the rural normal of El Mexe, Hidalgo, took place in February 2000, in response to the authorities' takeover of their campus. El Mexe's students had organized a strike protesting the governor's latest round of enrollment cuts, a creeping trend throughout the 1990s. Their protest had already resulted in so many student detentions that teachers and parents set up camp in the state capital demanding their release. When the governor sent a riot squad to dismantle the encampment and retake the normal, the repression meted out by the police elicited the ire of surrounding communities. Before long, residents had surrounded the school and detained about seventy policemen. Stripped of all but their trousers, the policemen were lined up, tied, and laid facedown on the public square. There the community members submitted them to a public judgment. So incensed was the crowd that the police risked a collective lynching. But cooler heads prevailed, and they were eventually exchanged for the detained normalistas. It was a pyrrhic victory. Three years later, the governor closed the school dorms, and shortly thereafter his successor turned the normal into a polytechnic university.

In the southern state of Chiapas, equally dramatic events unfolded in the rural normal of Mactumactzá in August 2003. There students, faculty, and parents organized numerous protests against Governor Pablo Salazar Mendiguchía's plan to implement competitive standardized tests to determine which graduates would be hired as teachers. Reportedly recommended by the World Bank, this measure replaced a key feature of the rural normal system: the guarantee of a job for their graduates.[13] Students organized marches, protests, and roadblocks and commandeered numerous public and private transport vehicles, which they held at their school. To recover the vehicles, the governor launched a police incursion into the normal, which housed not only students but faculty, staff, and their families. Captured video footage shows merciless police beatings, bloodied staff, and children wailing from the effects of tear gas.[14] One school-bus driver was killed. That fall, the governor cut enrollments by half and closed the school dorms and cafeteria.

In 2012 normalistas in the state of Michoacán waged an especially strong battle against the implementation of President Calderón's education reform bill. Student demand for spots in rural normales—valued as much for the

FIGURE E.1 Under the police boot is a student from the rural normal of Ayotzinapa who, together with his peers, had taken over tollbooths on the Mexico City–Acapulco highway demanding teaching jobs upon graduation. *La Jornada*, December 1, 2007. Photograph by Pedro Pardo.

free education they provided as for the guarantee of a job after graduation—began to falter, providing officials a justification to further cut their funding. Staunchly supported by business groups such as Mexicans First, the education reform bill included a change in the curriculum at normales placing a strong emphasis on English-language and computer skills. Dissident teachers and normalistas opposed an education curriculum that privileged English over indigenous languages and emphasized computer-based pedagogy when so many teachers were assigned to communities with no electricity. Such critiques, responded supporters of the reform, reflected an unwillingness to adopt the principles of progress and modernity.

The democratic teachers' union, the National Coordinator of Education Workers, protested the lack of teacher participation in the new curricular design and its universal quality, which meant that students in the indigenous sierra of Oaxaca, Guerrero, Chiapas, and Michoacán would be taught and tested on the same material as those in the cities of Guadalajara, Monterrey, and the country's capital. In an attempt to halt its implementation, representatives from Michoacán's eight normales demanded talks with the state governor, Fausto Vallejo. Especially militant were the students from the rural normal of Tiripetío, the indigenous normal of Cherán, and the regional education center of Arteaga. When the governor refused to engage in any sort of negotiations, students sequestered forty passenger and cargo vehicles. To recover them, Governor Vallejo raided their schools, leading to confrontations that left numerous students injured and 176 arrested; dramatic photos show transport vehicles in flames. But the show of force succeeded only in galvanizing more student and teacher mobilizations. At the risk of facing a repeat of the 2006 Oaxaca rebellion in the context of Enrique Peña Nieto's presidential inauguration, Governor Vallejo freed the detained students and postponed the implementation of the reform in Michoacán.[15]

The battles between teachers and the government would intensify during the next sexenio as the Peña Nieto administration implemented a new round of education reforms, most of which deepened the provisions of the previous initiative and enacted constitutional changes undermining teachers' labor rights. Testing would be increased and now had punitive consequences for teachers' tenure; an education at a normal would no longer be required to become a teacher; and collective bargaining rights were curtailed. At rural normales, graduates would no longer be guaranteed a job after graduation, a measure that today stands as the greatest threat to these schools (map E.1). Without the promise of labor security, applications to the schools have gone down dramatically, a tendency state governors have used to reduce their

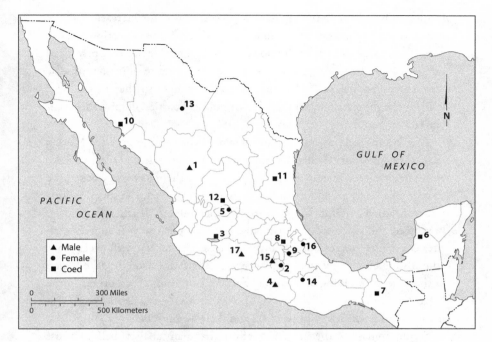

MAP E.I Rural Normales, 2019–2020

	SCHOOLS		SCHOOLS
1	Aguilera, Durango	10	El Quinto, Sonora
2	Amilcingo, Morelos	11	San José, Tamaulipas
3	Atequiza, Jalisco	12	San Marcos, Zacatecas
4	Ayotzinapa, Guerrero	13	Saucillo, Chihuahua
5	Cañada Honda, Aguascalientes	14	Tamazulapan, Oaxaca
6	Hecelchakán, Campeche	15	Tenería, Mexico State
7	Mactumactzá, Chiapas	16	Teteles, Puebla
8	El Mexe, Hidalgo	17	Tiripetío, Michoacán
9	Panotla, Tlaxcala		

Source: Compiled by author based on various sources, including SEP documents, news reports, and personal visits to schools.

Note: This map should be taken with a degree of caution since most sources contain errors and inconsistencies.

funding. Overall, Peña Nieto's reform paved the way for increasing school privatization by facilitating corporate sponsorship.[16] The education bill was part of a broader set of reforms known as the Pact for Mexico that privatized oil and eased restrictions on the extraction of natural resources. So drastic were these new measures that they required changes to the constitution, which were supported by all three major political parties, despite their general lack of popularity.

Few groups were as militant in their resistance to the Pact for Mexico as teachers. To counter their mobilizations, the state wielded massive force and implemented a media campaign so extensive that its costs exceeded the 2017 public relations allotment by 2700 percent. In fact, the spending surpassed funding amounts for the normales themselves.[17] Teachers, moreover, boycotted and protested the mandated tests, so much so that some testing sites counted a greater number of police than test takers, with evaluations administered under a virtual state of siege.[18] There was also bloodshed, such as the June 2016 killing of 8 people and the wounding of 150 others in the Mixtec community of Nochixtlán, Oaxaca, as armed police moved to dismantle roadblocks set up by teachers and their supporters.

So unpopular was the education reform that many analysts believe it cost Education Minister Aurelio Nuño the PRI's nomination for the presidency. More generally, the corruption scandals that plagued Peña Nieto's administration; the state's involvement in massacres such as those in Tlatlaya, San Fernando, Ayotzinapa, and Nochixtlán; the Pact for Mexico in general; and the education reform in particular help explain the landslide victory of the left-leaning candidate Andrés Manuel López Obrador in 2018. Among other promises, López Obrador vowed to overturn the education reform. To normalistas he pledged the reopening of the rural normal of El Mexe, a promise half borne out when in 2019 he reinaugurated it as a normal but without its boarding school.

A NATIONAL SECURITY PRIORITY

At the dawn of the twenty-first century, as the populations of most Latin American countries rebelled against neoliberalism by electing progressive and even socialist governments, Mexico's presidential administrations proceeded to deepen the structural reforms begun in the 1980s. It is not that Mexicans did not protest. On the contrary, the Chiapas indigenous rebels who on January 1, 1994, launched an armed revolt against the government inaugurated a global resistance to neoliberalism. But Mexico's technocratic elites weathered the storm, moving in fact more to the right, first with the election of the National Action Party in 2000, whose candidate, Vicente Fox, touted his business expertise (he had been head of Coca-Cola in Mexico) as a chief qualification for running the country, and then with Felipe Calderón, who declared a war on drugs and brought the army into the streets to wage it. When, under a new and modern guise, the PRI returned to the presidency in 2012, Peña Nieto quickly revealed far more continuities than changes. These came in his administration's massive corruption scandals, the dismantling of what revolutionary gains remained, and the ignoring and then stonewalling of the investigation into the Ayotzinapa events, the largest attack on students since Tlatelolco.[19]

For close to a century, right-wing groups have persecuted, demonized, and attacked rural normales and their graduates. Starting with the Catholic Church and hacendados during the 1920s and 1930s, moving through mid-century elites, intensifying during the late 1960s and early 1970s period of faltering PRI legitimacy and economic crisis, and accelerating with the technocratic reforms of the 1980s through the 2010s, rural normales have incurred the ire of those intent on overturning the poor's revolutionary gains. But rural normalistas have shown that burying justice is no easy process. Perhaps because of this, when President Calderón's transition team prepared to hand over power to Peña Nieto in 2012, they listed the rural normal of Ayotzinapa as a "national security priority." Their classified seventeen-page report stated that the "activism of the Ayotzinapa normalistas" presented a major "governability" concern.[20]

Mexico's neoliberal decades intensified the threats to rural normales (figure E.2). Indeed, the schools' very logic violated every principle of a doctrine based on the primacy of the individual, the privatization of public goods, and the vulnerability of labor. Presented by its proponents as a system based on market efficiency that was inextricably democratic and required minimal government involvement, in practice neoliberal reforms bred corruption, were implemented through autocratic measures, and were accompanied by exorbitant state spending for military and police forces. As free-trade agreements created an environment that helped expand the drug economy—by devastating subsistence farming and massively increasing border traffic, to name but two examples—the war on drugs accelerated the process of accumulation by dispossession. Mining, logging, petroleum, fracking, and other extractive industries have benefited from the drug war as governments enact policies that displace populations, create industrial security zones, and finance elite guards to protect multinational corporations. The irony, of course, is

FIGURE E.2 Mural on a dorm wall of the rural normal of San Marcos, Zacatecas. The mural lists the sixteen rural normales that existed in 2015. It also lists the normales of Cedral and Cherán, which, while not rural normales, were affiliated with the FECSM. It does not list the rural normal of San José, Tamaulipas, since its students are not affiliated with the federation. Photograph by author.

that the very forces charged with battling organized crime are themselves intimately involved in the drug trade. In Mexico, where drug organizations were born and evolved from within the state, it is fitting that on the night of September 26, 2014, the authorities came to a drug lord's aid to, as one investigative line shows, recover the precious heroin cargo contained, unbeknownst to the normalistas, in one of their commandeered buses.[21]

"If the 1994 guerrilla uprising in Chiapas helped crack open a longer history of armed struggle and resistance against the PRI," writes Alexander Aviña, "then perhaps the recent 2014 forced disappearance of forty-three Ayotzinapa *normalista* students in the northern region of Guerrero could aid in the uncovering of a longer history of state-sponsored (or at the very least, state-enabled) terror in southwestern Mexico."[22] There is a third layer that both events lay bare, the persistent legacy of the revolution, especially in the right to land and education it bequeathed to the country's most marginalized. When the Chiapas rebels rose up against the government, they cited Salinas's reform of Article 27 as the final straw in its decision to take up arms against the government. The president's 1992 changes to the constitution—a prerequisite for the North American Free Trade Agreement—privatized the ejido and declared all pending land petitions null and void. In their outcry from the southern corner of Mexican territory and under the banner of the revolutionary hero Emiliano Zapata, Mayan rebels elicited massive national and international support.

In a parallel if distinctive manner, the attacks against the normalistas in Guerrero ignited the fury of the Mexican citizenry and brought public attention to the rural normales, institutions that heretofore had receded into the margins of recent history. Normalistas' uncanny evocation of Karl Marx, Friedrich Engels, Vladimir Lenin, and Rosa Luxemburg, not to mention the ever-ubiquitous hammer and sickle that adorns their school walls, raised the eyebrows of more than a few—especially foreign—media correspondents. That such old-left insignia were a central trope of the decades of revolutionary consolidation seemed largely forgotten, despite the national and international popularity of Mexican muralists who celebrated communist utopias. Ephemeral in its implementation, socialist education was expansive in its legacy, and the Marxists who once abounded in the SEP bequeathed a framework that, from below, the FECSM perpetuated. While historically modest in their goals—the preservation and improvement of their schools— rural normalistas have been radical in their ideology and daring in their actions, demonstrating the ambitious implication of the poor's right to an education. The state's 2014 response to Ayotzinapa students illustrated that if there was anything new in the twenty-first-century PRI, it was the extent to which it was infused by organized crime. The normalista youth who unintentionally laid this bare to the world did so because of their long-standing radical tradition.

Appendix:
Sample Rural Normal Class Schedules

Sample schedules were compiled from report cards and course listings from three individual normales. They likely varied from school to school depending on instructor, workshop, and land availability.

TABLE A.1 Rural Normal Class Schedules, 1937–1939

GRADE	CLASS
Elementary school completion	Agricultural Practice
	Arithmetic and Geometry
	Drawing
	Home Economics
	Language Arts
	Music and Choir
	Nature Studies
	Physical Education
	Social Sciences
	Trades and Industries
	Writing

(continued)

Agricultural and industrial, 1st year	Anatomy, Physiology, and Hygiene
	Arithmetic and Geometry
	Basic Agriculture
	Drawing and Popular Arts
	Home Economics
	Language Arts
	Music and Choir
	Natural Sciences
	Physical Education
	Rural Industries
	Rural Trades
	Social Sciences
Agricultural and industrial, 2nd year	Anatomy, Physiology, and Hygiene
	Applied Mechanics
	Arithmetic and Geometry
	Basic Agriculture
	Drawing and Popular Arts
	Hygiene
	Home Economics
	Language Arts
	Music and Choir
	Natural Sciences
	Physical Education
	Rural Accounting
	Rural Construction
	Rural Economy and Legislation
	Rural Industries
	Rural Trades
	Social Sciences
	Use of Natural Resources

Professional	Advanced Language Arts
	Basic Agriculture
	Drawing and Popular Arts
	Educational Psychology
	Home Economics
	Modern Teaching Methods
	Music and Choir
	Natural Sciences
	Organization and Administration of Rural Schools
	Physical Education
	Preparation and Organization of Didactic Material
	Rural Education
	Rural Industries
	Rural Life: Structure and Betterment
	Rural Trades
	Science of Child Rearing
	Social Guidance and Worker and Campesino Legislation

Source: Archivo Histórico de la Secretaría de Educación Pública, Dirección General de Enseñanza Normal, Completion Certificate, c34232, Exp.15-27-6-11.

Note: Hours per week not available.

TABLE A.2 Rural Normal Class Schedules, 1943–1948

GRADE	CLASS	HOURS
Junior high, 1st year	Agriculture and Husbandry	6
	Biology/Botany	4
	Civics	3
	Drawing	2
	Geography	3
	Mathematics	5
	Music	2
	Language and Literature	5
	Physical Education	2
	Rural Industries	2
	Rural Trades	2
	Writing	2
Junior high, 2nd year	Agriculture and Husbandry	2
	Biology/Zoology	3
	Civics	2
	Drawing/Drafting	2
	Geography of Mexico	3
	History of Mexico	3
	Language and Literature	5
	Mathematics	5
	Music	2
	Physical Education	2
	Physics	3
	Rural Industries	2
	Rural Trades	2

Junior high, 3rd year	Agriculture, Husbandry, Rural Industry, and Trades	18*
	Biology/Anatomy	3
	Civics	4
	Chemistry	4
	Drawing and Modeling	2
	English	3
	Geography	3
	History of Mexico	4
	Hygiene	3
	Language and Literature	4
	Mathematics	4
	Music	1
	Physical Education	2
Professional, 1st year	Biology	4
	Drawing and Plastic Arts	2
	Etymology	3
	Logic	4
	Mineralogy	3
	Music	2
	Pedagogical Theory	4
	Physical Education	2
	Political Economy	3
	Psychology	4
	Teaching Methods	6
	World Literature	3
	Writing	2

(continued)

Professional, 2nd year	Child Development	4
	Cosmography	3
	Drawing and Plastic Arts	2
	Ethics	4
	History of Education	4
	Music	2
	Pedagogical Theory	4
	Physical Education	2
	School Hygiene	4
	Sociology	3
	Teaching Methods	6
Professional, 3rd year	Art History and Aesthetics	3
	Drawing and Plastic Arts	2
	History of Education in Mexico	3
	Music	2
	Pedagogical Psychology	3
	Pedagogical Theory	3
	Physical Education	2
	Teaching Methods	6
	Theater and Dance	2
	School Organization and Administration	3
	Workshops	2

Source: Archivo Histórico de la Secretaría de Educación Pública, Dirección General de Enseñanza Normal, "Documentos relativos que amparan las asignaturas y calificaciones," C34247, Exp.15-27-24-63.

* Document lists three hours daily, which is much higher than other years and should thus be taken with caution.

TABLE A.3 Rural Normal Class Schedules, 1954–1955

GRADE	CLASS	HOURS
Junior high, 1st year	Agricultural Activity	8
	Biology	3
	Civics	3
	Drawing	2
	English	3
	Geography	3
	Language and Literature	4
	Mathematics	4
	Musical Education	2
	Physical Education	2
	Workshops	3
	World History	3
Junior high, 2nd year	Agricultural Activity	8
	Biology	3
	Civics	3
	Directed Reading	4
	Drawing	2
	English	3
	Geography	3
	History of Mexico	2
	Language and Literature	3
	Mathematics	3
	Music	2
	Physical Education	2
	Physics	3
	Workshops	4
	World History	2

(continued)

Junior high, 3rd year	Agricultural Activity	4
	Biology	3
	Civics	2
	Directed Reading	10
	English	3
	Geography	3
	History of Mexico	3
	Language and Literature	3
	Mathematics	4
	Music	2
	Physical Education	2
	Sculpture	3
	Workshops	4
Professional, 1st year	Agricultural Activity	4
	Directed Reading	5
	Drawing	2
	Economic Problems of Mexico	3
	Etymology	3
	Logic	3
	Mineralogy	3
	Music	2
	Pedagogical Theory	3
	Physical Education	2
	Psychology	3
	Teaching Methods	6
	Workshops	2
	World Literature	3
	Writing	3

Professional, 2nd year	Agricultural Activity	4
	Audiovisual	2
	Child Development	3
	Cosmography	3
	Directed Reading	9
	Drawing	2
	Ethics	3
	History of Education	3
	Music	2
	Pedagogical Theory	3
	Physical Education	2
	Sociology	3
	Teaching Methods	6
Professional, 3rd year	Art History and Aesthetics	*
	Drawing and Plastic Arts	*
	Elective	*
	History of Education in Mexico	*
	Musical Education	*
	Pedagogical Psychology	*
	Pedagogical Theory	*
	Physical Education	*

Table A.3, continued

	School Organization and Administration	*
	Teaching Methods	*
	Theater and Dance	*
	Workshops	*

Source: Archivo Histórico de la Escuela Normal Rural de San Marcos, Zacatecas, "Horario," C1955; and Archivo Histórico de la Secretaría de Educación Pública, Dirección General de Enseñanza Normal, "Certificato de Estudios," c34180, Exp.15-27-21-53.

* Hours not available.

TABLE A.4 Rural Normal Class Schedules, 1962–1963

GRADE	CLASS	HOURS
Junior high, 1st year	Agricultural Activity	6
	Biology	3
	Choir	5
	Civics	3
	Drawing	2
	English	3
	Geography	3
	Home Economics	4
	Language and Literature	4
	Mathematics	4
	Music	2
	Physical Education	2
	Sports	5
	World History	3
Junior high, 2nd year	Agricultural Activity	6
	Biology	3
	Choir	5
	Civics	3
	Drawing	2
	English	3
	Geography	2
	History of Mexico	3
	Home Economics	2
	Language and Literature	3
	Mathematics	3
	Music	2
	Physical Education	2
	Physics (and lab)	5
	Sports	3
	World History	3

Junior high, 3rd year	Agricultural Activity	6
	Biology	3
	Chemistry (and lab)	5
	Choir	5
	Civics	2
	Drawing	2
	English	3
	Geography	2
	History of Mexico	3
	Home Economics	4
	Language and Literature	3
	Mathematics	3
	Mathematics (option)	3
	Music	2
	Physical Education	2
Professional, 1st year	Agricultural Activity	4
	Choir	5
	Drawing	2
	Economic Problems	3
	Etymology	2
	Home Economics	2
	Logic	3
	Mineralogy (and lab)	5
	Music	2
	Pedagogical Theory	3
	Physical Education	2
	Psychology	3
	Sports	5
	Teaching Methods	6
	World Literature	3
	Writing	2

(continued)

Professional, 2nd year	Agricultural Activity	4
	Audiovisual	2
	Child Development	3
	Choir	5
	Cosmography	3
	Drawing	2
	Ethics	3
	History of Education	3
	Home Economics	2
	Music	2
	Pedagogical Theory	3
	Physical Education	2
	School Hygiene	3
	Sociology	3
	Sports	5
	Teaching Methods	6
Professional, 3rd year	Agricultural Activity	4
	Art History	3
	Choir	5
	Drawing	2
	History of Education	3
	Home Economics	2
	Music	2
	Statistics	3
	Pedagogical Theory	3
	Physical Education	2
	Psychology of Teaching Methods	3
	School Organization	3
	Sports	5
	Teaching Methods	6
	Theater and Dance	2

Source: Archivo Histórico de la Escuela Normal Rural de Cañada Honda, Aguascalientes, "Horario de clases," c30.

TABLE A.5 Rural Normal Class Schedules, 1971–1972

GRADE	CLASS	HOURS
Professional, 1st year	Agricultural Activity	6
	Anthropology	2
	Child Psychology	4
	Electives	2
	History of Culture	4
	Introduction to Philosophy	3
	Musical Education	1
	Orientation Education	1
	Physical Education	2
	Plastic Arts	3
	Social Anthropology	4
	Spanish	3
	Teaching Methods	6
	Technological Activity	3
Professional, 2nd year	Agricultural Activity	6
	Arithmetic and Geometry	3
	Didactics	6
	Electives	2
	Ethics and Aesthetics	6
	Music	2
	Physical Education	2
	Physics and Chemistry	3
	Plastic Arts	2
	Spanish	1
	Teaching Methods	7
	Technologies	2

(continued)

Professional, 3rd year	Agricultural Activity	6
	Dance	2
	Electives	1
	Geography and Cosmography	3
	History of Education in Mexico	6
	Pedagogical Psychology	6
	Physical Education	3
	School Hygiene	4
	Spanish	4
	Teaching Methods	7
	Theater	2

Source: Archivo Histórico de la Escuela Normal Rural de Cañada Honda, Aguascalientes, "Horario de labores docentes," C38.

Note: Junior high no longer offered at normales.

Notes

Abbreviations

AGN	Archivo General de la Nación
AHENR/CH	Archivo Histórico de la Escuela Normal Rural de Cañada Honda, Aguascalientes
AHENR/SM	Archivo Histórico de la Escuela Normal Rural de San Marcos, Zacatecas
AHENR/T	Archivo Histórico de la Escuela Normal Rural de Tamazulapan, Oaxaca
AHSEP	Archivo Histórico de la Secretaría de Educación Pública
C	Caja [Box]
CONALTE	Consejo Nacional Técnico de la Educación
DEANR	Departamento de Enseñanza Agrícola y Normal Rural
DFS	Dirección Federal de Seguridad
DGEN	Dirección General de Enseñanza Normal
DGIPS	Dirección General de Investigaciones Políticas y Sociales
EXP.	Expediente [Record]
H	Hoja [Page]
LEG.	Legajo [File]
NARA	National Archives and Records Administration
P-MAC	Presidentes, Manuel Ávila Camacho
SEP	Secretaría de Educación Pública

Introduction

1. Three other people were also killed, and twenty-four suffered gunshot wounds, including seven *normalistas*. On the army's tracking of the students, see Anabel Hernández and Steve Fisher, "La historia no official," *Proceso*, December 13, 2014. For a blow-by-blow account of the attack on the normalistas and the state's cover-up, see Hernández, *Verdadera noche*.

2. Human Rights Watch, "Vanished."

3. For example, just two and a half months earlier, the military had killed twenty-two people in Tlatlaya, Mexico State, claiming the casualties resulted from a confrontation with drug traffickers. Investigations soon revealed the military had executed at least twelve of the individuals who were unarmed or trying to surrender and altered the scene to look like a confrontation had taken place. A much larger massacre, of 193 people, mostly Central American migrants, took place in 2011 in San Fernando, Tamaulipas. It was perpetrated by the Zetas cartel, but investigations also revealed the participation of Mexican police. On Tlatlaya, see Human Rights Watch, "Mexico." On San Fernando, see "Mexican Police Helped Cartel Massacre 193 Migrants Documents Show," *NPR*, December 22, 2014, https://www.npr.org/2014/12/22/372579429/mexican-police-helped-cartel-massacre-193-migrants-documents-show.

4. While much of this violence took place under the presidential administrations of Vicente Fox (2000–2006) and Felipe Calderón (2006–12), both from the National Action Party, the violence itself resulted from the PRI's decreased hegemony and the ensuing turf battles. With the ascendance of opposition parties since the 1990s, the PRI no longer held a monopoly over regional drug-trafficking power arrangements.

5. During the summer and fall of 1968, students from campuses across Mexico City organized a series of protests. Initially sparked by the government's excessive use of force against a skirmish between two rival high schools, the movement that developed soon issued a demand list that, among other things, included freedom for political prisoners, the abolishment of Mexico City's riot squad, and respect for university autonomy. More generally, participants denounced the enormous amount of resources devoted to the Olympic Games Mexico was preparing to host that fall. On October 2, as students held a massive rally in Tlatelolco's plaza, the army surrounded them and fired into the crowd, leaving an estimated two hundred to five hundred dead. Although it was known primarily as a student massacre, the mobilizations included many other sectors of the population who were also victims of repression.

6. In the 1930s the rural normales became explicitly for the sons and daughters of campesinos as well as the children of rural teachers. The term *campesino* is itself expansive and generally refers to those from the countryside who are poor.

7. For a sample of these thinkers' writing, see Loyo Bravo, *Casa del pueblo*.

8. Paul Gillingham has studied this dynamic in Guerrero for the 1930s and 1940s, but there is little other work for subsequent decades or other regions. See "Ambiguous Missionaries."

9. Grandin, *Last Colonial Massacre*, xvi.

10. On critical pedagogy see Freire, *Pedagogy of the Oppressed*. Paulo Freire emphasized that the means of transmitting knowledge matter as much as the content. At rural normales the education process rarely followed the dialogic approach envisioned by Freire.

11. For an overview of theories of consciousness, see Carpenter and Mojab, "Adult Education."

12. See Thompson, *Making of the English Working Class*.

13. For a Latin American case study that looks at the diverse origins of consciousness among Chilean workers, see Winn, *Weavers of Revolution*.

14. See, for example, Choudray, *Learning Activism*; and Kelley, *Freedom Dreams*.

15. Organizations like the Black Panthers or the Young Lords, for example, devoted much time and energy to breakfast programs for Black and Brown children, community health care, or campaigns to bring attention to toxic or dilapidated inner-city housing.

16. See, for example, Gould, *To Lead as Equals*.

17. For two works that detail this process for dramatically different times and places, see Aviña, *Specters of Revolution*; and Hylton and Thomson, *Revolutionary Horizons*.

18. In the first chapter of *Insurgent Collective Action and Civil War in El Salvador*, Elisabeth Jean Wood provides a concise summary of various explanatory frameworks of this puzzle.

19. For the 1950s independent teachers' movement, see Loyo Brambila, *Movimiento magisterial*; for the 1970s, see Cook, *Organizing Dissent*.

20. In 1964, for example, only 2.9 percent of school-age children in the countryside completed the six years of elementary education, a number that also reflected the small proportion—one in ten—of schools in the countryside that went up to sixth grade. Greaves, *Del radicalismo a la unidad nacional*, 266–67.

21. Sanderson, *Agrarian Populism*, 144–55.

22. Wright, *Death of Ramón González*, 6–7. As Wright shows, such large-scale use of chemical fertilizers also had devastating effects on the environment and on the health of farmworkers.

23. Gollás, "Breve relato de cincuenta años," 232–33.

24. Latapí, *Análisis de un sexenio*, 140; and Torres, "Corporativismo estatal," 167.

25. Torres, "Corporativismo estatal," 164.

26. Muñoz Izquierdo and Lobo, "Expansión escolar," 10.

27. Cook, *Organizing Dissent*, 2n2. In the late 1970s, the SNTE had over half a million members; by 1985 it had 700,000 and by 1990 close to a million. Torres, "Corporativismo estatal," 162, 166.

28. For example, Carlos Jonguitud Barrios, himself a graduate of a rural normal who later studied law at the National Autonomous University of Mexico, headed the SNTE from 1974 to 1977. Before leading the official teachers' union, he served on the PRI's executive committee and was later a national senator for the party. He was also the director of the country's social security system and governor of San Luis Potosí in the early 1980s.

29. Torres, "Corporativismo estatal," 166.

30. Street, "SNTE," 47.

31. Greaves, *Del radicalismo a la unidad nacional*, 116; and Arnaut Salgado, *Historia de una profesión*, 96n4.

32. For example, Jackson Albarrán, *Seen and Heard in Mexico*; Civera Cerecedo, *Escuela como opción de vida*; Lewis, *Ambivalent Revolution*; Vaughan, *Cultural Politics in Revolution*; Vaughan, *State, Education, and Social Class*; Britton, *Educación y radicalismo*; Raby, *Educación y revolución social*; and Ruiz, *Mexico*.

33. Pensado, *Rebel Mexico*; Gómez Nashiki, *Movimiento estudiantil*; Carey, *Plaza of Sacrifices*; and Zolov, *Refried Elvis*.

34. Henson, *Agrarian Revolt*; McCormick, *Logic of Compromise*; Alegre, *Railroad Radicals*; Aviña, *Specters of Revolution*; Walker, *Waking from the Dream*; and Padilla, *Rural Resistance*.

35. While there is now an emerging historical literature on elections, with a few exceptions, such as Luis Javier Garrido's *El partido de la revolución institucionalizada*, the state party that emanated from the revolution and ruled Mexico continuously for seven decades has received scant historiographical attention. While historians acknowledge that what came to be known as the PRI underwent important shifts, power struggles, and changes, there have still been few historical studies about the institutions that played a key part in its function as a state party. For example, there is no historical study on the SNTE, Mexico's biggest and most powerful union, whose leadership was intimately tied to the party's corporatist structure. Thom Rath's *Myths of Demilitarization in Postrevolutionary Mexico, 1920–1960*, and Aaron W. Navarro's *Political Intelligence and the Creation of Modern Mexico, 1938–1954*, are important examples of works that have now begun to probe the state party's inner workings and its relationship to other institutions. María Muñoz's *Stand Up and Fight* likewise examines how a sector of the indigenous leadership became incorporated into and engaged with the PRI. For recent work on elections, see Gillingham, "Mexican Elections"; Magaloni, *Voting for Autocracy*; Gómez Tagle, *Transición inconclusa*; Servín, *Ruptura y oposición*; Loaeza, *Partido Acción Nacional*; and Pansters, *Política y poder en Puebla*. On the PRI's early years, Gillingham's *Unrevolutionary Mexico*.

36. This follows Greg Grandin and Gilbert Joseph's call to consider Latin America's century of revolution as a distinct historical period. See Grandin and Joseph, *Century of Revolution*.

37. Joseph, "Latin America's Long Cold War," 402.

38. Grandin, "Living in Revolutionary Time," 28.

39. Pensado and Ochoa, *México beyond 1968*.

40. Gillingham and Smith, *Dictablanda*.

41. How hard or how soft the state's heavy hand came down depended on a group's socioeconomic standing. Mexico's most marginalized—the rural poor—bore the brunt of the state's use of force. The 1968 Tlatelolco massacre was exceptional not in its brutality but in its attack against middle-class protesters in the nation's capital before the eyes of the international community as Mexico prepared to host the Olympic Games. State violence in the countryside—both selective and indiscriminate—was a constant feature of the PRI regime. See, for example, Aviña, *Specters of Revolution*; McCormick, *Logic of Compromise*; and Padilla, *Rural Resistance*.

42. Knight, "Peculiarities of Mexican History," 132–42.

43. Grandin, *Last Colonial Massacre*, 186.

44. Paul Gillingham and Benjamin T. Smith, for example, argue that "for the majority of Mexicans the Cold War may instead have depoliticized everyday life" because expressions of discontent "remained wedded to pre-existing rhetoric, alliances and organizational structures." "Introduction," 24.

45. Dubois, "Atlantic Freedoms."

46. Novick, *That Noble Dream*. See also Linda Gordon's critique of Peter Novick's framework, which, she writes, sets up an objectivity/relativism binary that "oversimplifies the meaning and tensions between structuralist determinism and emphasis on agency." "Comments," 685. These questions are thus not new, but it behooves us to keep them in mind as we take stock of the first post-1940s Mexicanist historiographical generation in a field that, as Jaime M. Pensado and Enrique C. Ochoa remind us, has long been inaccessible to working-class students of color. "Preface," xiii.

47. While noting an inherent tension in acknowledging our position as historians while taking distance from it, Trouillot rejects "both the naive proposition that we are prisoners of our pasts and the pernicious suggestion that history is whatever we make of it." *Silencing the Past*, xix.

48. Kelley, *Freedom Dreams*, ix.

49. Part of the General Directorate of Political and Social Investigations (Dirección General de Investigaciones Políticas y Sociales, DGIPS) and the Federal Security Directorate (Dirección Federal de Seguridad, DFS), these collections were formally declassified in 2002 (though the former collection had been partly accessible since 1999). Beginning in 2014, access was increasingly restricted, but as of February 2020, Mexico's National Archive (Archivo General de la Nación)

announced that these collections were once again open and available for consultation. My own research with the DFS collection took place in 2007.

50. The SEP archives have changed locations three times since I first began my work there in 2007. Their reference system has also undergone some modifications. My repeated inquiries about post-1940s documentation on rural normales never received a clear answer, other than these documents are still part of personnel files and therefore inaccessible.

51. Individual institutional particularities, themselves marked by regional context and histories, are beyond the scope of this study. Regional or comparative ethnographies will hopefully be the subject of future research. For two historical works on individual normales, see Hernández Santos, *Tiempos de reforma*; and Ortiz Briano, *Entre la nostalgia y la incertidumbre*. Students in education programs in Mexico have also written theses on individual rural normales, though neither these nor the historical studies cited here make claims about the particularities of the institutions that are the subject of their work. Examples of such theses include Reynoso Sánchez, "Ser estudiante normalista rural"; Pinto Díaz, "Formadores"; and Vite Vargas, "Formación docente."

52. Portelli, "Living Voices," 248.

53. Portelli, "What Makes Oral History Different," 67, 64.

54. For example, many participants cite the prominent leadership of rural normalistas in the challenge to the SNTE's authoritarianism and corruption in the 1970s and 1980s as resulting from the political formation at rural normales. There, mandatory FECSM marches, *boteos* (soliciting donations on buses or along highways), and political assemblies meant that many of their graduates had experience in the art of public speaking, political recruitment, and popular organizing. No such institutionalized practices existed in state and urban normales. Significantly, it was not just the left that tapped into such skills; rural normalistas also relate that these very qualities made them attractive among official circles eager to co-opt them.

55. Victoria Ramírez, interview.

One. Normales, Education, and National Projects

1. Fowler-Salamini, *Agrarian Radicalism*, xv.

2. On teacher resistance during the Díaz regime, see Vaughan, *State, Education, and Social Class*, 75–76; and Cockcroft, "Maestro de primaria."

3. Cockcroft, "Maestro de primaria," 568. Unless otherwise stated, all translations are my own.

4. Fell, *José Vasconcelos*, 119.

5. Fell, *José Vasconcelos*, 127.

6. Vaughan, *State, Education, and Social Class*, 140–42.

7. Vasconcelos, "Discurso pronunciado en el Teatro Arbeu en la Fiesta del Maestro," May 14, 1921, *Boletín de la Universidad* 2 (July 1921): 240, quoted in Fell, *José Vasconcelos*, 119–20.

8. Carr, "Fate of the Vanguard," 343.

9. Craven, *Art and Revolution*, 40.

10. Olcott, *Revolutionary Women*, 7.

11. Alma Gómez Caballero, phone interview, May 8, 2020.

12. Vasconcelos, *José Vasconcelos*, 292.

13. Palacios, *La pluma y el arado*, 150–51.

14. Palacios, *La pluma y el arado*, 46, 16.

15. See Vaughan, *Cultural Politics in Revolution*.

16. Interestingly, Vasconcelos became a harsh critic of action pedagogy. Writing in the 1930s, he objected to Dewey's conception that children be given substantial freedom to learn from their environment. Instead, argued Vasconcelos, teachers should play an active role in instilling—not awakening— the principles of humanity. Since, for him, these principles were Iberian in origin, he rejected Dewey's philosophy that upheld Anglo-Saxon pragmatism based on a reification of the natural. "We do not know the natural, only its appearance humanized since its origins," wrote Vasconcelos in "De Robinson a Odiseo." Vasconcelos, *José Vasconcelos*, 36.

17. Sáenz, "Algunos aspectos de la educación," 26–27.

18. Dewey, "What Mr. John Dewey Thinks," 6.

19. Rafael Ramírez, "Propósitos fundamentales," 31–36.

20. Bassols, "Programa educativo de México," 44–46.

21. Dawson, *Indian and Nation*, xxv.

22. De la Peña, "Educación y cultura," 62–63.

23. Giraudo and Furio, "Neither 'Scientific' nor 'Colonialist,'" 15–16.

24. This document also critiqued an indigenist policy based on charity and specifically censured attempts to redirect scholarship funds for indigenous students at rural normales to instead pay for public work brigades in their communities. Berzunza Pinto, *Indígenas y la república Mexicana*, 26, 8.

25. Account based on Newland, "Estado Docente and Its Expansion," 454–59.

26. For a volume that brings together historical, anthropological, and pedagogical studies of state and community initiatives on indigenous education in Mexico, see Bertely Busquets, *Historias*. On indigenous bilingual teachers in the latter part of the twentieth century, see Dillingham, *Oaxaca Resurgent*.

27. For the indigenous population—then defined as those who did not speak Spanish and were from heavily indigenous communities—the SEP created thirty-two indigenous boarding schools during the 1930s. While teaching literacy, Spanish, and hygiene, these schools, as Alexander Dawson writes, "endeavored to cultivate rather than break down ethnic affiliations" by training social leaders within specific ethnic communities and experimenting with bilingual education. Part of Cárdenas's leftward shift, these initial experiments in cultural pluralism later became Indigenous Coordinating Centers run by the National Indigenist Institute, which in the 1950s and 1960s began to train *promotores bilingües*, agents of bilingual education and development. Dawson, "Histories and Memories,"

83–84. On the radicalization and political involvement of these promotores as both students and teachers, see Dillingham, "Indigenismo Occupied."

28. In 1936, when the number of students who spoke an indigenous language was a little over 7 percent, rural normales began to provide supplementary instruction to those who did not speak Spanish and relaxed grade requirements, allowing them to remain enrolled even if they failed certain curricular offerings. Regional inspectors were also charged with devising plans to better recruit students from indigenous communities. Civera Cerecedo, *Escuela como opción de vida*, 157. In the 1960s one-third of spots at normales were to be reserved for indigenous bilingual students, to be selected by the communities themselves, but it is unclear whether this goal was met. "Convocatoria para el concurso de admission de nuevo ingreso," June 20, 1967, AHENR/SM, C "Varias, 1966–67."

29. On Lunacharsky and Vasconcelos, see Fell, *José Vasconcelos*, 662; on the Marxist content of the cultural missions' theater troupes, see Robert Herr, "Puppets and Proselytizing"; on *El Maestro Rural*, see Palacios, *La pluma y el arado*.

30. Vaughan, *Cultural Politics in Revolution*, 119.

31. Vaughan, *Cultural Politics in Revolution*, 28.

32. Dawson, "Histories and Memories," 83–84.

33. National integration was a cultural rather than a racial problem, according to Vasconcelos, who declared, "I can conceive of no difference between the ignorant Indian and the ignorant French or English peasant; as soon as one or the other is educated, they become auxiliaries of the civilized life in their countries and they contribute, each in their own way, to the betterment of the world." Vasconcelos, *José Vasconcelos*, 291–92.

34. Civera Cerecedo, *Escuela como opción de vida*, 155–56.

35. See Flores, *Backroads Pragmatists*.

36. Miñano García, *Educación rural en México*, 16.

37. Vilchis Cedillo, "Escuela-Ayllu de Warisata," 152. According to Mario Aguilera Dorantes, the principal of several rural normales in the 1930s, who in later decades occupied other high SEP positions, the central office of Warisata displayed an image of Cárdenas. See "Con Mario Aguilera Dorantes," in Bolaños, *Historia de la educación*, 145.

38. Mistral, "Reforma Educacional de México," 163.

39. Transnational connections may in fact have been stifled by governments' strong nationalist emphasis. Mistral herself later lamented, "I have learned bitter things, that men believe miserably in *pequeñas patrias*, in the Mexican or Chilean air, in the Mexican or Chilean pastures. I have not been convinced by such ferocious nationalism." Gabriela Mistral, "Motivos de la vida" (unpublished, 1924), Archivo del Escritor, Biblioteca Nacional, Chile, Santiago, s/n, quoted in Moraba Valle, "'Lo mejor de Chile,'" 1238.

40. The case of China, where in the 1930s rural normales became the principal institutions of secondary education in the countryside, offers some uncanny

similarities to Mexico. These schools also provided free room and board and a modest stipend and were principally attended by students from poorer, mostly peasant families. Their graduates, a large number of whom joined the Communist Party, "carried the torch of the urban-born communist movement to the country-side." Liu, "Prometheus of the Revolution," 567. In another striking comparison to Mexico, Xiaoping Cong writes about Chinese normales: "Teachers' schools became centres of radical discussion and activities. Discontented rural students supplemented the government-stipulated curriculum with radical texts and responded enthusiastically to the encouragement they got from an older generation of leftist intellectuals who had survived the Nationalist purges of the late 1920s. Organizers won over many students in teachers' schools, recruiting them to become grassroots workers for the Communist Party." *Teachers' Schools*, 168.

41. Cox and Gysling, *Formación del profesorado*, 89–93.

42. See, for example, Green, *Education Reconstruction*; Butchart, *Schooling the Freed People*; and Anderson, *Education of Blacks*.

43. In the case of El Salvador, Héctor Lindo-Fuentes and Erik Ching write, "Teachers were one of the most important and most unexpected sectors to emerge as part of the left-leaning opposition to the PCN [Partido de Conciliación Nacional, National Conciliation Party]. In the first half of the 1960s teachers developed a collective consciousness and began questioning their traditional position in the military's system of rule." Lindo-Fuentes and Ching, *Modernizing Minds*, 89. On Chile, see Cox and Gysling, *Formación del profesorado*, 88.

44. Vaughan, *State, Education and Social Class*, 16.

45. Vaughan, *State, Education, and Social Class*, 62; and Arnaut Salgado, *Historia de una profesión*, 58.

46. Miñano García, *Educación rural en México*, 37–41. See appendix for sample classes for this and subsequent decades.

47. Arnaut Salgado, *Historia de una profesión*, 61; and Civera Cerecedo, *Escuela como opción de vida*, 382.

48. Miñano García, *Educación rural en México*, 23–45.

49. Ibarrola, "Formación de los profesores," 245, 249.

50. In 1950, of the country's 65,000 teachers, 43,000 did not have a teaching degree. Arnaut Salgado, *Historia de una profesión*, 103n12. Through correspondence courses or weekend training at centers throughout the country, the Federal Institute for Teacher Training offered teachers the opportunity to gain their degree after six years of study. According to official figures, between 1959 and 1964, it enrolled an average of 24,472 teachers a year, for which it was termed "the largest normal school in the world." SEP, *Obra educativa*, 163–64.

51. Greaves, *Del radicalismo a la unidad nacional*, 192–95.

52. These included the Regional Normal Teaching Centers (discussed in chapter 4), the National School for Preschool Teachers, and the short-lived National

Schools for Industrial and Agricultural Work. Meneses Morales, *Tendencias educativas oficiales*, 3:487, 492.

53. Such were the declarations made by then minister of education Víctor Bravo Ahúja. Ahúja, *Diario de una gestión*, 2:201, quoted in Arnaut Salgado, *Historia de una profesión*, 129.

54. Arnaut Salgado, *Historia de una profesión*, 172–74.

55. This decentralization process actually began in the late 1970s but proceeded slowly, partly because of the fierce opposition of the SNTE, whose power it would weaken by fragmenting the teaching corps into state unions. The late 1980s saw tumultuous battles that resulted in the destitution of the previously dominant faction known as the Revolutionary Vanguard, led by Carlos Jonguitud Barrios. The new leadership, headed by Elba Esther Gordillo, agreed to support the decentralization efforts on the condition that the union retain national representation of education workers. For a detailed account of the process, see Arnaut Salgado, *Federalización educativa en México*, chap. 9.

56. For a discussion of how the SEP deliberately constructed this mystique, see Palacios, *La pluma y el arado*. In the 1980s the SEP sponsored a project to collect the experiences of these early educators "who, through multiple pedagogical experiences transmitted early civic values, knowledge, civics, art and culture . . . so they could be known and acknowledged by contemporary Mexican society." The testimonies were published as a five-volume work entitled *Los maestros y la cultura nacional, 1920–1952*, edited by Engracia Loyo Bravo, Cecilia Greaves, and Valentina Torres. Quote from "Presentación," 1:7.

57. As part of their application, students must present proof of their poor background. This documentation often comes in the form of a letter from the municipal or ejido authorities. Undoubtedly, a portion of the students have come from what would more accurately qualify as the lower rungs of the middle class and used either false documentation or political connections to gain entrance. Normalistas themselves often denounced such practices and—as discussed throughout much of this work—sought to mitigate the numbers of such students by demanding a voice in the admissions process. In recent years, at some schools, members of the student association travel to students' homes to verify their living conditions.

58. Since the 1950s and 1960s, there have been important networks of indigenous teachers, operating under the category of promotores bilingües. Because they were hired on a piecemeal basis and had no union representation, they were paid less and often disparaged by normal graduates as second-class teachers. In the 1970s promotores bilingües successfully fought for formal recognition within the SEP, a status that entitled them to membership in the official union. From there, as Alan Shane Dillingham shows for Oaxaca, they mounted a dual struggle for equality within the teaching profession and for union democratization. The more radical ones engaged in theories of anticolonialism and antiracism, providing an important basis for subsequent proposals for indigenous

education that challenged long-standing assimilationist frameworks. See Dillingham, *Oaxaca Resurgent*.

59. Known as Escuelas Normales Indígenas Interculturales Bilungües (Intercultural Bilingual Indigenous Normal Schools), these institutions gained official recognition thanks to the combined organizing efforts of indigenous activists and dissidents of the official teachers' union. These normales recruit students speaking indigenous native tongues and privilege a curriculum focused on indigenous history, culture, and language. Despite their official recognition, the indigenous normales face ongoing battles with the SEP about resources, the nature of the courses they offer, and a guarantee of jobs for their graduates. Additionally, about twenty normales currently offer a specialization in bilingual and intercultural education. See Baronnet, "De cara al currículo nacional."

60. The halls of the SEP in Mexico City are themselves covered with Rivera's frescos; in the three-story building, a series of 120 panels depict an epic narrative of rural struggles for liberation, proletarian revolution, and the popular power brought about by ejido councils, unions, and rural schools. The celebration of such radical traditions, some scholars argue, enhanced the state's revolutionary image as a guarantor of worker and campesino rights. See Coffey, "'All Mexico on a Wall'"; and Carr, "Fate of the Vanguard."

61. On rural normales as an imagined community, see Luis Hernández Navarro, "Ayotzinapa y la fuerza del normalismo rural," *La Jornada*, October 28, 2014.

62. Examples of these works include Cortés Martínez et al., *Educación rural en México*; Aguayo Álvarez, *Paseo por los recuerdos*; Arias Delgado, *Saltando la cerca*; Quintal Martín, González Salazar, and Pacheco Hidalgo, *Historia de la benemérita Escuela Normal Rural "Justo Sierra Méndez"*; Zúñiga Castillo, *Normalismo rural en Tamaulipas*; *Soy normalista*; Bustos García, *Ximonco*; and Fabre Baños, *Normal rural de Galeana*.

63. During the Porfiriato, for example, the percentage of Mexico City's teachers who were women went from 56.8 in percent in 1875 to 76.2 percent in 1905. Gónzalez Jiménez, "De cómo y por qué las maestras llegaron a ser mayoría," 756.

64. Other than in this type of reference, northward migration, otherwise so ubiquitous in rural Mexico, is relatively absent in the documentation and interviews of rural normalistas. Like so many people in Mexico, those I interviewed had at least one relative living in the United States, but their own trajectories did not involve seeking work *del otro lado* (on the other side), an indication of how much the teaching profession constituted a sound economic option. In fact, in their educational profile, normalistas differed from the average migrant to the United States, whose years of schooling tended to be far less. See Durand, Massey, and Zenteno, "Mexican Immigration to the United States," 116.

65. Like migration to the United States, for most of the decades covered by this study, references to narco-trafficking are absent from the documentation and interviews of rural normalistas. This is likely due to two factors. First, Mexico's

drug trade and cultivation networks have historically taken place in locales separate from rural normales. Drug cartels' pervasive hold on vast sectors of rural Mexico—including the dynamics leading to the 2014 attack on Ayotzinapa's students—is a phenomenon more characteristic of the early twenty-first century. Second, the historiography on Mexican drug trafficking is relatively new, with scholars only recently turning their focus to the middle decades of twentieth century. As more historical studies emerge on both drug trafficking and the postrevolutionary period, scholars may uncover overlap between what we currently hold as distinct sectors.

Two. A New Kind of School, a New Kind of Teacher

1. Balam, "José Hernández Delgadillo," 58–61; and Hernández Zamora, "Prefacio," 11.

2. Ruiz, *Mexico*, 89.

3. SEP, *Misiones culturales*, 381.

4. Raby, *Educación y revolución social*, 23–24.

5. Vaughan, *State, Education, and Social Class*, 143–45.

6. Civera Cerecedo, *Escuela como opción de vida*, 88.

7. Loyo Bravo, "¿Escuelas o empresas?," 89.

8. Civera Cerecedo, *Escuela como opción de vida*, 91; and Loyo Bravo, "¿Escuelas o empresas?"

9. According to a 1928 examination of enrollments, 20 percent of pupils' families were ejidatarios, 39 percent were small-scale property owners and campesinos, and the remaining 41 percent were merchants, professionals, artisans, large landowners and cattle ranchers, members of the military, and industrialists. Civera Cerecedo, *Escuela como opción de vida*, 94.

10. Civera Cerecedo, *Escuela como opción de vida*, 97.

11. SEP, *Misiones culturales*, 226.

12. SEP, *Misiones culturales*, 226.

13. Civera Cerecedo, *Escuela como opción de vida*, 73.

14. Britton, *Educación y radicalismo*, 67.

15. Britton, *Educación y radicalismo*, 67–68.

16. Civera Cerecedo, *Escuela como opción de vida*, 140.

17. Loyo Bravo, "¿Escuelas o empresas?," 79.

18. Raby, *Educación y revolución social*, 47; and Civera Cerecedo, *Escuela como opción de vida*, 154.

19. Civera Cerecedo, *Escuela como opción de vida*, 159–60, 157. Language was of course not the only marker of indigenous identity, but in its efforts to recruit indigenous students, the SEP used it to differentiate indigenous from mestizo pupils.

20. Civera Cerecedo, "Coeducación en la formación de maestros rurales," 273.

21. Raby, "Principios de la educación rural," 576–78.

22. Raby, "Principios de la educación rural," 557–58.

23. "Informe que el ciudadano Gral. de División Lázaro Cárdenas rinde al H. Congreso del Estado al terminar su periodo constitucional 1928–1932 y contestación del presidente mismo," Tip. Arte y Trabajo, Morelia, Mich., September 15, 1932, 11–12, quoted in Córdoba, "Maestros rurales," 78.

24. Raby, "Principios de la educación rural," 558–59.

25. Raby, "Principios de la educación rural," 562. Tacámbaro's rural normal was not the first federally sponsored institution, but it is the oldest one to survive and is today located in Tiripetío, Michoacán.

26. See Villela Buenrostro, *Maestro del pueblo.*

27. SEP, *Misiones culturales,* 225–353.

28. SEP, *Misiones culturales,* 260.

29. Raby, *Educación y revolución social,* 47.

30. Antonieto Rodríguez, "El maestro como verdadero líder social de las comunidades," July 26, 1933, AHSEP/DGEN, C34256, Exp.15-27-20-7.

31. Maurillo García, "Influencia de la escuela rural en la comunidad," July 25, 1933, AHSEP/DGEN, C34272, Exp.15-27-30-56.

32. José Ma. Villanueva, "La escuela rural como factor de engrandecimiento y progreso del pueblo mexicano," July 26, 1933, AHSEP/DGEN, C34178, Exp.15-27-16-44.

33. María de la Luz Rodríguez, "La educación del adulto: Medio eficaz para la acción socializante de la escuela rural," July 26, 1933, AHSEP/DGEN, C34265, Exp.15-27-20-22.

34. José Ma. Villanueva, "La escuela rural como factor de engrandecimiento y progreso del pueblo mexicano," July 26, 1933, AHSEP/DGEN, C34178, Exp.15-27-16-44.

35. Manuel López Cienfuegos, "Prueba de técnica de la enseñanza de lectura y escritura," May 9, 1942, AHSEP/DGEN, C34236, Exp.15-27-19-41.

36. Rafael Ramírez, *Escuela rural mexicana,* 65.

37. SEP, *Misiones culturales,* 281.

38. SEP, *Misiones culturales,* 349.

39. Vidal Ramírez, "La escuela rural como agencia de mejoramiento económico, social y cultural," November 24, 1932, AHSEP/DGEN, C34263, Exp.15-27-26-62.

40. Maurillo García, "Influencia de la escuela en la comunidad," July 25, 1933, AHSEP/DGEN, C34272, Exp.15-27-30-56; see also Alejandro Sendejas, "¿Es ventajosa la coeducación?," 1933, AHSEP/DGEN, C34253, Exp.15-27-2-23.

41. Olcott, *Revolutionary Women,* 96–97.

42. Vaughan, *Cultural Politics in Revolution,* 16.

43. See Vaughan, *Cultural Politics in Revolution;* and Joseph and Nugent, *Everyday Forms of State Formation.* On revolutionary citizenship, see Olcott, *Revolutionary Women.*

44. Cecilia Rodríguez, "La educación integral del niño campesino único medio de lograr una patria mejor," July 26, 1933, AHSEP/DGEN, C34275, Exp.15-27-27-182.

45. Antonieto Rodríguez, "Maestro como verdadero líder," July 26, 1933, AHSEP/DGEN, C34275, Exp.15-27-20-7.

46. Palacios, *La pluma y el arado*.

47. Butler, "'Liberal' *Cristero*," 658.

48. Raby, "Principios de la educación rural," 565–66, 574–75.

49. Meyer, *Cristiada*.

50. See Purnell, *Popular Movements*.

51. Butler, *Popular Piety*.

52. Bassols "Programa educativo de Mexico," 51.

53. Bassols, "Programa educativo de México"; Britton, *Educación y radicalismo*, 1:53–54; and Raby, *Educación y revolución social*, 51–52.

54. Britton, *Educación y radicalismo*, 1:100–101; and Rubenstein, "Raised Voices," 315.

55. See Valdés Silva, "Educación socialista y reparto agrario."

56. Britton, *Educación y radicalismo*, 1:121–22; and Raby, *Educación y revolución social*, 37–38.

57. Civera Cerecedo, "Pedagogía alternativa y revolución," 9.

58. *Memoria*, 1933, 1:52–58, cited in Raby, *Educación y revolución social*, 39.

59. These were the Federation of Regional Education Workers Union, the left-wing group of the Confederation of Mexican Teachers, as well as the National Teachers League. Britton, *Educación y radicalismo*, 1:131.

60. "Manifesto a los campesinos," November 1934, AHSEP/DGEN, C34177, Exp.344/11.

61. See Valdés Silva, "Educación socialista y reparto agrario."

62. "Educación socialista y la escuela rural," 59, 63, 65.

63. Gabino Bautista and E. Dávila R., "La escuela socialista ante los problemas del hogar," *El Maestro Rural* 7, no. 6 (September 15, 1935): 31–32.

64. "Prueba de admisión," January 1940, AHSEP/DGEN, C34231, Exp.15-28-18-3.

65. "Pruebas extraordinarias educación rural," n.d., AHSEP/DGEN, c34254, Exp.15-27-25-19.

66. Isabel Nava, "Examen de aptitud," December 17, 1935, AHSEP/DGEN, C34207, Exp.15-28-5-66; and Manuel Castro, "Prueba práctica," December 16, 1935, AHSEP/DGEN, C34203, Exp.15-27-40-28.

67. Pascual Orozco García, "La escuela rural," January 22, 1946, AHSEP/DGEN, C34231, Exp.15-28-18-13.

68. Evancio Ocampo Sandoval, "La escuela rural mexicana y la actitud del maestro ante los problemas sociales," December 19, 1945, AHSEP/DGEN, C34231, Exp. 15-28-18-16.

69. Ma. Guadalupe Ortega, "Examen de aptitud," December 18, 1935, AHSEP/DGEN, C34258, Exp.15-28-17-50; Castro, "Prueba práctica," December 16, 1935; and Macario Pantaleón, "Informe de las labores desarrolladas," August 20, 1935, AHSEP/DGEN, C34236, Exp.15-27-19-18.

70. Máximo Xochipa, "Examen de aptitud," December 3, 1935, AHSEP/DGEN, C34148, Exp.15-28-32-30.

71. Nava, "Examen de aptitud," December 17, 1935.

72. See Vaughan, *Cultural Politics in Revolution*.

73. "Padre de familia," Instituto de Acción Social Destinado a la Regional Campesina de Tenería, 1934, AHSEP/DGEN, C34177, Exp.37.

74. Raby, *Educación y revolución social*, 126–27.

75. Raby, *Educación y revolución social*, 127–37.

76. Raby, *Educación y revolución social*, 147. The five-volume collection of rural teachers' memories, *Los maestros y la cultura nacional, 1920–1952*, edited by Engracia Loyo Bravo, Cecilia Greaves, and Valentina Torres, also recounts numerous anecdotes about Cristero violence and priest-led hostilities.

77. Raby, "Principios de la educación rural," 580–81.

78. Lewis, *Ambivalent Revolution*, 93–94.

79. SEP, *Misiones culturales*, 238, 307.

80. Castro, "Prueba práctica," December 16, 1935.

81. Civera Cerecedo, *Escuela como opción de vida*, 207.

82. García Téllez, *Socialización de la cultura*, 234, quoted in Civera Cerecedo, *Escuela como opción de vida*, 219.

83. Ing. Emilio F. Ferreira, "Plan mínimo de acción," January 15, 1937, AHSEP/DEANR, C3081, Exp.16-3-8-171, quoted in Civera Cerecedo, *Escuela como opción de vida*, 241.

84. Sociedad de Alumnos de la Escuela Regional Campesina, "Manifiesto," August 1934, Tamatán, Tamaulipas. Document transcribed in Calderón López-Velarde, "Escuela normal rural," 170–73.

85. Mariano Orozco Álvarez, interview. Established in Tacámbaro in 1922, Michoacán's first rural normal changed location several times, first to Erongarícuaro, then to Huetamo, and finally to Tiripetío.

86. Sociedad de Alumnos de la Escuela Regional Campesina, "Manifiesto."

87. "Conclusiones del Primer Congreso de Estudiantes Campesinos de la República," Exp.509: 4–8–8–30, AHSEP, quoted in Civera Cerecedo, *Escuela como opción de vida*, 217.

88. Civera Cerecedo, *Escuela como opción de vida*, 217.

89. FECSM, "Convocatoria a las sociedades de alumnos," 6.

90. Morales Jiménez, "Evocaciones de un profesor de banquillo," 208–9.

91. FECSM, "Convocatoria a las sociedades de alumnos."

92. "Circular de Luis Villarreal, jefe del DEANR, a los directores de las escuelas regionals campesinos," March 18, 1936, AHSEP/DEANR, C3015, Exp.16-1-2-97, quoted in Civera Cerecedo, *Escuela como opción de vida*, 223.

93. "Bases para la organización y funcionamiento del gobierno escolar en las escuelas regionales campesinas," AHSEP/DEANR, C3015, Exp.16-1-2-97, cited in Civera Cerecedo, *Escuela como opción de vida*, 224–25.

94. Civera Cerecedo, *Escuela como opción de vida*, 223–24.

95. Civera Cerecedo, *Escuela como opción de vida*, 234.

96. Santos Valdés, "Democracia y disciplina escolar," 104.

97. Santos Valdés, "Democracia y disciplina escolar," 86.

98. With the onset of the conservative administrations of the 1940s and 1950s, this characteristic, Santos Valdés noted, was dismissed as communist. "Democracia y disciplina escolar," 100–101.

99. Civera Cerecedo, "Pedagogía alternativa y revolución," 10. By the 1960s, however, some student activists mentioned the importance of maintaining a high grade point average so as not to give the school authorities an excuse to expel them.

100. Civera Cerecedo, *Escuela como opción de vida*, 242–48.

101. Fabre Baños, *Normal rural de Galeana*, 42.

Three. "And That's When the Main Blow Came"

1. Felipe Cortés Martínez, interview.

2. Blancarte, "Intransigence, Anticommunism, and Reconciliation," 85, 75.

3. See the articles in Padilla and Walker, "Spy Reports."

4. Servín, "Propaganda y Guerra Fría," 12, 22.

5. Greaves, *Del radicalismo a la unidad nacional*, 87.

6. Greaves, *Del radicalismo a la unidad nacional*, 143.

7. See Hamilton, *Limits of State Autonomy*.

8. *Novedades*, July 10, 1940, translated and quoted in Blancarte, "Intransigence, Anticommunism, and Reconciliation," 75.

9. *Novedades*, July 10, 1940, translated and quoted in Blancarte, "Intransigence, Anticommunism, and Reconciliation," 75.

10. *El Universal*, January 20, 1941, quoted in Greaves, *Del radicalismo a la unidad nacional*, 43.

11. "Discurso pronunciado por el Sr. Licenciado Luis Sánchez Pontón, Secretario de Educación Pública," April 23, 1941, AGN/P-MAC, Exp.708.1/6, quoted in Greaves, *Del radicalism a la unidad nacional*, 47.

12. Civera Cerecedo, *Escuela como opción de vida*, 360.

13. For example, Jesús Melo, David Téllez, and 120 other signatories to Manuel Ávila Camacho, May 14, 1941; Extracto: Carlos F. Carranco Cardoso to C. Presidente, May 3, 1941; Comité Directivo Nacional del Frente Zapatista de la República to C. Presidente de la República, July 24, 1941; Asociación Nacionalista de los Estados Unidos Mexicanos to Congreso de la Unión, May 12, 1941; and Julio Godoy to Manuel Ávila Camacho, n.d., all in AGN/P-MAC, Exp.549.11/6.

14. Sindicato de Trabajadores de la Enseñanza Pública Méxicana (STERM) Sección XVI, Michoacán, to Manuel Ávila Camacho, July 2, 1941, AGN/P-MAC, Exp.549.11/6; and Miembros del ejido de Cuajinicuilapa, Guerrero, to Presidente de la República, November 5, 1941, AGN/P-MAC, Exp.549.11/6.

15. H. Cárdenas, *Caso Ayotzinapa*, 167–68.

16. Sociedad de Alumnos Ricardo Flores Magón to Manuel Ávila Camacho, May 28, 1941, AGN/P-MAC, Exp.549.11/6. Despite Ávila Camacho's conservatism, he was Cárdenas's handpicked successor, which gave him legitimacy among many progressive forces. The 1940 right-wing candidacy of Juan Andreu Almazán further accentuated the left's support for Ávila Camacho.

17. In 1938, in accordance with Article 27 of the Mexican Constitution, which declared all subsoil resources property of the nation, President Cárdenas had nationalized the oil industry, which until then was held by U.S. and British companies. The act became a powerful nationalist rallying cry as it made good on the revolution's promises and asserted Mexico's sovereignty against two powers with a history of foreign intervention.

18. Sociedad de Alumnos Ricardo Flores Magón to Manuel Ávila Camacho, May 28, 1941.

19. Meneses Morales, *Tendencias educativas oficiales*, 3:248–51; and Greaves, *Del radicalismo a la unidad nacional*, 49.

20. "La labor del Nuevo Srio. de Educación Licenciado Octavio Véjar Vázquez," *Excélsior*, December 1, 1941.

21. H. Cárdenas, *Caso Ayotzinapa*, 149, 163–64.

22. Civera Cerecedo, *Escuela como opción de vida*, 370–74.

23. "La escuela rural mexicana," June 30, 1959, AHSEP/Conalte, C56, Exp.1496, Leg.1.

24. Civera Cerecedo, "Coeducación en la formación de maestros rurales," 273.

25. "Código disciplinario," Fall 1964, AHENR/SM, C1965-2. It is difficult to determine when this specific regulation came into place.

26. As Alicia Civera Cerecedo explains, it is unclear whether school staff actually ran underwear checks. Students resisted them, and nurses were reluctant to take on this battle. *Escuela como opción de vida*, 372.

27. "Informe general de labores," November 30, 1952, AHENR/T.

28. Greaves, *Del radicalismo a la unidad nacional*, 183.

29. López Pérez and Hernández Santos, "Mujeres campesinas," 47.

30. "La función del maestro rural," *Novedades*, February 14, 1942.

31. "20,000 escuelas rurales llamadas a desaparecer," *Novedades*, December 10, 1941.

32. Of the seventeen thousand members the Mexican Communist Party reported having in 1937, almost a third were teachers. Raby, *Educación y revolución social*, 91–92.

33. Carr, "Fate of the Vanguard," 337n14.

34. Greaves, *Del radicalismo a la unidad nacional*, 52.

35. "Arde en fantástica pira un millión de libros escolares," *Excélsior*, December 4, 1941.

36. Pope Pius XI, "*Divini Redemptoris*: Encyclical of Pope Pius XI on Atheistic Communism," March 19, 1939, http://www.vatican.va/content/pius-xi/en /encyclicals/documents/hf_p-xi_enc_19370319_divini-redemptoris.html.

37. Greaves, *Del radicalismo a la unidad nacional*, 57.

38. Greaves, *Del radicalismo a la unidad nacional*, 63.

39. Álvarez García, "Difusión de las ideas," 153, 178.

40. Miñano García, *Educación rural en México*, 119; and Meneses Morales, *Tendencias educativas oficiales*, 3:314.

41. "Informa visita a la Escuela Normal Rural de Comitancillo, Oax.," February 9, 1959, AHSEP/Conalte, C40, Exp.1065.

42. "Informa visita a la Escuela Normal Rural de Comitancillo, Oax.," February 9, 1959; and Hernández Santos, *Tiempos de reforma*, 148–54.

43. "Discurso pronunciado en la inauguración de la convención de educación normal, en Saltillo, Coah.," April 23, 1944, in Torres Bodet, *Educación mexicana*, 99–101.

44. SEP, *Junta Nacional de Educación Normal*, 1:168.

45. Civera Cerecedo, *Escuela como opción de vida*, 389–90.

46. During Cárdenas's administration, the average percentage spent on education was 12.7; during Ávila Camacho's administration, it was 10.2. See Wilkie, *Mexican Revolution*, 160–62. On Alemán's wealth, see Niblo, *Mexico in the 1940s*, 208.

47. Greaves, *Del radicalismo a la unidad nacional*, 65–66.

48. Greaves, *Del radicalismo a la unidad nacional*, 196; and "Strike of Students at Rural Normal Schools," March 31, 1950, NARA, Record Group 59, box 4496.

49. Greaves, *Del radicalismo a la unidad nacional*, 195; and Meneses Morales, *Tendencias educativas oficiales*, 3:377.

50. "Strike of Students at Rural Normal Schools," March 31, 1950; and Memorandum, March 24, 1950, AGN/DFS 9-27, Leg.2, H168–73.

51. An intelligence report noted that the FECSM had received a thousand letters of support from various organizations. Memorandum, March 24, 1950; and "Strike of Students at Rural Normal Schools," March 31, 1950.

52. Memorandum, April 14, 1950, AGN/DFS 9-27, Leg.2, H228–32.

53. Piedad Banuet Quero to Salvador Varela, April 15, 1950, AHENR/T.

54. Memorandum, April 14, 1950.

55. "Strike of Students at Rural Normal Schools," March 31, 1950.

56. Santos Valdés, "Breve historia de la FECSM," 31.

57. "Political Conditions in Mexico from April 16 through May 15, 1950," May 19, 1950, NARA, box 3230, General Records of the Dept of State 1950–54; and Memorandum, April 14, 1950.

58. "Strike of Students in Rural Normal Schools," March 31, 1950; "Public Education in Mexico," February 27, 1950, NARA, Record Group 59, box 4496; and Memorandum, March 24, 1950. Founded in 1939, the Confederation of Mexican Youth constituted the youth wing of the official party and included student organizations from universities as well as technical, agricultural, and teacher-training schools. Despite its ties to the official party, member groups included some with leftist tendencies that were affiliated with the Popular Party and the Mexican Communist Party.

59. Founded in London in 1945 and headquartered in Prague, the International Union of Students maintained a pro-Soviet position in world affairs. It came to have an important presence in Latin America, where it defended the Cuban Revolution and supported clandestine student organizations. Also founded in 1945, the World Federation of Democratic Youth included communist youth groups from around the world as well as nationalist organizations from Asia and Africa.

60. "Página editorial," *Excélsior*, February 11, 1950, in "Public Education in Mexico," February 27, 1950, NARA, Record Group 59, box 4496.

61. Francis White to Henry Holland, August 25, 1954, NARA, Record Group 59, box 4496.

62. "Dismissal Under-Secretary Mexican Ministry of Education," May 21, 1953, NARA, Record Group 59, box 4496; and "El plan comunista de Gómez Robleda," *Excélsior*, February 16, 1953 (newspaper clipping in same NARA folder).

63. Santos Valdés, *Autobiografía*, 61.

64. This is not only a reoccurring theme in countless normalista testimonies but a fact recognized by education officials themselves. For example, one SEP official wrote, "In spite of the deficiencies we frequently denounce in our schools, more often than not, youngsters eat better there than they do in their homes." In SEP, *Junta Nacional de Educación Normal*, 2:188.

65. Mariano Orozco Álvarez, interview.

66. José Ángel Aguirre Romero, interview.

67. José Luis Aguayo Álvarez, interview.

68. Conversely, education officials worried that parents sent their kids to the junior high school component of the normal only "to rid themselves of an additional mouth to feed" but withdrew them from school once old enough to earn their keep, so they could join the labor market and contribute to the household income. Hernández Ruiz, "El problema de la deserción escolar," in SEP, *Junta Nacional de Educación Normal*, 2:188. See also "Informe final," December 9, 1954, AHENR/SM, C79.

69. Ruiz del Castillo, *Othón Salazar*, 105.

70. Manuel Arias Delgado, interview.

71. Felipe Cortés Martínez, interview.

72. Reynaldo Jiménez, interview.

73. Felipe Cortés Martínez, interview.

74. José Ángel Aguirre Romero, interview.

75. "El problema de la deserción de los alumnos," July 2, 1954, AHENR/SM, C53, 1959–60.

76. Rosalva Pantoja Guerrero, interview.

77. Graciela Cásares, interview.

78. "La reforma educativa en la enseñanza normal," November 10, 1963, AHENR/SM, C1963. The name sometimes began with "Club" rather than "Committee."

79. Vicente Estrada, interview.

80. Felipe Cortés Martínez, interview.

81. Vela Gálvez, "Organización estudiantil y su acción formadora," 233.

82. José Ángel Aguirre Romero, interview.

83. SEP, *Junta Nacional de Educación Normal*, 1:175.

84. SEP, *Junta Nacional de Educación Normal*, 1:169.

85. "Oficio circular," March 23, 1954, AHENR/CH, C28, 1954–57.

86. "Proyecto de planes de studio para las escuelas normales primarias," n.d., AHSEP/Conalte, C31, Exp.885, Leg.1.

87. Aguayo Álvarez, *Salaices*, 105.

88. Specific classes, activities, and times varied from school to school and changed over time.

89. See appendix for list of courses and subject areas.

90. "Expediente General del Proyecto de Plan de Estudios," 1959, AHSEP/Conalte, C48, Exp.1288, Leg.1.

91. "Expediente General del Proyecto de Plan de Estudios," 1959.

92. The number, types, and names of committees varied from school to school and often changed over time. Other committees included those on work, reforestation, recreation, sports, professional development, regional arts and crafts, and school annexes. "Informe que rinde el C. Director de la Escuela Normal Rural de Cañada Honda, Ags.," May 1954, AHENR/CH, C27b, 1950–54; "Ponencia que presenta la dirección general de enseñanza normal," 1964, AHSEP/Conalte, C52, Exp.1343, Leg.1; and Consejo Escolar, [ca. 1962–63], AHENR/SM, C10, 1962.

93. "Carta de Dirección General de Enseñanza a Directores," June 12, 1954, AHENR/SM, C1955.

94. "Carta de Dirección General de Enseñanza a Directores," June 12, 1954. See also "Informe que rinde el C. Director de la Escuela Normal Rural de Cañada Honda, Ags.," May 1954; "Ponencia que presenta la dirección general de enseñanza normal," 1964; and Consejo Escolar, 1962–63, AHENR/SM, C10, 1962.

95. "Informe que rinde el Sr. Director," May 1954, AHENR/CH, C27b; "Código disciplinario," June 19, 1954, AHENR/CH, C28, 1954–57; and "Código disciplinario," Fall 1964, AHENR/SM, C1965.

96. For example, Vela Gálvez, "Sistema democrático disciplinario," 257; and Quintal Martín, González Salazar, and Pacheco Hidalgo, *Historia de la benemérita Escuela Normal Rural "Justo Sierra Méndez,"* 154.

97. Santos Valdés, "Democracia y disciplina escolar," 100–101.

98. "Circular #21/53," April 15, 1953, AHENR/CH, C28, 1954–57; and "Instructivo de la Dirección General de Enseñanza Normal," January 24, 1954, AHENR/SM, C53.

99. "Forma en que deben estar concebidos y redactados los escritos de la Sociedad de Alumnos," November 9, 1954, AHENR/CH, C27, 1950–54.

100. Santos Valdés, "Democracia y disciplina escolar," 100–101.

101. Director Miguel Silva Sánchez and Subdirector Fernando Segura Basaure to Guadalupe de Zavaleta, November 15, 1959, AHSEP/Conalte, C40, Exp.1065.

102. For example, a 1942 Aguascalientes newspaper reported that several students had been unjustifiably expelled from the rural normal of Cañada Honda, accounts a school inspector's investigation revealed to be false. Civera Cerecedo, *Escuela como opción de vida,* 370n20.

103. "Discurso pronunciado en la inauguración de la convención de educación normal, en Saltillo, Coah.," April 23, 1944, in Torres Bodet, *Educación mexicana,* 100–101.

104. Santos Valdés, "Democracia y disciplina escolar," 112.

105. SEP, *Educación rural mexicana,* 245. See also Arnaut Salgado, *Federalización educativa en México,* 238; Ruiz, *Mexico,* 84; SEP, *Junta Nacional de Educación Normal,* 2:60–61; and Hernández Ruiz, "Problema de la deserción escolar," 182–83.

106. Arnaut Salgado, *Historia de una profesión,* 103n12.

107. SEP, *Educación rural mexicana,* 243, 261, 265.

108. "Instructivo de la Dirección General de Enseñanza Normal," January 25, 1954, AHENR/CH, C27, 1950–54.

109. "Circular #8," March 1955, AHENR/SM, C1955.

110. "Los problemas de la selección de alumnos," June 27, 1954, AHSEP/Conalte, C53, Exp.1374, Leg.1.

111. I was unable to locate federal records on the establishment of new rural normales during the 1950s due to the inaccessibility of post-1940 documentation at the Ministry of Public Education Archive.

112. Ceniceros, "Política educativa del regimen," 351.

113. Carlos María Peralta Oropeza to Celerino Cano Palacios, March 10, 1959, AHSEP/Conalte, C4, Exp.17, Leg.1.

114. "El problema de deserción de los alumnos," July 1954, AHENR/SM, C53.

115. "Resoluciones de la Segunda Comisión," in SEP, *Educación rural mexicana,* 241.

116. "Resoluciones de la Segunda Comisión," in SEP, *Educación rural mexicana,* 242.

117. "Enseñanza Primaria en los Estados y Territorios," 1953, AHSEP/Conalte, C29, Exp.801.

118. Wilkie, *Mexican Revolution*, 160–61.

119. Medina, *Hacia un nuevo estado*, 170.

120. Gillingham and Smith, "Introduction," 2–3.

121. Gollás, "Breve relato de cincuenta años," esp. 232.

122. For detailed studies on this process, see Sanderson, *Transformation of Mexican Agriculture*; Barkin and Suárez, *Fin de la autosuficiencia alimentaria*; and Hewitt de Alcántara, *Modernización de la agricultura mexicana*.

123. "Guión para la elaboración," November 5, 1957, AHSEP/Conalte, CII, Exp.286.

124. Walker, *Waking from the Dream*, 3.

125. See Padilla, *Rural Resistance*; Grammont, "Unión General de Obreros y Campesinos"; and Bartra, *Guerrero bronco*.

Four. Education at a Crossroads

1. Ruiz del Castillo, *Othón Salazar*, 113–14, 120, 124, 131–32, 133; and Othón Salazar, interview.

2. "Instructivo de la Dirección General de Enseñanza Normal," January 25, 1954, AHENR/CH, C27; and "Sobre inscripción de alumnos en las escuelas normales rurales," January 21, 1955, AHENR/SM, CI955.

3. On the rail workers' movement, see Alegre, *Railroad Radicals*; on the National Polytechnic strike, see Pensado, *Rebel Mexico*; and on the press, see Servín, "Propaganda y Guerra Fría."

4. SEP, *Junta Nacional de Educación Normal*, 2:185.

5. Grandin, *Last Colonial Massacre*, 184–85.

6. Torres Bodet, *Jaime Torres Bodet*, 259.

7. Plutarco Emilio García Jiménez, interview.

8. Vicente Estrada, interview.

9. Charles Nash Myers calculated that by 1960 Mexico City "had 39.3 per cent of the national enrollment in middle education, but only 13.7 per cent of the total school age population." *Education and National Development*, 95.

10. "Strike in the Normal School for Elementary Teachers," April 16, 1953, NARA, Record Group 59, box 4496.

11. Cardiel Reyes, "Período de conciliación y consolidación," 2:357.

12. Loyo Brambila, *Movimiento magisterial*, 61.

13. Loyo Brambila, *Movimiento magisterial*, 62–63.

14. Loyo Brambila, *Movimiento magisterial*, 80.

15. Loyo Brambila, *Movimiento magisterial*, 82–85.

16. Othón Salazar, interview.

17. Loyo Brambila, *Movimiento magisterial*, 95.

18. The increases ranged from 15 to 57 percent, depending on rank and seniority. Loyo Brambila, *Movimiento magisterial*, 95, 98–99, 101.

19. Declaraciones del Comité Pro-Pliego Petitorio y Democratización de la IX: "Razón de ser del movimiento," August 10, 1956, quoted in Loyo Brambila, *Movimiento magisterial*, 39–40, 95.

20. Quoted in Caballero and Medrano, "Segundo período de Torres Bodet," 364.

21. Amembassy Despatch 1193, April 8, 1960, NARA, Central Decimal File, 1960–63, 812.43, box 2337.

22. "Circular #32," January 9, 1962, AHENR/CH, C30, 1960–64.

23. Torres Bodet, *Jaime Torres Bodet*, 243–44.

24. Torres Bodet, *Jaime Torres Bodet*, 243–44.

25. Aboites, "Salario del educador," 71.

26. Normalistas with scholarships were to serve three years or pay back their financial aid.

27. Arnaut Salgado, *Historia de una profesión*, 116.

28. Ávila Carrillo and Martínez Brizuela, *Historia del movimiento magisterial*, 37.

29. Amembassy Despatch 1193, April 8, 1960.

30. Bernardo Ponce, "Perspectiva," *Excélsior*, April 5, 1960; and "El conflicto de la Normal," *Séñal*, April 3, 1960, quoted in Loaeza, *Clases medias*, 249.

31. Amembassy Despatch 1193, April 8, 1960. See also Loaeza, *Clases medias*, 248–49n9.

32. Loaeza, *Clases medias*, 248–49n9.

33. Amembassy Despatch 1193, April 8, 1960.

34. Amembassy Despatch 1193, April 8, 1960.

35. Torres Bodet, *Jaime Torres Bodet*, 271–72, 275.

36. SEP, *Obra educativa*, 149.

37. Plutarco Emilio García Jiménez, interview.

38. Loaeza, *Clases medias*, 216.

39. Inaugural address, December 1, 1958, quoted in Caballero and Medrano, "Segundo período de Torres Bodet," 360.

40. Torres Bodet, *Jaime Torres Bodet*, 272.

41. Amembassy Despatch 1193, April 8, 1960.

42. Plutarco Emilio García Jiménez, interview.

43. Loaeza, *Clases medias*, 186–88.

44. Ávila and Muñoz, *Creación de la Comisión Nacional*, 92–93.

45. Torres Bodet, *Memorias*, 387.

46. Loaeza, *Clases medias*, 235.

47. Convocatorias published in *Tiempo* quoted in Loaeza, *Clases medias*, 235.

48. Loaeza, *Clases medias*, 240–41, 236.

49. Greaves, *Del radicalismo a la unidad nacional*, 174; and Loaeza, *Clases medias*, 215.

50. Greaves, *Del radicalismo a la unidad nacional*, 154.

51. Loaeza, *Clases medias*, 306.

52. See, for example, "Bolchevizar al país es la meta othonista," *El Universal*, May 14, 1958, reproduced in Lobato, *Movimiento del magisterio*, 199–204.

53. *Señal*, October 5, 1958, quoted in Torres Septién, *Educación privada*, 203.

54. The Catholic newspaper *Señal* continuously published editorials about Cuban children being taken from their parents and sent to the Soviet Union as well as children being educated in prison-like schools with government-issued Marxist texts. See Loaeza, *Clases medias*, 305.

55. *El Universal*, January 18, 1961, quoted in Greaves, *Del radicalismo a la unidad nacional*, 161.

56. *Boletin de la UNPF*, no. 8 (April–May 1961): 6, quoted in Greaves, *Del radicalismo a la unidad nacional*, 161–62.

57. Loaeza, *Clases medias*, 271.

58. The president made this statement on July 1, 1960, shortly after Cuban president Osvaldo Dorticós visited Mexico. "Dentro de la Constitución, mi gobierno es de extrema izquierda," *Excélsior*, July 2, 1960, quoted in Loaeza, *Clases medias*, 262.

59. *Excélsior*, November 24, 1960, quoted in Loaeza, *Clases medias*, 285; see also 284–85.

60. Christlieb Ibarrola, *Monopolio educativo o unidad nacional*, 56.

61. Alejandro Avilés, "Extrema izquierda: Monopolios, capitalismo de estado," *La Nación*, July 10, 1960, 2, quoted in Loaeza, *Clases medias*, 265–66.

62. Loaeza, *Clases medias*, 274–75.

63. Greaves, *Del radicalismo a la unidad nacional*, 164.

64. "Un mentis a los detractores gratuitos del Dr. y Prof. Pablo Gómez Ramírez," *Índice*, October 21, 1964; and Torres Septién, *Educación privada*, 217.

65. Torres Septién, *Educación privada*, 202.

66. Cárdenas spearheaded Mexico's National Liberation Movement, which defended Cuban self-determination. The former president also criticized large industrial monopolies and latifundios, as well as the control the state exercised over unions. He had good relations with the MRM as well as the rail workers fighting for union independence. Loaeza, *Clases medias*, 263, 287.

67. Greaves, *Del radicalismo a la unidad nacional*, 165; and "Socio-Economic Aspects of Mexico's Public Education System: A Monterrey View," February 14, 1964, NARA, Record Group 59, box 369. The former puts the number of demonstrators at 150,000, while the latter gives 100,000.

68. Greaves, *Del radicalismo a la unidad nacional*, 169–70.

69. Greaves, *Del radicalismo a la unidad nacional*, 168; and Loaeza, *Clases medias*, 373.

70. Loaeza, *Clases medias*, 364, 372, 389, 393.

71. Loaeza, *Clases medias*, 377.

72. In fact, the free-textbook program recalls Vasconcelos's initiative to print and disseminate a massive number of classic works of literature, a measure by which the state positioned itself as a guide of national cultural development. Loaeza, *Clases medias*, 225.

73. See Latapí, "Pensamiento educativo de Torres Bodet."

74. SEP, *Acción educativa del gobierno mexicano*, 29–30.

75. Torres Bodet, "Técnica y educación," in Torres Septién, *Pensamiento educativo de Jaime Torres Bodet*, 113–20, quote on 113. In 1955 Mexico spent 1.1 percent of its gross domestic product on education, less than half what poorer countries such as Jamaica, Ivory Coast, Sri Lanka, and Uganda did. This amount had increased to 2.1 percent by 1965 but was still less than in countries like Chile and Argentina, which spent 3.6 and 3.3 percent respectively. Cuba spent 5.6 percent of its gross domestic product on education. For 1955 figures, see Navarrete, "Financiamiento de la educación pública," 48. For 1965 figures, see Centro de Estudios Económicos y Demográficos, *Dinámica de la población*, 220.

76. The committee Torres Bodet convened argued that the budget necessary to ensure school access for the three million children who by the SEP's calculation did not attend school in 1950 would never be approved by the finance ministry. To make the goal more tenable, the SEP proposed to meet educational demand rather than need. Thus, those who had dropped out or did not attend school because of chronic illness would not be included in the target population. This logic reduced the number almost by half, to 1,700,000, a figure that did not account for population growth. That problem, President López Mateos told Torres Bodet, would be dealt with by future administrations. Torres Bodet, *Jaime Torres Bodet*, 253–55.

77. Navarrete, "Financiamiento de la educación pública," 35. The number was far higher in the countryside, where, in 1960, 76 percent of rural primary schoolteachers taught without certificates. Myers, *Education and National Development*, 55.

78. SEP, *Obra educativa*, 163.

79. Caballero and Medrano, "Segundo período de Torres Bodet," 385–86.

80. SEP, *Obra educativa*, 163.

81. Greaves, *Del radicalismo a la unidad nacional*, 116n75.

82. "Instructivo al que se sujetará la expedición y registo de títulos para maestros normalistas," 1961, AHENR/CH, C30, 1960–64.

83. Arnaut Salgado, *Historia de una profesión*, 96; and Greaves, *Del radicalismo a la unidad nacional*, 88–89.

84. Myers, *Education and National Development*, 52.

85. Navarrete, "Financiamiento de la educación pública," 31.

86. Caballero and Medrano, "Segundo período de Torres Bodet," 372.

87. Arnaut Salgado, *Historia de una profesión*, 114.

88. Arnaut Salgado, *Historia de una profesión*, 114.

89. Over the coming decades, fourteen more CRENs would be established throughout Mexico. Today, their numbers equal that of rural normales.

90. SEP, *Obra educativa*, 150.

91. Torres Bodet, *Jaime Torres Bodet*, 259.

92. "Dictamen sobre el punto dos de la convocatoria," [ca. late March 1959], AHENR/CH, C29, 1957–61.

93. "Informando semana de guardia," May 5, 1958, AHENR/CH, C29, 1957–62; "Dando a conocer paro," May 6, 1958, AHENR/SM, C164, Administración Académica; "Dando a conocer paro," September 10, 1958, AHENR/SM, C164; and Loyo Brambila, *Movimiento magisterial*, 53.

94. "Dictamen sobre el punto dos de la convocatoria," [ca. late March 1959].

95. "Dictamen sobre el punto dos de la convocatoria," [ca. late March 1959].

96. "Dictamen sobre el punto dos de la convocatoria," [ca. late March 1959].

97. "Se contesta Pliego de Peticiones," April 29, 1959, AHENR/CH, C29, 1957–62.

98. "Relativo a la superación del sistema en todos sus aspectos," March 31, 1958, AHENR/CH, C29, 1957–62.

99. Examples of purportedly unfounded student mobilizations against directors included those at the rural normales of Misantla (Veracruz), Tamazulapan and Comitancillo (both in Oaxaca), and Panotla (Tlaxcala). Union officials cited conflicts between school directors and staff at Hueyapan (Puebla), Atequiza (Jalisco), and Ayotzinapa (Guerrero) as further evidence of a system in crisis. "Circular #002," May 11, 1959, AHENR/CH, C28, 1954–57.

100. "Relativo a la superación del sistema en todos sus aspectos," March 31, 1958.

101. "Relativo a la superación del sistema en todos sus aspectos," March 31, 1958.

102. SNTE, "Circular 30," April 1959, AHENR/CH, C28, 1954–57.

103. "Relativo a la superación del sistema en todos sus aspectos," March 31, 1958.

104. "Se presentan consideraciones respecto al personal comisionado," July 23, 1958, AHENR/CH, C28, 1954–57.

105. "Proponiendo una modalidad de trabajo," January 15, 1958, AHENR/CH, C28, 1954–57.

106. Greaves, *Del radicalismo a la unidad nacional*, 193–94. Until then normalistas took thirty-eight different courses divided into three general areas: cultural literacy (knowledge of the classics), the science of education (pedagogical methods), and hands-on training, often in the form of workshops. Hernández Santos, *Tiempos de reforma*, 197–98. See appendix for sample schedules.

107. "Ponencia que presenta la Dirección General de Enseñanza Normal," [ca. late 1950s], AHSEP/Conalte, C52, Exp.888, Leg.1.

108. "Relativo al acuerdo de fecha 26 del actual," August 29, 1960, AHENR/CH, C29, 1957–61.

109. "Circular #15," [ca. 1964], AHENR/CH, C30, 1960–64; and Greaves, *Del radicalismo a la unidad nacional*, 193–94. In the rural normales, Torres Bodet

implemented the curricular changes that the National Meeting of Normal Education had proposed since 1954. Meneses Morales, *Tendencias educativas oficiales*, 3:488–92.

110. "Circular #32," January 9, 1962, AHENR/CH, C30, 1960–64.

111. The SEP issued the CRENs' working-group reports with instructions on the new course structure, pedagogical methods, and changes in grading practices. "Cuarto Seminario de Estudio de los Centros Regionales de Enseñanza Normal," August 24, 1963, AHENR/CH, C31, 1963–66.

112. Minutes of meeting between director and teachers at the rural normal of Cañada Honda, September 5, 1962, AHENR/CH, C30, 1960–64; "Reunión de Colegio de Maestros," September 2, 1964, AHENR/SM, C1965; and "Oficio Circular," September 5, 1964, AHENR/SM, C1965.

113. Comité Ejecutivo Nacional de la FECSM to Agustín Yáñez, March 8 1965, AHENR/SM, C1965.

114. For example, "Pidiendo salida del maestro de literatura," December 10, 1965, AHENR/CH, C31, 1963–66. The poor teaching quality that resulted from such situations was often a cause of student protest. "Magisterio," July 4, 1963, AGN/DFS 40-1, Exp.36, H202–5.

115. "La reforma educativa en la enseñanza normal," November 10, 1963, AHENR/SM, C "Varios 1963."

116. Sometimes referred to as a committee, sometimes a club, the Political and Ideological Orientation Club also organized cultural events related to song, theater, and poetry. "Club de Orientación Política e Ideológica 'Valentín Gómez Farías,'" March 17, 1959, AHENR/SM, C52.

117. "La reforma educativa en la enseñanza normal," November 10, 1963.

118. "Proyección de las actividades agropecuarias," November 1964, AHENR/CH, C30, 1960–64.

119. Ing. Carlos M. Peralta O. to Prof. Celerino Cano Palacios, March 10, 1959, AHSEP/Conalte, C4, Exp.17, Leg.1.

120. The SEP expanded and renamed the branch that oversaw agricultural practices. Previously the Office of Economic Development, it would now be the Office of Agricultural Extension and Education to reflect the link between production and education. "Circular #69," December 9, 1963, AHENR/CH, C30, 1960–64.

121. "Instrucciones en relación con las prácticas agropecuarias," September 20, 1966, AHENR/CH, C33, 1966–69.

122. "V Seminario de Estudio de las Escuelas Normales del Calendario B," August 1964, AHENR/CH, C33, 1966–69.

123. "V Seminario de Estudio de las Escuelas Normales del Calendario B," August 1964.

124. "V Seminario de Estudio de las Escuelas Normales del Calendario B," August 1964.

125. "Cuarto Seminario de Estudios de los Centros Regionales de Enseñanza Normal," [ca. 1963], AHENR/CH, C31, 1963–66.

126. "Sobre la promoción escolar," June 25, 1959, AHENR/CH, C29, 1957–61.

127. "Normas para calificar las asignaturas," June 17, 1964, AHENR/CH, C30, 1960–64.

128. "Normas para calificar las asignaturas," June 17, 1964.

129. "Sobre la promoción escolar," June 25, 1959.

130. Minutes of meeting between director and teachers at the rural normal of Cañada Honda, September 5, 1962, AHENR/CH, C30, 1960–64. This latter statute was a point of contention with the FECSM since its delegates' responsibilities involved travel to other schools and they thus often missed many classes. "Acta Num. 3," October 23, 1962, AHENR/SM, C10, 1962.

131. "Sobre la promoción escolar," June 25, 1959; "Circular #16," March 19, 1964, AHENR/CH, C30, 1960–64; and "Las tareas del seminario," February 12, 1964, AHENR/CH, C30, 1960–64.

132. "La reforma educativa en la enseñanza normal," November 10, 1963.

133. While in the projected budget Adolfo López Mateos assigned larger educational expenditures than Cárdenas, the actual amount spent was consistently lower. Wilkie, *Mexican Revolution*, 160–64, esp. table 7-2 and n.5. Significantly, as James Wilkie notes, the SEP's publication *La obra educativa en el sexenio, 1958–1964*, was based on projected rather than actual spending.

134. Torres Bodet, "Técnica y educación," in Torres Septién, *Pensamiento educativo de Jaime Torres Bodet*, 114.

135. Latapí, "Pensamiento educativo de Torres Bodet," 37–38.

136. See, for example, McGinn and Street, "Has Mexican Education"; Muñoz Izquierdo, "Análisis e interpretación"; and Muñoz Izquierdo and Lobo, "Expansión escolar."

137. In 1960, for example, when the army ended a student strike at the University of Guerrero by killing at least twenty people, the social outrage led to the resignation of Governor Raúl Caballero Aburto. In 1966 a student protest over a hike in bus fares in Morelia triggered an army takeover of the University of Michoacán San Nicolás de Hidalgo. In Sonora, when students joined widespread state protests in 1967 over the imposition of an unpopular PRI gubernatorial candidate, the army occupied the campus of the state university. That same year students at the Agricultural School Hermanos Escobar in Chihuahua sought an expansion of educational access for the poor by demanding that this heretofore private school be made public. And, of course, the 1968 student movement in Mexico City coalesced around a broad set of political demands; its two months of demonstrations ended in an army massacre in the Tlatelolco plaza.

Five. "The Infinite Injustice Committed against Our Class Brothers"

1. "Un mentis a los detractores gratuitos del Dr. y Prof. Pablo Gómez Ramírez," *Índice*, October 21, 1964. An earlier, significantly abridged version of this chapter appeared in *México beyond 1968: Revolutionaries, Radicals, and Repression during the Global Sixties and Subversive Seventies*, edited by Jaime M. Pensado and Enrique C. Ochoa (Tucson: University of Arizona Press, 2018).

2. Wasserman, *Capitalists, Caciques, and Revolution*, 165.

3. Wasserman, *Capitalists, Caciques, and Revolution*, 6.

4. Wasserman, *Persistent Oligarchs*, 165, 77, 111–13.

5. Wasserman, *Persistent Oligarchs*, 82, 173.

6. Boyer, *Political Landscapes*, 44, 145–46.

7. "Estado de Chihuahua," September 20, 1964, AGN/DGIPS, C1025, Exp.22; and Vargas Valdés, *Madera rebelde*, 81–82.

8. The three industries were Celulosa de Chihuahua, Industrias Madera, and Maderas de Pino Industrializadas. "Estado de Chihuahua," September 20, 1964.

9. Henson, *Agrarian Revolt*, 50; and García Aguirre, *Revolución que llegaría*, 69–70.

10. José Ibarra was one of four partners in the Cuatro Amigos livestock company, which bought fourteen thousand hectares from Bosques de Chihuahua. The other three were Alejandro Prieto, Tomás Vega, and Roberto Schneider. Henson, *Agrarian Revolt*, 51.

11. Memorandum, October 8, 1964, AGN/DFS 100-5-1, Leg.10, H246–54; and Daniel Reyes, "Guerrillas en la sierra chihuahuense de Madera," *Sucesos para todos*, September 11, 1964.

12. Grammont, "Unión General de Obreros y Campesinos," 225–28.

13. Memorandum, September 18, 1964, AGN/DFS 100-5-1, Leg.10, H56–58.

14. García Aguirre, *Revolución que llegaría*, 52–53.

15. The Normal Night Schools provided accreditation courses for educators who already worked as teachers but did not have the proper credentials. Founded toward the end of the nineteenth century, the Arts and Trade School and Ladies' Industrial School imparted courses in various trades. The former included classes in bookmaking, carpentry, mechanics, shoemaking, and technical skills for radio and television work, and the latter instructed women in cooking, sewing, and secretarial work. These schools, as opposed to the rural normales, were under state jurisdiction.

16. García Aguirre, *Revolución que llegaría*, 53–54.

17. "Organizan la Federación de Estudiantes de Chihuahua," *El Heraldo*, May 12, 1962.

18. Vargas Valdés, *Madera rebelde*, 96.

19. Quoted in Vargas Valdés, *Madera rebelde*, 99–100.

20. "Bosques de Chihuahua, S.A., Asesinos," *Índice*, February 27, 1960.

21. Reyes, "Guerrillas en la sierra chihuahuense"; Henson, *Agrarian Revolt*, 51–52, 59; and García Aguirre, *Revolución que llegaría*, 144.

22. Memorandum, October 8, 1964, AGN/DFS 100-5-1, Leg.10, H246–54.

23. "Bosques de Chihuahua, S.A., Asesinos"; and "'Bosques Asesinos S.A.' condenados en México por Renato Leduc en 'Siempre,'" *Índice*, April 21, 1960.

24. "Eliminación total de cacicazgos piden los jóvenes," *El Norte*, March 7, 1960.

25. "Ritmo de libertad y de progreso que ha sido detenido," *El Norte*, March 7, 1960.

26. "Llegó la caravana de campesinos de Madera," *El Norte*, November 20, 1960; and García Aguirre, *Revolución que llegaría*, 41.

27. "Dentro de la ley . . . lo que quieran . . . fuera nada," *El Norte*, November 27, 1960.

28. "Gobernadorcillo Constitucional de Chihuahua," *Índice*, October 22, 1960.

29. From a Sonoran family, Ríos was active in the UGOCM and like Gámiz spent time in Mexico City, where he met numerous PP activists. He became a UGOCM delegate and moved to Madera after Luján Adame's assassination. Gaytán came from a large campesino family from Dolores, Chihuahua; his was one of the many families dispossessed of their land by Bosques de Chihuahua. Also a UGOCM leader, Gaytán led the union's commissions to Mexico City demanding land and education reform. In 1962 he was elected sectional president of Mineral de Dolores, where, together with Gámiz, he helped set up a school and spearheaded other community projects. See Vargas Valdés, *Madera rebelde*, 121–22; and López Rosas, "Pensamiento y estrategia política," 74.

30. Vargas Valdés, *Madera rebelde*, 184; and López Rosas, "Pensamiento y estrategia política," 42–46.

31. Pensado, *Rebel Mexico*, 85–89.

32. Vargas Valdés, *Madera rebelde*, 186–87.

33. Pensado, *Rebel Mexico*, 107–8.

34. Henson, *Agrarian Revolt*, 60.

35. Salvador Gaytán, interview by López Rosas, June 30, 2007, Mexico City, quoted in López Rosas, "Pensamiento y estrategia política," 59.

36. Santos Valdés, *Madera*, 82; and López Rosas, "Pensamiento y estrategia política," 72.

37. "Reportaje de la sierra de Temosachic, Madera y del viejo Mineral de Dolores," *La Voz de Chihuahua*, May 12, 1963.

38. Toro Rosales, *Testimonios*, 40–42.

39. Alma Gómez Caballero, interview.

40. Santos Valdés, *Madera*, 166.

41. Alma Gómez Caballero, interview.

42. Memorandum, June 5, 1963, AGN/DFS 100-5-1, Leg.6, H307; "Información sobre el estado de Chihuahua," June 6, 1963, AGN/DFS 100-5-1, Leg.6, H310; and "Un mentis a los detractores gratuitos."

43. Alma Gómez Caballero, interview; and Santos Valdés, *Madera*, 167.

44. Alma Gómez Caballero, interview. To avoid confusion, in this chapter I refer to Alma by her first name.

45. Alma Gómez Caballero, interview. Alma joined the Revolutionary Action Movement in 1971 and was captured and jailed in 1973.

46. José Luis Aguayo Álvarez, interview.

47. Jose Ángel Aguirre Romero, interview. Bosques de Chihuahua owned 615,445 hectares from its purchase of Northwestern Railway and had a concession of 563,393 hectares from Alemán's presidential decree, giving it control of over a million hectares. "Estado de Chihuahua," September 20, 1964.

48. Jose Ángel Aguirre Romero, interview.

49. Manuel Arias Delgado, interview.

50. Silvina Rodríguez, interview.

51. Alma Gómez Caballero, interview.

52. "Estado de Chihuahua," June 15, 1967, AGN/DFS 100-5-1, Leg.20, H391.

53. "Cobarde actitud de los comunistas emboscados," *El Heraldo*, April 29, 1961; and "Todos son alumnos de la Escuela Normal de Salaices, desde donde fueron traidos," *El Heraldo*, May 1, 1961.

54. García, "Fui secretario general," 77–78; and García Aguirre, *Revolución que llegaría*, 63.

55. "Chihuahua, agresión sinarquista," *Política*, May 15, 1961.

56. As Eric Zolov writes, while the United States framed its concern over the Cuban Revolution as a matter of national security in the battle against communism, in Mexico conservative sectors used it to further contain Cardenismo. See "¡Cuba sí, Yanquis no!"

57. "Todos son alumnos de la Escuela Normal de Salaices."

58. García, "Fui secretario general," 77–78; and García Aguirre, *Revolución que llegaría*, 63.

59. García, "Fui secretario general," 77; and "Chihuahua, agresión sinarquista."

60. Gámiz, "Participación de los estudiantes."

61. Aguayo Álvarez, "Prólogo," 13.

62. Manuel Arias Delgado, interview.

63. Gámiz, "Participación de los estudiantes."

64. "Del 7 al 12 de octubre será el encuentro en la sierra," *Acción*, September 18, 1963.

65. Vargas Valdés, *Madera rebelde*, 245, 255–56.

66. "Fue detenido por la policía en Cuauhtémoc," *El Heraldo*, October 20, 1963.

67. Vargas Valdés, *Madera rebelde*, 250–51.

68. Gámiz, "La participación de los estudiantes en el movimiento revolucionario," *Índice*, November 7, 1963. This is a somewhat modified version of the text appearing in *Ediciones Linea Revolucionaria*.

69. Gámiz, "Participación de los estudiantes."

70. Henson, *Agrarian Revolt*, 97.

71. Contreras Orozco, *Informantes*, 90; García Aguirre, *Revolución que llegaría*, 118; and "Violento choque entre campesinos y tropas federales en la zona de Janos," *El Norte*, January 19, 1964.

72. "La versión de los campesinos," *El Norte*, January 19, 1964.

73. "Golpe final a invasiones," *El Heraldo*, January 21, 1964.

74. Memorandum, February 20, 1964, AGN/DFS 100-5-3, Leg.1, H413–16.

75. "Torres Bodet decidirá la situación del grupo estudiantil de Saucillo," *El Heraldo*, February 23, 1964.

76. "Tratarán de disuadir a estudiantes de Saucillo de participar en las asonadas," *El Heraldo*, February 23, 1964.

77. Memorandum, February 20, 1964.

78. "Tratarán de disuadir a estudiantes de Saucillo."

79. "Torres Bodet decidirá la situación."

80. Memorandum, February 19, 1964, AGN/DFS 100-5-3, Leg.1, H406–7; and Memorandum, February 20, 1964 AGN/DFS 100-5-3, Leg.1, H424–25.

81. "Última hora: Tres estudiantes y dos profesores detenidos y consignados," *El Norte*, February 23, 1964; "Motín de estudiantes normalistas disuelto con bombas lacrimógenas," *El Norte*, February 23, 1964; "La intervención enérgica de las autoridades se hizo necesaria," *El Heraldo*, February 23, 1964; Memorandum, February 22, 1964, AGN/DFS 100-5-3, Leg.1, H441–44; "El mitin por la tarde abundó en amenazas," *El Heraldo*, February 23, 1964; and quote from "Actúan agitadores profesionales," *El Heraldo*, February 23, 1964.

82. Toro Rosales, *Testimonios*, 24–25.

83. "Intervención enérgica de las autoridades."

84. "Última hora."

85. "Intervención enérgica de las autoridades."

86. Toro Rosales, *Testimonios*, 28–30.

87. "Antecedentes sobre los distintos problemas que presentan las escuelas normales rurales en el estado," April 15, 1964, AGN/DFS 100-5-1, Leg.8, H52–54.

88. Toro Rosales, *Testimonios*, 27.

89. "Carta abierta al Sr. Presidente de la República Lic. Gustavo Díaz Ordaz desde la penitenciaria del estado," *Índice*, September 27, 1965.

90. "La UGOCM cumplió y cumplirá mientras exista con el papel histórico q'le corresponde," *Índice*, November 7, 1963.

91. "Antecedentes sobre los distintos problemas que presentan las escuelas normales rurales en el estado," April 15, 1964, AGN/DFS 100-5-1, Leg.8, H52–54.

92. "Antecedentes sobre los distintos problemas que presentan las escuelas normales rurales en el estado," April 15, 1964, AGN/DFS 100-5-1, Leg.8, H52–54.

93. Gral. de Div. Praxedes Giner Durán, "Al pueblo del estado," *El Heraldo*, February 25, 1964.

94. Toro Rosales, *Testimonios*, 11–67.

95. "Atenderá el agrario el problema campesino, sin prejuicios de tipo político o ideológico," *El Norte*, March 5, 1964; and "Declaran a los agentes de la procuraduría," *El Heraldo*, March 5, 1964.

96. Henson, *Agrarian Revolt*, 102; and Contreras Orozco, *Informantes*, 94–95.

97. Contreras Orozco, *Informantes*, 95; Santos Valdés, *Madera*, 87; and Reyes, "Guerrillas en la sierra chihuahuense."

98. Henson, *Agrarian Revolt*, 127–29.

99. Memorandum, October 8, 1964, AGN/DFS 100-5-1, Leg.10, H246–54.

100. Memorandum, April 6, 1964, AGN/DFS 10-26, Leg.8, H17–23; "Gran presencia de animo en medio de un desorden," *El Heraldo*, April 7, 1964; Oscar Viramontes, "Un incidente que hizo temblar a Chihuahua," *El Heraldo de Chihuahua*, October 12, 2009, http://www.oem.com.mx/elheraldodechihuahua/notas/n1360455.htm; and "Por una ventana escaparon el alcalde y catorce personas más," *El Heraldo*, April 7, 1964. Newspaper accounts and intelligence documents disagree about whether Mariñelarena was a student from Chihuahua's State Normal or from the rural normal of Salaices.

101. Intelligence note attached to "Circular No. 1" of the Ejército Popular Revolucionario, September 2, 1964, AGN/DFS 100-5-3, Leg.2, H125.

102. "Gran presencia de animo."

103. "Manifiesto," May 5, 1965, AGN/DFS 11-142, Leg.1, H120.

104. "Antecedentes sobre los distintos problemas que presentan las escuelas normales rurales en el estado," April 15, 1964; intelligence note attached to "Circular No. 1" of the Ejército Popular Revolucionario, September 2, 1964; and description of political affiliations of some teachers from the rural normales of Salaices and Saucillo, August 24, 1964, AGN-DFS 100-5-1, Leg.2, H110–11.

105. "Información sobre el estado de Aguascalientes," November 3, 1964, AGN/DFS 100-1-1, Leg.3, H147–48.

106. "El cierre de internados y de las escuelas normales," *Índice*, September 12, 1964; "Clausuran las normales nocturnas de Chihuahua, Juárez, Ojinaga y Parral," *El Heraldo*, August 25, 1964; and Memorandum, November 11, 1964, AGN/DFS 100-5-1, Leg.11, H80–83.

107. "No han llegado los 103 que ofreció la SEP," *El Heraldo*, August 25, 1964.

108. Memorandum, September 12, 1964, AGN/DFS 100-5-1, Leg.10, H2–3; Memorandum, November 8, 1964, AGN/DFS 100-5-1, Leg.11, H37–40; Memorandum, November 11, 1964, AGN/DFS 100-5-1, Leg.11, H80–83; and Memorandum, October 29, 1964, AGN/DFS 100-5-1, Leg.10, H345–47; and "Carta abierta al Sr. Presidente de la República."

109. Memorandum, October 29, 1964; description of political affiliations of some teachers from the rural normales of Salaices and Saucillo, August 24, 1964, AGN-DFS 100-5-1, Leg.2, H110–11; and Memorandum, September 18, 1964, AGN/DFS 100-5-1, Leg.10, H56–58.

110. "Huelga en 16 escuelas normales rurales," *Índice*, November 21, 1964; Memorandum, November 22, 1964, AGN/DFS 100-5-1, Leg.11, H258–60; Memorandum, November 4, 1964, AGN/DFS 100-5-1, Leg.10, H417–19; and Memorandum, November 29, 1964, AGN/DFS 100-5-1, Leg.11, H275.

111. Memorandum, November 8, 1964.

112. Memorandum, December 2, 1964, AGN/DFS 100-5-1, Leg.11, H277–78.

113. Miguel Quiñónez to Javier Flores, reproduced in Aguayo Álvarez, *Paseo por los recuerdos*, 178–79.

114. Santos Valdés, *Madera*, 173–75.

115. Flores Torres, González García, and Ruiz Hernández, "Homenaje a Miguel," 176.

116. Santos Valdés, *Madera*, 172; and Vargas Valdés, *Madera rebelde*, 335–36.

117. "Manifiesto," January 15, 1965, reproduced in Vargas Valdés, "Los Gaytán y el movimiento guerrillero."

118. "Manifiesto," January 15, 1965.

119. López Rosas, "Pensamiento y estrategia política," 151.

120. Memorandum, May 20, 1965, AGN/DFS 100-5-3, Leg.2, H223–26.

121. "Boletín de prensa," *Índice*, June 12, 1965.

122. "Único camino a seguir."

123. Aleida García Aguirre traces how, during the early 1960s, numerous graduates from Chihuahua's rural normales, especially Salaices, taught in the Sierra Tarahumara. García writes that this concentration took place partly because of personal recruitment networks but also because of the region's federal education inspector, Manuel Reynaldo Gaytán, a member of the Communist Party and a supporter of those trying to democratize the teachers' union, who created an environment favorable to progressive and radical teachers. *Revolución que llegaría*, chapter 4.

124. Flores Torres, González García and Ruiz Hernández, "Homenaje a Miguel," 178.

125. José Ángel Aguirre Romero, interview.

126. Elizabeth Henson's *Agrarian Revolt* and Jesús Vargas Valdés's *Madera rebelde* are two recent exceptions.

127. This captain, Lorenzo Cárdenas Barajas, reportedly trained members of Fidel Castro's group during their stay in Mexico before the Cuban Revolution. Henson, "Madera 1965," 33.

128. Vargas Valdés, *Madera rebelde*, 350.

129. Henson, *Agrarian Revolt*, 174–75.

130. According to Javier Contreras Orozco, the military may have known of the group's plan. *Informantes*, 137–38.

131. "Panorama nacional," *Política*, October 1, 1965. This detachment included four T-33 jets, one C-54, and one D-54 with sixty-eight parachuters. Henson, *Agrarian Revolt*, 182.

132. The Jaramillista movement, for example.

133. Alma Gómez Caballero, interview.

134. Alma Gómez Caballero, interview.

135. Alma Gómez Caballero, interview.

136. Henson, *Agrarian Revolt*, 142.

137. "Panorama nacional"; Toro Rosales, *Testimonios*, 96; Vargas Valdés, *Madera rebelde*, 356; and Santos Valdés, *Madera*, 120.."

138. "Panorama nacional."

139. "Estado de Chihuahua," October 12, 1965, AGN/DFS 100-5-1, Leg.14, H206–10.

140. "Estado de Chihuahua," October 12, 1965; and "Estado de Chihuahua," October 5, 1965, AGN/DFS 100-5-1, Leg.14, H160–62.

141. "Estado de Chihuahua," October 12, 1965.

142. "Estado de Chihuahua," October 29, 1965, AGN/DFS 100-5-1, Leg.15, H78–81.

143. "Estado de Chihuahua," October 12, 1965. Quote from Jaime Canelas López, *10 años de guerrilla*, 26.

144. "Estado de Chihuahua," November 24, 1966, AGN/DFS 100-5-1, Leg.18, H265.

145. José Ángel Aguirre Romero, interview.

146. "Federación de Estudiantes Campesinos Socialistas de México," January 20, 1966, AGN/DFS 100-5-1, Leg.17, H290–96.

Six. Learning in the Barricades

1. "Estado de Morelos," March 14, 1965, AGN/DGIPS, C448, Exp.1; "Estado de Morelos," March 15, 1965, AGN/DGIPS, C448, Exp.1; and "Estado de Morelos," March 18, 1965, AGN/DGIPS, C448, Exp.1.

2. On students and modernity, see, for example, Manzano, *Age of Youth*; and Zolov, *Refried Elvis*.

3. Grandin, *Last Colonial Massacre*, 181.

4. Ramiro Arciga, interview.

5. Grandin, *Last Colonial Massacre*, xv.

6. César Navarro, interview.

7. Pedro Martínez Noriega, interview.

8. Reynaldo Jiménez, interview.

9. Proceso Díaz, interview.

10. Accounts of novatadas are remarkably absent from the archival documentation but consistently appear in the oral histories of male normalistas. In some schools that had recently become coeducational, women also underwent initiation rituals although they were separate from, and less aggressive than, those organized by their male counterparts. In two all-women normales I visited,

students did mention initiation rituals, referred to as the *semana de pruebas* (week of proving yourself). The student committee organized various physical activities such as cleaning the school grounds, weeding the fields, or participating in long marches. The novatadas are likely recent in female normales.

11. Novatadas are frequently invoked by officials and the mainstream media as an example of the rural normales' toxic environment.

12. Despite such demeaning components, continues Pensado, "many newcomers willingly participated in these rituals, which celebrated a cosmopolitan notion of youth through a temporary appropriation of the streets." *Rebel Mexico*, 53–55.

13. Aristarco Aquino Solís, interview.

14. Herminia Gómez Carrasco, interview.

15. Elsa Guzmán, electronic communication, May 15, 2019.

16. César Navarro, phone interview, May 15, 2019. Significantly, when some rural normales became coed in the 1990s, at schools like El Mexe, Hidalgo, novatadas did extend to female students. Rather than shaving their heads, however, the initiation ritual included identifying anyone who was conceded dressing her up in a princess outfit, and dowsing her in dirty water. The goal was to show that at rural normales no one was better than anyone else. Vite Vargas, "Reconfiguración de la cultura institucional," 153.

17. Isidro Rodríguez, interview.

18. Augusto Carrasco Orozco, interview.

19. Isidro Rodríguez, interview.

20. Aristarco Aquino Solís, interview.

21. Augusto Carrasco Orozco, interview.

22. Aristarco Aquino Solís, interview.

23. See Dillingham, *Oaxaca Resurgent*.

24. Aristarco Aquino Solís, interview.

25. López de la Torre, *Guerras secretas*, 199.

26. Hermenegildo Figueroa García, interview.

27. César Navarro, interview. Issued in 1962 by Fidel Castro in the wake of the Bay of Pigs invasion and Cuba's expulsion from the Organization of American States, the Second Declaration of Havana reiterated Cuba's commitment to socialism and affirmed Latin America's revolutionary possibilities.

28. César Navarro, interview.

29. Cañas Loya, "La FECSM y el golpe," 87.

30. Belén Cuevas, interview; and Pedro Martínez Noriega, interview.

31. Manuel Arias Delgado, interview.

32. García Arellano, in Zúñiga Castillo, *Normalismo rural*, 33.

33. Graciela Cásares, interview.

34. Olademis Leyva, interview.

35. Catalina Calderón, interview.

36. Bustos García, *Ximonco*, 30.

37. Alma Gómez Caballero, interview.

38. Memorandum, April 2, 1965, AGN/DFS 100-19-1, Leg.9, H147–48.

39. Guevara Niebla, "Antecedentes y desarrollo." Mónica Naymich López Macedonio, whose study ignores normalistas' long process of organizing, politicization, and struggles, portrays the FECSM as a clientelist affiliate of the PRI. See Naymich López Macedonio, "Historia de una relación institucional."

40. Comité Ejecutivo Nacional de la FECSM to Agustín Yáñez, March 8, 1965, AHENR/SM, C1965; "Pliego General de Peticiones," January 27, 1968, AGN/DFS 63-19, Leg.2, H306–12; and "Marcha estudiantil por la ruta de la libertad," February 16, 1968, AGN/DFS 11-142, Leg.3, H264–72.

41. Ernesto Enríquez to Eleno Medina Vázquez and Eusebio Mata Mejía, October 29, 1963, AHENR/CH, C30, 1960–64.

42. Comité Ejecutivo Nacional de la FECSM to Agustín Yáñez, March 8, 1965; and "Estado de Morelos," April 2, 1965, AGN/DGIPS, C448, Exp.2. Members of the student body also participated in the committee administering student funds. When directors at individual schools charged illegal fees—such as at Mactumactzá, where students were asked to make registration payments—the FECSM denounced it, leading the SEP to notify all rural normales that such transactions were illegal. "Circular #11," March 3, 1964, AHENR/CH, C30, 1960–64.

43. Comité Ejecutivo Nacional de la FECSM to Agustín Yáñez, March 8, 1965.

44. Ernesto Enríquez to Eleno Medina Vázquez and Eusebio Mata Mejía, October 29, 1963; and Memorandum, October 29, 1963, AGN/DFS 63-19, Leg.1, H270–71.

45. Comité Ejecutivo Nacional de la FECSM to Agustín Yáñez, March 8, 1965.

46. "Magisterio," July 4, 1963, AGN/DFS 40-1, Exp.36, H202–25.

47. "Magisterio," July 4, 1963.

48. "Se informa en relación con el magisterio," August 19, 1963, AGN/DFS 63-19, Exp.1, H188–90.

49. Comité Ejecutivo Nacional de la FECSM to Agustín Yáñez, March 8, 1965.

50. "Se informa en relación al magisterio," March 3, 1964, AGN/DFS 63-19, Leg.1, H283.

51. Memorandum, October 29, 1963, AGN/DFS 63–19, Leg.1, H270–71.

52. "Los normalistas rurales en lucha," *Voz de México*, April 4, 1965; "Comité Ejecutivo de la Sociedad de Alumnas to C. Director Silverio Díaz," March 26, 1965, AHENR/CH, C31, 1963–66; Memorandum, March 27, 1965, AGN/DFS 100-5-1, Leg.12, H386–87; "Normales rurales," March 29, 1965, AGN/DFS 63-19-65, Leg.1, H337–40; and "Estado de Durango," April 1, 1965, AGN/DGIPS, C448, Exp.2.

53. "Normales rurales," March 29, 1965.

54. "Estado de Morelos," April 2, 1965.

55. Memorandum, March 23, 1965, AGN/DFS 100-15-1, Leg.6, H152.

56. Memorandum, March 23, 1965; "Estado de Morelos," April 9, 1965, AGN/ DGIPS, C448, Exp.2; "Estado de Morelos," April 2, 1965; and "Estado de Morelos," March 23, 1965, AGN/DGIPS, C448, Exp.1.

57. Comité Ejecutivo Nacional de la FECSM to Agustín Yáñez, March 8, 1965.

58. "Acta de Constancia," August 13, 1954, AHENR/CH, C28, 1954–57.

59. Rosalva Pantoja Guerrero, interview.

60. "Estado de Morelos," March 16, 1965, AGN/ DGIPS, C448, Exp.1.

61. "Estado de Morelos," April 7, 1965, AGN/DGIPS, C448, Exp.2; and "Estado de Morelos," March 19, 1965, AGN/ DGIPS, C448, Exp.1.

62. "Estado de Morelos," March 24, 1965, AGN/DGIPS, C448, Exp.1; Memorandum, March 23, 1965; and "Estado de Morelos," March 18, 1965.

63. "Estado de Morelos," April 9, 1965.

64. "Estado de Morelos," April 12, 1965, AGN/DGIPS, C448, Exp.2.

65. "Estado de Morelos," April 24, 1965, AGN/DGIPS, C448, Exp.2.

66. "Circular No. 21," April 26, 1965, AHENR/SM, C1965; "Convocatoria," June 3, 1965, AHENR/SM, C1965; "Relacionado con la inscripción de los alumnos de nuevo ingreso," April 26, 1965, AHENR/SM, C1965; and "Estado de Puebla," April 25, 1965, AGN/DGIPS, C448, Exp.2.

67. "Se contesta a pliego de peticiones," March 19, 1965, AGN/DFS 63-19, Leg.1, H300; and "Estado de Durango," May 6, 1966, AGN/DFS 100-8-1, Leg.4, H36–38.

68. "Normales rurales," April 23, 1965, AGN/DFS 63, Leg.1, H300.

69. "Estado de Durango," May 6, 1966, AGN/DFS 100-8-1, Leg.4, H36–38.

70. "Estado de Guerrero," May 10, 1966, AGN/DFS 100-10, Leg.20, H278.

71. "Pliego general de peticiones," January 27, 1968.

72. "Contestación al pliego general de peticiones," February 8, 1968, AGN/DFS 63-19, Leg.3, H14–18; and "Normales rurales," February 14, 1968, AGN/DFS 63-19, Leg.3, H27–28.

73. "Marcha estudiantil por la ruta de la libertad," February 16, 1968.

74. "Marcha estudiantil por la ruta de la libertad," February 16, 1968.

75. "Problema de las escuelas normales rurales," March 5, 1968, AGN/DFS 63-19, Leg.3, H160–61.

76. "Problema de las escuelas normales rurales," March 4, 1968, AGN/DFS 63-19, Leg.3, H140–44; and "Problema de las escuelas normales rurales," March 5, 1968. The head of the confederation was even present at the final negotiating meeting. "Problema de las escuelas normales rurales," March 8, 1968, AGN/DFS 63-19, Leg.3, H199–204.

77. "A todos los padres de familia," November 11, 1968, AHENR/SM, C7, Movt. October 2, 1968.

78. "Necesaria desaparición de las escuelas normales rurales," *El Universal*, March 14, 1968, in AGN/DFS 63-19, Leg.4, H11.

79. El Comité Ejecutivo de la Sociedad de Padres de Familia to Compañeros Padres de Familia, March 6, 1968, AHENR/CH, C33, 1966–67/68/69.

80. "Problema de las escuelas normales rurales," March 5, 1968; "Problema de las escuelas normales rurales," March 8, 1968; "Normales rurales," February 14, 1968; "Problema de las escuelas normales rurales," March 2, 1968, AGN/DFS 63-19, Leg.3, H124–26; "Marcha estudiantil por la ruta de la libertad," February 16, 1968; "Problema de las escuelas normales rurales," March 13, 1968, AGN/DFS 63-19, Leg.4, H6–8; "Estado de Chiapas," May 25, 1968, AGN/DGIPS, C478, Exp.1; and "Distrito Federal," October 7, 1968, AGN/DGIPS, C484, Exp.02.

81. "Problema de las escuelas normales rurales," March 4, 1968; and "Estado de Chiapas," March 6, 1968, AGN/DGIPS, C1723A, Exp.01.

82. In the late 1960s, the authorities threatened students with suspension if they used their stipend for anything other than personal use. "Normas que regirán a los alumnos de esta institución y a los padres de familia o tutores," n.d., AHENR/CH, C34, 1968/69/70.

83. Alma Gómez Caballero, interview.

84. "Estado de Morelos," April 5, 1965, AGN/DGIPS, C448, Exp.2.

85. "Estado de Morelos," April 5, 1965.

86. "Estado de Morelos," March 17, 1965, AGN/DGIPS, C478, Exp.1; and "Estado de Morelos," March 18, 1965, AGN/DGIPS, C478, Exp.1.

87. Belén Cuevas, interview.

88. Esperanza Guzmán Gamboa, interview.

89. El Director to Comité Ejecutivo de la Sociedad de Alumnos, October 28, 1968, AHENR/CH, C4, 1968/69/70.

90. Herminia Gómez Carrasco, interview.

91. Silvina Rodríguez, interview.

92. "Más y mejor educación para los campesinos de México," August 1969, AHENR/CH, C36, 1970–71.

93. Memorandum, November 8, 1964, AGN/DFS 100-5-1, Leg.11, H37–40; Memorandum, September 12, 1964, AGN/DFS 100-5-1, Leg.10, H2–3; and "Más y major educación para los campesinos de México," August 1969.

94. "Escuelas normales rurales," August 8, 1969, AGN/DFS 63-19, Leg.5, H326–33.

95. "En defensa de las normales rurales contra la reforma antipopular y reaccionaria," August 8, 1969, AGN/DFS 63-19, Leg.7, H59–66; Memorandum, November 8, 1964; and Memorandum, September 12, 1964.

96. "Problema de las escuelas normales rurales," March 4, 1968; and "En defensa de las normales rurales contra la reforma antipopular y reaccionaria," August 8, 1969.

97. Memorandum, November 14, 1964, AGN/DFS 100-5-1, Leg.11, H111–15.

98. "Escuelas normales rurales," September 1, 1969, AGN/DFS 63-19, Leg.7, H302–37. As Pensado shows in *Rebel Mexico*, these agents were key to the government's authoritarian practices.

99. Olademis Leyva, interview.

100. "Estado de Chihuahua," October 29, 1965, AGN/DFS 100-5-1, Leg.15, H78–81.

101. "Estado de Durango," May 6, 1966, AGN/DFS 63-19, Leg.2, H70–73.

102. "Estado de Durango," May 7, 1966, AGN/DFS 100-8-1, Leg.4, H47–51.

103. "Estado de Durango," May 6, 1966, AGN/DFS 100-8-1, Leg.4, H36–38; and "Estado de Chiapas," May 10, 1968, AGN/DGIPS, C1732A, Exp.01.

104. "Escuelas normales rurales," April 25, 1973, AGN/DFS 63-19, Leg.11, H6.

105. "Concurso de oratoria en la escuela normal rural de Panotla, Tlax.," November 25, 1965, AGN/DFS 63-19, Leg.2, H1, 3, and 4.

106. "Escuelas normales rurales," September 4, 1969, AGN/DFS 63-19, Leg.8, H119–25; "Estado de Guerrero," April 27, 1969, AGN/DFS 100-10-1, Leg.33, H294–95; "Estado de Jalisco," February 15, 1969, AGN/DFS 100-12-1, Leg.19, H37–38; "Estado de Puebla," April 21, 1969, DFS/AGN 100-19-1, Leg.19, H296–97; "Estado de Durango," May 8, 1966, AGN/DFS 100-8-1, Leg.4, H56–58; "Seminario sobre la educación normal rural," *Voz de México*, March 10, 1969; and "La marcha de obreros de triplay," *Voz de México*, March 23, 1969.

107. "Estado de Durango," May 8, 1966; and "Estado de Durango," May 7, 1966.

108. "Estado de Durango," May 8, 1966.

109. Gould, "Solidarity under Siege," 365–66, 366n81. As Gould notes, participation in political movements is often accompanied by festivity and personal fulfillment. See also Grandin, "Living in Revolutionary Time."

110. "Normales rurales," February 14, 1968; "Marcha estudiantil por la ruta de la libertad," February 16, 1968; "Marcha estudiantil por la ruta de la libertad," February 17, 1968, AGN/DFS 63-19, Leg.3, H60; and "Problema de las escuelas normales rurales," March 2, 1968.

111. "Tema II. De la supervición en las escuelas normales rurales," 1967, AHENR/SM, C8, 1966–67; and "Normales," 1969, AHSEP/Conalte, C89, Exp. Reforma Educativa.

112. SEP, *Memoria: Primera asamblea nacional*, 37.

Seven. "A Crisis of Authority"

1. SEP, *Memoria: Primera asamblea nacional*, 33–35.

2. SEP, *Memoria: Primera asamblea nacional*, 33–35, 38.

3. SEP, *Memoria: Primera asamblea nacional*, 54.

4. "Estado de Chiapas," May 24, 1968, AGN/DGIPS, C478, Exp.1.

5. Among the fourteen rural normales slated to become agricultural schools were El Perote, Veracruz, and El Roque, Guanajuato. The former, however, never reopened, and El Roque instead became an institution to train teachers for agricultural schools.

6. Prawda, *Teoría y praxis*, 69–70.

7. Álvarez García, "Difusión de las ideas," 159.

8. "Posibilidad para la reestructuración del sistema de enseñanza post-primaria rural," and "La reestructuración de la enseñanza pospirmaria rural," both [ca. 1967], AHENR/SM, C8, 1966–67.

9. "Estado de Morelos," July 1, 1967, AGN/DFS 63-19, Leg.2, H202–4.

10. "Normales rurales," June 24, 1967, AGN/DFS 63-19, Leg.2, H159.

11. "Estado de Guerrero," June 22, 1967, AGN/DFS 100-10-1, Leg.24, H245.

12. "Estado de Morelos," July 1, 1967.

13. Angel Posada Gil, Fermín Esparza Irabién, and Apolinar Ortíz Espinosa to C. Director Federal de Seguridad, June 29, 1967, AGN/DFS 63-19, Leg.2, H167; and SEP, *Memoria: Primera asamblea nacional*, 41–43.

14. "La organización del gobierno escolar," [ca. May–June 1967], AHENR/SM, C8, 1966–67; and SEP, *Memoria: Primera asamblea nacional*, 73–75.

15. "De la supervición en las escuelas normales rurales," [ca. May–June 1967], AHENR/SM, C8, 1966–67; and SEP, *Memoria: Primera asamblea nacional*, 90–92.

16. SEP, *Memoria: Primera asamblea nacional*, 85.

17. "La reforma educativa," [ca. May–June 1967], AHENR/SM, C8, 1966–67; and SEP, *Memoria: Primera asamblea nacional*, 84–88, 105–8, 128–31.

18. SEP, *Memoria: Primera asamblea nacional*, 122.

19. "El calendario escolar," [ca. May–June 1967], AHENR/SM, C8, 1966–67.

20. "El calendario escolar"; and SEP, *Memoria: Primera asamblea nacional*, 76–81, 101–2, 121–24 (quote on p. 124).

21. "El problema de la formación professional," [ca. May–June 1967], AHENR/SM, C8, 1966–67; and SEP, *Memoria: Primera asamblea nacional*, 89–90, 108–11, 131–35.

22. "Organización de la vida económica en las escuelas normales rurales," [ca. May–June 1967], AHENR/SM, C8, 1967.

23. "Organización de la vida económica en las escuelas normales rurales"; and SEP, *Memoria: Primera asamblea nacional*, 81–84, 103–4, 125–28.

24. SEP, *Memoria: Primera asamblea nacional*, 109–10; "La organización del gobierno escolar"; and "Posibilidades para la reestructuración," AHENR/SM, C8, 1966–67.

25. "Declaración de Atequiza," *Voz de México*, March 23, 1969; and "Estado de Chiapas," May 24, 1968.

26. Rivera Borbón, *Gasto del gobierno federal mexicano*, 77. Moreover, as Carlos Rivera Borbón notes, the SEP's projected spending was often less than its actual spending (70–80). See also "Educational Reform and the Mexican Education System," January 24, 1969, NARA, Central Foreign Policy Files, 1967–69, box 349. For 1965 figures, see Centro de Estudios Económicos y Demográficos, *Dinámica de la población*, 220.

27. "Declaración de Atequiza."

28. "Declaración de Atequiza"; emphasis in original.

29. "Hacia la Central Estudiantil Independiente," *Voz de México*, June 15, 1963.

30. For a list of these struggles, see Guevara Niebla, "Antecedentes y desarrollo," 6–8. See also "Pese a todo, los estudiantes no retroceden" and "La Voz editorial," *Voz de México*, April 23, 1967.

31. See Zolov, "¡Cuba sí, Yanquis no!"

32. Guevara Niebla, "Antecedentes y desarrollo," 13.

33. "Se informa en relación con el magisterio," May 7, 1964, AGN/DFS 63-19, Leg. 1, H298–99; "Se informa en relación con el magisterio," October 8, 1964, AGN/DFS 40-1, Leg.38, H1; and "Por la unidad de los estudiantes," *Voz de México*, December 12, 1965.

34. For example, "Sobre el encuentro nacional de dirigentes estudiantiles," *Voz de México*, October 30, 1966; and "Estado de Chihuahua," April 11, 1967, AGN/DFS 100-5-1, Leg.19, H357.

35. "Culminó la Jornada Nacional por la Reforma Democrática de la Educación," *Voz de México*, April 16, 1967; and "Balance de la jornada nacional estudiantil," *Voz de México*, April 30, 1967. The former articles cites 125,000 participants, while the latter puts the number at 150,000.

36. "Por la ruta de la libertad," *Voz de México*, February 11, 1968; and "Estado de Guanajuato," February 5, 1968, AGN/IPS, C519, Exp.04.

37. "Estado de Guanajuato," February 2, 1968, AGN/DGIPS, C519, Exp.04; and "Conjura contra la libertad," *Voz de México*, February 4, 1968.

38. "Estado de Guanajuato," February 3, 1968, AGN/DGIPS, C519, Exp.04.

39. Alma Gómez Caballero, interview.

40. "Nuestra marcha será una demostración pacífica," *Voz de México*, February 4, 1968; and "Estado de Guanajuato," February 2, 1968.

41. "Por la ruta de la libertad," *Voz de México*, February 11, 1968; and "Estado de Guanajuato," February 3, 1968.

42. Terán Olguín, *Marcha por la ruta de la libertad*, 26–27; "Por la ruta de la libertad"; "La disolución de la marcha estudiantil y las provocaciones anticomunistas," *Voz de México*, February 18, 1968; and "La verdad y la razón se impusieron," *Voz de México*, February 25, 1968.

43. "Se informa en relación con el magisterio," October 8, 1964.

44. "Universidad," December 17, 1963, AGN/DFS 100-10-1, Exp.15, H122; Memorandum, April 7, 1965, AGN/DFS 100-10-1, Leg.291, H18; "Estado de Guerrero," November 18, 1966, AGN/DFS 100-10-1, Leg.22, H88; "Estado de Guerrero," n.d., AGN/DFS 100-10-1, Leg.22, H410–11; "Normales rurales," March 20, 1967, AGN/DFS 63-19, Leg.2, H123; Memorandum, March 2, 1964, AGN/DFS 100-5-3, Leg.2, H46–49; "Información sobre el estado de Chihuahua," June 13, 1964, AGN/DFS 100-5-1, Leg.8, H296–97; Memorandum, October 27, 1964, AGN/DFS 100-5-1, Leg.10, H323–25; Memorandum, April 2, 1965, AGN/DFS 100-19-1, Leg.9, H147–48; "Estado de Nayarit," November 19, 1968, AGN/DFS 63-19, Leg.4, H255; and "Estado de Chiapas," June 21, 1969, AGN/DGIPS, C1723A, Exp.01.

45. "Estado de Morelos," March 24, 1965, AGN/DGIPS, C448, Exp.1; and "Solidaridad con los normalistas rurales en lucha," *Voz de México*, April 4, 1965.

46. "Datos Generales de la Central Nacional de Estudiantes Democráticos," September 15, 1966, AGN/DFS 11-142, Leg.2, H190–92.

47. José Luis Aguayo Álvarez, interview.

48. Gustavo Díaz Ordaz, "Cuarto informe de gobierno," reproduced in Ramón Ramírez, *Movimiento estudiantil*, 2:203–4.

49. "Carta al C. Director de La Sociedad de Alumnas," September 19, 1968, AHENR/CH, C34, 1968–70; "A todos los padres de familia," November 11, 1968, AHENR/SM, C7, Movt. 2 oct. 1968; "Estado de Chiapas," July 31, 1968, AGN/DGIPS, C1723A, Exp.01; "Estado de Chiapas," August 14, 1968, AGN/DGIPS, C1723A, Exp.01; "Distrito Federal," September 22, 1968, AGN/DGIPS, C484, Exp.02; "Estado de Guerrero," November 8, 1968, AGN/DFS 100-10-1, Leg.32, H178–79; and Bustos García, *Ximonco*, 13.

50. Ramón Ramírez, *Movimiento estudiantil*, 1:435, 471.

51. Proceso Díaz, interview.

52. José Francisco Casimiro Barrera, interview.

53. "Escuelas normales rurales," November 11, 1968, AGN/DFS 63-19, Leg.4, H167–68; "Información de Ciudad Victoria," November 9, 1968, AGN/DGIPS, C1475B, Exp.51; "Escuelas normales rurales," November 9, 1968, AGN/DFS 63-19, Leg.4, H147–48; "Escuelas normales rurales," November 13, 1968, AGN/DFS 63-19, Leg.4, H200–201; "Escuelas normales rurales," November 19, 1968, AGN/DFS 63-19, Leg.4, H253–55; "Estado de Nayarit," November 9, 1968, AGN/DGIPS, C1475B, Exp.51; and "Estado de Aguascalientes," November 9, 1968, AGN/DGIPS, C1475B, Exp.51.

54. Aristarco Aquino Solís, interview..

55. See Oikión Solano, "Movimiento de Acción Revolucionaria."

56. García Aguirre, *Revolución que llegaría*, chap. 4.

57. "Educational Reform and the Mexican Education System," January 24, 1969.

58. "La formación de maestros de enseñanza primaria," Dirección General de Enseñanza Normal, 1969, IV Congreso Nacional de Educación Normal, AHSEP/Conalte, C94, Exp.1169, Leg.3.

59. "Discurso de inauguración," April–May 1969, Saltillo, Coahuila, AHSEP/Conalte, C4, Exp.1169, Leg.3.

60. Pablo Latapí, "Reformas educativas," 1327.

61. Latapí, "Necesidades del sistema educativo nacional," 170.

62. "Educational Reform and the Mexican Education System," January 24, 1969.

63. Latapí, "Reformas educativas," 1327.

64. "Educational Reform and the Mexican Education System," January 24, 1969; and Latapí, "Necesidades del sistema educativo nacional," 136–37. In 1965 Mexico ranked last among Latin American countries in terms of its taxation as a percentage of the gross domestic product. Smith, "Building a State on the Cheap," 259–60.

65. Latapí, "Reformas educativas," 1329.

66. "En defensa de las normales rurales contra la reforma antipopular y reaccionaria," August 8, 1969, AGN/DFS 63-19, Leg.7, H59–66.

67. "En defensa de las normales rurales contra la reforma antipopular y reaccionaria," August 8, 1969.

68. "En defensa de las normales rurales contra la reforma antipopular y reaccionaria," August 8, 1969.

69. Greaves, *Del radicalismo a la unidad nacional*, 193; and Luis Herrera y Montes, "Crítica al plan de estudios para las escuelas normales," *Magisterio*, no. 106, December 1969.

70. "Se informa sobre la escuela normal rural Luis Villarreal," February 27, 1968, AGN/DFS 63-19, Leg.3, H230–31; "Estado de Chihuahua," February 28, 1968, AGN/DFS 63-19, Leg.3, H247–50; and "Escuelas normales rurales con sus zonas campesinas de afluencia," March 4, 1968, AGN/DFS 63-19, H313–23. While some ejidatarios were affiliated with nonstate associations such as the Independent Campesino Central or the General Union of Mexican Workers and Campesinos, the vast majority belonged to the PRI's National Campesino Confederation.

71. For example, "Escuelas normales rurales," July 29, 1969, AGN/DFS 63-19, Leg.5, H26–33; "Escuelas normales rurales," August 7, 1969, AGN/DFS 63-19, Leg.5, H297–302; and "Escuelas normales rurales," August 16, 1969, AGN/DFS 63-19, Leg.6, H210–15.

72. "Escuelas normales rurales," August 7, 1969; "Escuelas normales rurales," August 8, 1969, AGN/DFS 63-19, Leg.5, H326–33; "Escuelas normales rurales," August 16, 1969; "Escuelas normales rurales," August 18, 1969, AGN/DFS 63-19, Leg.6, H233–42; "Escuelas normales rurales," August 23, 1969, AGN/DFS 63-19, Leg.7, H116–19; "Escuelas normales rurales," August 13, 1969, AGN/DFS 63-19, Leg.6, H129; and "Se levanta acta," [ca. 1968], AHENR/CH, C34, 1968/69/70.

73. Aristarco Aquino Solís, interview.

74. Mauricio Alvarado and five other signatories to Prof. Luis Álvarez, [ca. mid-1969], AHSEP/Conalte, C101, Exp.1, Ref.201.3:25/1341/1; and Pedro Martínez and forty-two other signatories to Presidente Gustavo Díaz Ordaz, [ca. mid-1969], AHSEP/Conalte, C101, Exp.1, Ref.201.3:25/1341/1.

75. El Comisario Ejidal and twenty-seven other signatories to Luis Álvarez Barret, July 18, 1969, AHSEP/Conalte, C101, Exp.1, Ref.201.3:25/1341/1.

76. Roberto Andrade and seventy-eight other signatories to Sr. Lic. Gustavo Diaz Ordáz, [ca. mid-1969], AHSEP/Conalte, C101, Exp.1, Ref.201.3:25/1341/1.

77. Aristarco Aquino Solís, interview.

78. "Escuelas normales rurales," September 3, 1969, AGN/DFS 63-19, Leg.8, H73–79; "Escuelas normales rurales," September 4, 1969, AGN/DFS 63-19, Leg.8, H119–25; "Normales rurales," June 16, 1969, AGN/DFS 61, Leg.5, H1; "Escuelas normales rurales," July 12, 1969, AGN/DFS 63-19, Leg.5, H12, 64–69; "Escuelas normales rurales," September 1, 1969, AGN/DFS 63-19, Leg.7, H302–7; "Escuelas

normales rurales," September 2, 1969, AGN/DFS 63-19, Leg.8, H1–17; "Escuelas normales rurales," September 8, 1969, AGN/DFS 63-19, Leg.8, H227–33; and "Circular Num. 17-D," June 19, 1969, AHENR/CH, C34, 1968/69/70.

79. "Escuelas normales rurales," August 7, 1969.

80. "Escuelas normales rurales," 1969, AGN/DFS 63-19, Leg.6, H1–12; "Escuelas normales rurales," September 3, 1969; and "Escuelas normales rurales," September 9, 1969, AGN/DFS 63-19, Leg.8, H257–60.

81. "Escuelas normales rurales," September 5, 1969, AGN/DFS 63-19, Leg.8, H159–65.

82. José Francisco Casimiro Barrera, interview.

83. "Escuelas normales rurales," September 4, 1969; and "Escuelas normales rurales," September 2, 1969.

84. Morán López, "Recuerdos tristes," 97.

85. "Escuelas normales rurales," August 7, 1969; "Denuncian la ocupación de las normales," *El Día*, August 6, 1969, in AGN/DFS 63-19, Leg.5; and "Escuelas normales rurales," August 5, 1969, AGN/DFS 63-19, Leg.6, H177–85. One student, for example, described how he and his schoolmates were made to walk barefoot on the burning pavement. See Ruiz Valenzuela, "Cierre de nuestra escuela normal," 95–96.

86. Report issued by Fernando Gutiérrez Barrios, August 18, , AGN/DFS 63-19, Leg.6, H276–79.

87. "Escuelas normales rurales," 1969, AGN/DFS 63-19, Leg.6, H1–12; and Aristarco Aquino Solís, interview.

88. "Escuelas normales rurales," August 15, 1969, AGN/DFS 63-19, Leg.6, H177–85; and "Escuelas normales rurales," August 2, 1969, AGN/DFS 63-19, Leg.5, H156–61.

89. "Escuelas normales rurales," September 6, 1969, AGN/DFS 63-19, Leg.8, H119–25, 253–54.

90. "Escuelas normales rurales," September 8, 1969; and "Escuelas normales rurales," September 10, 1969, AGN/DFS 63-19, Leg.8, H298–301.

91. "Escuelas normales rurales," September 10, 1969.

92. "Escuelas normales rurales," September 10, 1969.

93. "Problema estudiantil," September 13, 1969, AGN/DFS 11-4, Leg.92, H154–55.

94. FECSM to C. Prof. Mario Aguilera Dorantes, September 29, 1969, AGN/DFS 63-19, Leg.9, H216–17.

95. López de la Torre, *Guerras secretas*, 228.

96. López de la Torre, *Guerras secretas*, 217.

97. González Villarreal and Amann Escobar, "Amilcingo," 78–79. Several recent ethnographic studies of individual rural normales detail the persistence of this unofficial curriculum that is structured, regulated, and reproduced by the students themselves. For example, Reynoso Sánchez, "Ser estudiante normalista rural"; Pinto Díaz, "Formadores"; and Vite Vargas, "Formación docente."

98. Of the teacher-training system, the report specified, "The normal schools of Mexico are a kind of seminary in which eager, dedicated young men and women are isolated from the mainstream of national life during the years of their instruction. They are in the hands, for the most part, of dedicated Marxists." "The Engagement with Mexican Higher Education Instruction," August 1, 1963, NARA, Record Group 59, box 3246.

Eight. "That's How We'd Meet . . . Clandestinely with the Lights Off"

1. Elsa Guzmán, interview.

2. "Estado de Jalisco," May 7, 1974, AGN/DFS 63-19, Leg.12, H147–48; "Escuelas normales rurales," May 22, 1974, AGN/DFS 63-19, Leg.12, H72–73; and "Escuelas normales rurales," April 25, 1973, AGN/DFS 63-19, Leg.11, H6.

3. On June 10, 1971, students in Mexico City marched in support of their peers at the Autonomous University of Nuevo Leon, whose campus had been occupied by the state police. This demonstration in Mexico City was the first major student mobilization since 1968, and many hoped it would revive the student movement.

4. See Aviña, *Specters of Revolution*.

5. On the conservative middle class, see Walker, *Waking from the Dream*, chap. 2.

6. "A los estudiantes de las escuelas normales rurales," October 16, 1974, AHENR/T.

7. Marcos José García, interview.

8. Aristarco Aquino Solís, interview.

9. Elsa Guzmán, interview. Once Guzmán finished her secundaria studies in Champusco, she went to the rural normal of Tamazulapan in Oaxaca.

10. "Minutarios," [ca. May 1973], AHENR/SM, CI, 1973–74, cited in Hernández Santos, *Tiempos de reforma*, 355.

11. "Escuelas normales rurales," May 22, 1974.

12. For example, "Escuelas normales rurales," May 13, 1974, AGN/DFS 63-19, Leg.12, H214–15; and "Escuelas normales rurales," May 21, 1974, AGN/DFS 63-19, Leg.13, H28–30.

13. "Escuelas normales rurales," September 25, 1972, AGN/DFS 63-19, Leg.10, H40–42.

14. "Estado de Chihuahua," December 4, 1972, AGN/DFS 63-19, Leg.10, H182.

15. "Estado de Guerrero," December 12, 1972, AGN/DFS 63-19, Leg.10, H295, 297, 314, 321.

16. "Estado de Jalisco," May 22, 1973, AGN/DFS 63-19, Leg.11, H10–11; and "Estado de Jalisco," November 24, 1972, AGN/DGIPS, C1188, Exp.01. The removal of López Iriarte likely had to do with more than just the FECSM's demand. The official teachers' union had accused him of contravening President Echeverría's vision and representing an obstacle to the general will of the country's teachers. See "Escuelas normales rurales," September 25, 1972.

17. "Estado de Chihuahua," October 13, 1970, AGN/DFS 100-5-1, Leg.30, H172–73; "Problemas que se han suscitado en las escuelas normales rurales de la república," May 9, 1974, AGN/DFS 63-19, Leg.12, H97–119; and Hernández Santos, *Tiempos de reforma*, 324.

18. Elsa Guzmán, interview.

19. "Se ratifican normas para evaluar a dirigentes estudiantiles," December 5, 1974, AHENR/T.

20. "Resoluciones finales a las peticiones presentadas por la Federación de Estudiantes Campesinos Socialistas de México," May 30, 1974, AGN/DFS 63-19, Leg.14, H54; "Distrito Federal," June 4, 1974, AGN/DGIPS, C964, Exp.2; and "Anuncia la SEP regularización de los predios de las normales rurales," *Excélsior*, May 21, 1974.

21. "Estado de Hidalgo," September 3, 1975, AGN/DFS 100-11-1, Leg.6, H222–23.

22. "Estado de Sonora," November 15, 1973, AGN/DGIPS, C1730B, Exp.05.

23. "Estado de Chiapas," October 16, 1974, AGN/DGIPS, C1131, Exp.1; and "Estado de Chiapas," October 18, 1974, AGN/DGIPS, C1131, Exp.1.

24. "Estado de Michoacán," January 10, 1973, AGN/DFS 63-19, Leg.10, H325; "Estado de Hidalgo," April 25, 1974, AGN/DFS 40-147, Leg.1, H290–91, 298–99; "Escuelas normales rurales," May 2, 1974, AGN/DFS 63-19, Leg.11, H223–24; . "Estado de Hidalgo," May 19, 1974, AGN/DFS 40-147, Leg.2, H72–74; "Problemas que se han suscitado en las escuelas normales rurales de la república," May 9, 1974; "Estado de Chihuahua," October 11, 1974, AGN/DFS 100-5-1, Leg.50, H26–27; and "Estado de Chihuahua," October 12, 1974, AGN/DFS 100-5-1, Leg.50, H31–33.

25. "Estado de Chiapas," November 11, 1974, AGN/ DGIPS, C1131, Exp.1; and "Problemas que se han suscitado en las escuelas normales rurales de la república," May 9, 1974.

26. "Estado de Chiapas," September 7, 1974, AGN/DGIPS, C1723A, Exp.01.

27. "Estado de Chiapas," October 17, 1974, AGN/DGIPS, C1723A, Exp.01; and "Estado de Chiapas," October 19, 1974, AGN/DGIPS, C1723A, Exp.01.

28. "Distrito Federal," February 25, 1975, AGN/DGIPS, C1667A, Exp.3; and "Escuelas normales rurales y escuelas tecnológicas agropecuarías," [ca. 1975], AGN/DFS 63-19, Leg.15, H62–64; on the students' expulsion, see "Magisterio," July 14, 1975, AGN/DFS 40-1, Leg.82, H47–49; and "A la opinion pública," August 1975, AGN/DFS 63-19, Leg.16, H134.

29. "II Congreso Ordinario de la Federación de Estudiantes Campesinos Socialistas de México," October 15, 1974, AGN/DFS 63-19, Leg.14, H220–24; and "Estado de Chiapas," October 16, 1974, AGN/DGIPS, C1723A, Exp.01.

30. Marcos José García, interview. The PST emerged in 1973 as a party that would bring together dispersed workers, campesinos and student leaders, and its organizers often delivered results by appealing to government offices for resources, subsidies, and supplies made increasingly available by Echeverría's social programs.

For the PST's recruitment efforts, see report by Luis de la Barreda Moreno on student leaders from various rural normales, [ca. October 1974], AGN/DFS 63-19, Leg.14, H239–44. On the PST, see Alonso, *Tendencia al enmascaramiento*.

31. "Magisterio," July 14, 1975.

32. Report by Luis de la Barreda Moreno on student leaders from various rural normales, [ca. October 1974].

33. "Escuelas normales rurales," May 21, 1974; and "Escuelas normales rurales," May 22, 1974.

34. "SEP," April 13, 1976, AGN/DFS 63-19, Leg.17, H121.

35. "A los estudiantes de las escuelas normales rurales y a la opinion pública," October 26, 1976, AHENR/T.

36. "Al consejo directivo de la Federación de Estudiantes Campesino Socialistas de México," November 12, 1976, AHENR/T; emphasis in original.

37. Two years later, in Tamaulipas, former students and teachers of the rural normal of Tamatán (closed in 1969) also established a new rural normal, named San José de las Flores. This new school, however, did not join the FECSM and, unlike Amilcingo, is virtually absent from the archival documentation, making it difficult to determine its history.

38. Report on various normales rurales, [ca. November 1974], AGN/DFS 63-19, Leg.12, H113–15.

39. Franco Solís, *¡Que se estén quietecitos!*, 32–33, 34, 38, 43, 35–36.

40. "Escuelas normales rurales," May 2, 1974; and "Estado de Chihuahua," May 22, 1974, AGN/DFS 63-19, Leg.13, H45.

41. Franco Solís, *¡Que se estén quietecitos!*, 46–47.

42. "Estado de Morelos," July 28, 1974, AGN/DGIPS, C1194, Exp.03; and Franco Solís, *¡Que se estén quietecitos!*, 48

43. "Escuelas normales rurales," May 2, 1974.

44. González Villarreal and Amann Escobar, "Amilcingo," 68.

45. "Problemas que se han suscitado en las escuelas normales rurales de la república," May 9, 1974.

46. "Resoluciones finales a las peticiones presentadas por la Federación de Estudiantes Campesinos Socialistas de México," May 30, 1974.

47. "Estado de Morelos," June 24, 1974, AGN/DGIPS, C1194, Exp.03.

48. "Estado de Morelos," May 30, 1974, AGN/DGIPS, C1194, Exp.03.

49. "Estado de Morelos," June 3, 1974, AGN/DGIPS, C1194, Exp.03; and González Villarreal and Amann Escobar, "Amilcingo," 70.

50. Franco Solís, *¡Que se estén quietecitos!*, 75, 166–67.

51. "La verdad sobre Temoac," *Correo del Sur*, July 22, 1979.

52. González Villarreal and Amann Escobar, "Amilcingo," 70.

53. "A los habitantes del municipio de Temoac, Mor.," *Correo del Sur*, July 8, 1979.

54. Franco Solís, *¡Que se estén quietecitos!*, 75–76, 80; and González Villarreal and Amann Escobar, "Amilcingo," 70.

55. González Villarreal and Amann Escobar, "Amilcingo," 77.

56. González Villarreal and Amann Escobar, "Amilcingo," 83.

57. Xóchitl García, interview.

58. García's father survived his nine stab wounds, but his companion did not. On the Jaramillista movement, see Padilla, *Rural Resistance*.

59. Xóchitl García, interview.

60. The small office that houses the school archive is named after Eva Rivera, who, unlike the other three leaders, died of natural causes.

61. Aguayo Quezada, "Impacto de la guerrilla," 92.

62. "Escuelas normales rurales," September 2, 1969, AGN/DFS 63-19, Leg.8, H1–17.

63. See Oikión Solano, "Movimiento de Acción Revolucionaria."

64. Young, *Guns, Guerillas*.

65. Aguayo, *Charola*, 311.

66. Herminia Gómez Carrasco, interview.

67. As Jeff Gould found across the Americas, youth who participated in political movements "recall high levels of personal fulfillment and intense political commitment." Some, as a Uruguayan student put it, conceived of their "devotion to the political struggle not as a free option but as an irrepressible moral obligation." Gould, "Solidarity under Siege, 364–67.

68. Alma Gómez Caballero, phone interview, May 8, 2020.

69. Robinet, "Revolutionary Group," 129–30.

70. "Problemas que se han suscitado en las escuelas normales rurales de la república," May 9, 1974; "Escuelas normales rurales," June 26, 1975, AGN/DFS 11-235, Leg.31, H38–39; "Escuelas normales rurales," September 30, 1975, AGN/DFS 63-19, Leg.17, H13–14; and "Estado de Morelos," October 25, 1975, AGN/DFS 100-11-1, Leg.7, H14.

71. Elsa Guzmán, interview.

72. For example, "Estado de Chiapas," April 29, 1974, AGN/DGIPS, C1723A, Exp.01.

73. Suárez, *Lucio Cabañas*, 53.

74. "Grupo Genaro Vázquez Rojas," n.d., AGN/DGIPS, C2760, Exp.único.

75. Elsa Guzmán, interview.

76. "Problemas que se han suscitado en las escuelas normales rurales de la república," May 9, 1974; "Escuelas normales rurales," June 26, 1975; "Escuelas normales rurales," September 30, 1975; "Estado de Morelos," October 25, 1975; and "Estado de Sonora," May 30, 1974, AGN/DGIPS, C1730B, Exp.05.

77. "Estado de México," May 21, 1974, AGN/DGIPS, C1070, Exp.03.

78. "Estado de Chiapas," May 31, 1974, AGN/DGIPS, C1723A, Exp.01.

79. "Estado de Hidalgo," February 13, 1976, AGN/DFS 100-11-1, Leg.7, H202; "Distrito Federal," May 13, 1974, AGN/DGIPS, C1157A, Exp.01; and "Problemas que se han suscitado en las escuelas normales rurales," May 9, 1974.

80. "Distrito Federal," May 9, 1974, AGN/DGIPS, C1157A, Exp.01.

81. "Hago del conocimiento de usted," August 16, 1976, AGN/DGIPS, C1660A, Exp.02.

82. "Escuelas normales rurales," October 26, 1977, AGN/DFS 63-17, Leg.19, H246–48.

83. "Estado de Hidalgo," May 4, 1974, AGN/DGIPS, C1183, Exp.03.

84. "Estado de Chiapas," October 15, 1974, AGN/DGIPS, C1131, Exp.1.

85. "Estado de Chiapas," October 13, 1974, AGN/DGIPS, C1723A, Exp.01.

86. "Informe sobre la situación en las escuelas normales rurales," October 16, 1974, AGN/DFS 63-19, Leg.14, H258–62.

87. "Escuelas normales rurales," October 13, 1974, AGN/DFS 63-19, Leg.14, H192–93; and Calderón López-Velarde, "Escuela normal rural," 103n2.

88. "Estado de Durango," February 27, 1975, AGN/DGIPS, C1667A, Exp.3.

89. For example, "Relación de alumnos dirigentes y activistas negativos de las escuelas normales rurales," [ca. February 1975], in AGN/DGIPS, C1660A, Exp.02; and "Estado de Chiapas," July 4, 1974, AGN/DGIPS, C1723A, Exp.01.

90. "Escuelas normales rurales," May 2, 1974.

91. "Escuelas normales rurales y escuelas tecnológicas agropecuarias," [ca. 1975]; and "Estado de Guerrero," [ca. 1975], AGN/DFS, 63-19, Leg.16, H179–85.

92. "Estado de Chiapas," May 16, 1974; "Estado de Chiapas," May 17, 1974; "Estado de Chiapas," August 28, 1974, all in AGN/DGIPS, C1723A, Exp.01; and "Estado de Sonora," May 6, 1974, AGN/DGIPS, C1730B, Exp.05.

93. "Estado de Guerrero," October 15, 1974, AGN/DFS 100-10-1, Leg.48, H261–62.

94. "Estado de Guerrero," July 20, 1978, AGN/DFS 100-10-1, Leg.75, H36–37; "Estado de Guerrero," September 13, 1978, AGN/DFS 100-10-1, Leg.75, H217–18; and "Estado de Guerrero," September 14, 1978, AGN/DFS 100-10-8, Leg.76, H1–4; and "Estado de Guerrero," September 29, 1978, AGN/DFS 100-10-1, Leg.77, H31–33.

95. "A los jóvenes estudiantes de las escuelas normales rurales," March 27, 1976, AHENR/T.

96. "A los jóvenes estudiantes de las escuelas normales rurales," March 27, 1976.

97. "Al consejo directivo de la Federación de Estudiantes Campesinos Socialistas de México," November 12, 1976; emphasis in original.

98. "A los jóvenes estudiantes de las escuelas normales rurales," March 27, 1976.

99. "Al consejo directivo de la Federación de Estudiantes Campesinos Socialistas de México," November 12, 1976.

100. "A los estudiantes de las escuelas normales rurales y a la opinion pública," October 26, 1976.

101. "A los jóvenes estudiantes de las escuelas normales rurales," March 27, 1976.

102. "A los estudiantes de las escuelas normales rurales," October 16, 1974.

103. "Al consejo directivo de la Federación de Estudiantes Campesinos Socialistas de México," November 12, 1976; emphasis in original.

104. Arnaut Salgado, *Historia de una profesión*, 145–46.

105. *Excélsior*, November 15, 1969, quoted in Meneses Morales, *Tendencias educativas oficiales*, 4:171.

106. McGinn and Street, "Has Mexican Education," 331.

107. Morales-Gómez and Torres, *State*, 51.

108. Latapí, "Reformas educativas," 1330.

109. In a two-step process—in 1971 and again in 1973—subjects at normales were condensed from five areas: scientific, humanistic, psychopedagogical, technological, and physical-artistic, to the following three: human-scientific; physical, aesthetic, and technological; and professional training. Latapí, *Análisis de un sexenio*, 74–75; and Calderón López-Velarde, "Escuela normal rural," 187. See appendix for specific classes.

110. Meneses Morales, *Tendencias educativas oficiales*, 4:173.

111. Recall that until 1969, at rural normales, junior high school education was part of their six-year coursework; students thus entered after finishing elementary school.

112. In 1969 normalistas had eight separate subject areas in which they had to take classes: cultural, pedagogical, psychological, social, philosophical, technological, artistic, and physical. Calderón López-Velarde, "Escuela normal rural," 107.

113. See Hernández Santos, *Tiempos de reforma*, 364–68.

114. Vera, "Reformas a la educación normal," 110.

115. Victoria Avilés Quezada, comments on Vera, "Reformas a la educación normal," 128. See also Othón Salazar and the Movimiento Revolucionario del Magisterio to Víctor Bravo Ahúja, Secretario de Educación Pública, July 14, 1972, AHSEP/Conalte, C150, Exp.333, Leg.1; and Movimiento Revolucionario del Magisterio, "La formación de maestros en la república mexicana" ponencia presentada a la Conferencia popular de educación, cited in Victoria Avilés Quezada, comments on Vera, "Reformas a la educación normal," 128.

116. Vera, "Reformas a la educación normal," 128–29.

117. "El problema de las normales rurales," *El Día*, April 23, 1977.

118. "Los buenos deseos hacia el maestro rural," *El Día*, April 23, 1977.

119. Othón Salazar and the Movimiento Revolucionario del Magisterio to Víctor Bravo Ahúja, Secretario de Educación Pública, July 14, 1972.

120. "El problema de las normales rurales."

121. Arnaut Salgado, *Historia de una profesión*, 128–30. In a similar vein, the SEP allowed teachers to occupy positions in both day and evening schools, a strategy that raised take-home pay by increasing work hours rather than wages— double exploitation—as one study characterized it. Ávila Carrillo and Martínez Brizuela, *Historia del movimiento magisterial*, 48.

122. Arnaut Salgado, *Historia de una profesión*, 145–46, 131n9.

123. "Escuelas normales rurales," May 22, 1974; Meneses Morales, *Tendencias educativas oficiales*, 5:263–64; and Calderón López-Velarde, "Escuela normal rural," 127.

124. Calderón López-Velarde, "Escuela normal rural," 127.

125. Robles, *Educación y sociedad*, 226.

126. Arnaut Salgado, *Historia de una profesión*, 132.

127. See Dillingham, *Oaxaca Resurgent*.

128. Torres, "Corporativismo estatal," 165.

129. Morales-Gómez and Torres, *State*, 30.

130. Morales-Gómez and Torres, *State*, 30–31.

131. Aboites, "Salario del educador," 89.

132. Schmelkes et al., *Participación de la comunidad*, 102–4.

133. Morales-Gómez and Torres, *State*, 31.

134. "Medio siglo de dictadura burguesa."

Epilogue

1. Street, "Lucha por transformar," 188–90.

2. Arnaut Salgado, *Federalización educativa en México*, 266.

3. Arnaut Salgado, *Federalización educativa en México*, 268–69.

4. Meneses Morales, *Tendencias educativas oficiales*, 5:101–4.

5. Meneses Morales, *Tendencias educativas oficiales*, 5:264.

6. Cook, *Organizing Dissent*, 108, 113, 132, 143, 157, 200–201.

7. Arnaut Salgado, *Federalización educativa en México*, 277–80.

8. Gilbert, "Rewriting History," 275–88.

9. Gilbert, "Rewriting History," 295.

10. Karina Avilés, "El SNTE pagó a televisa campaña de comunicación para la ACE," *La Jornada*, August 12, 2013. Gordillo had, in fact, played an important role in Calderón's election as she threw the union's weight behind him in what was a highly contested election, resulting in a razor-thin victory margin against the leftist candidate Andrés Manuel López Obrador. Santiago Igartúa, "Revela Elba Esther pacto con Calderón para apoyarlo hacia la presidencia," *Proceso*, June 29, 2011, https://www.proceso.com.mx/274462/revela-elba-esther-pacto-politico -con-calderon-para-apoyarlo-rumbo-a-la-presidencia/amp.

11. Laura Poy Solano, "Las normales rurales, semilleros de guerrilleros, afirma Gordillo," *La Jornada*, August 6, 2010, https://www.jornada.com.mx/2010/08 /06/sociedad/035n1soc; and Karina Avilés and Claudia Herrera, "Gordillo emite sentencia de muerte para escuelas normales," *La Jornada*, August 16, 2008, https://www.jornada.com.mx/2008/08/19/index.php?section=sociedad&article =043n1soc.

12. The events in Hidalgo, Chiapas, and Michoacán discussed later in this epilogue are based on numerous press accounts published at the time. Most are also chronicled in Luis Hernández Navarro's works *Cero en conducata* and *No habrá recreo*.

13. "Mactumactzá y el Banco Mundial," *Diario Este-Sur*, September 8, 2003, cited in Velasco Hernández, " 'Ciclo metabólico,' " 8.

14. See Jill Freidberg's documentary film *Granito de arena*.

15. In May 2006, what began as a protest of Oaxacan teachers for better pay and working conditions turned into a rebellion against Governor Ulises Ruiz (2004–10) as parents, youth, indigenous communities, and other popular sectors joined them to form the People's Popular Assembly of Oaxaca. Together they took over and barricaded the center of Oaxaca City, demanding the resignation of Governor Ruiz for his generalized corruption and acts of repression. The People's Popular Assembly held the capital until November, when President Fox dispatched federal police, army, and navy units to dismantle the popular camps. After six months, state and paramilitary repression had left about two dozen dead (including the U.S. filmmaker Brad Will) and many more beaten, raped, tortured, and incarcerated.

16. For more on Peña Nieto's Education Reform Law and its critics, see Bocking, "Mexican Teachers' Movement."

17. David Agren, "Mexico's Education Reforms Flounder as More Spent on PR than Teacher Training," *The Guardian*, May 15, 2018.

18. Ernesto Martínez Elorriaga, "Más policías que maestros en evaluación docente en Michoacán," *La Jornada*, July 9, 2017, http://semanal.jornada.com.mx/ultimas/2017/07/09/mas-policias-que-maestros-en-evaluacion-docente-en-michoacan; Javier Trujillo, "Más de 2 mil maestros de Guerrero se presentan a examen," *Milenio*, March 3, 2015, https://www.milenio.com/estados/2-mil-maestros-guerrero-presentan-examen; and Ángeles Mariscal, "Maestros y policías se enfrentan durante evaluación en Chiapas," *El Financiero*, June 20, 2015, https://www.elfinanciero.com.mx/nacional/maestros-y-policias-se-confrontan-durante-evaluacion-en-chiapas.

19. President Peña Nieto took ten days to make any pronouncements on Ayotzinapa and then dismissed it as a local affair. When mounting public pressure forced his administration to accept an international investigative team, its members were subjected to a defamation campaign from news outlets close to the government, their phones were targeted with sophisticated spyware sold by Israel to the Mexican government, and, despite pleas from the families of the Missing 43, they were ushered out of the country before their investigation was complete; the initial findings contradicted the government's version. Through its last days in office, the Peña Nieto administration insisted on what the Attorney General Jesús Murillo Karam called the "historic truth," that local police had handed the students over to members of a drug organization, who burned their bodies in a nearby dump. Independent national and international investigative teams, for their part, pointed to forensic evidence that rendered such a scenario impossible. Investigations such as Anabel Hernández's also revealed a chain of command in the government's actions the night of the attacks that reached high government and army levels. See Hernández, *Verdadera noche de Iguala*.

20. Hernández, *Verdadera noche de Iguala*, 52–53.

21. On capitalism by dispossession, see Harvey, *New Imperialism*. On its application to the war on drugs and the extent to which international antidrug agreements serve the logic of capital, see Paley, *Drug War Capitalism*. Dawn Paley also documents the links among the Colombian state, the paramilitaries, and the latter's involvement in drug trafficking and assassination of activists. For an account of the state-cartel operation to recover the drug cargo from one of the buses taken by the Ayotzinapa students, see Hernández, *Verdadera noche de Iguala*, chap. 12.

22. Aviña, "War against Poor People," 134.

Bibliography

Archives

Archivo General de la Nación, Mexico City

    Ramo Dirección Federal de Seguridad
    Ramo Dirección General de Investigaciones Políticas y Sociales
    Ramo Presidentes, Manuel Ávila Camacho

Archivo Histórico de la Escuela Normal Rural de Cañada Honda, Aguascalientes

Archivo Histórico de la Escuela Normal Rural de San Marcos, Zacatecas

Archivo Histórico de la Escuela Normal Rural de Tamazulapan, Oaxaca

Archivo Histórico de la Secretaría de Educación Pública, Mexico City

    Consejo Nacional Técnico de la Educación
    Departamento de Enseñanza Agrícola y Normal Rural
    Dirección General de Enseñanza Normal

National Archives and Records Administration, College Park, Maryland

Interviews

All interviews conducted by author.

Aguayo Álvarez, José Luis. Chihuahua City, Chihuahua, February 10, 2008.

Aguirre Romero, José Ángel. Chihuahua City, Chihuahua, February 12, 2008.

Aquino Solís, Aristarco. San Sebastián Tuxtla, Oaxaca, August 21, 2017.

Arciga, Ramiro. Tehuacán, Puebla, December 8, 2013.

Arias Delgado, Manuel. Chihuahua City, Chihuahua, February 13, 2008.

Blanco, Minerva. Mexico City, January 15, 2008.

Bravo Castellanos, Zenén. Cuilapan de Guerrero, Oaxaca, August 20, 2017.

Calderón, Catalina. Uruétaro, Michoacán, September 2, 2009.

Carrasco Orozco, Augusto. Oaxaca City, Oaxaca, August 20, 2017.

Cásares, Graciela. Morelia, Michoacán, September 2, 2009.

Cásares, Jorge. Morelia, Michoacán, January 12, 2020.

Casimiro Barrera, José Francisco. Morelia, Michoacán, September 20, 2008.

Cortés Martínez, Felipe. Mexico City, February 12, 2011.

Cuevas, Belén. Chihuahua City, Chihuahua, February 12, 2008.

Díaz, Proceso. Tula, Hidalgo, March 22, 2010.

Escamilla García, Humberta. Tulancingo, Hidalgo, March 22, 2010.

Escobedo, Tacho. Morelia, Michoacán, September 2, 2009.

Estrada, Vicente. Cuautla, Morelos, July 31, 2010.

Figueroa García, Hermenegildo. Tehuacán, Puebla, December 8, 2013.

García, Marcos José. Oaxaca City, Oaxaca, August 21, 2017.

García, Xóchitl. Cuautla, Morelos, January 15, 2012.

García Jiménez, Plutarco Emilio. Jiutepec, Morelos, July 30, 2010.

Gómez Caballero, Alma. Mexico City, February 3, 2008; phone interview, May 8, 2020.

Gómez Carrasco, Herminia. Chihuahua City, Chihuahua, February 13, 2008.

Gómez Sousa, Aníbal. Morelia, Michoacán, September 2, 2009.

Guzmán, Elsa. Cuilapan de Guerrero, Oaxaca, August 20, 2017.

Guzmán, Tapia Manuel. Morelia, Michoacán, September 2, 2009.

Guzmán Gamboa, Esperanza. Chihuahua City, Chihuahua, February 13, 2008.

Jiménez, Reynaldo. Morelia, Michoacán, September 2, 2009.

Juárez, Gloria. Chihuahua City, Chihuahua, February 11, 2008.

Leyva, Olademis. Mexico City, January 10, 2020.

López López, María de los Ángeles. Nochixtlán, Oaxaca, August 22, 2017.

Martínez, Jaime. Tulancingo, Hidalgo, March 22, 2010.

Martínez Noriega, Pedro. Oaxaca City, Oaxaca, August 24, 2017.

Mendoza Nube, Germán. Oaxaca City, Oaxaca, August 18, 2017.

Navarro, César. Mexico City, December 5, 2009; phone interview, May 15, 2019.

Orozco Álvarez, Mariano. Morelia, Michoacán, September 19, 2008.

Pantoja Guerrero, Rosalva. Tamazulapan, Oaxaca, August 19, 2017.

Ramírez, Victoria. Tlaxcala City, Tlaxcala, January 18, 2017.

Rea Iglesias, Margarita. Tehuacán, Puebla, December 8, 2013.

Reynoso Vázquez, Pedro. Morelia, Michoacán, September 2, 2009.

Rodríguez, Isidro. Morelia, Michoacán, September 4, 2009.

Rodríguez, Noel. Chihuahua City, Chihuahua, February 12, 2008.

Rodríguez, Silvina. Chihuahua City, Chihuahua, February 11, 2008.

Rodríguez García, José Antonio. Nochixtlán, Oaxaca, August 22, 2017.

Salazar, Othón. Mexico City, February 6, 2008.

Salinas Antonio, Roel. Oaxaca City, Oaxaca, August 8, 2017.

Vela Gálvez, Luciano. Mexico City, February 12, 2011.

Zaya, Guadalupe. Mexico City, April 16, 2018.

Other Sources

Aboites, Hugo. "El salario del educador en México (1925–1982)." *Coyoacán* 18, no. 16 (January–March 1984): 69–95.

Aguayo Álvarez, José Luis, ed. *Un paseo por los recuerdos*. Chihuahua: La Asociación Civil de Exalumnos de Salaices, 2007.

Aguayo Álvarez, José Luis. "Prólogo." In *Normalistas: Testimonios de la docencia*, edited by José Luis Aguayo Álvarez, 11–15. Chihuahua: Asociación Civil de Ex Alumnos de Salaices, 2009.

Aguayo Álvarez, José Luis. *Salaices: Escuela rural normal formadora de maestros*. Chihuahua: Ediciones del Azar, 2002.

Aguayo Quezada, Sergio. *La charola: Una historia de los servicios de inteligencia en México*. Mexico City: Grijalbo, 2001.

Aguayo Quezada, Sergio. "El impacto de la guerrilla en la vida mexicana." In *Movimientos armados en México, siglo XX*, edited by Verónica Oikión Solano and Marta Eugenia García Ugarte, 1:91–96. Zamora: El Colegio de Michoacán and Centro de Investigaciones y Estudios Superiores en Antropología Social, 2006.

Ahúja, Víctor Bravo. *Diario de una gestión*. Mexico City: Secretaría de Educación Pública, 1976.

Alegre, Robert F. *Railroad Radicals in Cold War Mexico: Gender, Class and Memory*. Lincoln: University of Nebraska Press, 2013.

Alonso, Jorge. *La tendencia al enmascaramiento de los movimientos politicos: El caso del Partido Socialista de los Trabajadores*. Mexico City: Ediciones de la Casa Chata, 1985.

Álvarez García, Isaías. "La difusión de las ideas y el cambio en la formación de maestros de primaria en México (un caso histórico exploratorio)." *Revista Latinoamericana de Estudios Educativos (México)* 44, no. 3 (2014): 139–209.

Anderson, James D. *The Education of Blacks in the South, 1860–1935*. Chapel Hill: University of North Carolina Press, 1988.

Arias Delgado, Manuel. *Saltando la cerca*. Chihuahua: Ediciones Empresa Familia Generaciones, 2007.

Arnaut Salgado, Alberto. *La federalización educativa en México: Historia del debate sobre la centralización y la descentralización educativa (1889–1994)*. Mexico City: El Colegio de México y Centro de Investigación y Docencia Económicas, 1998.

Arnaut Salgado, Alberto. *Historia de una profesión: Los maestros de educación primaria en México 1887–1994*. Mexico City: Centro de Investigación y Docencia Económicas, 1996.

Ávila, Ana Cristina, and Virgilio Muñoz. *Creación de la Comisión Nacional de Libros de Texto Gratuitos: La perspectiva escolar, 1958–1964*. Mexico City: Noriega Editores, 1999.

Ávila Carrillo, Enrique, and Humberto Martínez Brizuela. *Historia del movimiento magisterial (1910–1989): Democracia y salario*. Mexico City: Unión Tipográfica Editorial Hispano Americana, 1985.

Aviña, Alexander. *Specters of Revolution: Peasant Guerrillas in the Cold War Mexican Countryside*. Oxford: Oxford University Press, 2014.

Aviña, Alexander. "A War against Poor People: Dirty Wars and Drug Wars in 1970s Mexico." In *México beyond 1968: Revolutionaries, Radicals, and Repression during the Global Sixties and Subversive Seventies*, edited by Jaime M. Pensado and Enrique C. Ochoa, 134–52. Tucson: University of Arizona Press, 2018.

Balam, Benito. "José Hernández Delgadillo: Notas autobiográficas." In *José Hernández Delgadillo, 1928–2000*, edited by Francisco Hernández Zamora, 57–80. Hidalgo: Secretaría de Cultura del Estado de Hidalgo, 2017.

Barkin, David, and Blanca Suárez. *El fin de la autosuficiencia alimentaria*. Mexico City: Centro de Ecodesarrollo, 1985.

Baronnet, Bruno. "De cara al currículo nacional: Las escuelas normales indígenas en las políticas de formación docente en México." In *Construcción de políticas educativas interculturales en México: Debates, tendencias, problemas, desafíos*, edited by Saúl Velasco Cruz and Aleksandra Jablonska Zaborowska, 245–72. Mexico City: Universidad Pedagógica Nacional, 2010.

Bartra, Armando. *Guerrero bronco: Campesinos, ciudadanos y guerrilleros en la Costa Grande*. Mexico City: Era, 2000.

Bassols, Narciso. "El programa educativo de México." In *La casa del pueblo y el maestro rural mexicano: Antología*, edited by Engracia Loyo Bravo, 43–58. Mexico City: Secretaría de Educación Pública, 1985.

Bertely Busquets, María, ed. *Historias, saberes indígenas y nuevas etnicidades en la escuela*. Mexico City: Centro de Investigaciones y Estudios Superiores en Antropología Social, 2006.

Berzunza Pinto, Ramón. *Los indígenas y la república mexicana: La política indigenista del P.C.M.* Mexico City: n.p., 1941.

Blancarte, Roberto. "Intransigence, Anticommunism, and Reconciliation: Church/State Relation in Transition." In *Dictablanda: Politics, Work, and Culture in Mexico, 1938–1968*, edited by Paul Gillingham and Benjamin T. Smith, 70–88. Durham, NC: Duke University Press, 2014.

Bocking, Paul. "The Mexican Teachers' Movement in the Context of Neoliberal Education Policy and Strategies for Resistance." *Labor and Society* 22, no. 1 (2019): 61–76.

Bolaños, Víctor Hugo, ed. *Historia de la educación de México en el siglo XX contada por sus protagonistas*. Mexico City: Educación, Ciencia y Cultura, 1982.

Boyer, Christopher. *Political Landscapes: Forests, Conservation, and Community in Mexico*. Durham, NC: Duke University Press, 2015.

Britton, John A. *Educación y radicalismo en México*. 2 vols. Mexico City: Secretaría de Educación Pública, 1976.

Bustos García, Felipe. *Ximonco, la escuela normal rural de Perote*. Xalapa, Veracruz: Editora del Gobierno del Estado de Veracruz-Llave, 1995.

Butchart, Ronald E. *Schooling the Freed People: Teaching, Learning and the Struggle for Black Freedom, 1861–1876*. Chapel Hill: University of North Carolina Press, 2010.

Butler, Matthew. "The 'Liberal' *Cristero*: Ladislao Molina and the *Cristero* Rebellion in Michoacán, 1927–9." *Journal of Latin American Studies* 31, no. 3 (1999): 645–71.

Butler, Matthew. *Popular Piety and Political Identity in Mexico's Cristero Rebellion: Michoacán, 1927–29*. Oxford: Oxford University Press, 2004.

Caballero, Arquímedes, and Salvador Medrano. "El segundo período de Torres Bodet, 1958–1964." In *Historia de la educación pública en México*, edited by Fernando Solana, Raúl Cardiel Reyes, and Raúl Bolaños Martínez, 2:360–402. Mexico City: Fondo de Cultura Económica, 1982.

Calderón López-Velarde, Jaime Rogelio. "La escuela normal rural: Crisis y papel político (1940–1980)." Bachelor's thesis, Escuela Nacional de Antropología e Historia, 1982.

Canelas López, Jaime. *10 años de guerrillas en México, 1964–1975*. Mexico City: Editorial Posada, 1974.

Cañas Loya, Jesús. "La FECSM y el golpe a las normales rurales." In *Un paseo por los recuerdos*, edited by José Luis Aguayo Álvarez, 87–94. Chihuahua: Asociación Civil de Exalumnos de Salaices, 2007.

Cárdenas, Hipólito. *El caso Ayotzinapa o la gran calumnia*. Mexico City: Taller Gráfico de México, 1965.

Cardiel Reyes, Raúl. "El período de conciliación y consolidación: 1946–1958." In *Historia de la educación pública en México*, edited by Fernando Solana, Raúl Cardiel Reyes, and Raúl Bolaños Martínez, 2:327–59. Mexico City: Fondo de Cultura Económica, 1982.

Carey, Elaine. *Plaza of Sacrifices: Gender, Power and Terror in 1968 Mexico*. Albuquerque: University of New Mexico Press, 2005.

Carpenter, Sara, and Shahrzad Mojab. "Adult Education and the 'Matter' of Consciousness in Marxist-Feminism." In *Marxism and Education: Renewing the Dialogue, Pedagogy, and Culture*, edited by Peter E. Jones, 117–40. New York: Palgrave Macmillan, 2011.

Carr, Barry. "The Fate of the Vanguard under a Revolutionary State: Marxism's Contribution to the Construction of the Great Arch." In *Everyday Forms of State Formation: Revolution and the Negotiation of Rule in Modern Mexico*, edited by Gilbert Joseph and Daniel Nugent, 326–52. Durham, NC: Duke University Press, 1994.

Ceniceros, José Ángel. "La política educativa del regimen." In *La educación rural Mexicana y sus proyecciones: Resoluciones de la Junta Nacional de Educación Primaria*, 349–56. Mexico City: Secretaría de Educación Pública, 1954.

Centro de Estudios Económicos y Demográficos. *Dinámica de la población de México*. Mexico City: El Colegio de México, 1970.

Choudray, Aziz. *Learning Activism: The Intellectual Life of Contemporary Social Movements*. New York: University of Toronto Press, 2015.

Christlieb Ibarrola, Adolfo. *Monopolio educativo o unidad nacional: Un problema de México*. Mexico City: Editorial Jus, 1962.

Civera Cerecedo, Alicia. "La coeducación en la formación de maestros rurales en México (1934–1944)." *Revista Mexicana de Investigación Educativa* 11, no. 28 (2006): 269–91.

Civera Cerecedo, Alicia. *La escuela como opción de vida: La formación de maestros normalistas rurales en México, 1921–1945*. Toluca: El Colegio Mexiquense, 2008.

Civera Cerecedo, Alicia. "Pedagogía alternativa y revolución: La formación de maestros normalistas rurales en México, 1922–1945." Documentos de Investigación 93, El Colegio Mexiquense, Toluca, 2004.

Cockcroft, James D. "El maestro de primaria en la revolución mexicana." *Historia Mexicana* 16, no. 4 (1967): 565–87.

Coffey, Mary K. "'All Mexico on a Wall': Diego Rivera's Murals at the Ministry of Public Education." In *Mexican Muralism: A Critical History*, edited by Alejandro Anreus, Leonard Folgarait, and Robin Adèle Greeley, 56–75. Berkeley: University of California Press, 2012.

Cong, Xiaoping. *Teachers' Schools and the Making of Modern Chinese Nation-State, 1897–1937*. Vancouver: University of British Columbia Press, 2007.

Contreras Orozco, Javier H. *Los informantes: Documentos confidenciales de la guerrilla en Chihuahua*. Chihuahua: Universidad Autónoma de Chihuahua, 2007.

Cook, María Lorena. *Organizing Dissent: Unions, the State, and the Democratic Teachers' Movement in Mexico*. University Park: Pennsylvania State University Press, 1996.

Córdoba, Arnaldo. "Los maestros rurales en el cardenismo." *Cuadernos Políticos* 2 (1974): 77–92.

Cortés Martínez, Felipe, Tomás Hernández López, Javier Moreno Pichardo, and Luciano Vela. *La educación rural en México y la escuela del Mexe han cumplido*. Mexico City: n.p., 2009.

Cox, Cristián D., and Jacqueline Gysling. *La formación del profesorado en Chile, 1842–1987*. Chile: Centro de Investigación y Desarrollo de Educación, 1990.

Craven, David. *Art and Revolution in Latin America, 1910–1990*. New Haven, CT: Yale University Press, 2002.

Dawson, Alexander S. "Histories and Memories of the Indian Boarding Schools in Mexico, Canada, and the United States." *Latin American Perspectives* 39, no. 5 (2012): 80–99.

Dawson, Alexander S. *Indian and Nation in Revolutionary Mexico*. Tucson: University of Arizona Press, 2004.

de la Peña, Guillermo. "Educación y cultura en el México del siglo XX." In *Un siglo de educación en México*, edited by Pablo Latapí, 1:43–83. Mexico City: Fondo de Cultura Ecónomica and Consejo Nacional para la Cultura y las Artes, 1998.

Dewey, John. "What Mr. John Dewey Thinks of the Educational Policies of Mexico." *Publicaciones de la Secretaría de Educación Pública* 9, no. 13 (1926): 3–9.

Dillingham, Alan Shane. "Indigenismo Occupied: Indigenous Youth and Mexico's Democratic Opening (1968–1975)." *The Americas* 72, no. 4 (October 2015): 549–82.

Dillingham, Alan Shane. *Oaxaca Resurgent: Indigeneity, Development, and Inequality in Twentieth-Century Mexico*. Stanford, CA: Stanford University Press, 2021.

Dubois, Laurent. "Atlantic Freedoms." *Aeon*, November 7, 2016. https://aeon.co/essays/why-haiti-should-be-at-the-centre-of-the-age-of-revolution.

Durand, Jorge, Douglas S. Massey, and Rene M. Zenteno. "Mexican Immigration to the United States: Continuities and Changes." *Latin American Research Review*, 36, no. 36 (2001): 107–27.

"La educación socialista y la escuela rural." In *La casa del pueblo y el maestro rural mexicano: Antología*, edited by Engracia Loyo Bravo, 59–66. Mexico City: Secretaría de Educación Pública, 1985.

Fabre Baños, José Ángel. *Normal rural de Galeana*. Nuevo León: Archivo General del Estado, 1989.

Federación de Estudiantes Campesinos Socialistas de México. "Convocatoria a las sociedades de alumnos de las escuelas regionales campesinos, internados indígenas del país y normales rurales de los estados." n.p., 1937.

Fell, Claude. *José Vasconcelos: Los años del águila (1920–1925); Educación, cultura e iberoamericanismo en el México postrevolucionario*. Mexico City: Universidad Nacional Autónoma de México, 1989.

Flores, Rubén. *Backroads Pragmatists: Mexico's Melting Pot and Civil Rights in the United States.* Philadelphia: University of Pennsylvania Press, 2014.

Flores Torres, Javier, Adelina González García, and Jesús B. Ruiz Hernández. "Homenaje a Miguel." In *Un paseo por los recuerdos*, edited by José Luis Aguayo Álvarez, 174–78. Chihuahua: Asociación Civil de Exalumnos de Salaices, 2007.

Fowler-Salamini, Heather. *Agrarian Radicalism in Veracruz, 1920–38.* Lincoln: University of Nebraska Press, 1971.

Franco Solís, Guillermo A. *¡Que se estén quietecitos! Movimientos sociales en el oriente de Morelos.* Cuernavaca: Editorial la Rana Sur, 2006.

Freidberg, Jill, dir. *Granito de arena.* Seattle, WA: Corrugated Films, 2005.

Freire, Paulo. *Pedagogy of the Oppressed.* Translated by Myra Bergman Ramos. New York: Herder and Herder, 1970.

Gámiz, Arturo. "Participación de los estudiantes en el movimiento revolucionario." Resoluciones 6. Ediciones Línea Revolucionaria, 1965. http://www.madera1965.com.mx/res6.html.

García, Pedro. "Fui secretario general." In *Un paseo por los recuerdos*, edited by José Luis Aguayo Álvarez, 74–80. Chihuahua: La Asociación Civil de Exalumnos de Salaices, 2007.

García Aguirre, Aleida. *La revolución que llegaría.* Mexico City: n.p., 2015.

García Téllez, Ignacio. *La socialización de la cultura: Seis meses de acción educativa.* Mexico City: Secretaría de Educación Pública, 1935.

Garrido, Luis Javier. *El partido de la revolución institucionalizada: Medio siglo de poder político en México.* Mexico City: Siglo Veintiuno, 1982.

Gilbert, Dennis. "Rewriting History: Salinas, Zedillo and the 1992 Textbook Controversy." *Mexican Studies/Estudios Mexicanos* 13, no. 2 (1997): 271–97.

Gillingham, Paul. "Ambiguous Missionaries: Rural Teachers and State Façades in Guerrero, 1930–1950." *Mexican Studies/Estudios Mexicanos* 22, no. 2 (2006): 331–60.

Gillingham, Paul. "Mexican Elections, 1920–1994: Voters, Violence and Veto Power." In *The Oxford Handbook of Mexican Politics*, edited by Roderic Ai Camp, 53–76. Oxford: Oxford University Press, 2011.

Gillingham, Paul. *Unrevolutionary Mexico: The Birth of a Strange Dictatorship.* New Haven, CT: Yale University Press, 2021.

Gillingham, Paul, and Benjamin T. Smith, eds. *Dictablanda: Politics, Work, and Culture in Mexico, 1938–1968.* Durham, NC: Duke University Press, 2014.

Gillingham, Paul, and Benjamin T. Smith. "Introduction: The Paradoxes of Revolution." In *Dictablanda: Politics, Work, and Culture in Mexico, 1938–1968*, edited by Paul Gillingham and Benjamin T. Smith, 1–44. Durham, NC: Duke University Press, 2014.

Giraudo, Laura, and Victoria J. Furio. "Neither 'Scientific' nor 'Colonialist': The Ambiguous Course of Inter-American 'Indigenismo' in the 1940s." *Latin American Perspectives* 39, no. 5 (September 2012): 12–32.

Gollás, Manuel. "Breve relato de cincuenta años de política económica." In *Una historia contemporánea de México: Transformaciones y permanencias*, edited by Ilán Bizberg and Lorenzo Meyer, 223–312. Mexico City: Editorial Océano, 2003.

Gómez Nashiki, Antonio. *Movimiento estudiantil e institución: La universidad michoacana de San Nicolás de Hidalgo, 1956–1966*. Mexico City: Asociación Nacional de Universidades e Institutos de Enseñanza Superior, 2008.

Gómez Tagle, Silvia. *La transición inconclusa: Treinta años de elecciones en México, 1964–1994*. Mexico City: El Colegio de México, 2001.

González Jiménez, Rosa María. "De cómo y por qué las maestras llegaron a ser mayoría en las escuelas primarias de México, Distrito Federal." *Revista Mexicana de Investigación Educativa* 14, no. 42 (2009): 747–85.

González Villarreal, Roberto, and Ricardo Amann Escobar. "Amilcingo: Los desafíos de la tradición." In *Historias de normales: Memorias de maestros*, edited by María Adelina Arredondo, 63–109. Cuernavaca, Morelos: Universidad Autónoma del Estado de Morelos, 2009.

Gordon, Linda. "Comments on *That Noble Dream*." *American Historical Review* 96, no. 3 (1991): 683–87.

Gould, Jeffrey L. "Solidarity under Siege: The Latin American Left, 1968." *American Historical Review* 114, no. 2 (2009): 348–75.

Gould, Jeffrey L. *To Lead as Equals: Rural Protest and Political Consciousness in Chinandega, Nicaragua, 1912–1979*. Chapel Hill: University of North Carolina Press, 1990.

Grammont, Hubert C. de. "La Unión General de Obreros y Campesinos de México." In *Historia de la cuestión agraria*, vol. 8, *Política estatal y conflictos agrarios 1950–1970*, edited by Julio Moguel, 222–60. Mexico City: Siglo Veintiuno, 1989.

Grandin, Greg. *The Last Colonial Massacre: Latin America in the Cold War*. Updated ed. Chicago: University of Chicago Press, 2011.

Grandin, Greg. "Living in Revolutionary Time: Coming to Terms with the Violence of Latin America's Long Cold War." In *A Century of Revolution: Insurgent and Counterinsurgent Violence during Latin America's Long Cold War*, edited by Greg Grandin and Gilbert M. Joseph, 1–42. Durham, NC: Duke University Press, 2010.

Grandin, Greg, and Gilbert M. Joseph, eds. *A Century of Revolution: Insurgent and Counterinsurgent Violence during Latin America's Long Cold War*. Durham, NC: Duke University Press, 2010.

Greaves, Cecilia. *Del radicalismo a la unidad nacional: Una visión de la educación en el México contemporáneo, 1940–1964*. Mexico City: El Colegio de México, 2008.

Green, Hilary. *Education Reconstruction: African American Schools in the Urban South, 1865–1890*. New York: Fordham University Press, 2016.

Guevara Niebla, Gilberto. "Antecedentes y desarrollo del movimiento de 1968." *Cuadernos Políticos* 17 (July–September 1978): 6–33.

Hamilton, Nora. *The Limits of State Autonomy*. Princeton, NJ: Princeton University Press, 1981.

Harvey, David. *The New Imperialism*. Oxford: Oxford University Press, 2003.

Henson, Elizabeth. *Agrarian Revolt in the Sierra of Chihuahua: 1959–1965*. Tucson: University of Arizona Press, 2019.

Henson, Elizabeth. "Madera 1965: Primeros Vientos." In *Challenging Authoritarianism in Mexico: Revolutionary Struggles and the Dirty War, 1964–1982*, edited by Fernando Calderón and Adela Cedillo, 19–39. New York: Routledge, 2012.

Hernández, Anabel. *La verdadera noche de iguala: La historia que el gobierno trató de ocultar*. New York: Vintage Español, 2017.

Hernández Navarro, Luis. *Cero en conducata: Crónica de la resistencia magisterial*. Mexico City: Fundación Rosa Luxemburgo, 2011.

Hernández Navarro, Luis. *No habrá recreo: Contra-reforma constitucional y desobediencia magisterial*. Mexico City: Fundación Rosa Luxemburgo, 2013.

Hernández Ruiz, Santiago. "El problema de la deserción escolar." In *Junta Nacional de Educación Normal*, 2:179–89. Mexico City: Secretaría de Educación Pública, 1954.

Hernández Santos, Marcelo. *Tiempos de reforma: Estudiantes, profesores y autoridades de la Escuela Normal Rural de San Marcos frente a las reformas educativas, 1926–1984*. Zacatecas: Universidad Autónoma de Zacatecas, 2015.

Hernández Zamora, Francisco. "Prefacio." In *José Hernández Delgadillo, 1928–2000*, edited by Francisco Hernández Zamora, 11. Hidalgo: Secretaría de Cultura del Estado de Hidalgo, 2017.

Herr, Robert. "Puppets and Proselytizing: Politics and Nation-Building in Post-revolutionary Mexico's Didactic Theater." PhD diss., University of Massachusetts Amherst, 2013.

Herrera Calderón, Fernando, and Adela Cedillo, eds. *Challenging Authoritarianism in Mexico: Revolutionary Struggles and the Dirty War, 1964–1982*. New York: Routledge, 2012.

Hewitt de Alcántara, Cynthia. *La modernización de la agricultura mexicana, 1940–1970*. Mexico City: Siglo XXI, 1978.

Human Rights Watch. "Mexico: Events of 2015." Human Rights Watch. 2016. https://www.hrw.org/world-report/2016/country-chapters/mexico.

Human Rights Watch. "Vanished: The Disappeared of Mexico's Drug War." Human Rights Watch, January 8, 2014. https://www.hrw.org/news/2014/01/08/vanished-disappeared-mexicos-drug-war.

Hylton, Forrest, and Sinclair Thomson. *Revolutionary Horizons: Past and Present in Bolivian Politics*. London: Verso Books, 2007.

Ibarrola, María de. "La formación de los profesores de educación básica en el siglo xx." In *Un siglo de educación en México*, edited by Pablo Latapí, 2:230–75.

Mexico City: Fondo de Cultura Ecónomica and Consejo Nacional para la Cultura y las Artes, 1998.

Jackson Albarrán, Elena. *Seen and Heard in Mexico: Children and Revolutionary Cultural Nationalism*. Lincoln: University of Nebraska Press, 2014.

Joseph, Gilbert M. "Latin America's Long Cold War: A Century of Revolutionary Process and U.S. Power." In *A Century of Revolution: Insurgent and Counterinsurgent Violence during Latin America's Long Cold War*, edited by Greg Grandin and Gilbert M. Joseph, 397–414. Durham, NC: Duke University Press, 2010.

Joseph, Gilbert, and Daniel Nugent, eds. *Everyday Forms of State Formation: Revolution and the Negotiation of Rule in Modern Mexico*. Durham, NC: Duke University Press, 1994.

Kelley, Robin D. G. *Freedom Dreams: The Black Radical Imagination*. Boston: Beacon, 2002.

Knight, Alan. "The Peculiarities of Mexican History: Mexico Compared to Latin America, 1821–1992." *Journal of Latin American Studies* 24 (1992): 99–144.

Latapí, Pablo. *Análisis de un sexenio de educación en México, 1970–1976*. Mexico City: Editorial Nueva Imagen, 1980.

Latapí, Pablo. "Las necesidades del sistema educativo nacional." In *Disyuntivas sociales: Presente y futuro de la sociedad Mexicana, II*, edited by Miguel S. Wionczek, 133–77. Mexico City: Secretaría de Educación Pública, 1971.

Latapí, Pablo. "El pensamiento educativo de Torres Bodet: Una apreciación crítica." *Revista Latinoamericana de Estudios Educativos* 22, no. 3 (1992): 13–44.

Latapí, Pablo. "Reformas educativas en los cuatro últimos gobiernos (1952–1975)." *Comercio Exterior* 25, no. 12 (December 1975): 1323–33.

Lewis, Stephen. *The Ambivalent Revolution: Forging State and Nation in Chiapas, 1910–1945*. Albuquerque: University of New Mexico Press, 2005.

Lindo-Fuentes, Héctor, and Erik Ching. *Modernizing Minds in El Salvador: Education Reforms and the Cold War, 1960–1980*. Albuquerque: University of New Mexico Press, 2012.

Liu, Chang. "Prometheus of the Revolution: Rural Teachers in Republican China." *Modern China* 35, no. 6 (November 2009): 567–603.

Loaeza, Soledad. *Clases medias y política en México: La querella escolar, 1959–1963*. Mexico City: El Colegio de México, 1988.

Loaeza, Soledad. *El Partido Acción Nacional: La larga marcha, 1939–1994; Oposición leal y partido de protesta*. Mexico City: Fondo de Cultura Económica, 1999.

Lobato, Ernesto. *El movimiento del magisterio: Sus antecedentes, causas e implicaciones*. Mexico City: Talleres Gráficos de México, 1958.

López de la Torre, Saúl. *Guerras secretas: Memorias de un ex guerrillero de los setentas que ahora no puede caminar*. Mexico City: Artefacto Editor, 2001.

López Pérez, Oresta, and Marcelo Hernández Santos. "Las mujeres campesinas y su derecho a la educación en las normales rurales." In *Presencia de las mujeres en la construcción histórica del normalismo rural en México durante el siglo XX*, edited by Oresta López Pérez and Marcelo Hernández Santos, 43–68. San Luis Potosí: El Colegio de San Luis, 2019.

López Rosas, Abel. "El pensamiento y estrategia política del profesor Arturo Gámiz García en las luchas campesinas y estudiantiles de Chihuahua (1962–1965)." Bachelor's thesis, Universidad Nacional Autónoma de México, 2009.

Loyo Brambila, Aurora. *El movimiento magisterial de 1958 en México*. Mexico City: Ediciones Era, 1979.

Loyo Bravo, Engracia, ed. *La casa del pueblo y el maestro rural mexicano: Antología*. Mexico City: Secretaría de Educación Pública, 1985.

Loyo Bravo, Engracia. "¿Escuelas o empresas? Las centrales agrícolas y las regionales campesinas (1926–1934)." *Mexican Studies/Estudios Mexicanos* 20, no. 1 (Winter 2004): 69–98.

Loyo Bravo, Engracia, Cecilia Greaves, and Valentina Torres, eds. *Los maestros y la cultura nacional, 1920–1952*. 5 vols. Mexico City: Secretaría de Educación Pública, 1987.

Loyo Bravo, Engracia, Cecilia Greaves, and Valentina Torres. "Presentación." In *Los maestros y la cultura nacional, 1920–1952*, vol. 1, *Norte*, edited by Engracia Loyo Bravo, Cecilia Greaves, and Valentina Torres, 7–9. Mexico City: Secretaría de Educación Pública, 1987.

Magaloni, Beatriz. *Voting for Autocracy: Hegemonic Party Survival and Its Demise in Mexico*. Cambridge, UK: Cambridge University Press, 2009.

Manzano, Valeria. *The Age of Youth in Argentina: Culture, Politics, and Sexuality from Perón to Videla*. Chapel Hill: University of North Carolina Press, 2014.

McCormick, Gladys I. *The Logic of Compromise in Mexico: How the Countryside Was Key to the Emergence of Authoritarianism*. Chapel Hill: University of North Carolina Press, 2016.

McGinn, Noel, and Susan Street. "Has Mexican Education Generated Human or Political Capital?" *Comparative Education* 20, no. 3 (1984): 323–38.

Medina, Luis. *Hacia un nuevo estado: México, 1920–1994*. Mexico City: Fondo de Cultura Económica, 1994.

"Medio siglo de dictadura burguesa." Segundo Encuentro en la Sierra "Heraclio Bernal." Resoluciones 4. Ediciones Línea Revolucionaria, 1965. http://www.madera1965.com.mx/res4.html.

Meneses Morales, Ernesto. *Tendencias educativas oficiales en México*. Vol. 3, *1934–1964*. Mexico City: Universidad Iberoamericana, 1988.

Meneses Morales, Ernesto. *Tendencias educativas oficiales en México*. Vol. 4, *1964–1976*. Mexico City: Centro de Estudios Educativos, 1991.

Meneses Morales, Ernesto. *Tendencias educativas oficiales en México*. Vol. 5, *1976–1988*. Mexico City: Centro de Estudios Educativos, 1997.

Meyer, Jean A. *La cristiada*. 3 vols. Mexico City: Siglo XXI, 1973.

Miñano García, Max H. *La educación rural en México*. Mexico City: Ediciones de la Secretaría de Educación Pública, 1945.

Mistral, Gabriela. "La reforma educacional de México." In *Gabriela y México*, edited by Pedro Pablo Zegers B., 159–65. Santiago de Chile: RIL Editores, 2007.

Moraba Valle, Fabio. "'Lo mejor de Chile está ahora en México': Ideas políticas y labor pedagógica de Gabriela Mistral en México (1922–1924)." *Historia Mexicana* 63, no. 3 (January–March 2014): 1181–247.

Morales-Gómez, Daniel A., and Alberto Torres. *The State, Corporatist Politics, and Educational Policy Making in Mexico*. New York: Praeger, 1990.

Morales Jiménez, Alberto. "Evocaciones de un profesor de banquillo." In *Los maestros y la cultura nacional, 1920–1952*, edited by Engracia Loyo Bravo, Cecilia Greaves, and Valentina Torres, 3:195–227. Mexico City: Secretaría de Educación Pública, 1987.

Morán López, Cruz Alfonso. "Recuerdos tristes." In *Un paseo por los recuerdos*, edited by José Luis Aguayo Álvarez, 96–98. Chihuahua: La Asociación Civil de Exalumnos de Salaices, 2007.

Muñoz, María. *Stand Up and Fight: Participatory Indigenismo, Populism, and Mobilization in Mexico, 1970–1984*. Tucson: University of Arizona Press, 2016.

Muñoz Izquierdo, Carlos. "Análisis e interpretación de las políticas educativas: El caso de México (1930–1980)." In *Sociología de la educación: Corrientes contemporáneas*, edited by Guillermo González Rivera and Carlos Alberto Torres, 389–445. Mexico City: Centro de Estudios Educativos, 1981.

Muñoz Izquierdo, Carlos, and José Lobo. "Expansión escolar, mercado de trabajo y distribución del ingreso en México: Un análisis longitudinal; 1960–1970." *Revista del Centro de Estudios Educativos* 4, no. 1 (1974): 9–30.

Myers, Charles Nash. *Education and National Development in Mexico*. Princeton, NJ: Industrial Relations Section, Princeton University, 1965.

Navarrete, Ifigenia M. de. "El financiamiento de la educación pública en México." *Investigación Económica* 18, no. 69 (1958): 21–55.

Navarro, Aaron W. *Political Intelligence and the Creation of Modern Mexico, 1938–1954*. University Park: Pennsylvania State University Press, 2010.

Naymich López Macedonio, Mónica. "Historia de una relación institucional: Los estudiantes normalistas rurales organizados en la Federación de Estudiantes Campesinos Socialistas de México y el Estado mexicano del siglo XX (1935–1969)." PhD diss., Colegio de México, 2016.

Newland, Carlos. "The Estado Docente and Its Expansion: Spanish American Elementary Education, 1900–1950." *Journal of Latin American Studies* 26, no. 2 (1994): 449–67.

Niblo, Stephen. *Mexico in the 1940s: Modernity, Politics, and Corruption*. Wilmington, DE: Scholarly Resources, 1999.

Novick, Peter. *That Noble Dream: The "Objectivity Question" and the American Historical Profession.* Cambridge, UK: Cambridge University Press, 1988.

Oikión Solano, Verónica. "El Movimiento de Acción Revolucionaria: Una historia de radicalización política." In *Movimientos armados en México, siglo XX,* vol. 2, *La guerrilla en la segunda mitad del siglo,* edited by Verónica Oikión Solano and Marta Eugenia García Ugarte, 417–60. Zamora: El Colegio de Michoacán and Centro de Investigaciones y Estudios Superiores en Antropología Social, 2008.

Olcott, Jocelyn. *Revolutionary Women in Postrevolutionary Mexico.* Durham, NC: Duke University Press, 2005.

Ortiz Briano, Sergio. *Entre la nostalgia y la incertidumbre: Movimiento estudiantil en el normalismo rural mexicano.* Zacatecas: Universidad Autónoma de Zacatecas, 2012.

Padilla, Tanalís. *Rural Resistance in the Land of Zapata: The Jaramillista Movement and the Myth of the Pax Priísta, 1940–1962.* Durham, NC: Duke University Press, 2008.

Padilla, Tanalís, and Louise Walker. "Spy Reports: Content, Methodology and Historiography in Mexico's Secret Police Archives." Special issue, *Journal of Iberian and Latin American Research* 19, no. 1 (2013): 1–103.

Palacios, Guillermo. *La pluma y el arado: Los intelectuales pedagogos y la construcción sociocultural del "problema campesino" en México, 1932–1934.* Mexico City: El Colegio de México, 1999.

Paley, Dawn. *Drug War Capitalism.* Oakland, CA: AK Press, 2014.

Pansters, Wil G. *Política y poder en Puebla: Formación y ocaso del avilacamachismo en Puebla, 1937–1987.* Mexico City: Fondo de Cultura Económica, 1998.

Pensado, Jaime M. *Rebel Mexico: Student Unrest and Authoritarian Political Culture during the Long Sixties.* Stanford, CA: Stanford University Press, 2013.

Pensado, Jaime M., and Enrique C. Ochoa. "Introduction: México beyond 1968: Revolutionaries, Radicals, and Repression." In *México beyond 1968: Revolutionaries, Radicals, and Repression during the Global Sixties and Subversive Seventies,* edited by Jaime M. Pensado and Enrique C. Ochoa, 3–16. Tucson: University of Arizona Press, 2018.

Pensado, Jaime M., and Enrique C. Ochoa, eds. *México beyond 1968: Revolutionaries, Radicals, and Repression during the Global Sixties and Subversive Seventies.* Tucson: University of Arizona Press, 2018.

Pensado, Jaime M., and Enrique C. Ochoa. "Preface: Mexico Today." In *México beyond 1968: Revolutionaries, Radicals, and Repression during the Global Sixties and Subversive Seventies,* edited by Jaime M. Pensado and Enrique C. Ochoa, ix–xv. Tucson: University of Arizona Press, 2018.

Pinto Díaz, Iván Alexis. "Los formadores en la Escuela Normal Rural Mactumactzá, Chiapas: La configuración de un 'hacer escuela.'" PhD diss., Universidad Pedagógica Nacional, 2013.

Pius XI. "*Divini Redemptoris*: Encyclical of Pope Pius XI on the Atheistic Communism to the Patriarchs, Primates, Archbishops, Bishops, and other Ordinaries in Peace and Communion with the Apostolic See." March 19, 1939. http://www.vatican.va/content/pius-xi/en/encyclicals/documents/hf _p-xi_enc_19370319_divini-redemptoris.html.

Portelli, Alessandro. "Living Voices: The Oral History Interview as Dialogue and Experience." *Oral History Review* 45, no. 2 (2018): 239–48.

Portelli, Alessandro. "What Makes Oral History Different." In *The Oral History Reader*, edited by Robert Perks and Alistair Thomson, 63–74. London: Routledge, 1998.

Prawda, Juan. *Teoría y praxis de la planeación educativa en México*. Mexico City: Grijalbo, 1984.

Purnell, Jennie. *Popular Movements and State Formation in Revolutionary Mexico: The Agraristas and Cristeros in Michoacán*. Durham, NC: Duke University Press, 1999.

Quintal Martín, Fidelio, Adolfo González Salazar, and Mario Pacheco Hidalgo. *Historia de la benemérita Escuela Normal Rural "Justo Sierra Méndez" de Hecelchakán, Campeche*. Mérida, Yucatán: Ediciones de la Academia Mexicana de la Educación, A.C., 2003.

Raby, David. *Educación y revolución social en México, 1921–1940*. Mexico City: Secretaría de Educación Pública, 1974.

Raby, David. "Los principios de la educación rural en México: El caso de Michoacán, 1915–1929." *Historia Mexicana* 22, no. 4 (1973): 553–81.

Ramírez, Rafael. *La escuela rural mexicana*. Mexico City: Secretaría de Educación Pública, 1976.

Ramírez, Rafael. "Propósitos fundamentales que la educación rural Mexicana debe perseguir." In *La casa del pueblo y el maestro rural mexicano: Antología*, edited by Engracia Loyo Bravo, 31–42. Mexico City: Secretaría de Educación Pública, 1985.

Ramírez, Ramón. *El movimiento estudiantil de México*. 2 vols. Mexico City: Ediciones Era, 2008.

Rath, Thom. *Myths of Demilitarization in Postrevolutionary Mexico, 1920–1960*. Chapel Hill: University of North Carolina Press, 2013.

Reynoso Sánchez, Iris Monserrat. "Ser estudiante normalista rural: La construcción de una identidad colectiva en las estudiantes de la escuela normal rural de Amilcingo 'Gral. Emiliano Zapata' 1974–1984." Master's thesis, Universidad Autónoma del Estado de Morelos, 2016.

Rivera Borbón, Carlos. *El gasto del gobierno federal mexicano a través de la Secretaría de Educación Pública*. Mexico City: Talleres Gráficos de la Dirección General de Administración de la Secretaría de Educación Pública, 1970.

Robinet, Romain. "A Revolutionary Group Fighting against a Revolutionary State: The September 23rd Communist League against the PRI-State

(1973–1975)." In *Challenging Authoritarianism*, edited by Fernando Herrera Calderón and Adela Cedillo, 129–47. New York: Routledge, 2012.

Robles, Martha. *Educación y sociedad en la historia de México*. Mexico City: Siglo Veintiuno Editores, 1977.

Rubenstein, Anne. "Raised Voices in the Cine Montecarlo: Sex Education, Mass Media, and Oppositional Politics in Mexico." *Journal of Family History* 23 (July 1998): 312–23.

Ruiz, Ramón. *Mexico: The Challenge of Poverty and Illiteracy*. San Marino, CA: Huntington Library, 1963.

Ruiz del Castillo, Amparo. *Othón Salazar y el Movimiento Revolucionario del Magisterio*. Mexico City: Plaza y Valdés Editores, 2008.

Ruiz Valenzuela, Reyes. "El cierre de nuestra escuela normal." In *Un paseo por los recuerdos*, edited by José Luis Aguayo Álvarez, 94–96. Chihuahua: La Asociación Civil de Exalumnos de Salaices, 2007.

Sáenz, Moisés. "Algunos aspectos de la educación en México." In *La casa del pueblo y el maestro rural mexicano: Antología*, edited by Engracia Loyo Bravo, 19–30. Mexico City: Secretaría de Educación Pública, 1985.

Sanderson, Steven. *Agrarian Populism and the Mexican State*. Berkeley: University of California Press, 1981.

Sanderson, Steven. *The Transformation of Mexican Agriculture*. Princeton, NJ: Princeton University Press, 1986.

Santos Valdés, José. *Autobiografía y dos trabajos sobre la educación*. n.p., 1980.

Santos Valdés, José. "Breve historia de la FECSM." In *Obras completas*, 16:13–57. Zacatecas: n.p., 2014.

Santos Valdés, José. "Democracia y disciplina escolar." In *Obras completas*, 1:76–112. Mexico City: Federación Editorial Mexicana, 1982.

Santos Valdés, José. *Madera: Razón de un martirologio*. Mexico City: Laura, 1968.

Schmelkes, Sylvia, Roberto González, Flavio Rojo, and Alma Rico. *La participación de la comunidad en el gasto educativo*. Mexico City: Secretaría de Educación Pública, 1982.

Secretaría de Educación Pública. *Acción educativa del gobierno mexicano, 1959–1960*. Mexico City: Secretaría de Educación Pública, 1961.

Secretaría de Educación Pública. *La educación pública en México: Desde el 1o de diciembre de 1934 hasta el 30 de noviembre de 1940*. Mexico City: Secretaría de Educación Pública, 1941.

Secretaría de Educación Pública. *La educación rural mexicana y sus proyecciones: Resoluciones de la Junta Nacional de Educación Primaria, México, 1953*. Mexico City: Secretaría de Educación Pública, 1954.

Secretaría de Educación Pública. *Junta Nacional de Educación Normal*. Vols. 1 and 2. Mexico City: Secretaría de Educación Pública, 1954.

Secretaría de Educación Pública. *Memoria de la Secretaría de Educación Pública, 1949–1950*. Mexico City: Secretaría de Educación Pública, 1950.

Secretaría de Educación Pública. *Memoria de la Secretaría de Educación Pública, 1950–1951*. Mexico City: Secretaría de Educación Pública, 1951.

Secretaría de Educación Pública. *Memoria: Primera asamblea nacional de educación normal rural*. Mexico City: Secretaría de Educación Pública, 1967.

Secretaría de Educación Pública. *Las misiones culturales en 1927*. Mexico City: Secretaría de Educación Pública, 1928.

Secretaría de Educación Pública. *La obra educativa en el sexenio, 1958–1964*. Mexico City: Secretaría de Educación Pública, 1964.

Servín, Elisa. "Propaganda y Guerra Fría: La campaña anticomunista en la prensa mexicana del medio siglo." *Signos Históricos* 6, no. 11 (2004): 9–39.

Servín, Elisa. *Ruptura y oposición: El movimiento henriquista, 1945–1954*. Mexico City: Cal y Arena, 2001.

Smith, Benjamin T. "Building a State on the Cheap: Taxation, Social Movements, and Politics." In *Dictablanda: Politics, Work, and Culture in Mexico, 1938–1968*, edited by Paul Gillingham and Benjamin T. Smith, 255–75. Durham, NC: Duke University Press, 2014.

Soy normalista: Anécdotas y comentarios, Hecelchakán, Campeche; Normal Rural "Justo Sierra." Vols. 1 and 2. n.p., 1996.

Street, Susan. "La lucha por transformar el aparato burocrático de la Secretaría de Educación Pública: Fuerzas políticas y proyectos después de un quinquenio de desconcentración." *Revista Mexicana de Sociología* 47, no. 4 (October–December 1985): 183–212.

Street, Susan. "El SNTE y la política educativa, 1970–1990." *Revista Mexicana de Sociología* 54, no. 2 (April–June 1992): 45–72.

Suárez, Luis. *Lucio Cabañas, el guerrillero sin esperanza*. Mexico City: Roca, 1976.

Terán Olguín, Liberato. *Marcha por la ruta de la libertad*. Culiacán, Sinaloa: Serie Estudiantil June 7, 1973.

Thompson, E. P. *The Making of the English Working Class*. New York: Vintage Books, 1966.

Toro Rosales, Salvador del. *Testimonios*. Monterrey: Universidad de Nuevo León, 1996.

Torres, Carlos Alberto. "El corporativismo estatal, las políticas educativas y los movimientos estudiantiles y magisteriales en México." *Revista Mexicana de Sociología* 53, no. 2 (April–June 1991): 159–83.

Torres Bodet, Jaime. *Educación mexicana: Discursos, entrevistas, mensajes*. Mexico City: Ediciones de la Secretaría de Educación Pública, 1944.

Torres Bodet, Jaime. *Jaime Torres Bodet: Textos sobre educación*. Edited by Pablo Latapí. Mexico City: Consejo Nacional para la Cultura y las Artes, 1994.

Torres Bodet, Jaime. *Memorias*. 2nd ed. Mexico City: Editorial Porrua, 1981.

Torres Bodet, Jaime. "Técnica y educación." In *Pensamiento educativo de Jaime Torres Bodet*, edited by Valentina Torres Septién, 113–20. Mexico City: Secretaría de Educación Pública, 1985.

Torres Septién, Valentina. *La educación privada en México (1903–1976)*. Mexico City: El Colegio de México and Universidad Iberoamericana, 1997.

Torres Septién, Valentina. "El miedo de los católicos mexicanos a un demonio con cola y cuernos: El comunismo entre 1950–1980." In *Una historia de los usos del miedo*, edited by Pilar Gonzalbo Aizpuru, Anne Staples, and Valentina Torres Septién, 311–27. Mexico City: El Colegio de México and Universidad Iberoamericana, 2009.

Torres Septién, Valentina. "La Unión Nacional de Padres de Familia: La lucha por la enseñanza de la religión en las escuelas particulares." In *La ciudad y el campo en la historia de México: Memoria de la VII Reunión de Historiadores Mexicanos y Norteamericano*, edited by Roberto Moreno de los Arcos and Hugh M. Hamill Jr., 927–35. Mexico City: Universidad Nacional Autónoma de México, 1992.

Trouillot, Michel-Rolph. *Silencing the Past: Power and the Production of History*. Boston: Beacon, 1995.

"El único camino a seguir." Segundo Encuentro en la Sierra: Resoluciones 5. Ediciones Línea Revolucionaria, 1965. http://www.madera1965.com.mx /resol.html.

Valdés Silva, María Candelaria. "Educación socialista y reparto agrario en La Laguna." In *Escuela y sociedad en el periodo cardenista*, edited by Susana Quintanilla and Mary Kay Vaughan, 229–50. Mexico City: Fondo de Cultura Económica, 1997.

Vargas Valdés, Jesús. "Los Gaytán y el movimiento guerrillero, 1964–1965." *La Fragua de los Tiempos*, no. 959 (July 1, 2012). https://www.chihuahuamexico .com/images/stories/periodicos/PDFLaFragua/La%20Fragua%20de%20 los%20tiempos%20No.959.pdf.

Vargas Valdés, Jesús. *Madera rebelde: Movimiento agrario y guerrilla (1959–1965)*. Chihuahua: Ediciones Nueva Vizcaya, 2015.

Vasconcelos, José. *José Vasconcelos: Textos sobre educación*. Edited by Alicia Molina. Mexico City: Secretaría de Educación Pública and Fondo de Cultura Económica, 1981.

Vaughan, Mary Kay. *Cultural Politics in Revolution: Teachers, Peasants, and Schools in Mexico, 1930–1940*. Tucson: University of Arizona Press, 1997.

Vaughan, Mary Kay. *The State, Education, and Social Class in Mexico, 1880–1928*. DeKalb: Northern Illinois University Press, 1982.

Vela Gálvez, Luciano. "La organización estudiantil y su acción formadora." In *La educación rural en México y la escuela del Mexe han cumplido*, edited by Felipe Cortés Martínez, Tomás Hernández López, Javier Moreno Pichardo, and Luciano Vela, 228–40. Mexico City: n.p., 2009.

Vela Gálvez, Luciano. "Un sistema democrático disciplinario." In *La educación rural en México y la escuela del Mexe han cumplido*, edited by Felipe Cortés Martínez, Tomás Hernández López, Javier Moreno Pichardo, and Luciano Vela, 257–61. Mexico City: n.p., 2009.

Velasco Hernández, Francisco Antonio. "El 'ciclo metabólico' de la Escuela Normal Rural Mactumactzá: Métodos, metodologías y nuevas epistemologías en las ciencias sociales; Desafíos para el conocimiento profundo de Nuestra América." In *Memoria Académica del V Encuentro Latinoamericano de Metodología de las Ciencias Sociales, Mendoza, Argentina, November 16–18, 2016*. http://www.memoria.fahce.unlp.edu.ar/trab_eventos/ev.8605/ev .8605.pdf.

Vera, Rosa. "Reformas a la educación normal durante el sexenio, 1970–1976." In *Simposio sobre el magisterio nacional*, 101–29. Mexico City: Centro de Investigaciones Superiores del Instituto Nacional de Antropología e Historia, 1980.

Vilchis Cedillo, Arturo. "La Escuela-Ayllu de Warisata, Bolivia y sus relaciones con México." *De Raíz Diversa* 1, no. 1 (April–September 2014): 145–70.

Villela Buenrostro, Othón. *Un maestro del pueblo y la epopeya de la primera normal rural*. Morelia: Secretaría de Educación del Estado, 1997.

Vite Vargas, Marisol. "La formación docente en el marco de la cultura institucional de la Escuela Normal Rural 'Luis Villareal' de El Mexe, Hidalgo." PhD diss., Universidad Pedagógica Nacional, 2010.

Vite Vargas, Marisol. "La reconfiguración de la cultura institucional de la normal rural Luis Villarreal de El Mexe, Hidalgo a partir de la reinserción de las mujeres." In *Presencia de las mujeres en la construcción histórica del normalismo rural en México durante el siglo XX*, edited by Oresta López Pérez and Marcelo Hernández Santos, 131–60. San Luis Potosí: El Colegio de San Luis, 2019.

Walker, Louise E. *Waking from the Dream: Mexico's Middle Classes after 1968*. Stanford, CA: Stanford University Press, 2013.

Wasserman, Mark. *Capitalists, Caciques, and Revolution: The Native Elite and Foreign Enterprise in Chihuahua, Mexico, 1854–1911*. Chapel Hill: University of North Carolina Press, 1984.

Wasserman, Mark. *Persistent Oligarchs: Elites and Politics in Chihuahua, Mexico 1910–1940*. Durham, NC: Duke University Press, 1993.

Wilkie, James W. *The Mexican Revolution: Federal Expenditure and Social Change since 1910*. 2nd rev. ed. Berkeley: University of California Press, 1970.

Winn, Peter. *Weavers of Revolution: The Yarur Workers and Chile's Road to Socialism*. Oxford: Oxford University Press, 1986.

Wood, Elisabeth Jean. *Insurgent Collective Action and Civil War in El Salvador*. Cambridge, UK: Cambridge University Press, 2003.

Wright, Angus. *The Death of Ramón González*. Austin: University of Texas Press, 1990.

Young, Benjamin R. *Guns, Guerillas, and the Great Leader: North Korea and the Third World*. Stanford, CA: Stanford University Press, 2021.

Zolov, Eric. "¡Cuba sí, Yanquis no! The Sacking of the Instituto Cultural México-Norteamericano in Morelia, Michoacán, 1961." In *In from the Cold: Latin*

America's New Encounter with the Cold War, edited by Gilbert Joseph and Daniela Spenser, 214–52. Durham, NC: Duke University Press, 2008.

Zolov, Eric. *Refried Elvis: The Rise of Mexican Counterculture*. Berkeley: University of California Press, 1999.

Zúñiga Castillo, Enrique, ed. *El normalismo rural en Tamaulipas (entrevistas)*. Tamaulipas: Colegio de Bachilleres, 1998.

Index

Page numbers followed by *f* indicate figures.

Peña Nieto, Enrique, 4, 38, 248–51, 321n19
Pensado, Jaime, 169
People's Popular Assembly of Oaxaca, 321n15
Pérez Guerrero, Carlos, 72–73
Perote *normal*, Veracruz, 168*map*, 208, 308n5
Peru, 33
Pinochet, Augusto, 34, 213
Pius XI, Pope, 76
pluralism, cultural, 29, 275n27
point system for infractions, 66, 92–93
Political and Ideological Orientation Committee/Club, 87, 127, 295n116
Popular Guerrilla Group (GPG), 154, 160–61
Popular Socialist Party (PPS), 134, 136–37, 143, 222
Popular Socialist Youth, 137
Porras, Espino, 147
porros (agents provocateurs), 185
Portelli, Alessandro, 17
PPS (Popular Socialist Party), 134, 136–37, 143, 222
PRI (Institutional Revolutionary Party): about, 4; co-optation by, 174, 218; corporatist structure, 11, 100; *dictadura-dictablanda* false dichotomy, 14–15; influence after control of, 270n4; mobilization against *normalistas*, 181–82; MRM and, 100; neoliberalism, shift to, 242; SNTE support for, 11; textbook initiative and, 111. *See also* National Revolutionary Party
professionalism, 106, 195–96
professionalization, 77, 94–95, 116–19, 237
PST (Socialist Workers' Party), 218–19, 315n30

Quiñónez, Miguel, 157–59

Raby, David, 75–76
rail workers strike, 100
Ramírez, Rafael, 28–29, 52

Ramírez, Victoria, 18–19
rationalist education, 56
regional campesino schools, 46–49, 50*map*
regional *normales*, 37
Regional Normal Teaching Centers (CRENS), 102, 118, 121–23, 126, 294n89
regional student federations, 200
religious schools, FECSM demands on, 120–21, 123
Revolutionary Action Movement (MAR), 202, 225–26, 230–31
Revolutionary Teachers Movement (MRM), 100, 108, 186, 228, 236–37
Revolutionary Vanguard, 278n55
Reyes Mantecón *normal*, Oaxaca, 168*map*; 1968 strike and, 182; 1969 restructuring and, 207–8; *normalista* narratives, 170–71, 174, 215; political orientation classes, 169
Ricardo Flores Magón *normal*, Chihuahua, 50*map*, 79*map*
Ríos, Álvaro, 140, 149, 187, 298n29
Ríos, Carlos, 138, 154
Rivera, Diego: *La Maestra rural*, 23, 24*f*, 26, 42; SEP commissions, 26, 279n60
Rivera, Eva, 220–21
Rivera, Justo, 221
Rivera Crespo, Felipe, 222
Rodríguez, Isidro, 170–71
Rodríguez, Silvina, 146, 184
Rosales Olivar, Benedicto, 221–24
Ruiz, Ulises, 321n15
Ruiz Cortines, Adolfo, 81, 104
rural *normales*: 1969 reform and restructuring, 191, 193–94, 203–10, 212–13; about, 2; age of students, 47, 89; *bachillerato* requirement, 242–43; beginnings of, 45–46; Cardenista project and, 64; coeducational, 27; conditions as improvement on home life, 83; crisis in rural education, 94–98; daily schedule, 89–90; director ouster efforts, 123–25, 165–66, 178–79, 294n99; disciplinary code, 66–67, 91–93; disciplinary measures post-1969, 215–16;

and gender, 53; FECSM demands and SEP responses and concessions, 119–23, 165–66, 175–82, 216–17, 233–34; Federal Institute for Teacher Training and, 117; ideology, changing, 53; missionary duty rhetoric, 6, 11, 27–28, 52, 105–6; modernizing development framework, 196; murals commissioned by, 26, 279n60; National Assembly on Rural Normal Education (1967), 189–90, 192–97; *normalista* investment in schools and, 89; Palmira case and, 179; progressive thinkers and, 25; purge of leftists, 80–81; reforms under Echeverría, 233–39; SNTE appeals to, 123–26; socialist education and, 55, 57, 71; social service requirement and strike, 107–10; student leadership and, 64–65; technocratic appointments to, 241–42; textbook initiative and, 101–2, 111–16

service, spirit of, 87–88

sex education, 55

sexual misconduct, 178–79

sexual promiscuity rumors, 184

Sierra Partida, Alfonso, 165–66, 179

Sierra Tarahumara, 157–61, 302n123

Sinarquistas, 147

Sindicato Nacional de Trabajadores de la Educación. *See* SNTE

sisterhood, 170

Smith, Benjamin T., 273n44

SNTE (National Union of Education Workers): appeals to SEP, 123–26; corruption and, 9, 11; decentralization and, 241–42; founding of, 36; MRM and, 104–5; Palmira case and, 165–66; Section IX, 100, 103–5, 107

socialist education: deep roots in rural *normales*, 68; elimination of, 71–77; implementation of, 55–60; legacy of, 253; Santos Valdés on, 81

Socialist Workers' Party (PST), 218–19, 315n30

social justice: Cárdenas and, 39, 110; Cold War and, 141; FECSM and, 14,

82; muralists and, 26; national unity, shift to, 68–70; political culture and, 7; quid pro quo and, 190–91; SNTE and language of, 125; teachers and, 25, 31, 58, 101

social service requirement (SEP), 107–10

Soviet Union, 7, 31–32, 225

spending on education: corporatist logic of, 11–12; as percent of budget, 78, 286n46; as percent of GDP, 197, 293n75; Torres Bodet and, 116

State Normal School of Chihuahua, 137–42, 147, 156

strikes: in 1960s, nearly continuous, 175–76; 1968, 182; 1973, 218; FECSM and, 9, 175–80; logistical tactics for, 182–83; MRM, 104–5; national, 179–80; National Teachers School, 103; rail workers, 100; State Normal School of Chihuahua, 156

student governance, 60–65

Student-Teacher Councils, 65

Tacámbaro *normal*, Michoacán, 49, 281n25

Tamatán *normal*, Tamaulipas, 50*map*, 79*map*, 168*map*; 1968 strike and, 182; 1969 restructuring and, 208; FECSM and, 62; new *normal* in Tamaulipas and, 316n37

Tamazulapan *normal*, Oaxaca, 79*map*, 168*map*, 214*map*, 249*map*; 1968 strike and, 182; 1969 restructuring and, 207; Amilcingo *normal* and, 221; director, mobilization against, 294n99; guerrilla groups and, 227–28; *normalista* narratives, 86, 212; sexual misconduct, 178–79; strikes and, 80; student association office, 128*f*

teachers: as archetype, 27–28; Communist Party membership and, 75–76, 285n32; at day and evening schools, 319n121; incentives under Echeverría, 239; pay of, 11–12, 69, 96, 106, 238; in Rivera's *La Maestra rural*, 26; rural living conditions and, 10; social justice

Véjar Vázquez, Octavio, 73, 75–76
Vela Gálvez, Luciano, 87
Villa, Francisco "Pancho," 23, 135, 207, 231–32
Villistas, 23

Wasserman, Mark, 135
World Federation of Democratic Youth, 81, 287n59
writings of graduating students, 51–54, 58

Xalisco *normal*, Nayarit, 50*map*, 79*map*, 168*map*

Xochiapulco *normal*, Puebla, 50*map*, 79*map*
Xocuyucan *normal*, Tlaxcala, 168*map*, 178

Yáñez, Agustín, 178, 188–90, 203

Zapata, Emiliano, 23, 25, 207, 232, 244, 253
Zapatistas, 23
Zaragoza *normal*, Puebla, 168*map*
Zedillo, Ernesto, 244–45
Zolov, Eric, 299n56